THE LIFE OF
THOMAS JOHNSON

THOMAS JOHNSON AT THE AGE OF THIRTY-SIX
From a painting by John Hesselius

The Life of

Thomas Johnson

MEMBER OF THE CONTINENTAL CONGRESS
FIRST GOVERNOR OF MARYLAND
AND
ASSOCIATE JUSTICE OF THE
UNITED STATES SUPREME COURT

Edward S. Delaplaine

HERITAGE BOOKS
2007

HERITAGE BOOKS

AN IMPRINT OF HERITAGE BOOKS, INC.

Books, CDs, and more—Worldwide

For our listing of thousands of titles see our website
at
www.HeritageBooks.com

A Facsimile Reprint
Published 2007 by
HERITAGE BOOKS, INC.
Publishing Division
65 East Main Street
Westminster, Maryland 21157-5026

— Publisher's Notice —
In reprints such as this, it is often not possible to remove blemishes from
the original. We feel the contents of this book warrant its reissue despite
these blemishes and hope you will agree and read it with pleasure.

International Standard Book Number: 978-1-58549-687-7

FOREWORD

IN the various scenes of the drama that led to the foundation of our Republic—in the Colonial days, the Revolution, the adoption of the Articles of Confederation, the ratification of the Federal Constitution, the establishment of the Capital City and the stabilization of the Nation— Thomas Johnson played an important rôle.

In the issue of April 3, 1824, of the "Political Intelligencer"—a newspaper published in Frederick, Maryland, by Robert Ritchie—there appeared a letter to the editor which paid a glowing tribute to the late Governor Johnson; in it appeared the following suggestion:

"Of such a man some account ought to be transmitted to posterity; and, without doubt, it would be a public benefit, if the friends of Mr. Johnson would publish a sketch of his life, or furnish to some person the materials from which the same might be drawn up."

The suggestion was never followed. And recently, upon hearing that "The Life of Thomas Johnson" was ready for publication, Governor Albert C. Ritchie expressed a sentiment that has been entertained for more than a century by the people of Maryland when he said: "Biographical justice has not been done many of the great men of Maryland. Because of that, Governor Johnson's life and public services are not as familiar as they deserve to be.

The biography of Johnson is a want which has been too long unfilled."

Not only has Johnson failed to receive the recognition which he deserves in American History, but some of the honors to which he is entitled have actually been bestowed upon others. One glaring example of this is the nomination of George Washington for Commander-in-Chief of the Continental Army. President Calvin Coolidge, in a carefully prepared address delivered at Cambridge, Massachusetts, on July 3, 1925, gave the distinction of nominating Washington to John Adams. Said President Coolidge on this occasion: "It was a stroke of political genius that Adams, soul of Puritanic idealism, should have moved the adoption of the army by Congress and the selection of Washington as Commander-in-Chief. . . . In presenting his name to the Congress Adams described him in terms which seem prophetic, and which we can hardly improve. . . . Let it ever be set down to the glory of Massachusetts that John Adams made George Washington Commander-in-Chief of the Continental Armies and John Marshall Chief Justice of the United States. Destiny could have done no more." As a matter of fact, Adams himself admitted that Washington was nominated for Commander-in-Chief by Johnson.

The author of this volume hopes his efforts will do more than to bestow upon a Marylander the credit to which he is entitled. A second purpose of the biography is to emphasize the friendship between Johnson and George Washington. For many years they were compatriots as well as business associates. But they were more than that. They were bosom friends. The author hopes that the book will throw further light upon the life of the immortal Virginian.

Governor Harry Flood Byrd, of Virginia, recently made the following comment in this connection: "A leader in that patriotic movement which resulted in the independence of the United States, a friend of Washington, the first Governor of the State of Maryland, an Associate Justice of the United States Supreme Court, Thomas Johnson must ever stand forth as a leading and impressive figure in the history of the Nation and a son of whom Maryland and America can justly and jointly be proud. Governor Johnson was a prominent member of the Continental Congress. It was he who placed the name of Washington in nomination for Commander-in-Chief of the Continental Armies. It was he who urged upon Washington to accede to the demands of the people by accepting the presidency of the Republic. A National and historic figure, the life of Thomas Johnson belongs to the annals of the United States and the world."

A third purpose of this book is to show the prominent part that Maryland played in securing American Independence and in establishing the foundation of our National Government. No effort, of course, is made to minimize the importance of the part taken in the formative days of the Nation by the other States—notably Massachusetts and Virginia—but the author feels, as Winfield Scott Schley felt in the Spanish-American War, that there is glory enough for us all.

Lauding the Commonwealth of Virginia in an address at the College of William and Mary on May 15, 1926, President Coolidge said: "The resolutions [adopted by the Virginia Convention on May 15, 1776] did not fail to recognize the principle of Nationality. . . . It was the expression of a desire for a yet unformulated plan for a

Federal Government. How great a part Virginia was to play in the final adoption of such a Government was by this action already indicated. When that great test came some years later it was the known wish of the great Washington, aided by the superb reasoning powers of Marshall, notwithstanding the direct opposition of Henry, that caused Virginia to ratify the Federal Constitution at a time which was again decisive in the formulation of the Union. For a second time the action of this great Commonwealth was the determining factor in the destiny of America."

It is true that Virginia had many influential leaders at the time of the Revolution, but the author believes the pages of "The Life of Thomas Johnson" will show that it was the action of Maryland at the time of the adoption of the Articles of Confederation, by leading the way toward the creation of a National domain, that was "the determining factor in the destiny of America"; and again, according to the immortal Washington himself, it was Maryland—not Virginia, as President Coolidge avers—that ratified the Federal Constitution "at a time which was again decisive in the formulation of the Union."

EDWARD S. DELAPLAINE.

FREDERICK, MARYLAND,
February 22, 1927.

CONTENTS

ILLUSTRATIONS

THE
LIFE OF THOMAS JOHNSON

CHAPTER I

ANCESTRY

ABOUT the time of the "Glorious Revolution" in England—when William of Orange appeared at the head
of a Dutch Army to save England from Tory régime, and
King James II fled to France, after which William and
Mary in 1689 jointly ascended the throne—a vessel, commanded by Captain Roger Baker, clandestinely set sail for
America. Among those on board were Mr. and Mrs.
Thomas Johnson, a newly married couple. The groom was
a young barrister of Norfolk County. He came from a
splendid family, his ancestors having taken a prominent
part for more than a century in the affairs of Yarmouth.

$$*\qquad*\qquad*\qquad*\qquad*$$

The history of Great Yarmouth—distinguished from the
suburb, Little Yarmouth, on the opposite bank of the River
Yare—goes back to the days of the Roman invasion. For
many years its population consisted mainly of hardy sailors
and fishermen of the North Sea, who traded, smuggled, and
plundered along the coasts of England and Scotland. The
town was ruled by pirates, euphemistically styled "vikings,"
until the reign of King John, when it was given a Charter in-

corporating it is a borough with privileges of self-government. According to tradition, several members of the Johnson family commanded vessels in the fleet sent out from Yarmouth to meet the Grand Armada, fitted out in 1588 by Philip II of Spain against Queen Elizabeth.

Shortly after the time of the destruction of the "Invincible Armada," James Johnson was chosen one of the bailiffs of Yarmouth. Being the chief magistrates, the bailiffs were the most influential citizens of the borough. Mr. Johnson and his fellow bailiff, John Wheeler, distinguished themselves in 1589 and 1590 by erecting, for the protection of Yarmouth, sea-walls which proved to be far more substantial than any ever built there before. A few miles above the mouth of the Yare, the town stands on a slip of land, a mile and a half wide, washed on the East by the North Sea and by the River on the West. Back in the early days, sea-walls had been constructed time and again, only to be destroyed; so Johnson and his colleague devised the scheme of building two walls, inner and outer. The improvement was acclaimed everywhere, even in verse, as a great triumph of foresight and skill. So durably were the walls built that the ravages of three centuries were powerless to destroy them completely. When Bradley T. Johnson, a Confederate General in the Civil War, visited England in 1873, he saw at Yarmouth some of the remains of the sea-walls erected by his ancestor in the reign of Queen Elizabeth.

Thomas Johnson, the son of James, followed in the footsteps of his father by serving in 1624 as one of the bailiffs of Yarmouth. In 1625, he occupied a seat in the first Parliament of Charles I, which the new king speedily dissolved, when the Commons refused to grant him the full measure of support he demanded for the conduct of the War with Spain. In 1635 and 1636, Mr. Johnson served again as bailiff of Yarmouth.

The "Great Rebellion" between the Royalists, or *Cavaliers*, and the Parliamentary forces, called *Roundheads*—destined to divide the Nation on account of religion—was now approaching. In the Eastern Counties the *Roundheads* formed an organization which raised a well-disciplined army under the command of the Earl of Manchester and Oliver Cromwell. One of the prominent members of the "Eastern Counties Association" was Thomas Johnson, Jr. Chosen bailiff of Yarmouth in 1644, shortly after his father had held this office, the younger Thomas was selected by the Earl of Manchester in the same year to command the Yarmouth Militia. The Commonwealth and Protectorate, commencing when Charles I was beheaded in 1649, continued until 1660. Thought to have been disgusted at the execution of Charles I, Captain Johnson espoused the cause of the Royalists. He was confirmed in his command as Captain by Sir Edward Walker, the Lieutenant of the King. When in 1661, following the coronation of Charles II, the new Parliament passed an act which disqualified the incumbent bailiff of Yarmouth, Captain Johnson was appointed to take his place. For defending Yarmouth against the complaints of Lowestoft, a neighboring port, he was presented with a piece of plate as an evidence of the grateful appreciation of the people of the borough.

The gratitude of the Crown for Captain Johnson's separation from the Revolutionary forces is evidenced by the granting to him in 1661 of alteration and confirmation of arms by the Heralds' College, through Sir Edward

Walker, in recognition of the Captain's "great suffering and loyalty." The pedigree and family arms of Captain Johnson were recorded a few years later. The Johnson coat of arms is set forth in heraldry as follows:

> "*Argent; a fess, counter-embattled; between three lions' heads, erased, gules, ducally crowned, or. Crest: a leopard's head, gules, issuing from a ducal crown, or.*"

A translation into simpler language would be:

> "A silver shield; across the center, drawn horizontally, a band broken alternately above and below like battlements; between three red lions' heads, with jagged edges as if torn off the bodies, and with golden coronets. Crest: a red leopard's head issuing from a golden ducal crown."

In the United States the members of the Johnson family have used the words, *"Confide et Certa,"* or "Trust and Strive," in connection with the coat of arms; but General Bradley T. Johnson, on his return from England, declared that, while the arms as used in America by the descendants of Captain Thomas Johnson otherwise correspond with the description emblazoned in the Heralds' College, there is no record of any motto on the Johnson escutcheon.

Captain Johnson left two sons, Thomas and James. James, the younger, was destined to make a mark in his generation. He was deputed by the corporation to receive King Charles II, when he visited Yarmouth in 1671, and the sovereign was entertained by Mr. Johnson at his home on the South Quay. His Majesty showed his appreciation by knighting him. In 1681, during the reign of Charles II, he served as member of Parliament; but he declined to accept the wages or expenses which at that time it was the custom of the boroughs and shires to pay to their representatives. After the Duke of York was proclaimed James II, upon the death of Charles II in 1685, Sir James Johnson stood in confidential relations with the Court. Early in 1687, for example, he produced a Royal order in Council displacing some of the aldermen and common councilmen and another order appointing their successors. His arms and pedigree are recorded in the College of Arms among the Knights of Sir William Le Neve, who carried the proclamation of Charles I to the Earl of Essex the day after the first pitched battle of the "Great Rebellion." After reciting the pedigree, the record in the College of Arms says: "James Johnson of Yarmouth aforesaid, knighted as above, lived well, spent much, died poor."

Early in life, many years before he was knighted, Sir James was appointed to serve on a committee to settle some differences that had arisen relative to the appointment of a curate; and, when the dispute broke out again several years later, he was appointed to serve as a member of a delegation to journey to Norwich to present the claims of Yarmouth before the Lord Bishop. It was here that Sir James found his wife. He married Miss Dorothy Scotlowe, the daughter of Augustin Scotlowe, Mayor of Norwich. Sir James and Dorothy Johnson were the parents of two sons, James, born in 1650, and Thomas, born in 1656. Thomas died, unmarried, at the age of 28.

James Johnson, the elder son of Sir James, married, and one of his sons, during the turbulent reign of Anne, was elevated to a responsible position in the Office of Foreign Affairs.

*   *   *   *   *

Another son of James Johnson—named Thomas, the

young lawyer mentioned at the beginning of the Chapter—
had fallen in love with a chancery ward named Mary
Baker, and married her without the consent of the Lord
High Chancellor. Inasmuch as abduction and marrying of
maids in chancery constituted a high misprision, punishable
by heavy fine and imprisonment as a contempt of Court,
Johnson decided to flee with his bride from England. They appealed for help to Captain Roger Baker, the
bride's father, who was a mariner of Liverpool, and he
agreed to assist them in their romantic escape by allowing
them passage on his boat bound for the New World.

After the long journey across the Atlantic, Capt. Baker
entered the Chesapeake Bay about the year 1690. He
steered his vessel as far as the mouth of St. Leonard's Creek,
where Capt. Thomas Claggett, from the parish of St.
Leonard's, London, had settled some years before. Here,
in Calvert County, Maryland, the immigrants landed.

Thousands of miles away from the grip of the stern
British law, young Johnson felt he was safe from arrest for
his illegal marriage; but it was not long before his impulsive
nature and stubborn will brought him, charged with a penal
offense, before the bar of justice. The commission of this
crime came as a result of his deep political convictions. His
grandfather, Sir James Johnson, knighted by Charles II,
having been held in high favor at the Court of James II,
it was natural that the young Marylander sympathized with
King James, who had been compelled to flee to France,
rather than with William of Orange, who came at the head
of the Dutch Army to rescue England, it was said, from
arbitrary rule and Catholicism. Whilst the majority of
the Convention, which William summoned in 1689, was
fiercely Whig, the Tory admirers of James II vigorously

protested against the deposition of the sovereign who was entitled by divine right to be King. The Tories accordingly proposed the plan of allowing James to reign nominally as King and William of Orange to govern as Regent; but the Convention took the position that James, by reason of the fact that he had left England, had abdicated and hence William was lawfully entitled to ascend the vacant throne. And so when the "Declaration of Right," denouncing many of James's acts as illegal, was ratified by William and Mary, the throne was offered to them as joint sovereigns. Their accession exploded the old Tory theory of *Divine Hereditary Right.* Now a sovereign was subject to ejection, if he failed properly to perform his duties. The Seventeenth-Century struggle between King and subjects had ended: Parliament was now the most powerful element in the British state. Young Tom Johnson, however, in far-away Maryland, retained his loyalty to James II; as late as "the Sixth yeare of the Reign of our Soveraign Lord & Lady William & Mary King & Queen of England," he was arrested for uttering treasonable words against the King and Queen.

When the accusation was made against Johnson, the Government of the Colony was in a very unstable condition. Sir Thomas Lawrence, whom William and Mary had chosen for Secretary of Maryland, had been impeached and thrown into prison by Sir Lionel Copley, Royal Governor of Maryland. When Governor Copley died in 1693, the Governor of Virginia seized the Government of Maryland and assumed the authority of making Col. Nicholas Greenberry, President of the Council, the acting Governor. The impeachment proceedings against Lawrence were declared illegal and he was "appointed" by the Governor of

Virginia as the President of the Council and acting Governor of Maryland. Francis Nicholson, lawfully appointed Governor, did not arrive in Maryland to assume control until July, 1694, and so when the Council met at Battle Town, in Calvert County, in June, 1694, it consisted of both Sir Thomas Lawrence and Col. Greenberry as well as Thomas Tench, Esq., Capt. John Addison, Capt. John Courts, and Thomas Brooke, Esq. At the second session held on the 14th of June, commencing at 5 o'clock in the evening, a warrant was issued to the sheriff of Calvert County to arrest Thomas Johnson and to bring him forthwith before the Council "to answer to such things as on their Majesties' behalfe shall be objected against him." He was apprehended immediately and brought before the Council. A deposition, sworn to by Dr. Symon Wotton, was read aloud. It accused Johnson of uttering the following words: "All the people are rogues to the Government, and I will never swear to any king but King James!" The Council ordered [1] the accused to be kept in the sheriff's custody until he entered himself into recognizance in the sum of 500 pounds Sterling and his two sureties in the sum of 250 pounds each for his appearance at the next Provincial Court "and in the mean time to be of good behaviour." Dr. Wotton also had to give bond in the sum of 200 pounds that he would appear as a witness for the Crown.

It is believed that Johnson skipped his bail. On July 21, 1698—after a lapse of four years—John Broadhurst, another Calvert Countian, appeared before the Council in Annapolis to testify concerning the rebellious utterance. A day later, Capt. Richard Smith was haled before Governor Nicholson and his Council, under the charge that he was

---

[1] Proceedings of Council, XX *Archives*, 72.

in his own home when the utterance was made by Johnson and that he "countenanced him by laughing and grinning thereat." The Council required Capt. Smith to give security for his appearance at Court in 2,000 pounds Sterling.

Forced once more to flee for safety, Johnson trafficked in furs with the Indians. Some years later, when his brother had gained considerable influence at the Court of Anne, who became Queen in 1702 upon the death of William III, he decided to endeavor to make his way back to England. Believing that he could now visit England without any danger of arrest for his illegal marriage many years before, and taking with him a lot of fine furs and a quantity of gold, he set sail. But at this time a journey on the Atlantic was unusually perilous. Within a few weeks after Queen Anne's accession, war had commenced: England, Germany, and Holland formed an alliance against France and Spain —a conflict which saw no end until the Treaty of Utrecht in 1713—and sea and land were paraded by belligerents. While on the Atlantic, the vessel in which Johnson was traveling was captured by the Spaniards, and all on board were robbed of everything they had and imprisoned. After a considerable length of time, Johnson managed to escape on a Canadian ship and finally landed in Canada in a destitute condition. He then tramped, about the year 1714, all the way to Maryland on foot. When he came to the end of his long journey, he found that his home had been set on fire by the Indians. From anxiety and grief, Mrs. Johnson pined away; while her husband, weakened by exhaustion and exposure, followed her a short time later to the grave. They were buried side by side, near the spot where they had first set foot upon the soil of America.

Thus ends the pathetic story of the Johnson fugitives—

the Yarmouth barrister and the ward in chancery. Their
name was perpetuated, however, by an only son, Thomas,
born on the 19th of February, 1702. Left an orphan at the
age of twelve, the youngster was given food and clothing
by kind-hearted friends. He was given a good education, for, when in 1723, during the Administration of
Governor Charles Calvert, the Assembly passed the
Act "for the encouragement of Learning and erecting Schools in the several Counties within this Province"—the School Law that became the nucleus of the
County Academies—Thomas Johnson, Jr., was named as
one of the seven "visitors" or trustees in Cecil County to
carry out the provisions of the Act. The list of seven
trustees for each County, embodied by the Assembly in the
statute, shows who were considered "the better and more
intelligent sort of people at that early period." [2]

At the age of twenty-three—on March 12, 1725—young
Johnson was married to Dorcas Sedgwick, a girl of nineteen
Summers, who was the daughter of Mr. and Mrs. Joshua
Sedgwick, of Calvert County. The Sedgwicks were Puritans
who had been forced to leave Virginia. Shortly after his
marriage, Mr. Johnson was sent as a Delegate from Cecil
County to the Lower House of the Maryland Assembly, and
was reëlected from year to year up until about the time of
the birth of his distinguished son, his namesake, the first
Governor of the State of Maryland.

Thus, the favoring influence of heredity in the case of
Governor Johnson is quite apparent. It is quite true that
neither inherited predilection for a public career nor the
prestige of a family name has been a requisite for gaining
exalted official station; Lincoln, Jackson, Clay, Gar-

---

[2] Neill, *Terra Mariae,* p. 189.

field, and many other American statesmen were the children of poverty. "There is another list, however," says Theodore E. Burton, "quite as numerous, which tends to show that an inherited bias for public service is not without advantage. It is made up of those whose fathers held office, but in a theatre of action very limited in area, in many cases including only a township or a county, preferment having been given because of their sturdy common sense and unswerving integrity. Whatever inspiration descended to their sons, impelling them to participate in public affairs, was derived from such sources as the town meeting, the county court, the colonial or state legislature, or the command of the local militia." Johnson deserves to be placed in this class with such men as Jefferson, Marshall, Webster, Calhoun, and Blaine.

CHAPTER II

BIRTH AND EARLY LIFE

THOMAS JOHNSON, who was destined to become the patriot leader in Maryland during the Revolution, was born on the 4th of November, 1732. The birthplace, near the mouth of St. Leonard's Creek, was situated on an eminence that commanded a fine view of the Patuxent.

The year 1732 is also memorable as the date of birth of George Washington and Richard Henry Lee, both of whom became friends of Johnson in early life. It was Mr. Lee who, while serving as a member of the Continental Congress, offered the famous Resolution, "That the United Colonies are and ought to be free and independent States; that they are absolved from all allegiance to the British Crown; and that all political connection between them and the state of Great Britain is and ought to be totally dissolved." Mr. Lee's great-grandfather had emigrated from England to Virginia during the reign of Charles I, and Washington's great-grandfather settled in the same Colony during the Protectorate several years after the execution of the King. Although the Old Dominion lays claim to both George Washington and Richard H. Lee, their birthplaces, in Westmoreland County, are within a radius of a few miles from the home of Thomas Johnson on the Northern side of the Potomac. The birthplace of Johnson was destroyed by fire some years later and there was left standing only a small outbuilding, built by his brother, James, for a bakery, where bread was made to supply the ships that lay in the creek. Some years later, during the War of 1812, the Battle of the Barges, in which Commodore Joshua Barney met the British frigates, was fought near the old Johnson farm.

The first child of Thomas and Dorcas Johnson, born December 13, 1725, and christened Thomas—a name that had been used in the family through many generations— died when very young. All the other children—seven sons and four daughters—grew to maturity, remaining on the farm in Calvert County until they were able to take care of themselves.

The following were the eleven surviving children:

(1) Benjamin, the eldest, was born July 6, 1727, and served as a Major in the Maryland forces during the Revolutionary War. He was twice married.

(2) Mary, the eldest daughter, was born May 5, 1729. She was married to Walter Hellen, Esq.

(3) Rebecca was born on the 3rd of November, 1730. She became the wife of Thomas McKenzie, Esq., but died, on March 1, 1767, soon after the marriage.

(4) Thomas.

(5) Dorcas was born October 17, 1734. In August, 1783, when nearly 49 years old, she became the wife of Col. Josiah Clapham, of Loudoun County, Virginia.

(6) James was born September 30, 1736. He married Margaret Skinner, of Calvert County, and went to Indian Spring, in Frederick (now Washington) County. After constructing the "Green Spring" Iron Furnace, about a mile

from Fort Frederick, he settled in 1774 within the present borders of Frederick County. With the aid of his brothers, he managed "Catoctin" Furnace, "Bush Creek" Forge, "Johnson" Furnace, near the mouth of the Monocacy River, and the "Potomac" Furnace, in Loudoun County, Virginia, opposite Pt. of Rocks. He served as the Colonel of a battalion of infantry in the Flying Camp raised by his distinguished brother, and served in 1779 with Upton Sheredine and Alexander C. Hanson, as a member of the Court-martial which tried and ordered the execution of a number of Tories in Frederick Town.

(7) Elizabeth was born on the 17th of September, 1739. She became the wife of George Cook, who commanded a Maryland ship during the Revolution. Captain Cook is described as "a bold, blustering Scottish sea captain" with short queue and cocked hat, with many eccentricities, albeit honest and industrious and a good husband.

(8) Joshua was born June 25, 1742. He entered a countinghouse in London and eventually became a large dealer in tobacco. When the American Colonies declared their independence, he took up his residence in Nantes, France, and during the Revolution served as American Agent in France. From 1790 to 1797, he served, under the appointment of Washington, as the first American Consul at London. In 1797, his second daughter, Louisa Catherine, was married to John Quincy Adams, who was at that time Ambassador to the Court of Berlin. On his return to America, Joshua was appointed by President John Adams as Superintendent of Stamps in Washington, which position he held until the time of his death.

(9) John, born August 29, 1745, became a physician, and for some time occupied an office on West Patrick street,

in Frederick Town. He served as a surgeon in the Maryland Line during the Revolution.

(10) Baker was born on the 30th of September, 1747. After studying law in the office of his brother, Thomas, at Annapolis, he settled in Frederick to engage in the practice of his profession. He commanded a battalion with the rank of Colonel in the brigade of his brother, and was at the Battle of Paoli, near Philadelphia, famous for the slaughter of Wayne's men. He married Miss Catherine Worthington, the daughter of Col. Nicholas Worthington, of Anne Arundel County.

(11) Roger, the "baby" of the family, was born March 18, 1749. After studying under his brother, Thomas, he settled in Frederick County to engage in the iron business. With the aid of his brothers, he built "Bloomsbury" Forge, on Bennett's Creek, in Urbana District, and also managed the Forge on Bush Creek, at Riehl's Mill, in the Northern part of the District. He had the rank of Major in his brother James's Battalion. He was married to Elizabeth, daughter of Richard Thomas, of Montgomery County.

The good, Puritan mother who raised these eleven children lived long enough to see her youngest son, Roger, pass the age of twenty-one. Her death occurred on the 11th of December, 1770, several years before her son, Thomas, was chosen Governor. Thomas Johnson, Sr., died on April 11, 1777, thus living only three weeks after his distinguished son was first inaugurated Chief Executive of Maryland.

The Johnson children received elementary instruction in "the three R's"; but the Johnson parents, although enabled to live in comfortable circumstances, were precluded by the expense of raising such a large family from the possibility of affording their children a classical education in Europe.

While the advantages of education in the Colonies were of a very unpretentious character, the Johnsons were located within a few miles of Annapolis, which was not only the Capital of Maryland, but also, socially, intellectually, and commercially, one of the leading centers of American civilization. Thither—to the "Athens of America"—Thomas Johnson, the fifth child of Thomas and Dorcas (Sedgwick) Johnson, was sent at an early age to make his living.

The history of Annapolis dates back to 1649, when it was settled by Puritan refugees from Virginia, who came to Maryland to enjoy freedom of worship; but it was not until the year 1683 that the settlement was erected into a town, becoming the Capital of the Province in 1694. Between 1750 and the outbreak of the Revolution, Annapolis saw its most brilliant days. The following old record of Annapolis, preserved since 1749, indicates that the Puritanical character of the town had disappeared by that day:

"The outlook of the city was fair and promising, its merchants had secured the chief trade of the province; ships from all seas came to its harbour; its endowed school (King William's) educated its citizens for important positions; its thought made the mind of the province. The gayety of its inhabitants, and their love of refined pleasure had developed the race-course, the theatre, the ball-room; their love of learning, the *Gazette* and King William's school; creations and enterprises that made the province famous in after years as the centre of the social pleasures, of the culture and of the refinement of the American colonies."

Annapolis of pre-Revolutionary days has been described in detail by William Eddis, one of the Commissioners of the Loan Office of Maryland, who wrote great volumes of letters to his relatives and friends in England. In October,

1769, this prolific letter writer paints the following picture of Annapolis:

"At present the city has more the appearance of an agreeable village, than the metropolis of an opulent province, as it contains within its limits a number of small fields, which are intended for future erections. But in a few years, it will probably be one of the best built cities in America, as a spirit of improvement is predominant, and the situation is allowed to be equally healthy and pleasant with any on this side the Atlantic. Many of the principal families have chosen this place for their residence, and there are few towns of the same size, in any part of the British dominions, that can boast of a more polished society.

"The court-house, situated on an eminence at the back of the town, commands a variety of views highly interesting; the entrance of the Severn, the majestic Chesapeake, and the eastern shore of Maryland, being all united in one resplendent assemblage, vessels of various sizes and figures are constantly floating before the eye; which, while they add to the beauty of the scene, excite ideas of the most pleasing nature."

Another interesting bit of description of the gay life in Annapolis prior to the Revolution has been presented as follows by S. G. Fisher, in his "Colonial Men, Women and Manners":

"The men and women, who, like the rest of the Maryland gentry, ordered champagne from Europe by the cask, and madeira by the pipe, also dressed expensively in the latest English fashions, and French travellers said that they had seldom seen such clothes outside of Paris. They had French barbers, negro slaves in livery, and drove light carriages,—an extremely rare indulgence in colonial times. The clubs got up excursions, picnics, and fishing parties. Balls were given on all the great English anniversaries, and the birthday of the proprietor and saints' days were used as excuses."

Upon arriving in the Capital, Thomas Johnson, Jr., was given employment by Thomas Jennings, Register of the

Land Office. The lad's first employment, as a writer in the office of the Clerk of the Provincial Court, presented him the opportunity not only of becoming acquainted with Court procedure, but also of hearing some of the most brilliant American lawyers, headed by Daniel Dulany, the foremost lawyer of the New World, then engaged in active practice in Annapolis.

Young Johnson, deciding to take up the study of law, was given the privilege of studying in the office of Stephen Bordley. "As a lawyer," says Scharf, concerning Mr. Bordley, "he stood high in the Province and in Europe, and many distinguished lawyers of the Province studied under him." Although born in Annapolis, Mr. Bordley received his education in England. After a preliminary education at school followed by the study of law for a period of four years in the office of an English barrister, he sojourned for several years within the classical precincts of the Temple. In 1736, when he was 27 years old, his father, Thomas Bordley, one of the ablest lawyers of his time, died; and Stephen, the eldest son, thereupon assumed a commanding position at the Colonial Bar. He served as a member of the Assembly, in the Council, as Commissary General, Naval Officer at Annapolis, and Attorney-General of the Province. While Daniel Dulany was recognized both at home and in Europe as the foremost lawyer in the New World, Mr. Bordley was regarded as his nearest professional rival.

A glimpse into the character of Mr. Johnson's preceptor is presented by Governor Sharpe in his letters to Cecilius Calvert, the Secretary of Maryland. The following is an extract from a letter,[1] written July 7, 1760, in which the Governor describes the personnel of his Council:

[1] IX *Archives,* 425.

CONFIDE ET CERTA

THE JOHNSON COAT OF ARMS

"Of Mr. Bordley the other Gentleman who has a seat in the Council in consequence of my recommendation, I shall say the less as you seem to be already thoroughly satisfied of his ability and inclination to promote His Lordship's interest, indeed I am rather afraid that his earnest desire to do His Lordship acceptable service might sometimes carry him into extremes, he being of a very sanguine complection, and lest he should thereby prejudice the cause he would wish to serve than lest he should be deficient in point of duty. His abilities as a lawyer cannot be questioned and by this means he will I suppose be ever a check on Mr. Dulany of whom however he is perhaps too suspicious and jealous as they have always been at enmity, but as there is no man who is not liable to error and those of a warm temper are generally more liable than others, I shall never think it right to surrender myself up even to this Gentleman as to a Pilot, tho I assure you his opinion in matters of Law will always determine me; and his advice in other affairs will have great weight unless upon examining his propositions coolly and considering them maturely, I see good cause to decline carrying them into execution."

That Bordley was regarded as a peer of Dulany is indicated by another letter to Calvert, written by Governor Sharpe on May 8, 1764.

"How he [Dulany] behaved in England I know not," writes the Governor, "but he affects a great superiority here and indeed the only person in the Council that he seemed to consider as an equal was Mr. Bordley and as that gentleman is unhappily reduced to such a state by a paralytic disorder as to be almost disqualified for business Mr. Dulany who is now in perfect health seems to think himself of still greater importance than ever."

Mr. Bordley was never happier than when he was contributing to the happiness or advancement of young people. Mr. Johnson was only one of a number of young men whom he assisted on the highway to success. William Paca, one of the "Signers," who was eight years younger than Mr. Johnson, also received his legal training under Mr. Bordley.

John Beale Bordley, a half-brother, who was about five years older than Johnson, was another of his disciples.

But Stephen Bordley, though a diligent student of the law, was not a recluse. He had a jovial disposition and was famed for his hospitality. Remaining a bachelor his entire life, he was fond of young people's company. His home was constantly the scene of entertainments to the young ladies "of the first circle" in Annapolis, who "smiled at his primitive and precise politeness, but justly admired his wit, good sense, and good humor." [2]   In a letter written in 1750 to his relatives in England, Mr. Bordley said: "We live well, and cheerfully, with the enjoyment of all the necessaries and many of the little comforts of life. . . . We are all still single; a strange family! perhaps you'll say; but Beale is now in pursuit of a Dove, and I am apt to believe will soon break the enchantment." Beale married shortly afterwards. He did not, however, remain long in Annapolis; the practice of law did not appeal to him, and in 1753—the year Thomas Johnson became of age—he assumed the position of prothonotary, or clerk, of Baltimore County.

Mr. Johnson was admitted, in due time, as a member of the Bar. He had received an excellent preparation. The specimens of his pleading indicate that he was a diligent student and a master of the technicalities of law. Opening his office in Annapolis for the practice of his profession, he rapidly rose to the first professional rank in the Province. He became engaged as counsel in litigation arising in various sections of Maryland: in 1760 he was admitted to the Bar of Frederick County, where Mr. Bordley had first

[2] Gibson, *Biographical Sketches of the Bordley Family,* 48.

appeared in 1755. In the decade preceding the Revolution, Johnson held an enviable position in the legal profession, when Samuel Chase, William Paca, Thomas Stone, James Hollyday, Edward Dorsey, James Tilghman, and the Goldsboroughs adorned the Colonial Bar.

CHAPTER III

ASSAILING THE STAMP ACT

A T the age of 29, Johnson, recognized already as a leading member of the Bar, was elected one of the Delegates from Anne Arundel County to the Provincial Assembly. When he took his seat in the old Colonial Court House at Annapolis on the seventeenth of March, 1762, he started on a career in public life that covered a period of thirty years—a career which, for length, versatility and importance of service, is unparalleled in the annals of the State. The member of Assembly, during the Colonial days, occupied a very exalted station. Champion, as he was, of the people's cause, he unfailingly received, if he tried faithfully to perform his duty, the gratitude and the veneration of his constituents, if not, indeed, of all the subjects in the Province. The delegates who were true to their constituents deserved their popularity, for they were the only public officials who represented the people and, as such, they did what they could to stem the tide of oppression that flowed from Crown, Ministry and Parliament and from Lord Proprietary, Governor and Council.

It is true, under the Proprietary form of Government, Maryland, when compared with the other Colonies, had a Charter which operated with unusual beneficence. Unlike Virginia, a Royal Province, under the direct control and domination of the King, Maryland belonged to one person

—the Lord Proprietary—to whom the Crown delegated full control of the Province. Holding his domain as the patrimony of the family, the Proprietary stood in the relation of a *pater familias* to his Colony, which, if properly managed, would reflect glory upon him and bring wealth to his progeny. The comparative success of the Government of Maryland was thus largely attributable to the fact that the Province, like that of Pennsylvania, was vested in one family, for if these Colonies had been owned by several co-proprietors of different families, they would not have acted with the same sense of liberality and pride which animated a Proprietary, the name of whose family and the happiness of whose posterity were to be determined to a large extent by the wealth and prosperity of his Province. But even in Maryland, the subjects were at the complete mercy of the Proprietary and they looked to their chosen representatives as the guardians of their liberty. The Charter, which King Charles I granted to Cecilius Calvert, Second Lord Baltimore, on June 20, 1632—the most comprehensive grant of civil power that ever came from the throne of England—gave the Lord Proprietary the right to appoint not only the Governor but all the officers of the Province. Then, too, the Upper House of the Assembly— the Council—was composed of men who were on intimate terms with the Proprietary Governor and hence were necessarily oftentimes antagonistic to the will of the people. "The existence of the Upper House," says John V. L. McMahon, "as a coördinate branch of the Legislature constituted one of the most objectionable features of the Assembly. It had all the disadvantages without the advantages of the House of Peers. The latter, if it is independent of the people, is also independent of the Crown;

but the Upper House of the province, consisting of councillors appointed by the proprietary was an aristocracy of
the worst kind—an aristocracy wholly independent of and
irresponsible to the people, and at the same time the mere
creature and dependent of the proprietary."

But further than that, for twenty years prior to the
coronation of George III, the Lower House of the Maryland Assembly itself had been in control of a powerful
group of men, who, although pretending to be "patriots,"
really deluded their constituents in order to keep in power
and were actually inimical to the best interests of the
Colonists. This faction, led by Phil Hammond, was composed of men of very inferior calibre; and their obstinate
tempers and uncouth manners made their proceedings nothing short of disgusting. They did all they could to harass
the Proprietary Governor. It was, accordingly, not long
after Horatio Sharpe took the oath of office as Governor in
1753 that he warned the Lord Proprietary there were "too
many instances of the lowest persons, at least men of small
fortunes, no soul, and very mean capacity, appearing as
representatives of their respective Counties." Thinking
that the drudgery of electioneering had perhaps de-
terred the better class of citizens from running for the Legislature, Governor Sharpe suggested that a less frequent "can-
vass for seats" might produce an improvement in the House
personnel. The interim between elections, however, was
never lengthened.

On top of all this, in the year 1760, George III—one
of the most stubborn and stupid monarchs that ever wore
a crown since the dawn of civilization—ascended the throne
of England. Fortunate, indeed, therefore, were the people
of Maryland, when shortly after George III's accession, men

of the calibre of Thomas Johnson, Jr., secured control of the Lower House of the Provincial Assembly. The notorious Phil Hammond, the Opposition Leader in the House for over twenty years, died in 1760—the same year George was crowned King—and when the Assembly convened at Annapolis in March, 1762, as Thomas Johnson, Jr., took his seat in the House chamber for the first time, there was a change in its personnel that was most remarkable. The improvement was so noticeable that Governor Sharpe wrote to England: "We have had a general election, at which many well-behaved, sensible men were chosen in the stead of such as I have never desired to see again in the House." [1] Thus, the Radical faction was supplanted by a body of able and faithful Conservatives. The members of the Assembly were no longer demagogues: now they were conscientious guardians of the people's liberty. From this time until the outbreak of the War for Independence, the names of Tilghman and Hollyday, Ringgold and Ridgely, Goldsborough and Worthington, Johnson, Chase and Paca added luster to the annals of the Colonial Legislature. For an entire decade, Thomas Johnson served continuously as a Delegate from Anne Arundel County. In this period, most of the members were men of considerable brilliance. Mr. Eddis, the Englishman who served at Annapolis as Surveyor of the Customs, wrote as follows regarding the personnel of the Assembly in the day of Delegate Johnson:

"The Delegates returned are persons of the greatest consequence in their different Counties, and many of them are frequently acquainted with the political and commercial interests of their constituents. I have frequently heard subjects debated with great powers of eloquence and force of reason; and the utmost regularity and propriety distinguished the whole of their proceedings."

[1] Sharpe's *Correspondence,* Vol. III, p. 24.

When early in the reign of George III, the Parliament
considered the expediency of passing measures to raise
revenue in the Colonies of North America, Governor Sharpe,
aware of the "great powers of eloquence and force of reason" of the members of the Provincial Assembly in Maryland, was very slow in calling the Assembly together.
Under the Maryland Charter, the Lord Proprietary had
the right to convene, as well as to prorogue or adjourn, the
Provincial Assembly; and this prerogative was delegated to
the Governor, who used it as a sword over the heads of the
Assemblymen. If the Delegates were likely to cause trouble
for the Proprietary Government, they were not called together; if in session, they were speedily prorogued. This use
of prerogative, however, instead of driving the people from
their convictions, generally had the effect of making them all
the more defiant and their representatives eager to rally more
loyally to accomplish the desires of their constituents. But
while James Otis, in Massachusetts, and Patrick Henry, in
Virginia, were "touching the chord of public feeling, already
tremblingly alive," the Maryland House of Delegates was
prevented from officially pronouncing a single word of resentment.

Even the high dignitaries in England looked upon Maryland with suspicion. During the French and Indian War
—brought to an end by the Treaty of Paris in 1763—requisitions for men and money, recommended by the Governor of Maryland, were disregarded by the Assembly.
Maryland's passive course, however, was due neither to
selfish disregard nor to timid abandonment of the common
cause. She was ever anxious to provide for the general
defense and to promote the welfare of her sister Colonies.
But, at the outbreak of the French and Indian War, when

George Washington, Thomas Johnson and Richard Henry Lee were just arriving at man's estate, there unfortunately arose a dispute in Maryland over the *modus operandi* of raising the revenue to provide for the defense appropriations. Lord Baltimore claimed exemption from taxation and the representatives of the provincials insisted that the Proprietary ought to pay his share. Whilst fully cognizant of the obligations resting upon them to provide for the common defense, the members of Maryland's Colonial Legislature felt that to safeguard their constituents from the tyranny of unjust taxation was a more sacred duty; and they refused to let the discharge of a duty to the Crown and to the sister Colonies depend upon their disregard of the very birthright of the British subjects whom they represented. As "the power to tax is the power to destroy," the members of the House and, indeed, the people everywhere felt that upon the preservation by the Assembly of the power to impose taxes depended the very liberty of the Colonists. The demands of the Upper House could not have been granted without a surrender of those principles to which the Delegates stood unalterably pledged. A deadlock resulted and the appropriations were defeated.

The expenditures of the British Government in the prosecution of the war had added greatly to the debt of the Empire; and the Ministry took the position that the Colonists, for whom the war had been waged, could well afford to relieve England of a portion of the expense of running the Royal Government. But while imposed to help pay England's heavy indebtedness resulting from the conduct of the war and the payment of subsidies to the King of Prussia, the Stamp Act was also an experiment, prompted in large measure by the failure of several of the

Colonies—particularly Maryland—to comply with the requisitions of the King during the French War, to pave the way for more complete supremacy of the Crown over the recalcitrant Colonies. Indeed, William Pitt himself—later one of the champions of American liberty—was so incensed at Maryland's apathy that he avowed his intention of bringing the Colonies into such a state of subjugation that the Royal Government, upon the restoration of peace, would be enabled to compel obedience to every requisition of the Crown.

In the House of Commons, the celebrated Stamp Act was passed by a majority of 5 to 1, and in the House of Lords the vote in favor of the measure was unanimous. The King, seized by a fit of insanity, was unable to sign the bill; but a Board of Commissioners, acting on His Majesty's behalf, gave the Royal assent on March 22, 1765.

The Stamp Act provided that all legal documents in the Colonies had to bear British stamps. Colonial publications and advertisements were taxed, and contracts of every nature, unless written on paper bearing the Royal stamps, were declared to be unenforceable. The Act kindled the patriotic flame in the breasts of the Colonists. Soon after the news of its passage reached America, the resentment of the Colonists became malignant. Benjamin Franklin wrote to a friend: "The sun of American liberty has set. Now we must light the lamps of industry and economy." Immediately came the reply: "Be assured that we shall light torches of another sort!" This prediction, as Ridpath affirms, reflected the sentiment of the whole country. And it was a true prediction.

Nowhere in America was resentment more bitter against *Taxation without Representation* than in Maryland. Her

Charter declared that the subjects residing within the limits of the Province were entitled to all the liberties of British freemen. Accordingly, Marylanders contended that the covenants in the Charter expressly exempted them from taxation by Great Britain. And although Thomas Johnson and his colleagues in the Assembly were prevented, by repeated prorogations, from making an official remonstrance before final action had been taken by Parliament, the people throughout Maryland courageously indicated their indignation. When the news of the arrival of Zachariah Hood, an Annapolis merchant, whom the British Ministry had appointed stamp distributor for Maryland, spread through the Colony, the people in Annapolis, Frederick Town, and other places, burnt him in effigy. Describing the Annapolis demonstration, James McSherry, in his "History of Maryland," says: "The effigy of the stamp distributor was mounted on a one-horse cart. . . . The procession marched to the hill, tied the effigy to the whipping-post, and bestowed upon it nine-and-thirty lashes. . . . It was then hung upon a gibbet, erected for the purpose, a tar barrel placed under it, and set on fire, whence it ignited, and at length, fell into the blaze below and was consumed." On the 2nd of September, the people again showed their indignation by assembling in Annapolis and demolishing the stamp distributor's home. Forced to leave the Province, Hood fled to New York, where he resigned his commission.

Although the Maryland Assembly was in session only five weeks in 1762, and seven weeks in 1763, Governor Sharpe failed to convene it at all during 1764.

Finally, nearly six months after the Stamp Act had been adopted, Governor Sharpe issued a call for the

Assembly. The people assembled at various places, soon after this news was received, for the purpose of instructing their Delegates-elect to protest against the Stamp Act in the Maryland Assembly. In Anne Arundel County, for example, the freemen, assembling on September 7, 1765, passed a set of instructions for their representatives in the Lower House—Brice T. B. Worthington, Henry Hall, John Hammond and Thomas Johnson, Jr.—basing the claim to exemption from taxation by Parliament upon their rights and privileges as British subjects, the express provisions in the Maryland Charter, and the uninterrupted precedent established in the Province. Taxes could be imposed, they contended, only with the consent of the subjects themselves or their chosen representatives. "And," they continued, "we do unanimously protest against our being charged in any other manner, and by any other powers whatsoever; and we do request of you, our Representatives, that this Protest may be entered, and stand recorded, in your Journal, amongst the proceedings of your House, if it may be regularly done." Mr. Johnson and his colleagues were requested, in addition, to move an Address of Thanks to General Conway and Col. Isaac Barré for asserting the liberty of the Colonists; to advocate, in accordance with the proposal from the Assembly of Massachusetts Bay, a General Congress of the American Colonies; and to join in a Memorial to the Crown.

The members of the House met September 23, 1765, in a spirit little short of revolutionary. The fiat of public sentiment in uncompromising hostility to the Stamp Act had been issued, and the Delegates, after two years of inactivity, required little time for deliberation concerning the most expedient course to pursue. As soon as the House came to order, the members took up for consideration the Circular Letter from the Massachusetts Assembly; and, on the following day, the plan was unanimously endorsed. With the concurrence of the Council and the approval of Governor Sharpe, the Assembly appropriated £500 to pay the expenses of Maryland's Delegates to New York. The Assembly selected Col. Edward Tilghman of Queen Anne's, Thomas Ringgold of Kent, and William Murdock of Prince George's—three of the most brilliant and experienced statesmen of their day—as the Delegates from Maryland.

Up to this time, young Mr. Johnson had served only about 70 days, in all, as a Delegate in the Provincial Assembly; but in this short time his sound judgment had already been displayed. When, therefore, the Assembly appointed a committee of seven, with the able James Hollyday, of Queen Anne's County, as chairman, to draft a set of instructions for Maryland's representatives in the General Congress, the young Annapolis lawyer was chosen one of the members. The other members of the committee were: John Hammond, of Anne Arundel; John Hanson, Jr., of Charles; John Goldsborough, of Talbot; and Edmund Key and Daniel Wolstenholme, of St. Mary's. The seven Delegates framed their instructions with great haste, for on September 25, 1765, they brought in their report to the House. Tilghman, Ringgold and Murdock, they recommended, should repair immediately to the General Congress at New York "there to join in a general and united, dutiful, loyal, and humble representation to his Majesty and the British Parliament, of the circumstances and condition of the British Colonies; and to pray relief from the burdens and restraints lately laid upon their trade and commerce, and especially from the taxes imposed by the Stamp Act, whereby they are deprived, in some instances, of that invaluable privilege of Englishmen and British subjects, trials by jury; and to take care that such representation should humbly and decently, *but expressly*, contain an assertion of the right of the Colonists, to be exempt from all and every taxations and impositions upon their persons and property, to which they do not consent in a legislative way, either by themselves, or their representatives freely chosen and appointed." The committee's recommendations, it is needless to say, were accepted.

The plan of holding a General Congress of the Colonies having been speedily endorsed, the Maryland Assembly thereupon determined to enunciate, with more solemnity and with due formality, "the constitutional rights and privileges of the freemen of the Province." Again, Thomas Johnson was honored by being placed on this important committee. Colonel Tilghman and Messrs. Ringgold and Murdock—the Delegates who were preparing to leave for New York to represent Maryland at the General Congress —were named to assist in the preparation of the Resolutions. The other members of the committee were: James and Henry Hollyday, Samuel Chase, Brice T. B. Worthington, John Hammond, Edmund Key, Daniel Wolstenholme, Samuel Wilson, Charles Grahame and John Goldsborough. The committee reported its "Bill of Rights" on September 28, 1765, and it was adopted without a single dissenting vote. Referring to these Resolves, Mr. McMahon says: "Preëminent amongst all the legislative declarations of the Colonies, for the lofty and dignified tone of their remonstrance, and for the entire unanimity with which they were adopted, they form one of the proudest portions of our history." [2] If there were any doubts in the minds of the British Ministry as to whether Maryland would concur with the refractory Colonies, such doubts were now dispelled. Maryland had, in bold and uncompromising language, officially asserted her position.

This done, the legislators refused to entertain any other business and requested Governor Sharpe to give them "a short recess of a few weeks." This request was doubtless made for the purpose of awaiting the result of the General Congress at New York. The Governor indicated that he was willing to grant a recess; but added that, inasmuch as the British stamps would arrive before they reconvened, he was anxious to have advice as to what to do with the stamps when the British vessel anchored. Johnson was chosen as one of eleven members to draft a reply to the Governor. The committee recommended the following reply: "We should think ourselves extremely happy were we in circumstances to advise your Excellency on so new a subject; but it being a matter of importance, and such as we do not think ourselves at liberty to advise in, without the instructions of our constituents, which we cannot now obtain, we hope your Excellency will think us excusable for declining to offer you any advice upon the occasion." On September 28, 1765, after being in session only six days, the Assembly was prorogued. When the British sloop-of-war *Hawke* arrived with the stamped paper aboard, there was no person to receive it and no place in Maryland where it could be stored in safety. Governor Sharpe, in accordance with the suggestion of his Council, directed the commander of the vessel to keep it on board until instructions could be pro-

[2] John V. L. McMahon, *Historical View of the Government of Maryland* (1831), p. 345.

cured from the British Ministry concerning the disposal of the stamps. The stamps were never used in Maryland.

When the Assembly reconvened on November 1, Tilghman, Ringgold and Murdock presented a report of their course of action in the General Congress of the Colonies. The Congress had convened with 28 delegates in attendance in New York on the 7th of October, 1765. All the Colonies, with the exception of New Hampshire, Virginia, North Carolina and Georgia, were represented, and these four, although unrepresented, sympathized with the general cause. The Congress adopted a Declaration of Rights, an Address to the Crown, and a Memorial to Parliament. The course of action pursued at New York by Maryland's Delegates was heartily endorsed by the Maryland Assembly and a vote of thanks was given them for the able and faithful discharge of their duties.

The Stamp Art was to have become effective on the first day of November, 1765, but nowhere were any British stamps to be found in the Province. How was business to be carried on, if unstamped documents, under the Act of Parliament, had no legal value? This problem was soon to be solved by the Frederick County Court. The November Term convened on the nineteenth of the month. When the Clerk of the Court refused to issue process without British stamps, the "Immortal Twelve," on the 23rd of November, 1765, held that "all proceedings shall be valid and effective without the use of stamps." It was an important decision. The Parliament's authority had never before been questioned. "What Parliament doth," said Sir William Blackstone, "no authority on earth can undo." Everywhere throughout the Province the defiant action of the Court was acclaimed with great rejoicing.

One of the most memorable demonstrations was held at Frederick Town, where the people held a mock funeral of the Stamp Act, the effigy of Zachariah Hood being the sole mourner. After the funeral oration, the offensive document and the effigy were buried together "amid loud cheers and ruffs of the drums."

So bitterly did all the Colonies condemn the Stamp Act that Parliament at an early date took up the question of its repeal. Lord Mansfield stubbornly affirmed the absolute supremacy of the British Parliament in realm and dominions; but Camden and Pitt, the Earl of Chatham, pointing to the distinction between taxation and legislation, denied the right of Parliament to tax the Colonists. And later in the great Stamp Act debate in which Edmund Burke participated, William Pitt quoted freely from the essay published on October 14, 1765, by Daniel Dulany, the lawyer whose talents Johnson had the opportunity to observe at close range for many years during his residence at Annapolis. Woodrow Wilson paid the following tribute [3] to Dulany and his essay on the Stamp Act: "Mr. Daniel Dulany's 'Considerations on the Propriety of Imposing Taxes in the British Colonies for the Purpose of Raising a Revenue by Act of Parliament,' supplied the great Pitt with the chief grounds of his argument against taxing America. A Maryland lawyer had turned from leading the bar of a province to set up the true theory of the constitution of an empire with the dignity, the moderation, the power, the incommunicable grace of a great thinker and genuine man of letters." The Grenville Ministry having been succeeded by the Rockingham Administration, the fa-

[3] Woodrow Wilson, *History of the American People* (1902), Vol. III. p. 87.

mous Stamp Act was repealed on March 18, 1766—almost
exactly one year after its passage.

Maryland, on account of the prorogation of her
Assembly by Governor Sharpe until the Autumn of 1765,
was late in filing her official Remonstrance; but, when once
made, it was, indeed, "preëminent amongst all the legislative declarations of the Colonies." And Thomas Johnson,
Jr., of Annapolis, emerged from the controversy as one
of the outstanding champions of the American cause.

In the meantime, Johnson, at the age of 33, had asked
for the hand of Ann Jennings, the daughter of his old em-
ployer. They were married on February 16, 1766.

CHAPTER IV

AN APPEAL TO THE CROWN

EVERYWHERE in the American Colonies the news of the repeal of the Stamp Act was received with bound-less joy. When the tidings reached Annapolis the members of the Provincial Assembly adjourned in boyish glee and repaired to the Council chamber to drink patriotic toasts. The news spread like wildfire through the Colony. The happy subjects reasserted their loyalty to the Crown and quaffed wine and punch in great quantities to the health of the British statesmen who had advocated the American cause. It was the occasion for a jubilee such as had never before been known in the history of Maryland.

Portraits of Lord Camden, General Conway and Sir Isaac Barré were hung in Faneuil Hall. Statues to King George were authorized in New York and Virginia. Likewise in Maryland men of the Johnson type were anxious to honor the champions of American liberty. Reassembling toward the close of 1766, the House put forward the plan of adorning the walls of the Provincial Court with a portrait of Charles Pratt, Lord High Chancellor, and of memorializing William Pitt in marble. A resolution to this effect was carried with a unanimous vote. Assemblyman Johnson, of Anne Arundel, was one of the sponsors of an enabling Act introduced to carry this resolution into effect. The bill, like the resolution, met with instant and

37

hearty approval. But in His Lordship's Council the attitude toward the bill was somewhat different. On account of the failure of appropriation, Mr. Johnson and his associates never had the pleasure of hanging in the Court chamber the portrait of Lord Camden or of erecting in Annapolis the statue of Pitt. The Assembly could not be prevented, however, from sending through Charles Garth, the London Agent of the Province of Maryland, a note of thanks to King George, as evidence of the appreciation of the people in Maryland for His Majesty's assent to the repeal of the Stamp Act, and to the Earl of Chesterfield, Lord Shelburne, Colonel Barré, Secretary Conway, Sir George Saville, General Howard and any others who "acted the like glorious part" in defending the liberties of the American people.

A sort of Consul, Agent Garth had been transacting Maryland's provincial affairs faithfully and with great satisfaction to the people of the Colony. There now appeared in the Upper House at Annapolis a conspiracy to drive Mr. Garth out of office. Unless the Assembly would consent to impose a tax upon the people to provide a salary for the Clerk of the Council, *in addition to the fees of that office*, the Upper House declared it would refuse to provide the salary of the London Agent. Prorogation was imminent. There was little time to be lost. How could they secure £1,000 for Mr. Garth's salary and expenses? As an appropriation without the sanction of the Upper House was an impossibility, it was decided to conduct a lottery in order to raise the funds. Prominent members of the House were selected as promoters. Thomas Johnson, Jr., was called upon to serve as one of them. Others who helped to manage *The Maryland Liberty Lottery*, as it was called, were two young men who a decade later had the high distinction of signing the American Declaration of Independence—William Paca and Samuel Chase. William Murdock and Thomas Ringgold, both of whom were eminent as Colonial statesmen, were among those who helped to supervise the lottery, as were also John Hall and Brice T. B. Worthington, who long were colleagues of Mr. Johnson in the Lower House from Anne Arundel County. Five other Assemblymen—John Hammond, Thomas Sprigg, Henry Hall, Thomas Gassaway and John Weems—were chosen, making a total board of twelve. The lottery tickets were offered in all parts of Maryland.

Johnson was also called upon to serve on another recess committee at this time. This committee was asked to investigate the whole question of the *modus operandi* of raising revenue for the support of the Proprietary Government, and consisted of Speaker Robert Lloyd, Thomas Johnson, Thomas Ringgold, William Murdock, Edward Tilghman and John Hall. They were also authorized to present to the King, through Agent Garth, a full account of the controversy with the Upper House concerning appropriations for their Agent at the London Court. Accordingly, the committee drafted a letter to the Governor, in which they explained the need for an Agent in London. For example, they pointed out that the Province owned £30,000 of the capital stock of the Bank of England, but that many creditors were being denied their just claims, and that it was important to have an Agent in London to see that Bills of Credit were issued to pay such claims. The committee requested access to the Journals and Acts of the Assembly in order to secure certain data for Mr. Garth. On the 19th of February, 1767, Governor Sharpe presented the letter to the Council for consideration. Daniel Dulany, Secretary of the Province, was delegated to draft a reply. He replied on the same day that he would permit the Delegates to examine the official books and papers in his possession, but he reminded them that this permission would be granted them as *private gentlemen* only, and not as *officials.*

Policies were now in the making in England which were to give Thomas Johnson the opportunity to display his powers of leadership. In the Summer of 1766, the Administration of the Marquis of Rockingham ended; and in the following year Charles Townshend, Chancellor of the Exchequer, submitted to Parliament a new scheme for raising revenue in America, which made a distinction between "direct taxes" and "imposts to regulate commerce." William Pitt, now the Earl of Chatham, was prevented by ill health from taking an active part in the legislation, and the Acts passed with little opposition. They imposed new duties on tea, paper, glass and other articles imported into America and provided for a Board of Customs at Boston to collect the revenue throughout the Colonies. Receiving the Royal assent in June, the measures were intended to take effect on the 20th of November, 1767.

Again the smoldering fires of discontent were kindled in America. The Assembly of Massachusetts Bay called upon the other Colonies to unite in opposition to this most recent invasion of their Anglo-Saxon liberty. In Maryland the champions of the people's cause were eager openly and courageously to place themselves upon record in defiance of Crown, Ministry and Parliament; but the Provincial Assembly—the only official body representative of the people—was not in session. Furthermore, there was little likelihood of a session at an early date. Governor Sharpe, although bitterly condemned for proroguing the Assembly while the Stamp Act was before Parliament, continued his old tactics by preventing the Assembly from convening during the year 1767. The session was deferred until May 24, 1768—six months after the Acts of Parliament went into effect and a year after their passage. But when the House did finally reconvene, the members boldly resolved that the revenue measures infringed "the great and fundamental principles upon which the right of taxation is based." And they sent back to Massachusetts a message of warm sympathy and complete concurrence.

The Assembly also decided to state to the Crown in formal language the opinion of the freemen of Maryland regarding the latest measures. On the 8th of June, 1768, the Assembly selected a committee of seven to draft this Memorial to the King. The selection of Thomas Johnson on this committee presented him an enviable opportunity to render conspicuous service. Associated with him on the committee were Matthew Tilghman, Thomas Jennings, James Hollyday, William Murdock, Thomas Ringgold and John Hall.

About this time Governor Sharpe received an important circular letter from the Earl of Hillsborough, British Secretary of State, requesting immediate effort to forestall the "flagitious attempts [of Massachusetts] to disturb the public peace"; and in accordance with Lord Hillsborough's request, Sharpe asked the Assembly on the 20th of June to "confirm the favorable opinion His Majesty entertains of his Maryland subjects by taking no notice of such letter [from the Massachusetts Assembly], which will be treating it with the contempt it deserves." In reply to the Governor the Delegates declared they were surprised that memorials respectfully presented to the Crown could be regarded as seditious. "We cannot," they said, "but view this as an attempt, in some of his Majesty's Ministers, to suppress all communication of sentiments between the Colonies and to prevent the united supplications of America from reaching the Royal ear. We have the warmest and most affectionate attachment to our most gracious sovereign, and shall ever pay the readiest and most respectful regard to the just and constitutional power of the British Parliament; but we shall not be intimidated by a few high-sounding expressions from doing what we think is right." It was, indeed, a bold and uncompromising reply. Other Colonies expressed similar sentiments, but surely in language no more defiant.

The Memorial to George III, prepared by Johnson and his associates, was adopted by the Assembly with enthusiastic approval. Couched in language both fearless and respectful, and basing their arguments upon their inalienable rights as British freemen and upon their Charter, the Assemblymen's Remonstrance against the Acts of 1767 is a valuable commentary on the eventful years that preceded the dawn of the American Revolution. The Memorial has been described as a "lucid expression of Colonial rights and a convincing evidence of the firm principles and commanding abilities of the men to whom was then committed the peculiar care of the Province," which "may safely challenge a comparison with any similar paper of that period, as an eloquent and affecting appeal to the justice of the Crown."

CHAPTER V

A BUILDER OF THE STATE HOUSE

HORATIO SHARPE was Proprietary Governor of Maryland for fifteen years. Having served as commander-in-chief of the Royal forces operating against the French on the Ohio, Governor Sharpe was by nature militaristic; but, notwithstanding his impetuous and arbitrary disposition, he commanded the respect of the people of Maryland. Under Governor Sharpe's Administration, Johnson grew from a youth of 20 to a mature statesman, fully prepared to lead the cause of the people in the struggle for American independence.

On the first of August, 1768, Frederick Calvert, the Lord Proprietary of Maryland, commissioned his brother-in-law, Captain Robert Eden, then only 28 years of age, Governor of the Province. Young Sir Robert arrived in Maryland on the fifth of June, 1769. When the Provincial Assembly met on the 17th of November for the first time in his Administration, he had a number of experienced men in his Council to advise him, chief among whom were Daniel Dulany, Benedict Calvert and Richard Lee. In the popular branch Mr. Johnson was surrounded by a brilliant array of Colonial statesmen—men like Matthew and Edward Tilghman, James Hollyday, Chase and Paca. As soon as they assembled, the two Houses received a Message from Governor Eden, to which they returned Addresses couched in such courteous language that the young Governor wrote a few days later to Lord Hillsborough that indications pointed to an end of all trouble with the Colonists!

Up to this time the members of the Assembly held their sessions in the old Provincial Court House, on the site of the present State Capitol, while the Governor and his Council met in the tiny building used for many years afterwards as the office of the State Treasurer. In a letter to his friends in England in October, 1769, Mr. Eddis described the Colonial Court House and the Council building in the following manner:

"In the Court-house, the representatives of the people assemble, for the dispatch of provincial business. The courts of justice are also held here, and here likewise the public offices are established. This building has nothing in its appearance expressive of the great purposes to which it is appropriated, and by a strange neglect, is suffered to fall continually into decay, being, both without and within, an emblem of public poverty, and at the same time a severe reflection on the Government of this country, which, it seems, is considerably richer than the generality of the American provinces.

"The Council-chamber is a detached building, adjacent to the former, on a very humble scale. It contains one tolerable room, for the reception of the Governor and Council, who meet here during the sitting of the Assembly, and whose concurrence is necessary in passing all laws."

One of the first steps taken by the Maryland Assembly in Governor Eden's Administration was to provide for the erection of a new "Court House." A committee of seven members of the Assembly was chosen to superintend its construction. Dulany, the renowned leader in the Governor's Council, and Johnson, one of the leading members of the Lower House, were chosen to serve together on this committee. The other five members were Lancelot Jacques, Charles Wallace, William Paca, John Hall, and Charles

THE·MARYLAND STATE HOUSE

Carroll, barrister. An appropriation of £7500 Sterling was made by the Assembly to carry on the work, but the Building Committee was given the power to draw on the Treasurer of the Eastern or the Western Shore for any further amount that might be necessary to complete the building. Any four, being a majority, were authorized to proceed with the purchase of material and the employment of workmen. The committee had general supervision over the construction of the building.

The corner stone of the Maryland State House was laid by Governor Eden on March 28, 1772. It was a beautiful Spring day, when the trees of Annapolis were just beginning to bud. Although there was not a cloud in the sky, tradition says that when Governor Eden at noon rapped the corner stone of the State House with his mallet, a violent clap of thunder was heard. Dr. Bernard C. Steiner views this alleged meteorological phenomenon with suspicion, for in his biography of Governor Eden, he says that the newspaper account of the corner stone laying in the *Maryland Gazette* recounts the "three cheers" given by the workmen, the collation and the toasts, but makes no mention of the noise of thunder.

The State House, erected under the direction of Dulany, Johnson, Jacques, Wallace, Paca, Hall and Barrister Carroll, was built upon plans characterized by stateliness and yet by simplicity. It was in this building, on another March day five years later, that Johnson assumed the duties of Governor of Maryland as an independent State.

After the Revolution, a dome was added to the State House, and during the Administration of Governor Edwin Warfield, it was enlarged; but it still stands as one of America's most beautiful specimens of Colonial architecture.

Chapter VI

ASSERTING THE RIGHTS OF FREEMEN

THE subject of taxation had been the cause of frequent controversies in Maryland between the Proprietary Governor and the people. As early as 1650, the sacred principle of *No Taxation Without Representation* was recognized by the Provincial Assembly in a decree that no taxes should be levied without the assent of the people themselves or their representatives. Privileged to worship God in their own way, the British subjects in Maryland now took the position that the imposition of taxes in a manner objectionable to the Lower House constituted *economic* slavery. Taxes, duties, fees and fines—each gave rise to some important controversy. With each succeeding session of the Assembly, the Maryland freemen became more positive in their demand that the Lord Proprietary or the Governor should not interfere with the right of the people to regulate the taxes imposed within the Province. In 1743—when Thomas Johnson, Jr., was a lad ten years old—Daniel Dulany was protesting to Governor Bladen and his Council that the only measure which could possibly save the tobacco industry from threatened ruin in Maryland—the *Tobacco Inspection Act*—was prevented from being passed on account of bitter wrangling over fees.

The fees allowed public officials for their services had always been specified by the Assembly. In the session of 1763 —the second at which Mr. Johnson was a member—an Act providing for the fees of officials was passed; and it was continued from time to time until October 1, 1770, when the Fee controversy in which Mr. Johnson took a prominent part grew acute.

Johnson's first practical experience with the problems of taxation came in 1765. Chosen in the second session of that year to serve as chairman of a committee to examine the account of the Clerk of the Council, he made a thorough investigation of the revenues of the Proprietary Government. On the morning of December 10, Chairman Johnson presented his report to the House. The fines, forfeitures, etc., Mr. Johnson reported, exceeded 100,000 pounds of tobacco. Discussion of the subject was postponed several days, when the House decreed that the Clerk of the Council should thereafter be allowed no fees for (a) writing Inspector's Commissions, (b) recording bonds of Naval Officers, or (c) filing nominations of Vestrymen and Church Wardens. Delegate Johnson stood with the majority in the first instance, but in the second and third instances he voted in favor of the allowance of fees.

At the session of 1769, Delegate Johnson and Delegate Samuel Chase assailed the Fee Bill, but it was extended for another year.

When the Assembly met on September 25, 1770, the Fee Bill was again presented to the House for renewal. But it was contended that many of the Proprietary officials —especially the Provincial Secretary, the Commissary General, the Judges and the Register of the Land Office, all of whom were members of the Upper House, or Governor's Council—were receiving excessive fees; and the members

of the Lower House were indignant. Message after message, indicative of bitter animosity, went back and forth between the two chambers. The members of the Lower
House soon realized that it was impossible to fix the fees
in accordance with their own wishes, and they apprehended
that the members of the Council were designing to end the
deadlock by having Governor Eden issue a Proclamation
regulating the fees of all Provincial officers. The Delegates, intending to forestall such a step, resolved on November 1, 1770, that the representatives of the freemen of
Maryland, with the assent of "the other part of the Legislature," had the sole right to impose taxes and fees, and
that the imposition thereof by the Lord Proprietary or the
Governor or any other person not the representative of the
people was "arbitrary, unconstitutional and oppressive."

But the Governor, acting on the advice of his Council,
utterly disregarded the resolutions of the Lower House.
After nearly two months of bitter wrangling, the Assembly
was prorogued on November 21, 1770, without effecting
a renewal of the Fee Act, and on November 26, 1770, Governor Eden issued his Proclamation, reëstablishing the Fee
Act of 1763.

Throughout Maryland the Proclamation aroused great
indignation. Johnson and other leaders gravely denounced
the Governor's assumption of power.

The Assembly was not called together again until
October 2, 1771. The formal Remonstrance against the Fee
Proclamation was delayed several days by the contest of
Jonathan Hager for a seat in the House. The eligibility
of Hager (the founder of Hagerstown and a prominent
citizen of Western Maryland) was questioned by reason of
the fact that he was not a native-born subject. The Elec-

tions Committee having reported that he "came into America and was naturalized," the matter was set down for full discussion on the 8th of October, when Mr. Hager was represented by able counsel. Although the law seemed to be clearly against Mr. Hager, Delegate Johnson made a stubborn fight, probably on account of personal friendship, to have him seated. William Paca and William Smallwood—two brilliant young men, both of whom were destined to become Governor—were lined up with Johnson in behalf of Mr. Hager. The contestants were led by Samuel Chase, who contended that Hager was ineligible to sit in the Provincial Assembly. The contest aligned "Progressives" against "Conservatives." At that time, the House consisted of fifty-eight members. Delegate Johnson succeeded in mustering only eight votes from the Eastern Shore and fifteen from Western Maryland. By a vote of 24 to 23, the House declared Hager ineligible. After the announcement of the vote, he was informed that he was discharged from further attendance.

Jonathan Hager was not rejected from the Assembly by reason of any personal antipathy. The issue was based on the construction of the law. This was plainly indicated three days later, when a bill was introduced to repeal that portion of the law forbidding a naturalized subject to have a seat in the Provincial Assembly. Samuel Chase, who led the fight against Hager, was himself one of the delegates who brought in the bill. The measure was expeditiously passed, and on October 16, 1771—eight days after Hager was dismissed—the Speaker left his chair and repaired, in company with the members of the House, to the Council chamber to present the bill to Governor Eden, who forthwith signed and sealed it on behalf of the Lord Proprietary.

So speedily was this Act passed and approved that Mr.
Hager was enabled to take his seat in the House before
the close of the session. Reëlected a Delegate from
Frederick County, he qualified as a member of the Assembly
on the 16th of November, 1771, in time to vote for the
Remonstrance against the Fee Proclamation.

This memorable Remonstrance was prepared by Thomas
Johnson after it became plain that the passage of a new
Fee Bill was impossible. Early in October, soon after the
Assembly had convened, the Committee on Grievances reported that the fees of the Provincial officers were excessive
and a Fee Bill was passed by the Lower House for submission to the Council. The members of the Upper House,
on October 30, 1771, rejected the bill but suggested that
conferees be appointed to take the matter under consideration. Notwithstanding the fact that Thomas Johnson,
William Paca, Samuel Chase, Tilghman and Smallwood
were opposed to this proposition, the Lower House, by a
vote of twenty-eight to nineteen, decided in favor of a conference, and then selected Johnson, Chase, Tilghman, Hall,
Hammond, Grahame and Dennis to act as the conferees of
the Lower House.

On account of the uncompromising position of the
Delegates, on the one side, and the grim determination of
the Councillors to support Governor Eden and his Proclamation, on the other, the conferees clashed in deadlock. On
the 4th of November, 1771, the members of the Council
submitted a list of proposals, which was not entirely satisfactory to the Lower House; and two days later they submitted a second list, which was immediately rejected. The
Council and the House in turn asked that the conference
be discontinued, but proposals continued to fly back and

forth between the two chambers. At last, on the 22nd of November, the conference came to an end. The attempt to settle the controversy by compromise had unquestionably failed.

It was on the following day—the 23rd of November, 1771—that the Lower House took under consideration the Remonstrance against the Governor's Fee Proclamation, prepared by Delegate Johnson. In this masterly Protest, Johnson cited authorities to prove that the levying of fees for public officials constituted a tax upon the people. Under the Common Law, officers of justice were paid out of the revenues of the Crown and there was no precedent, he contended, for the regulation of fees by Proclamation. Inasmuch as the power to tax was reposed in the legislative branch of the Government, Delegate Johnson argued with great force and effect that the arbitrary regulation of fees by Governor Eden was "unconstitutional in the matter and shadowed in the manner, with the assigned reason to prevent extortion by the officers, in imitation of the practice of arbitrary kings, who, in their proclamations, which have been declared illegal, generally covered their designs with the specious pretence of public good."

The young Anne Arundel Delegate made it plain that the members of the Lower House were convinced that, although issued by Governor Eden, the Fee Proclamation had been schemed by ulterior advisers. "The advisers of the Proprietary," declared Mr. Johnson, "are enemies of the peace, welfare and happiness of this Province and of the laws and Constitution thereof!" He challenged the Governor to disclose to the Assembly the names of the men who had advised him to issue the Proclamation, or else issue a denial.

In a brilliant conclusion, Johnson presented the following logical argument:

"This act of power is founded on the destruction of constitutional security. If the Proclamation may rightfully regulate the fees, it has a right to fix any *quantum*. If it has a right to regulate, it has a right to regulate to a million; for where does its right stop? At any given point! To attempt to limit the right, after granting it to exist at all, is contrary to justice. If it has a right to tax us, then, whether our money shall continue in our own pockets depends no longer on us, but on the prerogative."

The Address to the Governor was adopted with only three dissenting votes. The positive language in which it was couched gave evidence of the unwavering attitude of the members.

Within six days—on November 29, 1771—Governor Eden issued a reply, in which he attempted to justify his position. The Executive declared that with the right to appoint public officials the Lord Proprietary had by implication the right to determine their emoluments. Governor Eden pointed to precedents, in other dominions, for the regulation of Officers' Fees by Royal prerogative.

Like Delegate Johnson's Remonstrance, Governor Eden's reply was skilfully framed. And it indicated that a compromise was impossible. Every Fee Bill proposed by the Lower House was speedily rejected by the Council. Indignant and exasperated, the Delegates were now ready to leave for their homes, and on the 30th of November, 1771, Governor Eden prorogued the Assembly.

During the next year and a half there was no session of the Provincial Assembly. During this time some of the people of Maryland paid the fees under protest while others refused to pay. The smoldering fires of discontent broke into a flame in 1773, when Charles Carroll, under the name of *First Citizen*, published in the *Maryland Gazette* a powerful attack against Governor Eden's Proclamation. His article was answered by Daniel Dulany, as *Antilon*. Having been appointed to the lucrative office of Provincial Secretary, Dulany had no other course to pursue than to endeavor to uphold the justice and the constitutionality of the Proclamation. Rebuttals and surrebuttals came from the pen of Carroll and Dulany. Replete with gems from the classics, and bulwarked with the most powerful arguments, and marked by bitterness restrained by the bounds of courtesy, the articles are masterpieces of logic and legal learning. They thoroughly aroused the people of the Colony. They made Carroll a hero and they spelt the doom of the popularity of the great Dulany. In Annapolis, a tumultuous crowd assembled in May, 1773, after the closing of the polls at the election for Delegates—the last election held under the Proprietary Government—and held a demonstration to indicate publicly the hostility of the people to the Proclamation. In accordance with the ancient Colonial custom, they decided to bury the despised Fee Proclamation at a mock funeral. The following description [1] has been written concerning this quaint ceremony: "To the sound of muffled drums, with the Proclamation in a coffin, with banners that bore inscriptions condemning it, with weapons of war and with a grave digger, the march was made from the polls to the gallows, where the offensive document was hanged, cut down, and buried, the ceremony being accompanied by a discharge of musketry."

In accordance with the request of the voters of Anne

[1] N. D. Mereness, *Maryland as a Proprietary Province,* 399.

Arundel County, the four Delegates-elect—Johnson, Chase, Hall and Worthington—wrote a letter of thanks to the *First Citizen* for his opposition to the "illegal, arbitrary and oppressive Proclamation."

When the Assembly reconvened on the 15th of June, the House once more denounced the Proclamation. Some of the Delegates proposed to bring the young Governor and his obdurate Councillors to their senses by refusing to make needful regulation of the tobacco industry. Calmer members, including Johnson, Chase and Paca, opposed this method of retaliation; but on the 18th of June, the House, by a vote of 24 to 12, determined to refuse to bring in the Tobacco Bill. It was not long, however, before it was perceived that this hasty action was ill advised, and five days later the House reconsidered its action and decided to appoint a committee to prepare the measure. But, at the same time, another committee was appointed to prepare a new Fee Bill.

One measure after another, passed by the Lower House, was killed in the Council. Even the bill for the support of the clergy was rejected in the Upper House. The Delegates were reduced to such a state of desperation that Governor Eden deemed it best to resort again to prorogation. Thus, on the 3rd of July, 1773, after being in session scarcely more than a fortnight, the Assembly was "for many important reasons" prorogued.

During the Summer and Autumn of 1773, there was a brief respite in the controversy. The Assembly convened on the 16th of November; but adjourned, on the 23rd of December, without producing any change in the situation.

The final session of the Assembly under the Proprietary

Government convened on March 23, 1774, and adjourned for the last time on April 19.

Governor Eden and his Council stood firm against the Remonstrance. Yet, while the freemen viewed the Proclamation with indignation, they hated the Councillors of the Government far more than the young Executive himself. "Easy of access, courteous to all and fascinating by his accomplishments," John V. L. McMahon explains, "he [Governor Eden] still retained his hold upon the affections even of his opponents, who, for the qualities of his heart and the graces of his manners, were willing to forgive the personal errors of his government."

Without an Assembly to serve as a safety valve by which to exhaust their resentment, the provincials had to rely upon the press and public meetings to display their hostility to the Proclamation. One illustration of the hostile sentiment of the people on the subject of taxation in Maryland prior to the Revolution was the institution of a suit for damages, in which the plaintiff contested the tax familiarly known as the *Forty Per Poll*. It had been collected under the provisions of a statute passed in 1702, and the imposition of the tax had caused great dissatisfaction for many years. Joseph H. Harrison, who had served as a member of the Assembly from Charles County, determined to test its legality and he refused to pay the tax. He was arrested, and when Sheriff Richard Lee, Jr., threatened to imprison him, he paid the tax under protest. Thereupon, Harrison sued the sheriff for £60 for assault and battery and for false imprisonment. His lawyers were Thomas Johnson, Samuel Chase and William Paca. Mr. Johnson's younger brother, Baker Johnson, assisted. Sheriff Lee, through Attorneys

Thomas Stone, John Rogers, and Cooke, pleaded "Not In-debted" and set up for defense the Act of 1702. As no aggravating circumstances, such as actual incarceration or ill treatment at the hands of the sheriff, were connected with the alleged assault, no punitive damages were asked. The sole purpose of the suit was to test the constitutionality of the tax. "Yet," says Scharf, "such was the idea which the Jury entertained of the liberty of the subject that they looked upon the sheriff's arrest and execution of the *Forty Per Poll* as an offence of the *first magnitude* against the rights of Englishmen, and brought in a verdict for the plaintiff, and gave him £60 damages, which was the whole sum in the declaration." [2]

Finally, Johnson, Chase and Paca, championing the cause of the people, prepared a reply to Mr. Dulany. In this masterly argument, published in the *Gazette*, the trio of brilliant young patriots laid down the *dictum* that the freemen of the Province—not the Crown or the Proprietary —were the *ultimate source of authority*. They took the position that the people themselves, or their representatives, had the power to pronounce final judgment on any question of Government. In the opinion of Dr. Bernard C. Steiner, the Johnson-Chase-Paca reply to Daniel Dulany was supe-rior to the argument advanced by Carroll. Says Dr. Steiner:

"The popular opinion has been that Charles Carroll had much the better of the argument with Dulany. In this opinion I do not join, though I admit most readily that in Carroll, Dulany found a worthy antagonist and that Carroll's success in arousing the people was most noteworthy, especially when we consider his religious faith. The last was by no means popular in Maryland at that time, and I regret to have to record the fact that Dulany strove in an unworthy manner to use that fact to Carroll's prejudice. My conclusion is that

[2] J. T. Scharf, *History of Maryland*, Vol. II, p. 127-8.

Dulany's arguments found their best refutation in the paper written by William Paca, Thomas Johnson, and Samuel Chase."

By this time, the controversy over Officers' Fees became overshadowed by the impending storm cloud of the Revolution. When the troubles around Boston were beginning to assume serious proportions in the Summer of 1774, Johnson sent to George Washington a copy of one of the issues of the *Maryland Gazette* containing the last "Controversial Piece" on the subject.

"I am sorry," Johnson wrote to the man at Mount Vernon, "to hear that your abrupt Dissolution has thrown you into difficulties about Officers' Fees. We have unhappily been for some time much embarrassed about the Fees of Office here and as you may remember have had some Controversial Pieces on the subject. I preserved a paper which contains the last, no Answer having been yet given to it, and inclose it to you—as, indeed, I would all on the subject if I had them—not from any opinion the matter may not be as well handled in Virginia as with us, but from an apprehension that any thing on the subject which may tend to an investigation of the truth will at this time be agreeable to you."

Thus, throughout the Fee controversy in Maryland both in and out of the Assembly, Johnson played the most prominent rôle of all the patriots of that day as the champion of the liberty of the people. It is true, the Proclamation was never repealed; but, as Mereness says in his *Maryland as a Proprietary Province*, "It is not improbable that the Proclamation, had the Proprietary Government continued a few years longer, would have fallen before this view as to the *Ultimate Source of Authority;* but, as it was, discontent was in a measure temporarily pacified by the revival of the old Inspection Act, without the table of fees, and then the Revolution soon followed." Moreover, in making the Remonstrance, the patriot leaders—notably Johnson, Carroll, Chase and Paca—did a valiant service in arousing the people of Maryland to a realization of the part they would have to play in resisting the oppressions of the Crown.

CHAPTER VII

ENDEAVORS TO PROMOTE NAVIGATION

IN the year 1732—memorable for the birth of George Washington, Thomas Johnson and Richard Henry Lee —there came the first step in the development of the Western part of Maryland. In that year vast areas of the fertile soil in the Western part of the Province were offered by Charles Calvert, fifth Lord Baltimore, to the subjects residing in tidewater. A number of wealthy men eagerly took advantage of Lord Baltimore's offer. Patrick Dulany acquired the soil upon which the city of Frederick now stands; Charles Carroll, father of the Signer, secured possession of 15,000 acres in Carrollton Manor; Benjamin Tasker received a patent for Tasker's Chance, embracing over 8,000 acres; and the renowned Daniel Dulany likewise obtained thousands of acres of the fertile soil in the valley of the Monocacy.

The following picturesque description of the forest land along the upper Potomac at the time of the birth of Thomas Johnson has been written by Scharf in the *History of Western Maryland:*

"The early settlers of Maryland and Virginia kept to the navigable streams, and it was many years afterwards before the fertile lands in the valleys in the neighborhood of the Blue Ridge and Alleghany Mountains began to be dotted with the log cabins of an advancing frontier. No pioneer had ventured into these solitudes, whose sleeping echoes were only waked by the scream of the eagle or the whoop of the painted warrior. Neither Gist nor Cresap had yet seen the wilds of Western Maryland. The Potomac then flowed in solitary grandeur for more than three hundred miles through an unbroken wilderness, its gentle surface only disturbed by the wing of the wild-fowl or the dip of the savage paddle."

In 1748—the year Washington caught his first vision of the upper Potomac and the West on Lord Fairfax's surveying trip—the Ohio Company was organized. In the following year this Company, composed of a small number of wealthy subjects of Virginia and Maryland, secured a grant of land West of the Alleghanies. Thomas Lee, at that time President of His Majesty's Council in Virginia, held two of the 20 shares and was the president of the Company. John Hanbury & Company, of London, holding two shares, were the London agents. John Mercer was secretary and counsel. George Mason was treasurer. Augustine and Lawrence Washington were among the shareholders. The organization of the Ohio Company was a signal of alarm for the French. The embers of hatred between Great Britain and France, which had been smoldering for many years as a result of conflicting territorial claims, burst forth into a flame when the frontiersmen of these two Nations attempted to colonize the Ohio Valley. So the great contest for supremacy between the Courts of Paris and London was destined to be decided in America.

Undaunted, the members of the Ohio Company commenced at once eagerly to explore the country. In 1750 a storehouse was constructed at Will's Creek—the present site of Cumberland—and it was stocked with goods which they ordered from London to be bartered with the Indians. The following year Colonel Thomas Cresap selected an

Indian to lay out a road from there to the mouth of the Monongahela. Then in 1752 Robert Dinwiddie became Crown Governor of Virginia and in the following year he heard the news of the imprisonment of a number of British traders and the order of the French military commanders to erect forts from Lake Erie to the headwaters of the Allegheny. All students of American history are thoroughly familiar with the aftermath—how Governor Dinwiddie, a prominent member of the Ohio Company, picked George Washington to carry the message of warning to the French against further intrusion of the Ohio Valley. "The person whom he [Gov. Dinwiddie] had selected," one author says of Washington, "was about twenty-one years old, six feet two inches in height, and the swiftest runner, the longest thrower, the best wrestler, the most skilful horseman, the strongest swimmer, and the finest athlete in all the country round."

Frederick County, Maryland, was crossed by Washington in November, 1753, on this memorable journey to Lake Erie, where General St. Pierre, the commander of the French forces in the West, was stationed. France, it will be remembered, claimed the valley of the Ohio by virtue of discovery and occupation; and St. Pierre replied that he was acting under military instructions. Of Washington's return trip, most of the time with Christopher Gist as his sole companion, another writer gives the following vivid description:

"It was one of the most solitary marches ever made by man. There in the desolate wilderness was the future President of the United States. Clad in the robe of an Indian, with gun in hand and knapsack strapped to his shoulder, struggling through interminable snows; sleeping with frozen clothes on a bed of pine-brush; breaking through the treacherous ice of rapid streams; guided by day by a pocket compass, and at night by the North Star, seen at intervals through the leafless trees; fired at by a prowling savage from his covert not fifteen steps away; thrown from a raft into the rushing Allegheny; escaping to an island and lodging there until the river was frozen over; plunging again into the forest; reaching Gist's settlement and then the Potomac—the strong-limbed young ambassador came back without wound or scar to the capital of Virginia. For his flesh was not made to be torn with bullets or to be eaten by the wolves. The defiant despatch of St. Pierre was laid before Governor Dinwiddie, and the first public service of Washington was accomplished."

Upon reaching Williamsburg, January 16, 1754, Washington made a report to the Governor and Council, and doubtless suggested the great importance—from a military, however, rather than from a commercial standpoint—of opening a communication between tidewater and the Western settlements. At all events Washington at an early day conceived the idea of connecting the East and the West.

As early as the Spring of 1755 Washington and General Braddock met in Frederick Town Governor Sharpe and Benjamin Franklin, the British Postmaster-General of the Colonies, and discussed plans for forwarding supplies to the frontier. This was the first time that the Philadelphia philosopher clasped hands with the great soldier-statesman of Virginia. In the same year Stephen Bordley, Johnson's legal preceptor, was admitted to the bar of Frederick County; but it was not until five years later—1760—that Johnson himself was admitted to practice in the Frederick County Court. On his trip to Frederick in his twenty-eighth year, Johnson was deeply impressed by the beauties and the wonderful latent resources of Frederick County and it was not long afterwards—on March 20, 1761—that he exhibited his faith in the future of Western Maryland by purchasing a piece of Frederick County land.[1]

Before the close of the French and Indian War, Mr. Johnson was considering the subject of promoting "water carriage" on the Potomac. About a month before he entered the Provincial Assembly as a Delegate from Anne Arundel County, there appeared in the *Maryland Gazette*, in the issue of February 11, 1762, the following announcement:

"The opening of the river Patowmack and making it passable for small craft, from Fort Cumberland at Will's Creek to the Great Falls, will be of the greatest advantage to Virginia and Maryland, by facilitating commerce with the back inhabitants, who will not then have more than 20 miles land carriage to harbour, where ships of great burthen load annually, whereas at present many have 150; and what will perhaps be considered of still greater importance, is the easy communication it will afford with the waters of the Ohio. The whole land carriage from Alexandria or George Town will then be short of 90 miles; whereas the Pennsylvanians (who at present monopolize the very lucrative skin and fur trades) from their nearest sea port have at least 300: a circumstance which must necessarily force that gainful trade into this channel, should this very useful work be affected; and that it may, is the unanimous opinion of the best judges, and at moderate expense compared with the extraordinary convenience and advantages which must result from it."

The advertisement announced that 22 managers had been appointed—11 for the colony of Maryland and 11 for the colony of Virginia—and that subscriptions would be solicited from the public. On the 10th of June, 1762, the *Gazette* contained the following announcement:

The managers have now the pleasure to inform the public, that subscriptions are filling very fast, and that people in general, but

[1] *Land Records of Frederick County*, Liber G, folio 142.

more especially in the back countries, and those bordering on the Patowmack, discover so much alacrity in promoting the affair, that there is not the least doubt that sum will be raised, sufficient to carry on the work by the day appointed for the meeting, 20th of July next."

Shortly afterwards Washington and Johnson heard with amazement and alarm reports of outrages committed by the savages in the Western part of Frederick County. After the Treaty of Paris brought the contest between England and France to a close, the British traders began again to move westward over the Alleghanies. This vanguard aroused Pontiac, an Ottawa chief, who journeyed stealthily among the tribes and obtained their solemn pledge to massacre the white men in order to put a stop to the encroachments. In June, 1763, the blow was struck. "Another tempest has arisen upon our frontiers," wrote Washington, "and the alarm spreads wider than ever. In short, the inhabitants are so apprehensive of danger that no families remain above the Conococheague road, and many are gone below. The harvests are, in a manner, lost, and the distresses of the settlements are evident and manifold." In a state of destitution the fugitives crowded to Frederick Town, where they received food and shelter. The Maryland Assembly convened in the Fall of 1763. It was Delegate Johnson's second session. Governor Sharpe pictured the outrages in vivid language, and the Lower House made further provision for the protection of the western settlers.

Even as late as July, 1764, the Indians committed a number of massacres along the Conococheague, and in the same month an expedition of five hundred men was sent to reënforce Fort Pitt, which had been cut off from all communication with the interior. In this expedition against

the Delawares, Mingoes and Shawnees, there were two companies of Maryland volunteers. And the Colonel who led
them wrote to Governor Sharpe the following November,
urging that he request the Assembly to pay these gallant
volunteers for their military services. "As such a public
spirit ought to be encouraged in our Colonies," said the
Colonel, "I beg leave to recommend them to your notice,
that they may obtain pay, if possible, from your Assembly."

As a member of the Provincial Assembly, Delegate
Johnson was one of the most liberal of all the members
in making appropriations. He appreciated deeply the hardships of the pioneers who ventured out into the Alleghanies.
When, for example, a motion was made in the House on
the 16th of November, 1765, to pay Capt. Evan Shelby
for his "spirited conduct" in the war, Delegate Johnson
voted in favor of the appropriation. The motion prevailed by the vote of 22 to 19. A motion was then offered
by the parsimonious faction that Capt. Shelby should be
allowed only 200 pounds. Believing that the appropriation to Capt. Shelby ought not to be restricted to this
amount, Mr. Johnson opposed the reduction and voted in
the negative. The sum of 200 pounds, however, was all
that the House allowed.

While the Assembly was in session, a report reached
Annapolis that Colonel Cresap had gathered together in
Frederick a force of over 300 men—many of them armed
with guns and tomahawks—and threatened to march his
band to Annapolis to bring the lawmakers to their senses,
unless speedier measures were taken to protect the settlers
from the Indians. As soon as he received the report, Governor Sharpe warned the Assembly. When it assembled at
two o'clock on the afternoon of December 10, 1765, the

Message from His Excellency was read and a committee of five of the ablest Delegates was appointed to frame a reply. Mr. Johnson was chosen to serve as chairman of the committee. His associates were: James Hollyday, Thomas Ringgold, William Murdock, and Brice T. B. Worthington. The House adjourned to meet at eight o'clock the next morning, when Mr. Johnson submitted the following reply:

"In answer to your Message of last Night, we assure your Excellency, we are very sensible of the bad Consequences of large Bodies of People coming hither, with a view to Intimidate either Branch of the Legislature, or to lay them under any Restraint. We shall therefore immediately take every Step in our Power to prevent any Measures that may have such Tendency: To which End, we pray your Excellency to lay before us the Evidences you have received of the Arming or Assembling of any Bodies of People with that Intention.

"We are very sorry to find such an Imputation on a Member of our House, as that laid on Col. Cresap; and we yet have Hope, your Excellency's Information, in that Particular, is without just Foundation, as it appears by our Journals, that he has not attended the House since the 22d of November, at which Time we conclude he left this Place; and when it could not be foreseen that any Difficulties would arise between the Two Houses in relation to the Payment of any Public Claims.

"As we should be very far from Countenancing, in any of our Members, a Conduct tending to disturb the Public Peace, and deprive any Branch of the Legislature of that Freedom of Debating and Judging, which is essential to the Constitution, we think it a Justice to the Public, as well as to Col. Cresap, that this Charge against him should be examined and set in a True Light; and therefore hope your Excellency will communicate to this House the Evidence on which the Charge contained in your Message, is founded."

Mr. Johnson read the Report to the House and it was adopted and engrossed for delivery to the Governor. But the rumors were groundless. All apprehensions were set at rest on December 14th, when a resident of Frederick County testified at the bar of the House that Frederick Town was calm and that Colonel Cresap himself averred that he expected the troubles in the Assembly proceedings to be removed and the Journal to pass.   It does not appear that "Cresap's Army" ever marched to Annapolis.

By this time there had commenced a friendship between Thomas Johnson and a Huguenot named Lancelot Jacques. Coming to America as a refugee, Jacques had settled in Annapolis, where his industry and inherent business acumen brought him considerable success.   Johnson and Jacques became associates in business enterprises and they obtained out of the High Court of Chancery a writ directing the sheriff of Frederick County to inquire, by the oath of twelve men, into the mineral lands lying on Green Spring Run, about two miles below Fort Frederick, "as might be the most convenient for setting up a Forge Mill and other conveniences, as shall be necessary for carrying on an Iron Work."   The sheriff made his return to the Court on December 23, 1766.   Johnson and Jacques gave security for the erection of a forge on the land within the time limited by the Act of the Assembly.   On April 11, 1768, Governor Sharpe countersigned Lord Baltimore's patent for 15,000 acres at Indian Spring (now in Washington County) to the two Annapolitans, as tenants in common; and here Mr. Jacques came to reside, not far from Fort Frederick. They erected Green Spring Furnace and the pig iron which they manufactured there was pushed down the Potomac River to George Town by Negro slaves.

Later Mr. Johnson, together with Leonard Calvert, obtained a patent from Lord Baltimore for 7,000 acres of mineral land in Frederick County, constituting the Catoctin

Furnace property. Accordingly, about the time of the arrival of Sir Robert Eden to take up the duties of Governor, Thomas Johnson, as well as Washington, had become thoroughly impressed with the mineral wealth and the immense productivity of the soil in the valleys of the Monocacy and the Antietam. Both Washington and Johnson were impressed also by the utter desolation of the back country. They saw that with the exception of rude trails —and even they were impassable a great part of the year— there was absolutely no mode of communication with the country West of the Alleghanies. Naturally, therefore, with clear perception of the future possibilities of the Western wilderness, George Washington and Thomas Johnson were leading advocates of the project to make the Potomac the means of communication between the East and the West. The Assemblies of Maryland and Virginia were urged to give support to the project. But, securing little encouragement, Johnson, on June 18, 1770, suggested to Washington the plan of promoting navigation by means of private subscriptions.

Washington's reply follows: [2]

GEORGE WASHINGTON TO THOMAS JOHNSON

Virginia, 20th July, 1770.

Sir:

I was honored with your favor of the 18th of June, about the last of that month, and read it with all the attention I was capable of; from that time till now I have not been able to inquire into the sentiments of any of the gentlemen of this side in respect to the scheme of opening the inland navigation of Potowmack, by private

[2] *House Reports,* 19th Congress, 1st Session, No. 228.

subscription, in the manner you have proposed—and, therefore, any opinion which I may now offer on this head will be considered I hope as the result of my own private thinking, not of the public.

That no person concerned in this event wishes to see an undertaking of the sort go forward with more sincerity and ardour than I do, I can truly assure you; and I will, at all times, give any assistance in my power to promote the design; but I leave you to judge from the trial, which before this you have undoubtedly made, how few there are, (not immediately benefited by it,) that will contribute any thing worth while to the work; and how many small sums are requisite to raise a large one.

Upon your plan of raising money, it appears to me there will be found but two kinds of people who will subscribe much towards it. Those who are actuated by motives of public spirit; and those again, who from their proximity to the navigation, will reap the salutary effects of it, clearing the river. The number of the latter, you must be a competent judge of; those of the former, is more difficult to ascertain; for which reason I own to you, that I am not without my doubts of your scheme falling through, however sanguine your first hopes may be from the rapidity of subscribers, for it is to be supposed that your subscription papers will probably be opened among those whose interests *must* naturally incline them to wish well to the undertaking, and consequently will aid it; but when you come to shift the scene a little, and apply to those who are unconnected with the river, and the advantage of its navigation, how slowly will you advance!

This, sir, is my sentiment, generally, upon your plan of obtaining subscriptions for extending the navigation of the Potowmack; whereas I conceive, that if the subscribers were vested by the two legislatures with a kind of property in the navigation under certain restrictions and limitations, and to be reimbursed their first advances with a high interest thereon, by a certain easy toll on all craft proportionate to their respective burthens, in the manner that I am told works of this sort are effected in the inland parts of England—or upon the plan of turnpike roads; you would add thereby a third set of men, to the two I have mentioned, and gain considerable strength by it. I mean the monied gentry; who, tempted by lucrative views, would ad-

vance largely on account of the high interest. This, I am inclined
to think, is the only method by which this desirable work will ever
be accomplished in the manner it ought to be; for, as to its becoming
an object of public expense, I never expect to see it. Our interests
(in Virginia, at least), are too much divided. Our views too confined, if our finances were better, to suffer that, which appears to
redound to the advantage of a part of the community only to become
a tax upon the whole—though in the instance before us, there is the
strongest speculative proof in the world to me of the immense advantages which Virginia and Maryland might derive, (and at a very
small comparative expence) by making the Potowmack the channel
of commerce between Great Britain, and that immense Territory;
a tract of country, which is unfolding to our view the advantages of
which are too great, and too obvious, I should think, to become the
subject of serious debate, but which, through ill-timed parsimony and
supineness, may be wrested from us and conducted through other
channels, such as the Susquehanna, (which I have seen recommended
by some writer) the lakes, &c. How difficult it will be to divert it
afterwards, time only can show. Thus far, sir, I have taken the
liberty of communicating my sentiments on the different modes of
establishing a fund, but if from the efforts you have already made
on the North side of the Potowmack, it should be found that my views
are rather imaginary than real, (as I heartily wish they may prove),
I have no doubts but the same spirit may be stirred up on the South
side, if gentlemen of influence in the counties of Hampshire, Frederick,
Loudoun and Fairfax, will heartily engage in it, and receive all occa-
sional sums, received from those who may wish to see a work of this
sort undertaken, although they expect no benefit themselves from it.

As to the manner in which you propose to execute the work, in order
to avoid the inconvenience which you seem to apprehend from locks,
I profess myself to be a very incompetent judge of it. It is a general
received opinion I know, that, by reducing one fall, you too frequently
create many; but how far this inconvenience is to be avoided by the
method you speak of, those who have examined the rifts—the depth
of water above, &c. must be infinitely the best qualified to determine.
But I am inclined to think, that, if you were to exhibit your scheme
to the public upon a more extensive plan, than the one now printed,

it would meet with a more general approbation; for so long as it is considered as a partial scheme, so long will it be partially attended to—whereas, if it was recommended to the public notice upon a *more enlarged plan, and as a means of becoming the channel of conveyance of the extensive and valuable trade of a rising empire;* and the operations to begin at the lower Landings, (above the Great Falls), and to extend upwards to as high as Fort Cumberland; or as far as the expenditure of the money would carry them; from whence the portage to the waters of Ohio must commence; I think many would be invited to contribute their mite, that otherwise will not. It may be said the expence of doing this will be considerably augmented. I readily grant it, but believe that the subscribers will increase in proportion; at any rate I think that there will be at least an equal sum raised by this means, and that the end of your plan will be as effectually answered by it.

G^o WASHINGTON.

Despite this reply from Washington—a reply all but encouraging—Mr. Johnson continued with enthusiasm his efforts to clear the Potomac and with the aid of his friend, Lancelot Jacques, secured numerous private subscriptions.

On August 18, 1770, Rev. Dr. Jonathan Boucher, who was a personal friend of Thomas Johnson and other Assembly leaders and was for some time Chaplain of the Lower House, wrote a letter to Washington in which he explained the excellent results Johnson and Jacques were securing in the sale of subscriptions of stock at Annapolis. The clergyman also announced in his letter that the two stock salesmen were ready to set off on the morrow for Frederick Town to seek further subscriptions in that town.

"They are still going on," Rev. Dr. Boucher wrote Washington, "with their Subscriptions for clearing the Potomac, and, as I am told, with spirit. Four hundreds pounds are subscribed in this City; nor have they got all they expect. Messrs. Jacques and Johnson set off for Frederick tomorrow, and talk of fixing a day for a general meeting, before they return. Will it be convenient and agreeable to you to attend—about a month hence, if you have notice in time—at the Spot, *i. e.*, at, or near Semple's?"

The trip to Frederick Town—in those days a long and tiresome journey from the Capital—was made by Johnson and his French companion in accordance with their schedule. That they arrived in due time is evidenced by the Land Records of Frederick County, which show that Thomas Johnson, Jr., of Annapolis, made his appearance on August 22, 1770, before "two of His Lordship's Justices of the Peace for Frederick County."

In the same year Washington sent a letter to Governor Eden pointing out the great benefits that would result from making the Potomac a channel of commerce between the Atlantic and the Western territory. But Thomas Johnson and George Washington and their business associates found out that they were undertaking a gigantic task. The people were skeptical, even antagonistic. In 1772, the Virginia Assembly passed an act for "opening and extending the Navigation of Potowmack from the Tidewater to Fort Cumberland." Johnson exerted himself to secure the passage by the Maryland Assembly of a similar measure, but failed on account of the opposition of Baltimore merchants. Governor Eden was appealed to for aid, but young Sir Robert was timid about the proposition, apprehensive that the passage of an Act by the Maryland Assembly might result in impairing the Proprietary's legal title to the bed of the river.

In the following letter to Colonel Washington, Johnson

declares that an appeal for help ought to be made to the Crown:

THOMAS JOHNSON TO GEORGE WASHINGTON

Annapolis, 10th May, 1772.

Sir.

Mr. Tilghman the Speaker of our House of Assembly, not being in town I could not procure a receit from him. I sent you one from myself for £6. as recd. for his use if that is not sufficient I will get one from himself and inclose it to you: as soon as I have an opportunity.—I inclose you a receit from the Clerk of the Upper House and another from the Clerk of the Lower House for £3. each. I thought there was the like ffee to the President of the Upper House as to the Speaker but on inquiry finding myself mistaken I return you 16 Dollars.

Mr. Ballendine has been here two or three days but Mr. Mason has not yet come. I fear our Governor is still under an impression that a concurrence by our Assembly in a scheme with yours for clearing Potowmack may weaken the proprietary claim of jurisdiction over that River and consequently that he is not at liberty to assent to such Bill tho' I believe in his own judgment clearing the River is an object which deserves immediate attention and that he wishes to see it effected. If the Governor should be under such impression and should not write home to be set more at large or should write unsuccessfully as the delay that might be thereby occasioned would at all events be highly prejudicial I would submit to your consideration whether it might not be prudent that a strong representation should be sent to England, to be made use of in case it should be necessary, to procure an intimation from thence that a Bill ought to pass here. If instructions ought at all to be sent to Governors as the rule of their conduct, I have no idea but that propry [proprietary] instructions might properly be superseded by instructions from the King in Council and if so I cannot apprehend there would be the least difficulty in obtaining an order for the passage of a Bill in which the Trade and Subjects are so much interested though it might possibly collaterally affect the proprs [proprietary's] claim of jurisdiction. I shall be glad that our Governor's letters to Virginia may evince that my apprehensions are groundless but if my conjectures are well founded I must wish that no time may be lost.

I am Sir
Your most obedient Servant,
THS JOHNSON, JUNR.

In October, 1772, Colonel Washington visited in Annapolis, and it is highly probable that Washington and Johnson discussed at length the Potomac River enterprise at this time.

In the following year the Maryland Assembly appropriated £3,000 to improve the Western roads and Delegate Johnson was selected one of seven commissioners to superintend the work and to disburse the money. An explanation of the status of this project and the backwardness of the movement to establish "water carriage" in the Potomac is presented in the following letter sent by Johnson to Colonel Washington shortly before the last session of the Provincial Assembly: [3]

THOMAS JOHNSON TO GEORGE WASHINGTON

Annapo. 21 Feby. 1774.

Sir

A Servant just now delivered me your Letter of yesterday and told me he was to go out of Town in a few Hours. I expect Mr. Calvert will be here tomorrow or the next Day at farthest by whom I imagine I may contrive you a more particular and satisfactory answer than I can instantly—If you have the Instrument by which Mr. Adams engaged his Vessel for your Security or a copy of it I should be obliged to you if any oppty offers witht any extraordinary Trouble that you would send it to me.—Your Attachment was received—instantly on the Return of it.

I have a particular pleasure in your approbation of our Grant of £3000 for the Western Roads—the commrs are left very much at

[3] *Washington,* Manuscript Division, Library of Congress, Vol. XIV.

large mislead we were not well enough acquainted with the circumstances of the country to be very precise in directing the expenditure of the Money—I have the Hon[r] to be one of seven intrusted in laying out the Money and am so far from a self sufficiency in the matter that I shall most gladly receive any information on the Subject— permit me to assure you I think myself honored by any mark of your confidence or attention and that instead of thinking your Hints unseasonable I should be very much obliged by an enlargem[t] on the Subject—I made a show of pushing for a further sum for improving the River with a View to secure more certainly the £3000 for the Road for some people look on any Thing less given than requested as so much saved. We had a smart struggle for the 3000 £ but I have not been idle since. I have been endeavouring and I hope with success to impress my Ideas of the advantages and practicability of water carriage. We are to have a session about the 20th of next month and I now expect we shall then do something effectual—I am determined never to cease trying till some thing is done—As soon as the Bill passed I took my measures to give an Impression in the Back Country that the laying out the money on the Road was left much in the Discretion of the Courts who would govern themselves much by the spirit and exertion of the Back people. I have the pleasure to understand it has so far answered my Expectation that 4 or 500 £ is already subscribed to be laid out in assisting with the Road. I wish there may be a Surplus not that I think any saving in £3000 is of much consequence to the Province but if any Thing is saved I think there will be no Difficulty in getting the Application changed to the River.—If I was less interested in Carriage from above and an early communication with the Back Country I dare say I should be better attended to but being fully satisfied of the general advantage of cheap and early carriage through Potowmack it would be a false Delivery now to attempt a public Good for fear of suspicion of my being actuated solely by private Interest.—I purpose to write you fully by Mr. Calvert—and remain

  Sir

    Your most obed[t] humble Serv[t],

          Th[s] Johnson, Jun[r].

In the *Maryland Gazette* of September 8, 1774, John Ballendine announces that he has arrived from England "with a number of engineers and artificers in order to remove the obstructions to the navigation of the Potowmack River at and above the Lower Falls," and that he is desirous of having a meeting of his principal subscribers at George Town to lay before them "an accurate plan and estimates of the expence, also an Act of the Virginia Assembly, and likewise a subscription from some of the principal proprietors, &c. of the Province of Vandalia now residing in England, for the further encouragement of the proposed undertaking."

On the 10th of October, 1774, Johnson, Washington and other prominent men of Maryland and Virginia assembled at George Town to discuss the Potomac enterprise. At this meeting the following pledge [4] was signed:

"We, the subscribers, have considered John Ballendine's plan and proposal for clearing Potowmack River and do approve it; to enable him to set about that useful and necessary undertaking we do hereby agree and promise severally to contribute such assistance or pay such sums as we respectively subscribe to the trustees named in said proposals, or to their order, at such times and places and in such proportions as shall be required for the purpose of clearing said river."

"N. B. As nothing effectual can be properly done for less than £30,000, this subscription is not binding unless the value of £30,000 Pennsylvania currency, be subscribed."

A total of £8,000, in the various currencies in use at that time, was subscribed at the meeting. George Washington headed the list with a subscription of £500, Virginia currency.

[4] Hugh Taggart, *Old Georgetown*, Columbia Historical Society, May 13, 1907.

Mr. Ballendine appointed the following men to serve as Trustees "to adjust and settle all matters" relating to the movement to open the Potomac:

Maryland—Thomas Johnson, Jr., Lancelot Jacques, Daniel Carroll, Thomas Cresap, Jonathan Hager, Charles Beatty, John Hanson, Jacob Young, Adam Stewart, Thomas Richardson, Robert Peter, John Murdock, William Deakins, John Cary, James Marshall, John Stall, David Ross, Thomas Johns, Richard Thompson, and Dan. and Sam. Hughes.

Virginia—George Washington, George Mason, Thompson Mason, Bryan Fairfax, William Ellzey, John Hough, Isaac Lane, Robert Rutherford, Daniel McCarty, William Ramsey, Robert Adam, Abraham Hite, Joseph Neville, John Carlyle, Joseph Janney and John Dalton.

In the issue of October 25, 1774, of the *Maryland Gazette*, Mr. Ballendine announced the approval of the "plan and estimate for opening the navigation of Potowmack River above the Falls," and the appointment of the Trustees, and requested the Trustees to meet at George Town to elect "a small and convenient number of the Trustees which shall be a committee to act for the whole."

A number of trustees met in December, 1774, first at George Town and later at Alexandria and authorized Ballendine to hire 50 Negroes to dig canals around the Falls of the Potomac. In an announcement, dated December 22, 1774, printed in the *Virginia Gazette*, January 14, 1775, Mr. Ballendine issues the following notice:

"At a meeting of the Trustees for opening the navigation of Potowmack River held at George Town Dec. 1, 1774, Thos. Johnson, Jr., Attorney-at-law, Wm. Deakins, Adam Stewart, Thos. Johns, Thos. Richardson, of Georgetown, merchants; Wm. Ellzey,

Robt. Alexander, Philip Alexander of Virginia present, who ordered and directed that the subscriber should on the credit and at the risk of the above named Trustees hire fifty slaves to labor in cutting the canals around the several Falls of said River; and at another meeting of Trustees for the purpose aforesaid held at Alexandria 19th inst., present Geo. Washington, John Carlyle, John Dalton, Wm. Ramsay, Gentlemen of Virginia together with many of the Trustees at the former meeting, who recognized & approved of the order for hiring fifty slaves and agreed to become equally liable. In consequence of which order of the Trustees I hereby give notice that I want to hire negro men for the ensuing year for the purpose above mentioned. Any person inclining to hire the whole or any part of them may see the proceeding of the said Trustees subscribed with their respective hands in my custody."

This advertisement seemed to indicate that the first real step had at last been taken and that the work of clearing the Potomac would begin immediately. But Johnson realized, if no one else did, the difficulties that confronted the undertaking. He knew the opposition that had arisen in Central Virginia to the Potomac bill in the House of Burgesses and he saw opposition on every hand in Maryland. Bitter jealousies existed between the merchants of George Town and Baltimore. Johnson was firmly convinced that unless the Provincial Assembly of Maryland loaned money to the people who were favorable to the movement, they would not be able to give sufficient assistance. In the following letter, Mr. Johnson explains that times were hard, that he himself was unable to raise any cash without selling a part of his estate and that other people were in the same predicament:

THOMAS JOHNSON TO GEORGE WASHINGTON

Annapo 24 Jany 1775.

Dear S^r.

Our printer assuring us in his last weeks paper that there would be a further prorogation of our Assembly and the very doubtful state of American affairs induced me to think that nothing would probably be attempted in your Assembly the ensuing session. This morning about 11 o'clock I reced your two letters by Mr. Stewart dated the 20 instant and this afternoon Mr. Ballendine came to see me on the subject of them.

I should have needed nothing more than your desire to have waited on the Gent. at Alexandria on Thursday if it was in my power but I am so circumstanced that I cannot oblige you. My time has been lately so much engrossed with Committee business and things of the kind that I have been obliged for a week or ten days past to be plodding over my Law Affairs every opportunity with more than common assiduity and I shall with great difficulty be able to get my Terms pleading done by the last day of this month against which day they must be finished. I believe owing to an anxiety which I cannot quiet on public matters I am in but an indifferent state of health nor could I, if for that reason alone, just now undertake the proposed journey with tolerable convenience. I had resolved therefore to send you off my thoughts tomorrow which I do by Mr. Ballendine though the time will not allow me to reduce them to the full draft of a Bill and despairing of ever seeing Pot^o. made navigable on the plan I most wished it you may depend on my best endeavours to get a Bill passed here similar to yours whether upon giving a fee simple in fixt and invariable tolls or having the tolls ascertained anew from time to time with an Eye to a limitted profit per cent in the cost and repairs of the work or giving a term only with a still higher profit. I may possibly be insensibly led by my own particular interest to view the advantages of navigation on the River as more general and extensive than I ought, but I really believe if I had not a Foot of land above the Falls I should be as warm a Friend to the scheme. Unless our Assembly will so far assist us as to emit a sum of money for loan to the subscribers I do assure you I do not think that those on our Side who would most willingly subscribe will be able to do anything clever. I myself am in such a situation that I cannot raise any sum of money without selling a part of the very Estate to be benefited by the scheme on very low terms at present and many with whom I have spoke on the subject are circumstanced as myself. I should think nothing of risking a good deal and might prudently do it all chances considered but in these times many want to borrow and but few to lend money. I do not know where 500 £ could be got on the Secty of 5000.

General Lee's plan has been delayed some time for a plate. I am told it is now nearly done and I hope to have the pleasure of sending you some copies soon.—There has been more alacrity shown by our people than I expected but we are but illy prepared with arms &c. I am apprehensive that the vigilance of the Govt. at home will make it necessary for us to turn our thoughts towards an internal supply of materials.

I am S^r. with the greatest Respect
Your most obed^t Servant
TH^s JOHNSON, JUN^R.

About a month later Johnson wrote Washington that there were some "rogues" who were scheming to have the delegates from Anne Arundel County instructed by their constituents to vote against any and all bills that might be introduced on behalf of the Potomac. Mr. Johnson's statement in this letter that although he was "much averse from engaging in a more active way in politics," he would nevertheless "endeavor to counteract such proceedings," shed a true light upon his character. He was not anxious to "play" politics, but he did not hesitate to try to counteract insidious political influence, if he felt that by doing so he was promoting the public weal.

This letter—in which he also inquires how Col. George

Mason is progressing with the work of framing the Potomac
River bill and moreover offers to draft it himself, if Washington so requests—is as follows: [5]

THOMAS JOHNSON TO GEORGE WASHINGTON

Annapo, 25 Febry 1775.

Sir

Mr. Jacques last night communicated to me your letter to him.
I sent to the post Office early this morning and got your letter from
thence of the 2d inst. Mr. Stewart generally sends me those letters
when the postage is paid but omitted this which is the occasion of my
not having answered it.—

Your suspicion or rather information that Adams is wasting the
timber I am apprehensive is too well founded. Major Jenifer's Discourse intimated as much as if he suspected or had heard the same
and he promised to interfere as far as he could to prevent it. If
Daniel J. Adams will not make a Conveyance of the Lands or his
sisters are determined not to quit their pretensions to the Land which
was not conveyed to old Adams in his lifetime you will not be able
to obtain a Remedy but in our Chancery Court the delay and trouble
of pursuing which to save only about 100 £ of your debt after an advance of near 500 £ Sterl more appears to me to be scarce worth your
while. But I cannot think but Major Jenifer will, as he always said
he would, prevail on the sisters to do you justice and if his endeavors
should not succeed I dare say it will be owing to the bad conduct of
D. J. Adams himself and the influence he may have on his sisters.
Our adjourned provincial Court is to sit the second Tuesday of next
Month when I shall make use of the oppty of talking with Major
Jenifer and Mr. Stone together and will inform you of what passes
on the subject.—The Loans in our Office are not for the 10 or 12
years that the money circulates. The borrowers may pay in as soon
as they please and the Consols are left at discretion to call in any par-
ticular Loan when they please whilst the securities remain good.
They have not called in any but securities may by the Act pay the

[5] *Washington*, Manuscript Division, Library of Congress, Vol. XV.

money at any time they please have an assignment of the bond for their use and stand in the same advantageous state as the Consols themselves. If the money has been actually paid into the Office, I think you would be obliged to an immediate repayment; if the Bond has been only changed, I suppose the Consols would permit another change of the Bond and so discharge the person whose name has been made use of. I am very sorry that this business of Adams has given and is likely to give you so much trouble and you may be assured Sʳ that it would be with very great pleasure to myself that I could oblige you in this or anything else.

General Lee's plan and directions are not yet done. If they are not likely to be soon finished I'll have a manuscript copy made for you—it is but short—from what I hear it is designed our Assembly should sit about the last of March. Against that time I should be glad to have through Mr. Calvert's hands or any other convenient conveyance Col. Mason's estimate, his remarks and the other pages I sent you by Mr. Ballendine. I shall in a day or two go to Baltimore and there hope to learn exactly what opposition is intended to our late Road Law or Potowmack; from what I have yet heard I expect some narrow designing men intend to get the people of Baltimore and a part of this as well as of Frederick County to petition for a repeal of the Road Law or to have such alterations made as will render it ineffectual—I have heard too that the rogues intentions for this County are to be instructed by their constituents to vote against any improvement of Potowmack but I do not believe that the people in general of this County are weak enough to be led into any Resolution which could reflect so much on themselves. If I am mistaken and such an instruction should be really made it will greatly embarrass me. I am much averse from engaging in a more active way in politicks, but if petitions or instructions should be sollicited either against the improvement of our Roads or the River I must endeavour to counteract such proceedings. If an attempt should be made against either the Roads or River I wish both may be attacked at once which will explain the motive as it truly is to shut out the Back people altogether from a Market. I shall most thankfully receive information of any further thoughts that may have occurred to you or Col. Mason relative to clearing Poto. and the draft of the Bill itself if Col. Mason has made it and if not I shall with pleasure do it as well as I am able—You will excuse Mr. Jacques' silence and my taking up the subject of your letter to him, as his lame arm will scarcely allow him to write his name.

I am s^r
>Your most obed^t hble Servant
>>Th^s Johnson, Junr.

Col. Mason finished the Potomac Bill early in March, 1775, and forwarded it to Mount Vernon for Washington's inspection. In his letter to Washington, dated March 9, 1775, Col. Mason says: "I have at last finished the Potomack River Bill; which I now send you, together with some very long remarks thereon; and a letter to Mr. Johnson; into which you'll be pleased to put a wafer when you forward the other papers to him. I also return the Act of Assembly, and Mr. Johnson's Notes, which you sent me. This affair has taken me five times as long as I expected; and I do assure you I never engaged in anything which puzzled me more; there were such a number of contingencys to provide for, and drawing up Laws a thing so much out of my way. I shall be well pleased if the pains we have bestowed upon the subject prove of any service to so great an undertaking; but by what I can understand, there will be so strong an opposition from Baltimore, and the Head of the Bay, as will go near to prevent its passage thro' the Maryland Assembly, in any shape it can be offered."

But the Maryland Assembly had long since adjourned. When the provincial lawmakers disbanded on the 19th of April, 1774, they separated for the last time in the history of the Proprietary Government. Consequently, Col. Mason's work was in vain. And Delegate Thomas Johnson never had the opportunity to present the Potomac River Bill to the Provincial Assembly.

This was the *status* of the project to open the Potomac to navigation when George Washington was nominated by Thomas Johnson at Philadelphia, on June 15, 1775, as Commander-in-Chief of the Army. And Washington thereupon hastened to Massachusetts to assume command of the Continentals.

Thomas Johnson had prophesied correctly. The Potomac scheme had failed on account of the inertia of the Maryland Assembly. This is the reason given by John Ballendine in a public announcement in the *Virginia Gazette*, October 28, 1775. He admits herein that while he endeavored, "at the earnest solicitation of many gentlemen on Potowmack and influenced by my own interest on that river," to open its navigation and underwent considerable expense in preparation for the work, the failure of the Maryland Assembly to pass an act coöperating with the one passed in Virginia obliged him to discontinue the work on the Potomac for the present. Mr. Ballendine thereupon gave his attention to the promotion of navigation of the River James.

But the lowering of the war clouds brought to an end all efforts for public improvements. The terrible struggle which followed the affair at Lexington drew the public mind to military objects of supreme importance. Thomas Johnson, as Revolutionary War Governor, and George Washington, as General, were deeply engrossed in the patriotic cause. Thus, for the ensuing decade, the efforts of Thomas Johnson and George Washington to promote "water carriage" on the Potomac River were entirely suspended.

CHAPTER VIII

ADVOCATE OF AMERICAN ASSOCIATION

THOMAS JOHNSON was only 33 years old at the time of the protest against the Stamp Act and 35 when the duties on tea and other articles went into effect; when the storm broke out again in America, he was approaching the age of 42, in the very vigor of his prime. The Provincial Assembly had adjourned for the last time on April 19, 1774. The opportunity which now came to Johnson was to arouse the freemen to resist the latest form of oppression from beyond the seas. He had been well schooled to assume this rôle. Serving continuously during a period of twelve years in the Assembly, he never held, and probably never sought, any one of the lucrative positions appointed by the Lord Proprietary or the Governor. It was natural, therefore, that he became a champion of the people's cause. The tinder which had caused the flames of hatred to break out again was the "Boston Tea Party." The duties on glass and a number of other articles had been withdrawn and the British Ministry notified the Colonists that the Empire would impose no additional taxes upon America; but a duty on tea still remained and the preamble of the Act of Parliament reaffirmed the necessity for raising revenue in the American Colonies. Three vessel loads of tea were cast into Boston harbor because it had to pay duty—an act which brought down upon the Pilgrims the wrath of the

King, Ministry and Parliament. As a means of revenge, a punitive measure was speedily passed to blockade the Boston port. The people of Boston were prepared for the worst. As soon as they heard the news they assembled in Faneuil Hall and resolved to resist the latest act of British tyranny. "If the other Colonies," they stated, "would come into a joint resolution to stop all importations from Great Britain and every part of the West Indies till the Act blockading up the harbor be repealed, the same will prove the salvation of North America and her liberties."

Copies of the Boston Port Bill and the Faneuil Hall Resolutions were received in Maryland about two months after the punitive measure was passed by Parliament. When the message reached Baltimore Town, a meeting was held in the Court House when a committee was appointed to communicate with the leaders at the Colonial Capital and in other towns of Maryland. Two days later the patriots assembled in Annapolis. At this meeting the following set of resolutions was adopted:

"At a meeting of the inhabitants of the city of Annapolis, on Wednesday, the twenty-fifth day of May, 1774, after notice given of the time, place, and occasion of this meeting,—

"*Resolved,* That it is the unanimous opinion of this meeting, that the town of Boston is now suffering in the common cause of America, and that it is incumbent on every colony in America, to unite in effectual measures to obtain a repeal of the late act of Parliament, for blocking up the harbour of Boston.

"That it is the opinion of this meeting, that if the colonies come into a joint resolution to stop all importation from, and exportation to Great Britain, till the said act be repealed, the same will preserve North America, and her liberties.

"*Resolved, Therefore,* That the inhabitants of this city will join in an association with the several counties of this province, and the principal provinces of America, to put an immediate stop to all exports to Great Britain, and that after a short day, hereafter to be agreed on, that there shall be no imports from Great Britain, till the said act be repealed, and that such association be on oath.

"That it is the opinion of this meeting, that the gentlemen of the law of this province bring no suit for the recovery of any debt due from any inhabitant of this province, to any inhabitant of Great Britain, until the said act be repealed.

"That the inhabitants of this city will, and it is the opinion of this meeting, that this province ought immediately to break off all trade and dealings with that colony or province, which shall refuse or decline to come into similar resolutions with a majority of the colonies.

"That Messieurs John Hall, Charles Carroll, Thomas Johnson, jun., William Paca, Matthias Hammond, and Samuel 'Chase, be a committee for this city to join with those who shall be appointed for Baltimore Town, and other parts of this province, to constitute one general committee; and that the gentlemen appointed for this city immediately correspond with Baltimore Town, and other parts of this province, to effect such association as will secure American liberty."

Mr. Johnson had had some slight experience in communicating with the sister Colonies. During the days of the Provincial Assembly he had been chosen (along with Matthew Tilghman, Edward Lloyd, Brice T. B. Worthington, John Hall, James Lloyd Chamberlaine, Joseph Sim, Matthias Hammond, Josiah Beale, William Paca and Samuel Chase) to represent the Assembly on a standing Committee of Correspondence and Enquiry. But a new day had arrived. The Committee of Correspondence chosen at the Annapolis Meeting was delegated not only to *correspond and enquire* but also to *effect such association* as would be necessary to secure their rights as British freemen.

Hardly had the Town Meeting adjourned before several

"gentlemen of influence" commenced to ridicule the Resolutions. Furthermore, said the cynics, if the sentiment of the people had been properly secured, the Resolutions would never have been adopted. In order to put an end to these unfriendly rumors it was decided to call another Town Meeting on the evening of May 27, to reconsider the entire subject. Here the proceedings of the first meeting were fully sustained. But still there was criticism. This time the principal complaint was levelled against the clause resolving,

"That it is the opinion of this meeting, that the gentlemen of the law of this province bring no suit for the recovery of any debt due from any inhabitant of this province, to any inhabitant of Great Britain, until the said act [Boston Port Bill] be repealed."

Fully 135 of the prominent subjects of Annapolis and vicinity signed a Protest against this Resolve. The Protest declared that the Resolve did pass by the narrow margin of 47 to 31, but that its passage was a grave mistake, being "big with bankruptcy and ruin." The Resolve, it said, spelt disregard of just obligations and that it would jeopardize commercial credit because other countries would no longer place any confidence in the New World. One of the signers was Daniel Dulany. In the list of objectors appeared the names of members of the Hammond, Ross, Tilghman, Howard, Worthington and other prominent Colonial Maryland families. The name of Thomas Johnson, Jr., however, was conspicuous for its absence.

But the greatest obstacles came not from within their own ranks. The chief difficulty was the fact that standing over the people in open antagonism to the people's will was the Proprietary Government, including all of the high and mighty officials of the Colony. There was no public official to whom they could appeal for help and guidance. A call from the Governor for a session of the Provincial Assembly was out of the question. The solution of the problem came on the last day of May, 1774, when the suggestion was advanced at Baltimore Town that the people send *deputies* from all the Counties of Maryland to a *General Convention* in Annapolis in order to decide on concert of action. This plan was heralded with universal acclaim. The subjects residing in Anne Arundel County assembled in Annapolis on the 4th of June and selected 13 deputies. Thomas Johnson, Jr., was one of the number. His colleagues were Samuel Chase, William Paca, Charles Carroll, barrister, Matthias Hammond, Brice T. B. Worthington, John Hall, Thomas Dorsey, John Hood, Jr., Samuel Chew, John Weems, Thomas Sprigg and Rezin Hammond.

There were very few British officials who looked upon the actions of the American Colonists with alarm. Sir Robert Eden had complacently left for a trip to England, unmindful of the bitter hostility of the subjects. Scarcely any member of the House of Commons, except Edmund Burke, saw the portentous results hidden in the Boston Port Bill. The Irish statesman declared the retaliatory measure gave him heartfelt sorrow not only because it was unjust and severe, but also because it was fraught with danger to British authority. This was a memorable instance of his clear political vision. It proved, as Mr. Burke expected it would, the great turning-point in American politics. The subjects in Maryland were as eager and determined as any in North America to defy the mighty menace of oppression from the throne. With faces set and fists clinched, 92 defiant deputies assembled in Annapolis to attend the first Provincial Convention.

The deputies organized on the 22nd of June, 1774, by calling Matthew Tilghman, of Talbot, to the chair. The several Counties were represented by their most influential citizens. The Anne Arundel County delegation was second to none in ability. Thomas Johnson, while not loquacious as an orator, was able, fearless and splendidly equipped for leadership in the Convention. After deciding that each County should have but one vote and that each question should be decided by a majority of votes, the members proceeded to business by taking under consideration the messages from the sister Colonies.

The result of the Convention was far-reaching. The deputies did not quibble. They did not waver for a moment on the course Maryland should pursue. They resolved that the recent Acts of the British Parliament were "cruel and oppressive invasions" of the natural and constitutional rights of England subjects and paved the way to the "utter destruction of British America." In the meantime the venerated Charter of Massachusetts had been annulled by Act of Parliament; General Gage had been appointed Governor of Massachusetts to see that the law was enforced; and the people of the Colony had been declared Rebels. The heart and hand of Maryland went out to their stricken brothers in the North. The Maryland Convention resolved to take subscriptions in every County for their relief. The deputies at Annapolis lost no time in considering the plan to sever all commercial relations with Great Britain. It met with instant approval. They resolved not only that all intercourse with the parent realm should be broken off, but that the people of Maryland would have no dealings with any Colony which refused to join in "the general plan." Thereupon the Convention went upon record in favor of a *General Congress of Deputies*, from all of the "Original Thirteen," for the purpose of giving ample relief to the people of Boston, of agreeing on one general plan of action with reference to the commercial relations between the Colonies and the Mother Country, and in other ways of preserving American liberty.

Early in June, Virginia and Massachusetts had proposed such a Congress. The Maryland Convention selected a committee of five to communicate with Pennsylvania and Virginia on the subject. Mr. Johnson was one of the deputies charged with the duty of conducting the correspondence. The other four were Matthew Tilghman, William Paca, Samuel Chase and Robert Goldsborough. The Convention authorized "any two or more of them" to attend the Congress, in case they were successful in making the arrangements; and, upon their return, to give an account of their stewardship.

The Convention accomplished its work within four days. The recess committee also did its work expeditiously, for on June 26, 1774—the day following adjournment of the Convention—Mr. Johnson and his associates drafted and sent off their message to the adjacent Colonies. In their letter to the Virginia Committee of Correspondence, they said:

"To save America from destruction, it is our most fervent wish and sanguine hope, that your Colony has the same disposition and spirit, and that, by a General Congress, such a plan may be struck out as may effectually accomplish the grand object in view. We are also directed to propose that the General Congress be held at the City of Philadelphia, the twentieth of September next. The limits of our Province, and the number of its inhabitants, compared with yours, afforded an opportunity of collecting our general sense, before the sentiments of your Colony could be regularly ascertained, and, therefore, as this Province had the first opportunity, it has taken the liberty of making the first proposition."

Being intimately acquainted with George Washington, one of the members of the Committee of Correspondence of the Old Diminion, and knowing that he wielded considerable influence South of the Potomac, Mr. Johnson also wrote him a personal note on the subject. Said he: [1]

THOMAS JOHNSON TO GEORGE WASHINGTON

Annapolis, 28 June 1774.

Sir—

I take the freedom to inclose you the Resolutions of our General Committee for the Province on the Bills respecting the Massachusetts Governm^t and the Act for blocking up the Harbour of Boston. If our general scheme of conduct should be adopted by the Congress I think even so strict an Association will be kept by the people of Maryland with good faith. I have sanguine hopes that your Colony will readily join in effectual measures . . . I have strong expectations from Pennsylvania but have heard nothing material from New York.

I am sir
Your most obed^t Servant
TH^s JOHNSON, JUN^R.

On the 5th of August, Colonel Washington sent to Thomas Johnson the views of Virginia concerning the General Congress. The letter from Washington to Johnson said:

"As the resolves of all the Colonies which had come to hand in this meeting, adopted your appointment of Philadelphia as the place to hold the Congress in; as the first of September or thereabouts hath

---

[1] *Washington,* Manuscript Division, Library of Congress, Vol. XV, 1867. *Vide* a portion of this letter near the end of Chapter V.

been fixed upon by all of them (except your province) as a fit time; and as the time is now so near at hand as to render it difficult if practicable, to change it, without putting too much to the hazard; it was resolved here to abide by the general choice of Philadelphia, though judged as an improper place, and to fix upon the 5th of September (as the South Carolinians have done) for the time."

On receiving this message from Washington, Mr. Johnson conferred without delay with Chase, and they then advised the Committee of Correspondence at Baltimore Town of its contents. The following memorandum was attached to their dispatch to the Baltimore Committee:

"The letter of Col. Washington to Mr. Johnson, you'll perceive, was not designed for public view. We are sorry that the meeting is so early as the 5th of September, but perhaps it will be better then, and at Philadelphia, than to run the risk of a new appointment."

CHAPTER IX

THE FIRST CONTINENTAL CONGRESS

U P to this time, Johnson's public work had been confined to the borders of his own Colony. But on the
6th of September, 1774, he took a seat in Congress and his
career in the broader field of politics began. Three of the
Maryland delegates—Chase, Paca, and Goldsborough—
were on hand when Congress convened the day before. So
was George Washington, who journeyed up from Mount
Vernon in company with two of his colleagues, Edmund
Pendleton and Patrick Henry. But the remaining member
from Maryland, the venerable Matthew Tilghman, did not
put in his appearance until a week later. Peyton Randolph,
who was chosen President of Congress, Richard Bland, and
Richard Henry Lee, completed the delegation from the
Old Dominion. The five delegates from Maryland and the
six from Virginia blended wisdom with eloquence, prudence
with courage, and conservatism with youthful fire. In Car-
penters' Hall, Johnson saw about him a brilliant array of
Colonial statesmen, the most powerful orators, the most
distinguished leaders, men of the most commanding ability
then to be found in all America. But with a long experience in the Provincial Assembly, he was well equipped to
play a conspicuous rôle in the proceedings of the General
Congress. His keen, analytical mind, his sound judgment
and common sense, his unflinching courage and incorrupt-

ible integrity brought him immediately forward as one of the leaders of the House.

The day Johnson arrived, Congress determined upon the plan to select a committee "to state the rights of the Colonies in general, the several instances in which those rights are violated or infringed, and the means most proper to be pursued for obtaining a restoration of them." And on the following day it was decided to place on the first committee—called the "Great Committee"—two delegates from each Colony. One of Maryland's representatives was Johnson. The following were the members of the committee:

Massachusetts, John Adams and Samuel Adams; Rhode Island, Samuel Ward and Stephen Hopkins; New Hampshire, John Sullivan and Nathaniel Folsom; Connecticut, Roger Sherman and Eliphalet Dyer; New York, John Jay and James Duane; New Jersey, William Livingston and John Dehart; Pennsylvania, Edward Biddle and Joseph Galloway; Delaware, Caesar Rodney and Thomas McKean; Maryland, Thomas Johnson and Robert Goldsborough; Virginia, Edmund Pendleton and Richard Henry Lee; South Carolina, John Rutledge and Thomas Lynch.

The appointment of Mr. Johnson on this committee gave him an opportunity to come in close contact with a score of the most eminent statesmen of the New World. With harmony so essential, they faced a task of supreme importance to America. John Adams said that during their first day's conference [September 8] the Great Committee had "a most ingenious, entertaining debate." Business on the floor of Congress was entirely suspended until the 14th of September; and the sessions of the Committee were so protracted that it was whispered in many quarters that the balance of the members were beginning to grow "jealous." But finally the Committee reached a decision and on September 22 reported the *Rights of the American Colonies*—rights based upon the laws of Nature, the principles of the English Constitution, and Charters and Compacts—and two days later the *Infringements of American Rights*. The first important duty of Congress had been performed.

The delegates were now ready to determine upon a common course of action. The first proposal was to stop all importations from the parent realm. This plan had been strongly endorsed in the Maryland Convention at Annapolis three months before; yet the Maryland delegates proceeded with caution. Although as ardently devoted to the American cause as any patriot in the Colonies, Johnson remained conservative and prudent in dealing with the soul-stirring problems which appeared before him at Philadelphia. Both he and George Washington advocated a courageous statement of American rights; but both, according to F. N. Thorpe, viewed the controversy, like John Adams, with the lawyer's eye: they did not display the impetuosity of Patrick Henry and the flaming zeal of Richard Henry Lee. Concerning the course Johnson and Washington pursued at Philadelphia, Mr. Thorpe says: [1]

"The Maryland delegates, Matthew Tilghman, Thomas Johnson, William Paca and Samuel Chase, were neither united nor divided on any administrative measures, but yet were unanimously desirous of formulating the American cause more clearly. Thomas Johnson, the ablest man among them, was not ready to go further than John Adams. The Maryland delegates, however, were instructed 'to effect one general plan of conduct bearing on the commercial connection of the Colonies with the mother country.' . . .

[1] Francis Newton Thorpe, *The Constitutional History of the United States*, Vol. I, 82-84.

Washington, one of the Virginia members, thus early appearing in the councils of his country, was not committed to radical measures, for as yet he was confident that harmony would ultimately prevail and he did not share the strong opinions of Henry, John Rutledge and Samuel Adams. Like John Adams and Thomas Johnson, he took a legal rather than an economic view of public affairs."

The *non-importation* agreement was assented to rather readily and on September 27 it was unanimously resolved, "That there be no importation, from and after December 1, 1774, into British America from Great Britain or Ireland, of any goods, or from any other place of any goods as shall have been exported from Great Britain or Ireland; and that no such goods, wares or merchandise imported after December 1 be used or purchased."

But *non-exportation* brought forth considerable opposition. All the delegates realized that this plan would be distasteful to Great Britain, but the Southern delegates maintained that their Colonies would thereby be injured more seriously than the others. North Carolina exported pitch, tar and turpentine; South Carolina large quantities of rice and indigo; and Virginia tobacco. Unless these products could be shipped to the foreign markets, the Southern statesmen insisted that their Colonies would suffer disastrously. Samuel Chase, coming from a "tobacco colony," gravely predicted that non-exportation would send the entire country into bankruptcy. But all the delegates realized that harmony should prevail; and when South Carolina acceded after securing an exception of rice, Virginia withdrew her opposition, Maryland supported the measure and North Carolina rapidly fell in line. Thereupon, on September 30, it was resolved "That from and after September 10, 1775, the exportation of all merchandise and every commodity to Great Britain, Ireland and the

West Indies, ought to cease, unless the grievances of America are redressed before that time."

Then came Johnson's appointment on a committee to devise a plan to make the resolutions effective. It was agreed in the non-exportation resolution that the Annapolis attorney, together with Thomas Cushing (Massachusetts), Isaac Low (New York), Thomas Mifflin (Pennsylvania) and Richard H. Lee (Virginia), should constitute a committee "to bring in a plan for carrying into effect the non-importation, non-consumption, and non-exportation resolved on." Recommendations were made by this committee for an *American Association*—a course which Mr. Johnson had warmly espoused in the first Maryland Convention.

Mr. Johnson, it seems, was conspicuous in the debates on the severance of commercial relations with the Mother Country. This fact can be inferred from the statement made by John Adams on October 10, 1774, that Johnson of Maryland possessed "an extensive knowledge of trade as well as law." Adams's opinion of Johnson is contained in the following estimate of the more prominent members of the first Congress:

"The deliberations of the Congress are spun out to an immeasurable length. There is so much wit, sense, learning, acuteness, subtlety, eloquence, &c. among fifty gentlemen, each of whom has been habituated to lead and guide in his own Province, that an immensity of time is spent unnecessarily. Johnson of Maryland has a clear and a cool head, an extensive knowledge of trade as well as law. He is a deliberating man, but not a shining orator; his passions and imagination don't appear enough for an orator; his reason and penetration appear, but not his rhetoric. Galloway, Duane, and Johnson are sensible and learned, but cold speakers. Lee, Henry, and Hooper, are the orators; Paca is a deliberator too; Chase speaks warmly; Mifflin is a sprightly and spirited speaker; John Rutledge don't exceed in learning or oratory, though he is a rapid speaker; young Edward Rutledge is young and zealous, a little unsteady and injudicious, but very unnatural and affected as a speaker; Dyer and Sherman speak often and long, but very heavily and clumsily." [2]

The observation of Mr. Adams that Delegate Johnson was "not a shining orator," in comparison with Patrick Henry and Lee, recalls the contrast Thomas Jefferson made fifty years later between the delegates from Maryland and the Virginia representatives in the Continental Congress. When Daniel Webster visited Jefferson at Monticello toward the close of the year 1824, the aged Virginian told that distinguished orator from New England that Patrick Henry and Lee "opened the general subject" in the Continental Congress with such gripping eloquence that Samuel Chase and William Paca, delegates from Maryland, shook their heads and said: "We shall not be wanted here. Those gentlemen from Virginia will be able to do everything without us." But, Jefferson explained, neither Henry nor Lee was a man of business, and, having made strong and eloquent general speeches, they had done all they could. [3] A slightly different account says that after Henry and Lee had made their maiden speeches in Congress, Mr. Chase said to one of his colleagues from Maryland: "We might as well go home. We are not able to legislate with these men." But later, during the debates on American commerce, Chase declared: "After all, I find these are but men, and, in the mere matters of business, very common men."

Manifestly, "reason and penetration" at this time were as much in demand as "passions and imagination." At least,

[2] *The Works of John Adams*, Vol. II, 395-6.
[3] George T. Curtis, *Life of Daniel Webster*, Vol. I, 588.

when Congress determined to make a plea to the King for reconciliation, the deliberating man, with the "clear and cool head," from Maryland, was again called upon to render assistance in the preparation of the paper. It was on the first day of October, 1774, when Congress unanimously resolved, "That a loyal address to his majesty be prepared, dutifully requesting the royal attention to the grievances that alarm and distress his majesty's faithful subjects in North-America, and entreating his majesty's gracious interposition for the removal of such grievances; thereby to restore between Great Britain and the Colonies that harmony so necessary to the happiness of the British Empire, and so ardently desired by all America." Whereupon Congress placed the burden of the work upon Richard Henry Lee and Patrick Henry of Virginia, John Adams of Massachusetts Bay, John Rutledge of South Carolina, and Thomas Johnson, Jr., of Maryland. For several weeks these five American statesmen devoted profound thought to the preparation of the document, which they desired to be respectful to the Crown and at the same time clear and emphatic. John Adams says that on the night of October 11 after dining with Caesar Rodney, Samuel Chase, William Paca, Thomas Johnson, and others, at the home of Mr. McKean, he went to Patrick Henry's "lodgings," to discuss the petition to the King. When Congress selected the committee, ability had been recognized, but geographical distribution had been sadly overlooked. Adams was the only Northern man on it. Lee, Henry, Rutledge, and Johnson came from the South. The Central Colonies—the most backward in general sentiment —were not represented. The report from the committee did not prove acceptable to the Middle Colonies; it was apparent that a mistake had been made. Accordingly, John Dickinson, of Pennsylvania, who had entered Congress a few days before, was added to the committee. On October 24 a second draft was reported, and two days later the *Petition of Congress to the King's Most Excellent Majesty* was signed by the delegates and prepared for transmission to Europe. Included among the signatures were those of *Mat. Tilghman, Th^s Johnson Junr., Wm. Paca*, and *Samuel Chase*. Like the Great Committee's report of American Rights and Infringements, the Address to King George III was a masterly presentation of the American cause, which "when laid upon the table of the House of Lords, drew forth the splendid encomium of Chatham."

The documents drafted by the members of the first Congress are state papers of great historical value. They will ever be regarded as among the ablest specimens of practical talent and wisdom in American politics. And while the Colonies were represented at this momentous session by statesmen of the highest order, none, according to the comparative estimates of the statesmen who served in it, had a keener vision or a firmer grasp of affairs than Johnson. In a body of more than fifty men representing over 2,000,000 people, Johnson had the distinction, enjoyed by only one other delegate [Richard Henry Lee] of serving on all three of the following committees of supreme importance: (1) the committee "to state the rights," or the Great Committee; (2) the committee to devise a plan to carry non-importation and non-exportation into effect; and (3) the committee to frame the Petition to the King. Very succinctly one authority [4] thus characterizes the leading statesmen in the First Congress:

---

[4] Frothingham, *The Rise of the Republic of the United States,* 361.

"New England presented, in John Sullivan, vigor; in Roger Sherman, sterling sense and integrity; in Thomas Cushing, commercial knowledge; in John Adams, large capacity for public affairs; in Samuel Adams, a great character, with influence and power to organize. The Middle Colonies presented, in Philip Livingston, the merchant prince of enterprise and liberality; in John Jay, rare public virtue, juridical learning, and classic taste; in William Livingston, progressive ideas tempered by conservatism; in John Dickinson, 'The Immortal Farmer,' erudition and literary ability; in Caesar Rodney and Thomas McKean, working power; in James Duane, timid Whiggism, halting, but keeping true to the cause; in Joseph Galloway, downright Toryism, seeking control, and at length going to the enemy. The Southern Colonies presented, in Thomas Johnson, the grasp of a statesman; in Samuel Chase, activity and boldness; in the Rutledges, wealth and accomplishment; in Christopher Gadsden, the genuine American; and in the Virginia delegation, an illustrious group,—in Richard Bland, wisdom; in Edmund Pendleton, practical talent; in Peyton Randolph, experience in legislation; in Richard Henry Lee, statesmanship in union with high culture; in Patrick Henry, genius and eloquence; in Washington, justice and patriotism. 'If,' said Patrick Henry, 'you speak of solid information and sound judgment, Washington unquestionably is the greatest man of them all.' "

John Quincy Adams and Charles Francis Adams, in editing the works of John Adams,[5] refer to Thomas Johnson, along with John Dickinson, Caesar Rodney, and several others of their calibre, as having "sincerity of purpose and cautious judgment as well as practical capacity, which would not have discredited the most experienced statesmen of their day."

Congress having adjourned on October 26, 1774, Mr. Johnson returned to his home in Annapolis; and on November 9th was placed on a Committee of Correspondence for

---

[5] *The Life of John Adams*, Vol. I, 217-8.

Anne Arundel County and authorized to attend the Second Provincial Convention. Assembling on the 21st of November, this body approved unanimously the proceedings of Congress, resolved that every person in Maryland ought strictly to observe the Articles of Association, and selected Tilghman, Johnson, Chase and Paca, Charles Carroll of Carrollton, Charles Carroll, barrister, and John Hall, on a Provincial Committee of Correspondence.

The Winter, which was now setting in, saw Maryland preparing with great haste for hostilities which seemed inevitable.

CHAPTER X

NOMINATES WASHINGTON FOR COMMANDER-IN-CHIEF

EVERYWHERE the Colonists awaited with bated breath the next move from abroad. Frequently holding meetings, they charged committees of their own selection to keep constant vigil for developments. For example, in the dead of Winter (on January 16, 1775) a mass meeting was held at Annapolis, at which Johnson was placed on a Committee of Observation for Anne Arundel County. Parliament, indignant and determined to retaliate for the interdiction of commerce, ordered General Gage to reduce the Colonists by force. The stirring antebellum days Ridpath describes in the following words which ring with martial music: "There was no longer any hope of a peaceable adjustment. The mighty arm of Great Britain was stretched out to smite and crush the sons of the Pilgrims. The Colonists were few and feeble; but they were men of iron wills who had made up their minds to die for Liberty. It was now the early spring of 1775, and the day of battle was at hand." The Maryland Convention reassembled on April 24th and on the 28th received the first word of bloodshed. The Maryland leaders of the patriot cause now had a new text from which to enthuse the people. As the pall of Lexington spread over the land, the people prepared more eagerly for defense. No event thus far had so strongly cemented the bonds of devotion to the American cause. The first volley of the Revolution had fired the whole country.

The second session of Congress was approaching, and the Maryland Convention proceeded to the choice of seven representatives. The five patriot leaders who had served so ably in the first Congress—Tilghman, Johnson, Paca, Chase, and Goldsborough—were authorized to return to the second. To the delegation were added John Hall and Thomas Stone. Any three or more were authorized to join with the sister Colonies in any measures deemed necessary for the defense of the American Colonies.

Mr. Johnson appeared in the State House at Philadelphia on Wednesday, May 10th, 1775, when the second Continental Congress convened. With him from Maryland were Delegates Samuel Chase, William Paca, John Hall and Matthew Tilghman. A few days later Mr. Goldsborough and Mr. Stone arrived. The Maryland delegation was now complete.

On the 2nd of June a message arrived from Massachusetts describing the "butcheries and devastations" committed by the Royal soldiers and asking for advice concerning the establishment of a Civil Government. It was then that John Adams delivered his speech urging the people in each Colony to assume the functions of Government. "The pride of Britain, flushed with late triumphs and conquests, their infinite contempt of all the power of America, with an insolent, arbitrary Scotch faction, with a Bute and Mansfield at their head for a Ministry," he said, would surely force the Americans to call forth every energy and resource of the country. He advocated a Confederacy, like that of Greece, declaring "No man would think of consolidating

this vast Continent under one National Government!"
Furthermore he advised that American emissaries should be
sent to Europe to seek aid at the Courts of France and
Spain. On the following day (June 3, 1775) Congress
resolved itself into a Committee of the Whole "to take into
further consideration the state of America." After discussion, it was decided that a committe of five should
recommend the proper advice that ought to be given to the
Convention of Massachusetts Bay. Johnson was one of
the members chosen by ballot to frame this important report. The members of the committee were: John Jay,
of New York; James Wilson, of Pennsylvania; Thomas
Johnson, Jr., of Maryland; Richard Henry Lee, of Virginia; and John Rutledge, of South Carolina. These five
able leaders, after conferring with the delegates from Massachusetts, drafted a set of recommendations which were
read to the House on the 7th of June. Two days later it
was resolved that Congress should advise the Convention of
Massachusetts that the offices of Governor and Lieutenant-
Governor should be considered vacant and that the people
should take possession of the Government until the Royal
officers acted in accordance with the Charter.

On the 3rd of June, Johnson was also chosen to take
part in framing a final appeal for reconciliation to the
Crown. Two of his colleagues on this committee—John
Rutledge and John Dickinson—had served with him in
drafting a similar paper in 1774. The two new members
were John Jay and Benjamin Franklin. Thus came Johnson's first opportunity to come in close touch officially with
"Poor Richard." The chosen five were authorized to prepare a "humble and dutiful" petition to the King, with a
view—forlorn though it may have been—of opening

negotiations for peace. So, during the month of June, the members of the committee gave careful thought to the petition.

But, in the meantime, the legislators at Philadelphia did not rest supine. While they earnestly hoped for peace, they considered liberty more important, and immediately took steps for defense. They determined to call upon the Committees of Pennsylvania, New Jersey, Maryland, and Delaware to send to Philadelphia without delay sulphur and saltpeter for gunpowder. Johnson and Dr. Franklin were again chosen together on June 10 "to devise ways and means to introduce the manufacture of salt petre in these Colonies," their associates being Robert Treat Paine, of Massachusetts; Philip Schuyler, of New York; and Richard Henry Lee. They also realized that no time was to be lost in sending off riflemen to join the camp at Boston, and provision was made on the 14th of June to organize troops immediately to serve for a period of one year.

But the Commander-in-Chief of the Continental forces had not yet been selected. Many names had been mentioned and it seemed inevitable that serious difficulty would be met before a choice could be made that would be satisfactory to all. To many of the members, it appeared most appropriate that the Army of New England should be commanded by a Northern General; to place it under the command of a Southerner, they argued, would be "an experiment of delicacy and hazard." On the other hand, the South—particularly Virginia—was very proud of its heritage and from an early day exhibited a marked suspicion, if not a jealousy, of the motives of the New England Colonies.

George Washington was then attending the sessions of

Congress in uniform—a fact which has led some writers to believe that he was modestly announcing his candidacy for some military office in the Continental Army. Although virile and courageous, and a good soldier, Col. Washington was openly opposed by many of the New England delegates. The Adamses seemed to be favorable to his appointment, but other members of the Massachusetts delegation held tenaciously to the view that a Northern man should be chosen. Then, too, some of the delegates from the South were not so very ardent in behalf of Washington. Indeed, some of the members of the Virginia delegation were "very cool" toward his appointment; while at least one of them was "very clear and full against it." It is safe to say, however, that "Dick" Lee and "Tom" Johnson were, from the very beginning, among the warmest supporters of their intimate friend from Mount Vernon. All three having been born in the same year along the Potomac, their friendship had grown stronger with each advancing year; and Lee and Johnson were in a position to appreciate from close contact the wonderful qualities of Washington as a man and as a soldier.

Finally, in an effort to test the sentiment of Congress, John Adams offered a motion to adopt the forces then besieging the British troops in Boston as the Continental Army. In support of the motion Adams casually remarked that it would not be difficult to secure a Commander-in-Chief with the necessary qualifications, for such a man, he felt sure, could be found on the floor of Congress. The allusions became so pointed that Col. Washington, who was occupying a seat near the door, darted with characteristic modesty into the library. Adams's remarks provoked many expressions of open hostility to Washington.

Thomas Cushing, of Massachusetts, avowed opposition to him, and warned that if a man from below the Potomac were picked for the position of Commander-in-Chief, the soldiers, and, indeed, the people of New England generally, would be greaty discontented. Mr. Paine expressed a strong preference for General Artemus Ward, an old college chum, who was already then in command of all the New England forces. Among others who declared that the selection of George Washington would be "highly inexpedient" was Roger Sherman, of Connecticut. Mr. Pendleton explained that to place his colleague at the head of the Army of the Revolution would be an "unwise course." The general trend of the argument was that the Continental forces were composed entirely of New England men, that they already had a General of their own, that he, General Ward, was very satisfactory, and that the American riflemen had proved themselves able to imprison the British— this was all that could be expected of them at this time.

George Washington's friends, observing the hostile sentiment, postponed final decision of the question. Overpowered for the time by the sense of responsibility, Washington is said to have declared to Patrick Henry: "I fear that this day will mark the down-fall of my reputation!" But his friends remained stanch for him and they made strenuous efforts out of doors to swing the delegations in line.

According to James Johnson, of Baltimore, one of Governor Johnson's nephews, who claimed that he heard the history of the nomination repeatedly from his uncle's lips,[1] Delegate Lee told Delegate Johnson that while he was in favor of George Washington, he preferred that the

[1] *Vide* Scharf, *History of Western Maryland*, Vol. I, 380, 390.

nomination be made by a member from some other Colony, as the delegates from Virginia felt "a delicacy" about nominating their own colleague Commander-in-Chief. Appreciating this position, Johnson met John Adams the morning of the nomination on the steps of the State House and after explaining that Mr. Lee had refused to nominate Washington asked the representative from Massachusetts if he would agree to make the nomination. "Mr. Adams," according to the story, "made no reply, turned on his heel, and left him."

The story of these conversations with Richard Henry Lee and John Adams evidently is not without foundation, for upwards of a half-century later Mr. Adams remembered that the delegates from Virginia had, from "delicacy," declined to place Washington's name before the House. In a letter written February 24, 1821, to Richard Henry Lee, grandson of the Richard Henry Lee who introduced the resolution in Congress to declare the United Colonies free and independent, Mr. Adams gave this explanation of why Thomas Johnson, of Maryland, made the nominating speech: "As such motions were generally concerted beforehand, I presume Mr. Johnson was designated to nominate a General, because the gentlemen from Virginia declined, from delicacy, the nomination of their own colleague. . . . It ought to be eternally remembered that the Eastern members were interdicted from taking the lead in any great measures, because they lay under an odium and a great weight of unpopularity. Because they had been suspected from the beginning of having independence in contemplation, they were restrained from the appearance of promoting any great measures by their own discretion, as well as by the general sense of Congress."

In a letter to Colonel Pickering, dated August 6, 1822, in which he told of his journey with Samuel Adams, Cushing, and Paine to Philadelphia in 1775, John Adams presented the following additional facts in this connection: "They were met at Frankfort by Dr. Rush, Mr. Mifflin, Mr. Bayard, and others who desired a conference, and particularly cautioned not to lisp the word 'Independence.' They added, you must not come forward with any bold measures; you must not pretend to take the lead; you know Virginia is the most populous State in the Union; they are very proud of their ancient dominion, as they call it; they think they have the right to lead, and the Southern States and Middle States are too much disposed to yield it to them. This was plain dealing, Mr. Pickering; and I must confess that there appeared so much wisdom and good sense in it, that it made a deep impression on my mind, and it had an equal effect on all my colleagues.   This conversation, and the principles and facts and motives suggested in it, have given a color, complexion, and character to the whole policy of the United States from that day to this.   Without it, Mr. Washington would never have commanded our armies, nor Mr. Jefferson have been the author of the Declaration of Independence, nor Mr. Richard Henry Lee the mover of it, nor Mr. Chase the mover of foreign relations.   If I have ever had cause to repent of any part of this policy, that repentance ever has been and ever will be unavailing.   I had forgot to say, nor Mr. Johnson ever have been the nominator of Washington for General."

From these statements written nearly fifty years after the Declaration of Independence, it appears that Adams considered it advisable, on the score of policy, that the nomination should proceed from a Southern delegate.   And thus the duty fell upon Johnson. The opportunity for this distinguished service came on Thursday, June 15, 1775, when after some discussion the following motion was adopted:

> "*Resolved,* That a General be appointed to command all the Continental forces, raised, or to be raised, for the defence of American liberty.
> "That five hundred dollars, per month, be allowed for his pay and expenses."

After the passage of this resolution, Johnson arose; and upon being recognized by John Hancock, who had been chosen presiding officer when Randolph left for Virginia, delivered a brief address in which he placed the name of his friend, George Washington, in nomination for General of "all the Continental forces." [2] It is true, Col. Washington and Mr. Johnson had been personally intimate for a great many years and had engaged in business enterprises together; but it was not friendship alone which induced the nomination. It is problematical whether Washington's nearest friends at this time foresaw the full extent of his greatness. Indeed, Washington openly declared that he doubted his ability to fulfill the arduous duties of Commander-in-Chief. General Bradley T. Johnson says: "Colonel Washington himself deprecated Johnson's action. He was of opinion that Andrew Lewis, the hero of Point Pleasant, was better qualified for the place." But Mr. Johnson felt that his friend from Mount Vernon had given ample proof of his generalship in actual warfare, and ignoring Washington's diffidence, moved his appointment with genuine zeal and enthusiasm, and so successfully was his

[2] *Journals of the Continental Congress* (edited by W. C. Ford) Vol. II, page 91.

work performed that Washington was elected unanimously! In moving Washington's appointment, at a time when less courageous souls hesitated from embarrassment, Thomas Johnson won an immortal distinction. Pointing to the importance of the rôle Mr. Johnson had thus enacted, Hampton L. Carson says:[3]

"To-day it matters not from what State a man may come, but then, narrow, local and contracted views predominated. Remember that this was but two months after the affair at Lexington, and more than a year before the Declaration of Independence. Reflect on the significance of this act, by which a Maryland man, recognizing the commonness of the danger and the essential unity of the cause, threw aside his provincial and colonial prejudices, and boldly faced the responsibility of naming, in the presence of disunited delegates from thirteen colonies, a Virginian, to command at Cambridge, an army which henceforth was to be known as the Continental Army, subject to the regulations and control of the Continental Congress, freed from purely local restraints, and thereby forced to the front the ideas of identity of grievances and unity of action, transmuting the loneliness of Massachusetts in matters once local into a common partnership interest in all questions affecting the general welfare, and placing in the van a man from a far distant colony whose rank would be superior to that of Ward, Thomas and Putnam even on the heights of Bunker Hill. It was a bold conception and national in its character. It is true that the suggestion of this nomination had come from John Adams, supported by Samuel Adams, and Joseph Warren, who three days later became the first great martyr in the American cause, had written a letter urging the appointment, but Pendleton, of Virginia, Washington's personal friend, had disclaimed any wish that the Massachusetts commanders should be superseded. It detracts nothing from the honor due to Maryland in thus distinctly adopting a national idea, to suggest that Massachusetts was under the pressure of an invading army, and her forces, as well as those of her New England allies, were plainly unequal to the task of resisting

[3] *Maryland's Contribution to Federalism*, Report, Third Annual Meeting (1898), Maryland State Bar Association.

alone for any length of time the power of the Crown. The nomination was unanimously approved with a liberality which reflects
credit upon all who participated, but the distinction which belongs to
the actor, the moving spirit in the cause, is clearly Maryland's."

When the delegates assembled on the following day
—June 16, 1775—the President formally notified Washington of his appointment as Commander-in-Chief and expressed the earnest hope that he would serve. Washington
then arose and, with great dignity and feeling, replied:

"*Mr. President,* Though I am truly sensible of the high honor
done me, in this appointment, yet I feel great distress, from a con-
sciousness that my abilities and military experience may not be equal
to the extensive and important trust. However, as the Congress
desire it, I will enter upon the momentous duty, and exert every power
I possess in the service, and for the support of the glorious cause. I
beg they will accept my most cordial thanks for this distinguished
testimony of their approbation. But lest some unlucky event should
happen, unfavourable to my reputation, I beg it may be remembered
by every gentleman in the room, that I, this day, declare with the
utmost sincerity, I do not think myself equal to the command I am
honored with. As to pay, Sir, I beg leave to assure the Congress,
that as no pecuniary consideration could have tempted me to accept
this arduous employment, at the expense of my domestic ease and
happiness, I do not wish to make any profit from it. I will keep an
exact account of my expenses. Those, I doubt not, they will discharge; and that is all I desire."

General Washington was commissioned on Saturday,
June 17th, and after bidding farewell to his friends set
out for Massachusetts.

The members of Congress now proceeded to take under
consideration the selection of Major-Generals. Among
those who hovered about the State House in quest of high
military honor was Charles Lee. Born in England in 1731,
he saw service in Braddock's ill-fated expedition against

Fort Duquesne, in the assault on Ticonderoga, in the attack against the French fort at Niagara, and in the conquest of Canada. On his return to England he was promoted to Lieutenant-Colonel and rendered conspicuous service in Portugal, where he aided in repelling the Spanish invasion. He expected promotion on his return home; but, instead, he was put on half pay. Greatly rankled, he offered his services to the King of Poland; but the hostilities he looked for did not develop and he journeyed to Turkey. Some time later he returned to London and again sought promotion; but, disappointed once more, he returned in disgust to Poland, where he received the commission of Major-General. He served in Russia against the Turks, and afterwards wandered through France, Italy, Germany, and Switzerland. Having bitterly denounced the British Government, Lee could not hope for any favors in England and in 1773 he sailed for America. Feeling that he might have a good chance of being appointed Commander-in-Chief of the American Army, he bought an estate in Virginia and espoused the cause of the Colonies with characteristic enthusiasm. It was a distinct disappointment to him when he failed to secure the highest command, but he now sought with great eagerness the post of first Major-General.

James Johnson declared that while he never heard his uncle boast of the honor of having nominated George Washington, there was one peculiar merit he always claimed—that of preventing Charles Lee from being chosen by Congress second in command. Says he: "When he [General Charles Lee] was nominated Mr. Johnson, in a speech of some length, portrayed his character as a *disappointed foreigner*, and not to be trusted. When he sat down the whole delegation from New York arose in a body, and said that every word the gentleman from Maryland had said was true." Artemus Ward, of Massachusetts, was thereupon chosen to head the list of Major-Generals. Lee, by nature vain and jealous, was enraged at this selection and called General Ward "a fat, old church warden" and "a joke as a warrior."

In order to appease Lee, Congress appointed him second Major-General and directed John Adams, Patrick Henry, and Thomas Lynch to find out whether he would accept this command. After an interview with Lee, they reported that he wanted to serve the American cause, and that he appreciated the honor conferred upon him, but he desired before entering upon the service to confer with a committee consisting of one delegate from each of the Colonies "to whom he desired to explain some particulars respecting his private fortune." The Congress acceded to his request, and Mr. Johnson was chosen to represent Maryland. The entire personnel was as follows:

Massachusetts, Samuel Adams; New Hampshire, John Sullivan; Rhode Island, Stephen Hopkins; Connecticut, Eliphalet Dyer; New York, Philip Livingston; Pennsylvania, George Ross; New Jersey, William Livingston; Maryland, Thomas Johnson, Jr.; Delaware, Caesar Rodney; Virginia, Patrick Henry; North Carolina, Richard Caswell; South Carolina, Thomas Lynch.

General Lee gave to the committee an estimate of the estate which he risked by entering the service. His property in England, he claimed, yielded him an income of some six or seven thousand dollars per annum. He told the delegates that if Congress would agree to indemnify him for any loss of property he might sustain by reason of his service, he would accept the command. The committee reported to the House the result of their interview, and Congress decided to protect Lee from any loss he might sustain. General Lee then hurried to Cambridge. On the recommendation of General Washington, Horatio Gates was appointed Adjutant-General with the rank of Brigadier. Philip Schuyler was chosen third Major-General, and Israel Putnam fourth. It turned out that General Ward resigned his command after the British evacuated Boston, and General Lee became senior Major-General, second only in command to General Washington. After the repulse of the attack on Charleston, Lee returned North in high popular favor, and after being captured laid before the British a scheme to crush the Revolution within sixty days. Lee's treason was not discovered among the documents of the British War Office until about seventy years after his death. After betraying his country, he had the brazen effrontery to return to the American service. At the battle of Monmouth, he deliberately planned the slaughter of his own soldiers, and was tried by Court-martial for disobedience of orders, misbehavior before the enemy in making an unnecessary retreat, and disrespect to the Commander-in-Chief. Found guilty on all three charges, he was sentenced to be suspended from the army for one year. After trying to supplant Washington in the highest command and after making many bitter attacks upon Congress, he was finally expelled from the army. He died in disgrace in a tavern in Philadelphia. Incidentally, Congress paid General Lee $30,000, when his property had been confiscated in England. If it is true that Delegate Johnson predicted on the floor of Congress, as his nephew alleges, that Charles Lee was "not to be trusted," the Maryland statesman saw into the future with prophetic vision. For this impudent British officer became the arch traitor of the Revolution, more despicable even than Benedict Arnold.

On the 23rd of June, 1775, Congress decided to adopt a Declaration to be published by General Washington at his Headquarters in New England. The work of drafting this document was referred to a committee, upon which Tom Johnson and Dr. Franklin once more served together. Their associates were John Jay, William Livingston, and John Rutledge. The committee worked with great haste, for it reported the very next day. This draft met with objection, and finally it was referred back to the committee, to which had been added John Dickinson, of Pennsylvania, and Thomas Jefferson, of Virginia. Then came the first association of Johnson and Jefferson on one of the Congressional committees. One of the chief objections to the first draft was that it was too harsh. Mr. Jefferson retouched it, and after being reported in its "softened" condition was adopted by the House.

With provisions made for the military establishment, and the Commander-in-Chief and the Major-Generals selected, Congress was now ready to hear a report from the committee chosen "to draught a Petition to the King." For a month Dr. Franklin, Jay, Johnson, Dickinson, and Rutledge had been devoting careful thought to this document, and when the "dutiful and humble" Petition was presented it was received with enthusiastic approval. On the 8th of July it was signed by the representatives of the various Colonies. The Maryland members who had signed the Petition of 1774, together with Mr. Stone, subscribed their names. In Ministry and Parliament, the position of Maryland was no longer in doubt.

Thomas Johnson's work at Philadelphia, at first chiefly

literary and legal, was now about to become more practical.
His ability was soon recognized in the realm of finance. On
the 19th of July, he was chosen, with Cushing of Massachusetts and Deane of Connecticut, "to estimate the expenses incurred by the votes and resolves of this Congress."
And when, shortly before adjournment, it was deemed advisable to select a recess committee of one member from
each of the "Original Thirteen," to make an exhaustive
search for lead ore and to ascertain the best method of having it smelted and refined, Johnson was chosen to head the
campaign in Maryland. This was the complete committee:
John Adams (Massachusetts); Stephen Hopkins (Rhode
Island); John Langdon (New Hampshire); Silas Deane
(Connecticut); George Clinton (New York); Stephen
Crane (New Jersey); Benjamin Franklin (Pennsylvania);
Caesar Rodney (Delaware); Thomas Johnson (Maryland); Patrick Henry (Virginia); Joseph Hewes (North
Carolina); Christopher Gadsden (South Carolina); and
Lyman Hall (Georgia). Mr. Johnson, in Maryland, and
his associates in their respective Colonies, were also directed
to investigate the most economical method of making salt.
After the selection of the recess committee, Congress ad-
journed on the 1st of August, 1775.

CHAPTER XI

FOUNDER OF A NEW RÉGIME

THE Second Continental Congress was still in session when one of the members, after bidding good-bye to his associates at the State House, set out from Philadelphia. Down through dense forests and over roads almost impassable, he pushes his way toward the South. His stature is a trifle under normal size. On his cheeks a color glows, matching his hair of reddish brown. He is as active as a man of 21, but in reality he is twice that age. Solemn of countenance but sanguine in spirit, he is overflowing with Rooseveltian energy and enthusiasm. Six weeks ago we saw him on the floor of the Congress, with Rutledge, Jay, Wilson and Lee, urging the House to advise the Convention of Massachusetts Bay to assume the functions of Government. He is now approaching Annapolis as fast as his horse can bring him, fired with zeal to inspire the Maryland Convention immediately to follow the same advice. No one hoped more ardently for peace than Delegate Thomas Johnson; but the general course of events was against reconciliation upon a firm basis of constitutional freedom. And so, Johnson was eager to teach the people of his own Colony the gospel of Opposition by force of arms to the British Crown.

Mr. Johnson had been away from home the greater part of three months. Arriving in Annapolis July 26, 1775, he beheld the capital throbbing with bustle and excitement. The Maryland Convention was ready to convene the same day, and deputies were arriving from all sections of the Province to attend the momentous session.

As the Provincial Convention opened, Thomas Johnson, by this time regarded as one of the most influential statesmen in all the United Colonies, took his seat as a Deputy from Anne Arundel County. It is natural to suppose that on the first day of the session, devoted mainly to preliminaries of organization, Mr. Johnson and his colleagues from Philadelphia were heralded with hearty cheers and sought for information and advice.

On the second day, the Convention proceeded without delay to business and appointed a committee "to consider of the ways and means to put this Province into the best state of defence." Johnson and his colleagues—Tilghman, Paca, Chase, Goldsborough and Stone—were placed on this important committee together with Charles Carroll of Carrollton, Charles Carroll, barrister, and James Hollyday —men equally signalized for their influence, general ability and devotion to the Common Cause.

To the general subject of preparation for war the committee devoted two weeks of careful thought and discussion. The members often assembled at daybreak, Mr. Johnson says, and continued work until darkness brought out their candles. Finally, on the 9th of August, they reached a decision. The Convention accepting their report, passed the following flaming resolutions:

"The long premeditated, and now avowed, design of the British Government to raise a revenue from the property of the Colonists without their consent, on the gift, grant and disposition of the Commons of Great Britain; the arbitrary and vindicative statutes passed under color of punishing a riot, to subdue by military force and by famine the Massachusetts Bay; the unlimited power assumed by Parliament to alter the Charter of that Province and the Constitution of all the Colonies, thereby destroying the essential securities of the lives, liberties and properties of the Colonists; the commencement of hostilities by the ministerial forces and the cruel prosecution of the War against the people of the Massachusetts Bay, followed by General Gage's Proclamation declaring almost the whole of the inhabitants of the United Colonies, by name or description, *rebels* and *traitors*—are sufficient causes to arm a free people in defence of their liberty and to justify resistance, no longer dictated by prudence merely, but by necessity, and leave no alternative but base submission or manly opposition to uncontroulable tyranny. The Congress chose the latter, and for the express purpose of securing and defending the United Colonies and preserving them in safety against all attempts to carry the above-mentioned acts into execution by force of arms,

"*Resolved,* That the said Colonies be immediately put into a state of defence and now supports, at the joint expence, an Army to restrain the further violence and repel the future attacks of a disappointed and exasperated Enemy.

"We, therefore, inhabitants of the Province of Maryland, firmly persuaded that it is necessary and justifiable to repel force by force, do approve of the Opposition by Arms to the British troops, employed to enforce obedience to the late acts and statutes of the British Parliament, for raising a revenue in America, and altering and changing the Charter and Constitution of the Massachusetts Bay, and for destroying the essential securities for the lives, liberties and properties of the subjects in the United Colonies.

"And we do unite and associate, as one band, and firmly and solemnly engage and pledge ourselves to each other, and to America, that we will, to the utmost of our power, promote and support the present Opposition, carrying on, as well by Arms as by the Continental Association, restraining our commerce.

"And as in these times of public danger and until a reconciliation with Great Britain on constitutional principles is effected (an event we most ardently wish may soon take place) the energy of government may be greatly impaired, so that even zeal unrestrained may be productive of anarchy and confusion; we do in like manner unite, associate and solemnly engage in maintenance of good order and the public peace to support the civil power in the due execution of the laws, so far as may be consistent with the present plan of Opposition, and to defend with our utmost power all persons from every species of outrage to ourselves or their property, and to prevent any punishment from being inflicted on any offenders other than such as shall be adjudged by the civil magistrate, Continental Congress, our Convention, Council of Safety, or Committees of Observation."

This *Association of the Freemen of Maryland*, as it was called, was a Declaration of Rights for a new régime. It was signed by the deputies in Convention assembled on Monday, August 14, 1775, after which it was distributed throughout the Colony to be signed as a pledge of loyalty to the patriot cause. On the same day, just before adjournment, sixteen members of a Council of Safety were chosen to carry on the Government until the close of the next succeeding Convention. The provisional machinery was now complete and, as we shall see, was soon to be put in motion.

A few days later Mr. Johnson sent off to Major-General Horatio Gates a lengthy letter in which, after stating his views concerning the Petition to George III, he explained how there was no longer any "real force or efficacy" in the Proprietary Government of Maryland for the reason that during the recess of the Convention the Council of Safety was to have the "supreme direction." As Mr. Johnson was one of the leading figures in the Convention and was selected one of the members of the Council of Safety, let us secure first-hand information of the condition of affairs existing in Maryland at that time by reading Johnson's own words: [1]

---

[1] *Letters of Members of Continental Congress* (Edited by E. C. Burnett). Vol. I, p. 190; Force, *American Archives*, 4th Series, Vol. III, p. 157.

THOMAS JOHNSON TO HORATIO GATES

Annapolis, August 18, 1775

My dear Sir:

I received yours of the 21st July, and in a day or two afterwards forwarded your letter to Mrs. Gates, by my brother, with directions, if she had left Frederick Town, where she then was on a visit, and had no immediate good opportunity, to send a servant on purpose.

I shall be very unhappy that petitioning the King, to which measure I was a friend, should give you or any one else attached to the cause of America and liberty the least uneasiness. You and I, and America in general, may almost universally wish in the first place to establish our liberties; our second wish is a reunion with Great Britain; so may we preserve the empire entire, and the constitutional liberty, founded in Whiggish principles handed down to us by our ancestors. In order to strengthen ourselves to accomplish these great ends, we ought, in my opinion, to conduct ourselves so as to unite America and divide Britain; this, as it appears to me, may most likely be effected by doing rather more than less in the peaceable line, than would be required if our petition is rejected with contempt, which I think most likely. Will not our friends in England be still more exasperated against the Court? And will not our very moderate men on this side of the water be compelled to own the necessity of op-posing force to force? The rejection of the New York petition was very serviceable to America. If our petition should be granted, the troops will be recalled, the obnoxious acts repealed, and we restored to the footing of 1763. If the petition should not be granted, but so far attended to as to lay the ground-work of a negotiation, Britain must, I think, be ruined by the delay; if she subdues us at all, it must be by a violent and sudden exertion of her force; and if we can keep up a strong party in England, headed by such characters as Lord Chatham and the others in the present opposition, Bute, Mansfield and North, and a corrupt majority cannot draw the British force fully into action against us. Our friends will certainly continue such as long as they see we do not desire to break from a reasonable and beneficial connection with the mother country; but if, unhappily for the whole Empire, they should once be convinced by our conduct that we design to break from that connection, I am apprehensive they will thenceforth become our most dangerous enemies—the greatest and first law of self-preservation will justify, nay compel it. The cunning Scotchman and Lord North fully feel the force of this reasoning; hence their industry to make it believed in England that we have a scheme of Independence, a general term they equivocally use, to signify to the friends of liberty a breaking off of all connection, and to Tories that we dispute the supremacy of Parliament. In the Declaratory Act is the power of binding us by its acts, in all cases whatever—the latter we do most certainly dispute, and I trust shall successfully fight against with the approbation of every honest Englishman. Lord North's proposition, and consequent resolution of Parliament, were insidiously devised to wear the face of peace, and embarrass us in the choice of evils—either to accept and be slaves, or reject and increase the number and power of our enemies. I flatter myself that your petition will present to him only a choice of means injurious to his villainous schemes.

Our Convention met the very day of my getting home; the meeting was very full; we sat close many days, by six o'clock in the morning, and by candle light in the evening. Our people were very prompt to do everything desired; they have appropriated £100,000 for the defence of this Province, a great part of it to be laid out in the military line immediately, part contingently, and the rest for establishing manufactories of salt, saltpetre, and gunpowder.

We have an Association, ascertaining the necessity and justifiableness of repelling force by force, to be universally signed; and strict resolutions with regard to our militia, which is to be as comprehensive here as perhaps in any country in the world, when called into action. We are to be subject to the Congressional rules and regulations for the army. A Committee of Safety, composed of sixteen, is, in the recess of the Convention, to have the supreme direction. We yet retain the forms of our Government, but there is no real force or efficacy in it; if the intelligence we have from England looks towards war, I dare say this Province will not hesitate to discharge all officers, and go boldly into it at once.

I have not lately heard anything particular from Virginia that can be depended on; their convention has had a long setting, and I have no doubt but spirited measures, becoming themselves, and adequate to their circumstances, are adopted. We have the pleasure, now and then, to hear of your successful skirmishes. I long to hear that you have all your riflemen, and am particularly anxious as to their conduct. The spirit has run through our young men so much, that if the business proceeds, notwithstanding the scarcity of men in this and the other Southern Provinces, I believe we must furnish you with a battalion or two; if, as I hope, those who are gone acquire reputation, many of our youth will be on fire. The difficulty now is to regulate and direct the spirit of the people at large; and I verily believe that, instead of their being discouraged by a check on our military achievements, a sore rub would inflame them nearly to madness and desperation. I have already solicited your notice of several young gentlemen from Maryland: Lieut. Griffith and Daniel Dorsey, volunteers with Captain Price's, and Frederick Ridgely with Capt. Cresap's company, are all young men of connection with us; their fathers, with whom I have an intimacy and friendship, are ambitious that they should be regarded by you, and desire I should make a favorable mention of them with that view. You must not be surprised, the rank you hold in the opinion of my countrymen must make you the military father of the Maryland youth; I have not a personal acquaintance with these three young gentlemen, but their passion for the service is a powerful recommendation.

Our Convention set one example of banishment. Our Association, I believe, will occasion a good many, chiefly Scotch, to return again to their own country.

On a late alarm, twelve out of thirteen North Britons, enrolled in one company, refused to march, on which they were disarmed; the alarm proved false, within an hour after the fatal discovery. I am very unwilling to do any thing harsh, but it is surely time to know who may be depended on. Under pretence of Neutrality, our inveterate Enemies will remain silent till we are on the hip, and then fall on like Devils to overthrow us.

I have done myself much pleasure in writing you this loose unconnected letter, and I shall have more in knowing the length of it
does not tire you. My best wishes attend you.

I am, my dear Sir,
Your most affectionate Servant,
Th. Johnson, Jun.

Gates, like Generals Lee, Conway and Montgomery,
was a native of England and had fought under the British
flag. Fame came to him later on the capture of Burgoyne,
but his laurels were undeserved, for he never stirred from
camp during the two bloody battles from which he won
renown. General Gates goes down in American History
as a selfish, small-souled and conceited man. If Thomas
Johnson saw with prophetic vision the future career of
Charles Lee, albeit he failed absolutely to gauge the character of Horatio Gates. Mr. Johnson would never have
characterized General Gates, as he did, "the military
father of the Maryland youth" had he known that Gates
was destined later to conspire with General Lee to oust
his beloved friend, Washington, from his high command
at the head of the American forces. As it was, Horatio
Gates, in his despicable effort to undermine General
Washington, lighted a fuse to a bomb which, had it not
been extinguished, would have shivered the United Colonies into fragments.

Whether by design or accident, the personal communication which Mr. Johnson forwarded to Major-
General Gates met with wide publicity. "The letter"
[from Johnson to General Gates] says Scharf,[2] "created
a considerable stir in the Colonies at the time, and in England it was published in nearly all the papers of the day."

[2] J. Thomas Scharf, *History of Maryland,* Vol. II, 186.

All of which seems to indicate not only the lack of censorship in "the times that tried men's souls," but also the high regard in which were held the opinions of Thomas Johnson, Jr., on both sides of the Atlantic.

On Tuesday, August 29, 1775, when the Council of Safety assembled for the first time under the new régime, Mr. Johnson appeared as one of the members from the Western Shore. Each Shore of Maryland had been given eight members on the Council. The Western Shore representatives, in addition to Mr. Johnson, were Chase, Paca, Alexander and Stone, Daniel of St. Thomas Jenifer, Carroll of Carrollton, and Carroll, barrister. The Eastern Shoremen on the Council were Tilghman, Goldborough, James Hollyday, Henry Hooper, John Beale Bordley, Thomas Smyth, and Edward and Richard Lloyd. From the Western Shore, on the day of organization, came Johnson, Chase, Paca, Alexander, Jenifer and the Carrolls. James Hollyday and Edward Lloyd, from the peninsula, made up the quorum. All of the nine took the oath prescribed by the Convention. The absence of Mr. Bordley was explained by a letter in which he promised to exert every effort as a private individual in the interest of his country but declined his appointment to the Council of Safety for the reason that he felt unable to measure up to the expectations of the Convention in the discharge of the duties of the office.

There lay before Mr. Johnson a mass of work to be done on the Council of Safety. On the last day of August, for example, he was authorized to purchase "stocks, steel ramrods, bayonets, double screws, priming wires, and brushes, and brass mounting for 500 musquets." And on the first day of September he was authorized to contract for the manufacture of not more than 1000 "good substantial proved musquets."

But at the time of his appointment to the Council of Safety, Mr. Johnson was also reappointed to the Continental Congress. The time arrived when the work on the Council had to be assigned to his colleagues. The Treasurer of the Western Shore had been ordered to pay 500 pounds common money to Johnson, Chase, Paca, Stone and Hall and the Treasurer of the Eastern Shore 200 pounds to Tilghman and Goldsborough in order to defray their expenses in attending the approaching session. "Any three or more of them," the Convention decreed, "have full and ample power to consent and agree to all measures, which such Congress shall deem necessary and effectual to obtain a redress of American grievances."

Feeling relieved that the important task of organizing the provisional régime had been accomplished, Mr. Johnson left Annapolis early in September and once more started on his way to Philadelphia.

Chapter XII

A DEBATER IN CONGRESS

THE successful effort made by Delegate Thomas Johnson to win for Washington the appointment of Commander-in-Chief during the Revolution will no doubt be regarded forever by the American people as one of the chief claims to fame of the first Governor of Maryland. Nevertheless there were many other outstanding features of Johnson's career in the Continental Congress which justly entitle him to National distinction. During the First and Second Congresses the need of the hour was the keen, thoughtful, analytical mind coupled with a bold, fluent pen. With such attainments Mr. Johnson was richly endowed. We have already seen how he was sought frequently to take an active part in drafting those early state papers which won the admiration of the British statesmen who at that time adorned the London Court.

The most important work of the legislators assembled at Philadelphia, it seems, up to this time was the preparation by select committees of remonstrances and resolutions. But when Johnson stepped forward on Wednesday, September 13, 1775, to present his credentials as delegate from Maryland, he entered upon a new period in his career as member of the Continental Congress. From now on, the scene of most arduous work at the State House changed from the committee room to the floor of the

House. Hardly had Delegate Johnson been sworn in
before he jumped into the debate concerning the purchase
of clothing for the little army of shreds and patches, over
which Washington had been called to assume supreme
command. Winter was approaching and Thomas Mifflin,
whom Washington had appointed Quartermaster-General,
applied at the door of Congress for a supply of woolen
goods. The controversy arose over Mifflin's application.
A motion was made by Delegate Nelson to advance
Quartermaster-General Mifflin £5,000 Sterling with
which to buy clothing for the Continentals. Mr. Sherman,
of Connecticut, offered an amendment that any soldier
should be allowed to supply himself in a different way, if
he so desired. At that point Mr. Read arose to explain
that there was already on hand a large supply of clothing
in Massachusetts; whereupon Sherman declared that he
was in favor of an investigation into the prices of goods
as well as the needs of the American Army along this line.
Apprehending the danger in unnecessary delay and with
a view to placate the dissentient delegates, Delegate
Thomas Johnson arose and addressed the Chair. He
admitted that the United Colonies had no centralization
of purchasing authority. "We don't know," said he,[1]
"what has been supplied by Massachusetts; what from
Rhode Island; what from New York; or what from Connecticut." But in a spirit of compromise, the Maryland
delegate offered a motion to limit the amount to be spent
for supplies to £5,000. Sherman's proposal to investigate
the needs of the Continentals was defeated, and to this
extent Johnson was satisfied. But Johnson's suggestion
that the amount of expenditure should not be definitely

[1] Adams, *Works,* Vol. II, 38.

set, but should be *limited* to £5,000, seems not to have been vigorously pushed, for on September 23rd, Congress resolved that a quantity of woolen goods, of the value of £5,000, should be secured.[2]

But while Mr. Johnson henceforward took a more conspicuous part in the debates on the floor of Congress, he still received a number of important committee assignments. On Monday, September 25, after Congress had been advised that claims were arriving somewhat different from the bills referred to the Committee of Accounts for liquidation, Johnson's ability in "trade as well as the law" was again recognized: he was chosen to represent Maryland on the reorganized Committee of Claims, composed of one member from each Colony, to examine all accounts against the Continent.

Again, the same week—on September 30—after Congress had decided to send Benjamin Harrison, Thomas Lynch and Dr. Franklin on a Northern trip to confer with General Washington and with a number of officials in the New England Colonies, "touching the most effectual method of continuing, supporting and regulating a Continental Army," Mr. Johnson was chosen—along with Samuel Adams, Robert R. Livingston, Richard Henry Lee and John Rutledge—to draw up a set of instructions for the three members who were about to start on the journey.

Mr. Johnson had also been serving since September 22 on a committee "to take into consideration the state of the trade of America." This was a committee of seven, the other members being Silas Deane (Connecticut), John Jay (New York), Benjamin Franklin and Thomas Willing (Pennsylvania), Peyton Randolph (Virginia), and John

[2] Adams, *Works,* Vol. II, 38.

Rutledge (South Carolina). The committee reported on the last day of September. It was not, however, until October 4 that Congress resolved itself into a Committee of the Whole to consider the trade of the Colonies—particularly the scheme of non-exportation, to which there had arisen considerable objection. The First Continental Congress, we have seen, after adopting the plan of non-importation, resolved that exportation to Great Britain, Ireland and the West Indies should cease September 10, 1775, unless the grievances against which the American people complained were redressed before that time.

Among all the advocates in Congress of firm adherence to the policy of non-exportation, there was none more stanch than Delegate Johnson. The British Ministry and the Imperial Parliament had firmly held their ground, and the valiant Maryland statesman, taking the floor of Congress, avowed his violent opposition to any plan that would weaken the barriers against commerce with the parent realm. At the same time, he made a strong plea in favor of building up the American merchant marine.

"I am in favor of the Resolutions on Imports and Exports standing until further order of Congress," said Mr. Johnson.[3] "But I am not in favor of giving up our [water] carriage. While it may not concern the planter, the community as a whole is vitally interested in knowing who are the exporters. If our carriers are owned by foreigners and manned by foreign seamen, then the shipwright, the hemp-grower, the rope-maker, the shipbuilder, the profits of the merchants—all are lost! I am for the Report standing. I am in favor of continuing the American Association."

[3] Adams, *Works*, Vol. II, 452.

Mr. R. R. Livingston took issue with the Delegate from Maryland. He declared that he could not see a single advantage in bottling up the American ports. On the contrary, he pointed out the many injuries that would result from such a policy. Non-exportation, said the New Yorker, was destructive to the farmers as well as to the merchants; and therefore would bring decay to business in the American Colonies. "I believe," he cried, "that the Non-Exportation Agreement should immediately be repealed."

When Livingston concluded, Mr. Johnson arose to explain that he did not favor making the terms of the Non-Exportation Agreement any more rigid than they already were.

"In the Winter," said Johnson, "our merchants will venture out to foreign countries. And in the event that Parliament should order the seizure of American merchant ships, the United Colonies can organize a Navy to guard and protect the American vessels. Foreign Nations could be invited to assist in protecting their own commerce. If we allow the Non-Exportation Agreement to remain as it is now, we can obtain powder by way of New York, the lower counties and North Carolina."

Delegate Willing, of Pennsylvania, warned that American paper would lose its circulation and credit, if commerce were stopped. Whereupon Richard Henry Lee declared that foreign Nations should be invited to come to the New World to aid in exporting goods for America. Chase advocated an adherence to the American Association, asserting that he was in favor of postponing the question for further discussion. The Resolutions were finally passed by Congress on November 1, 1775.

Another debate in which Mr. Johnson participated at this session revolved upon the attitude Congress ought properly to assume toward Lord Dunmore, deposed Governor of Virginia. The King's authority was overthrown throughout the Colonies in the summer and autumn of 1775. Nowhere in America did the Royal Governor exhibit such rank vindictiveness and cause so much alarm, when the Provisional Government was established, as in Virginia. Crazed with anger and spite, Governor Dunmore fled upon a man-of-war; and, supported by a considerable fleet, cruised up and down the coast, burning and ravaging towns and plantations. Toward the close of September, Dunmore ordered a bombardment of Hampton Roads; but a hundred Culpeper County men came to the rescue, and so deadly was their fire that the Dunmore boats were almost totally dismanned. Three vessels were sunk. Two drifted ashore and were captured. Left with only a few loyalist troops, the Royal Governor in a rage ordered all able-bodied men to repair to his standard under pain of forfeiture and death; and offered freedom to all Negro slaves and indented whites who would enlist under his banner. From these slaves was organized and equipped "Lord Dunmore's Ethiopian Regiment."

It was on October 6, 1775, that a resolution was offered in the Continental Congress recommending that each Colony seize all persons whose "going at large" might endanger the safety of the Colony or the liberties of America. The resolution was aimed at Lord Dunmore. Delegate Chase described how Dunmore had been committing hostilities along the coast of Virginia and had begun to extend his piracies into Maryland. Mr. Chase said that although the Governor should have been seized months

ago, Virginia did not possess a Naval force and was unable
to raise one. Accordingly, Chase said, the request contained in the resolution would amount to nothing in the
Old Dominion but a "mere piece of paper." Therefore he
opposed the resolution. Mr. Zubly also opposed it, but
for other reasons. He predicted that the seizure of the
King's representatives would so enrage the British officials
that they would conduct hostilities in the Colonies with
greater intensity. Mr. Dyer, on the contrary, said it was
impossible to irritate the people in England any more than
they were already and that they had fully decided on the
destruction of America.

At that point the little Marylander arose. Cool and
collected, Mr. Johnson began his argument by admitting
that Lord Dunmore was "a very bad man," and then went
on to describe the details of some of Gov. Dunmore's
piracies South of the Potomac. But instead of criticizing
the people of Virginia, as Mr. Chase had done, for being
unable to raise a Naval force, Johnson diplomatically explained that the Virginia Convention, after due consideration, had elected the plan of "defensive conduct" toward
Dunmore instead of a more direct campaign. "I am for
leaving it to Virginia," declared the representative from
Maryland.

Mr. Johnson continued with the following statement
which rings with righteous conviction:

"We ought not to lay down a rule in a passion. I see less and less
prospect of a reconciliation every day; but I would not render it impossible. If we should render it impossible, our Colony would take
it into their own hands, and make concessions inconsistent with the
rights of America. North Carolina, Virginia, Pennsylvania, New
York, at least, have strong parties in each of them of that mind. This

would make a disunion. Five or six weeks will give us the final
determination of the people of Great Britain. Not a Governor on
the Continent has the real power, but some have the shadow of it.
A renunciation of all connection with Great Britain will be understood by a step of this kind. Thirteen Colonies connected with Great
Britain in sixteen months have been brought to an armed opposition
to the claims of Great Britain. The line we have pursued has been
the line we ought to have pursued; if what we have done had been
proposed two years ago, four Colonies would not have been for it.
Suppose we had a dozen Crown officers in our possession, have we
determined what to do with them? Shall we hang them?"

When Mr. Johnson took his seat, Richard Henry Lee
arose to thunder a reply. Ridiculing the Marylander's
plea for delay, the Cicero of Virginia interrogated whether
the Colonists had acted fast enough when they allowed the
red coats to fortify themselves in Boston. "If six weeks
will furnish *decisive* information," he cried in derision,
"the same may bring *decisive* destruction to Maryland and
Virginia!"

Wythe, of Virginia, stated that the reason why the
Virginia Convention had not essayed to capture Governor
Dunmore was "a reverence for this Congress." Delegate
Wythe said he was unable to see how the seizure of the
Royal Governors would produce any more hostility on the
part of Great Britain than had already been exhibited.
And if Maryland wants to share in the glory of seizing
Dunmore, he said, Virginia will gladly share this honor
with her sister Colony.

Once more addressing the chair, Mr. Johnson asserted
that as far as he was concerned, Virginia could have un-
restricted permission to capture the frenzied nobleman;
but he was opposed to the resolution for the reason that it
dictated to Virginia the course she had to follow. Fur-

thermore, declared Johnson, he did not include himself in the same class with those who opposed the arrest of the Crown Governors from a fear that such action would be followed by reprisals.

"Maryland," he cried, "does not regard the connection with Great Britain as the first good!"

Thomas Johnson indicated plainly that he was ready to take any step necessary to protect America and her liberties. Johnson's arguments made a deep impression upon the members of Congress. His colleague, Mr. Stone, echoed his thought by suggesting that it might possibly be best to signify to Virginia that "it will not be disagreeable to us, if they secure Lord Dunmore." Whereupon Mr. Johnson's ideas were incorporated in an amendment providing that Congress should advise the Virginia Council of Safety to take any measures deemed proper to secure the Colony from the practices of Lord Dunmore.

From the course of this debate, it is apparent that Johnson took a conservative stand, holding in mind the possibility of reconciliation. At the same time he rendered a service to the House by telling the members how to escape from the paths of controversy and delay. That his views concerning Lord Dunmore and the Old Dominion were regarded with great respect by the members of the House is evident from the fact that he was selected as one of a committee of five out of the whole assembly "to enquire into the state of the Colony of Virginia, to consider whether any and what provisions may be necessary for its defence, and to report the same to the Congress." The five members were chosen on November 10, his associates being Samuel Adams of Massachusetts, James Wilson of

Pennsylvania, Samuel Ward of Rhode Island, and Thomas Lynch of South Carolina.

It was not long before the Continentals came to aid the Virginia Militia in an effort to drive Lord Dunmore from the waters of Virginia. When they arrived in December, 1775, Dunmore escaped to his fleet; but a few weeks later, remaining close off shore in search of revenge, he asked the American soldiers to send him provisions and to stop firing on his vessels. The Americans refused; and for two days and nights Dunmore bombarded Norfolk until the town was wiped out of existence. In the Summer of 1776, Dunmore's camp was broken up by General Andrew Lewis. Dunmore later offered his services to the British Naval forces at New York, and his Negroes were sent to the West Indies to be sold to the Spaniards.

During November, 1775, Delegate Johnson was placed by Congress on a number of important committees. On the 16th of that month, he was assigned to a committee of seven, one of whom was Thomas Jefferson, to consider "sundry papers from the General Court of the Colony of Massachusetts Bay." On the 17th, he was chosen on a committee of the same size, along with John Adams, Dr. Franklin and others, to consider a communication from the Commander-in-Chief with reference to the disposition of British vessels and their cargoes captured in Canada. On the 23rd, he was selected—with Sherman, Lynch, Lee and Samuel Adams—to investigate frauds alleged to have existed in connection with certain contracts with the Continent; and on the same day he was appointed—together with Wythe, Jay, Edward Rutledge, Samuel Adams, Jefferson and Franklin—to investigate reports that various persons in Philadelphia had refused to accept bills emitted by order of the Pennsylvania Assembly.

But probably the most important of all the assignments which the Annapolis lawyer received at this session of Congress came to him on Wednesday, November 29. His appointment on this day came in pursuance of the following resolution:

"*Resolved,* That a committee of five be appointed for the sole purpose of corresponding with our friends in Great Britain, Ireland, and other parts of the world; and that they lay their correspondence before Congress when directed.

"*Resolved,* That this Congress will make provision to defray all such expenses as may arise by carrying on such correspondence, and for the payment of such agents as the said committee may send on this service."

Mr. Johnson's colleagues on this committee were Benjamin Harrison (Virginia), John Dickinson and Dr. Franklin (Pennsylvania), and John Jay (New York). Charged with complete authority to conduct diplomatic correspondence and to employ confidential "agents" in the Courts of Europe, the members of the committee determined at the beginning upon a policy of rigid censorship. The five delegates were accordingly called by their colleagues at Philadelphia "The Secret Committee," and their names are inscribed in the Secret Journals of Congress, published in 1820 under the direction of the President. Here, on these early Journals of Foreign Affairs, more than seven months before the birth of the Nation, is to be found the germ of American Diplomacy.

CHAPTER XIII

AT THE HEAD OF THE MILITIA

ON the 2nd of December, 1775, announcement was made on the floor of Congress [1] that Delegate Johnson had left for home. The work of the "Secret Committee," headed by Benjamin Franklin, was in capable hands. Johnson knew this. And moreover he was anxious to attend the approaching session of the Provincial Convention. So, when the Convention opened at Annapolis on December 7th, Johnson was in his seat.

Among the new tasks assigned to Johnson during December, 1775, were: (1) "to devise the best ways and means to promote the manufacture of salt-petre"; (2) "to draw the form of commissions for the officers of the militia of this province"; (3) "to consider and report the most effectual method of establishing a gun lock manufactory, and the expense thereof"; and (4) "to consider what alterations and amendments are necessary in the regulation of the militia of this province, and report their opinion thereon."

The advent of the year 1776 saw Maryland in the midst of preparations for war. On Saturday, January 6, the deputies, assembled in the city on the Severn, were ready to name the superior officers of the Maryland

[1] *Journals of the Continental Congress,* Vol. III, p. 395.

Militia. The following minute is included in the proceedings of that day:

"The convention elected by ballot the following persons field officers for the militia: Mr. Henry Hooper brigadier-general of the lower district on the eastern shore. Mr. James Lloyd Chamberlaine of the upper district. Mr. John Dent of the lower district on the western shore. Mr. Andrew Buchanan of the middle district. Mr. Thomas Johnson, jun., of the upper district." [2]

Thereupon it was resolved that the said Brigadier-Generals rank in the following manner: *first*, Brigadier-General Johnson; *second*, Brigadier-General Hooper; *third*, Brigadier-General Dent; *fourth*, Brigadier-General Chamberlaine; *fifth*, Brigadier-General Buchanan. A lawyer, without military experience, thus became the supreme commander of the Militia.

Johnson's acceptance of the commission of senior Brigadier-General did not, however, release him from his obligations as a member of the Convention. For example, on the following Tuesday, January 9th, when it was resolved "that a committee be appointed to prepare and report a scheme for the emission of bills of credit, to defray the expenses of defending this province," General Johnson was elected by ballot to serve on the committee with James Tilghman, Hollyday, Rumsey and Hooe.

Nor was Gen. Johnson released from his duties as a member of the Continental Congress. For when the Convention, on January 12th, instructed the Maryland members of Congress to keep in mind the "avowed end and purpose for which these Colonies originally associated—the redress of American grievances and securing the rights of the Colonies," Thomas Johnson, Jr., was specifically

2 *Proceedings of the Conventions,* 1774-6, p. 78.

named, along with Tilghman, Goldsborough, Chase, Stone, Paca, Alexander and Rogers, as being bound by the instructions. Brigadier-General Johnson's position was a peculiar one. The same Convention that called him into the field to lead the Maryland Militia against the British requested him to strive for "reconciliation with the mother country upon terms that may ensure to these Colonies an equal and permanent freedom."

Many *advanced* statesmen in other Colonies were amazed at the *backwardness* of the Maryland Convention. They could not understand why many of the leading Maryland patriots were opposed to American Independence. But the Convention explained its action in this way: "The experience which we and our ancestors have had of the mildness and equity of the English Constitution, under which we have grown up and enjoyed a state of felicity not exceeded by any people we know of, until the grounds of the present controversy were laid by the Ministry and Parliament of Great Britain, has most strongly endeared to us that form of government from whence these blessings have been derived. . . . To this Constitution we are attached, not merely by *habit* but by *principle*, being in our judgments persuaded it is of all known systems best calculated to secure the liberty of the subject and to guard against despotism on the one hand and licentiousness on the other."

The popularity of Governor Eden also had much to do with the tranquillity of the Maryland subjects. While Lord Dunmore was ravaging coastal towns and plantations of Virginia, young Sir Robert—diplomatic and affable under all circumstances—remained cordial to all the Maryland patriots and, in turn, received every mark of courtesy and respect from the people of the Province. Even as late as the middle of January, 1776, Governor Eden was being hospitably entertained at Stepney by Daniel of St. Thomas Jenifer, President of the Council of Safety. When the Governor heard that the Provincial Convention, notwithstanding the appeal to arms, still felt attached to the British Government and ardently hoped for reconciliation, he suggested to Mr. Jenifer the plan of inviting the most distinguished leaders of the Province to meet for a talk over their difficulties. In compliance with this suggestion, Jenifer wrote to Charles Carroll, barrister, on the 15th of January that Gov. Eden desired to confer with the members of the Council of Safety and several other of the "most distinguished members of the Whig party," who might be "willing to disperse the cloud that has almost overshadowed and is ready to burst upon us." According to the accepted tradition, Carroll was requested by President Jenifer to invite the leading patriots to dine *with the Governor;* but Brigadier-General Johnson, when asked what he thought of the proposal, advised Mr. Carroll to invite such friends as he desired to his own home and then include the Governor as one of the guests. Carroll, so the story goes, accepted Johnson's suggestion as a lucky thought and began at once to prepare for the Executive, members of the Council of Safety and the other guests. Serving on the new Council— organized January 18, 1776, upon the adjournment of the Convention—in addition to President Jenifer and Carroll were James Tilghman, Benjamin Rumsey, Thomas Symth, Thomas B. Hands and John Hall. Among others invited to Carroll's mansion were General Johnson, Chase, Stone, Matthew Tilghman and James Hollyday.

The dinner was set for January 19th. This was Friday; hence, as one writer suggests, Mr. Carroll, a Roman Catholic, was prohibited from offering any flesh meat to his guests on that day. No doubt, with this exception, all the delicacies of food and drink afforded at that time by the waters and fields of Maryland were found in abundance on the banquet table.

After the guests had been "helped around," Governor Eden opened the all-important subject of discussion.

"It is understood in England," said the Governor, "that the Continental Congress is about to form a Treaty of Alliance with France."

Johnson was the first to respond.

"Your Excellency," he said, "we will answer your question, if you will answer one for us."

Governor Eden assented.

"Well," said the new Brigadier-General, "we will candidly acknowledge that overtures have been made to France but, as yet, they have not been accepted. Now, Sir, we understand that your master, King George III, is planning to hire an army of Hessians to join the Royal forces."

The Governor admitted that he had heard the report.

Whereupon General Johnson declared: *"The first Hessian soldier who puts his foot on American soil will absolve me from all allegiance to Great Britain!"*

Among the authorities who accept the story of the dinner party as reliable is Scharf, who takes occasion to add that Mr. Chase, inspired by General Johnson's exclamation, declared outright that he was in favor of a Declaration of Independence. "Thus," says Mr. Scharf,[3] "we see

---

[3] Scharf, *History of Maryland*, Vol. II, 218.

that the resolution to become independent was expressed long before it was done in Congress."

It was doubtless in Barrister Carroll's home that Governor Eden indicated his desire to send to England several copies of the resolutions of the Convention expressing "the mildness and equity of the English Constitution." The Governor promised to show the contents of his letters, if the Council of Safety would undertake to secure passports to New York for his messenger.

Governor Eden's request was granted. So he prepared letters to William Eden, Lord Dartmouth and Mr. Foxcroft, wherein he assured the British Ministry that the Resolutions of the Maryland Convention expressed the real sentiments of the people of his Province. "Far from desiring an Independency, the subjects in Maryland would," he said, "consider it a most happy event to be in precisely the same relation to the parent State as at the conclusion of the last war."

Under date of January 23, the Council of Safety requested the Maryland members of Congress to allow Governor Eden's messenger to pass through Philadelphia.

"The Governor has taken this measure," the Council explained, "in consequence of a free conversation with Messrs. Matthew Tilghman, Thomas Johnson, Thomas Stone and James Hollyday and ourselves on the subject. The step cannot be productive of an ill effect; it may be of the greatest service; it may possibly bring about some overture to a general reconciliation. He has promised you shall have the perusal of what he has wrote, when you come to Maryland. We intimate this to you to prevent the letter being stopt on suspicion of its containing any information or intelligence unfriendly to America." [4]

---

[4] XI *Maryland Archives*, 109.

In the meantime, however, the Maryland patriots had been continuing their preparations for defense. The Convention had decided to fortify Annapolis and Baltimore, and the Council endeavored to borrow from Congress thirty or forty 18-pounders for the purpose.

Immediately after Mr. Carroll's dinner-party, Brigadier-General Johnson left Annapolis to assume his military duties in Western Maryland. He went to Frederick Town, where he gave instructions to George Stricker, Captain of Infantry; and on Monday sent the Council of Safety the following letter explaining the situation in the "Upper District": [5]

GENERAL JOHNSON TO THE COUNCIL OF SAFETY

Gen[t]

Fred. Town
Jan[y] 22[d] 1776.

Stricker has accepted his commission & has had and I expect will have good success in inlisting. He proposes to be very particular in the men he takes & much wishes his, the Light Infantry Company, to be armed with Rifles. Both M[r] Price & he think Rifles for a company may be soon got. Considering the difficulty of speedily arming our troops I think with them it will be advisable to lodge a sum of money in the hands of some body here. No body will do more justice to the public than C. Beatty, to purchase up what Rifles can be got. My Brother this morning let Stricker have 100 of the 200 which he brought up for building the town Jail, to assist him in recruiting. M[r] Ford will be a very proper hand to bring up what money you may think proper to send Stricker. I imagine the 250£ he applies for is not too much as well as what you may think proper for Cap[t] Barrett many of whose Company I expect will be very good Riflemen, if collected in his neighborhood from where I think they may be best spared. Major Price tells me a good many public arms, some of which have been repaired at the expence of

[5] XI *Maryland Archives*, 120.

those who have them, may be collected with industry. I should be glad you^d send up an order for the Committee to collect all they can and if you think as I do to allow the people the reasonable expence of necessary repairs where the musquets came to their hands out of order. I understand about 100 gunlocks fit for Rifles—and that would do well enough to put to repaired muskets—are to be had in town. I wish you^d send up about 60£ to purchase them. Mr Beatty my Brother or myself will do it if you please.

Price tells me he gained an acquaintance with one Royston at the Camp of the Artillary, who was a very clever young man & desires to come to the South and from Price's account of him he would be very serviceable in our second artillery Comp^y & he would be well satisfied with a first Lieutenancy. I wish if there's still room that he may be prefered to it, a trifling circumstance prevented his coming with Price and he even talked of following him. Maj^r Price writes to him that troops are raising in this province & that it is likely he will be employed which he says he dare say will bring him with a strong recommendation from Genl Gates to whom he is well known.

I am Gen^t y^r most ob^t

TH. JOHNSON, JUN^R.

Within 24 hours, General Johnson's letter was in the hands of the Council of Safety. His recommendations were promptly adopted. On Tuesday, January 23, the Council issued an order on the Treasurer of the Western Shore to deliver to Benjamin Ford 100 pounds currency, to be used in securing rifles for Captain Stricker's Company of Light Infantry, and 60 pounds currency for the purchase of gunlocks, to be lodged at Frederick Town with General Johnson—or, in his absence, with Baker Johnson and Charles Beatty.

During the month of February, 1776, the senior Brigadier-General remained in Frederick County directing military preparations. Life in the undeveloped, but potentially rich, regions of Western Maryland appealed to Johnson; and while he realized that as long as the War with Great Britain continued he would be required to spend most of his time at Annapolis and Philadelphia, he longed for the day when he could settle with his wife and children in the "back country." His mother had died some years before, and his father, 74 years old on the 19th of February, was near his end. His brothers, Roger, Baker, and James, were permanently established in profitable business in Frederick County; and he believed that, after the war, opportunities in the law would be particularly bright in the fertile virgin country which was now being developed.

These are perhaps the reasons why Thomas Johnson, Junior, *of the City of Annapolis*, signed himself, in a deed on February 18th, as Thomas Johnson, Junior, *now of Frederick County.*[6]

Toward the close of February, Delegate Alexander became worried over the absence of his colleagues in Congress. General Johnson and Mr. Stone were still in Maryland; Chase had been selected for the mission to Canada; Tilghman had not yet been heard from; Rogers had been granted a leave of absence; and Alexander, too, wanted to leave for home to attend to private affairs. But feeling that it was his duty to remain until some of his "brethren" arrived, Mr. Alexander wrote the Council of Safety to request Johnson and Stone to hurry on up to Philadelphia.

Johnson, immediately upon receiving this summons to civil duty, dropped his military work in the environs of Frederick Town; and early in March was hastening, with all possible speed, to the seat of the General Government.

---

[6] *Land Records of Frederick County,* Liber W, Folios 644, etc.

At the Head of Elk he stopped, to inform Lt.-Col. Henry Hollingsworth that the Council had ordered him a supply of guns, and to receive a supply of money raised by subscription in Cecil County for the purchase of powder. Off again he hurried toward Philadelphia.

Back in Congress after three months' absence, General Johnson was given a warm reception and was showered with congratulations upon his election as commander-in-chief of the Maryland Militia. Among the new duties assigned him in March and April, 1776, were: (1) "to take into consideration the state of the Colonies in the Southern Department"; (2) "to enquire and report the best ways and means of raising the necessary supplies to defray the expences of the war for the present year, over and above the emission of bills of credit"; (3) "to consider the propriety of a War Office"; (4) "to examine and ascertain the value of the several species of gold and silver coins, current in these Colonies, and the proportion they ought to bear to Spanish milled dollars"; and (5) "to take into consideration the state of the Eastern Department and report thereon." He was also asked to consider messages from General Washington, General Schuyler, the Maryland Council of Safety, and the Commissioners to Canada, together with a number of other communications.

Johnson cheerfully rendered these duties for the United Colonies. But the responsibilities that fell upon him as Brigadier-General now took a large part of his time and attention. Immediately upon his arrival in Philadelphia he searched high and low for powder; but he learned that not a single pound could be secured anywhere in the city. Only a few days later, however, there arrived a vessel laden with 2,000 pounds of powder, six tons of lead and various other supplies. It was about this time that Philadelphia received the news that a man-of-war had appeared in the Chesapeake. Johnson and Alexander lost no time in making application for a ton of powder. Their request was granted. The Virginia delegation, apprehensive that the ship might cause great damage in the Bay, offered to Maryland an additional ton. Johnson and Alexander gladly accepted this load, too, and late Saturday night (March 9, 1776) they sent off a dispatch advising the Maryland Council of the shipping of the two tons of powder.

One effort General Johnson and Mr. Alexander made at this session of Congress was to dispose of the Maryland ship, *Defence*. They went before the Marine Committee and urged the purchase of the vessel from Maryland. The offer of sale, however, did not appeal to the committee; and General Johnson felt it was advisable to let the matter rest until a later date. Writing to the Council on March 26th, Alexander and Johnson said by way of consolation: "T. J. confirms our Opinion that if any Depredations should take place after we had parted from the vessell it would be imputed to the sale of her."

Each day brought news of distress in the South—and growing appeals for help. One of the causes for alarm in Maryland was the lack of money. Collectors were sent through the Counties to collect gold and silver coin with the promise that Continental money would be given in exchange. The supply of provincial money was about exhausted. On March 17, the Council of Safety wrote the Maryland delegates that it was looking every day for the Continental money and for the plates and paper for the new emission. "Unless the plates and paper are furnished in a very short time," said the Council, "the Treasury will be exhausted and the credit of the Province must fail."

On March 26, Delegates Johnson and Alexander replied: "Mr. Rittenhouse has been pressed to get the plates done. He has been lately chosen into the Assembly, which has been sitting a good while past. He promises to let us have plates to begin, enough for one sheet, next week. The paper was to be finished about this time." On the 2nd of April, Johnson, Alexander, Paca and Stone assured the Council that their messenger would set out from Philadelphia within a few days with a supply of Continental money. "We hope," they said, "the plates and the paper may be sent off about the same time." Finally, on April 9, Johnson, Stone and Alexander explained that 51 reams of paper were on the way to Annapolis. "The plates," they wrote, "are not yet done. Mr. Rittenhouse now promises they shall be done by next Saturday and as the Assembly is adjourned we hope he will fulfill his promise. They shall be forwarded by the post or some safe hand as soon as done." [7]

This is but one instance of the myriad of harassing difficulties and delays encountered during the Revolutionary War by the members of the Continental Congress. They worked unremittingly, by day and by night, trying to locate muskets and powder, knapsacks and haversacks, linen and duck, leather breeches, hunting shirts, stockings and shoes. The day of resolutions and debate was past. The thirteen Colonies were now on a wild chase for arms and ammunition, for clothing and other supplies, as well as for money.

[7] XI *Maryland Archives*, 290, 306, 319.

CHAPTER XIV

THE END OF THE PROPRIETARY

IN the Spring of 1776, General Charles Lee came into possession of a packet of papers from England, addressed to Governor Robert Eden of Maryland. The packet was taken from a messenger on his way from Dunmore's fleet to Annapolis. Included in the papers were: An offer of pardon to everyone who ceased resistance to the Crown; an appeal from Lord Dartmouth to give aid to the British; letters from Governor Eden's brother; and a communication from Sir George Germain, Lord Dartmouth's successor in the Colonial office. Lord Germain disclosed that a great armament of land and sea forces was preparing to proceed toward the South, in his Lordship's expression, "in order to attempt the restoration of legal government in that part of America." Governor Eden was urged to render "facility and assistance to its operations" by coöperating with Lord Dunmore.

General Lee sent copies of the intercepted letters to Samuel Purviance, chairman of Baltimore County Committee of Observation, together with a confidential message, pompously authorizing Mr. Purviance to seize Governor Eden *in the name of General Lee.*

Mr. Purviance sent copies of the letters to John Hancock, president of the Continental Congress, and attached an unsigned letter of his own, in which he severely condemned the Council of Safety and avowed that he would, on his own responsibility, send off an expedition to Annapolis to arrest Governor Eden. The anonymous letter was intended as a personal note for Mr. Hancock. Mr. Purviance's plans, however, did not materialize as he expected—as is shown by General Johnson in the following letter: [1]

GENERAL JOHNSON TO THE COUNCIL OF SAFETY

Gentlemen.

Philadelphia
17 April 1776.

Yesterday morning just before the meeting of Congress, the letters from Balt. which occasioned the Resolution of yesterday came to the hands of the President. By the same express, and as I believe under the same cover came an Anonymous letter referring to a copy therein inclosed from Genl Lee to Mr Samuel Purviance. I saw and read the copy which was in Purviances hand writing. Lee strongly urged the immediate seizing and securing of the Govr. After the minutes of the preceeding day were read the President began reading the Anonymous letter, but he had not proceeded far before he came to a part desiring that it might not be made known to the Congress but, as I think, to such only as the President might think proper to trust with the contents, the President hesitated, for he had not before read the letter, and seemed desirous of running his Eye over it but on being desired to read out he did so, from the inclosure above mentioned as well as many expressions in the letter and Mr Purviances being the Heroe of the tale which was told in the first person, I had not the least doubt but that Purviance was the Author and Mr Andrew Allen who saw the letter and is acquainted with Purviances hand writing says it was his.

The letter informs that the writer of it had impressed on Genl Lee, in his way to Virg^a an Idea that the Council of Safety was timorous and inactive and represents the Council of Safety and Con-

[1] XI *Maryland Archives,* 347.

vention too as being afraid to execute the Duties of their Stations, his own and the conduct of the Convention on an affair that you must remember he contrasts to the Disadvantage of the latter whose inaction he imputes to want of spirit. He speaks of the orders *he* gave Capt Nicholson on the late alarm and how the Council of Safety was alarmed and frightened at the spirit and boldness of them—represents himself as an object against whom the intentions of the Council of Safety are levelled and in proof recites a conversation with, or saying of, one of them to the effect that he was a warm man or a hot headed man whose power must be pulled down or he would throw things into Confusion. As I heard the letter read but once I cannot undertake to repeat expressions with exactness but I think I have preserved the sentiments and have not exaggerated in any thing and on the whole I esteem it a vile injurious calumny calculated like his conversation with Genl Lee to spread suspicion and distrust of the only executive in our province. If I am not mistaken the letter mentions further that some Gen^t were sent from Balt. or were by him proposed to be sent to Annapolis, who should engage the officer commanding the troops there to secrecy under Oath and their endeavour to get his assistance to execute what you are requested to do by the resolution, this I suppose may be easily traced.

As soon as the letter was read a motion was made to send the original or a copy of it to you which was warmly supported but it was put off till to day to make way for the Consideration of the subject of the Express and in the meantime all was ordered to be secret. Messrs Stone and Alexander who had been delayed in writing letters for the post, came into the Congress, in this stage of the affair and are, as well as myself, privy to the after transactions:

I am Gen^t Your mo obed^t Servant,

TH. JOHNSON, JUN^R.

General Johnson renewed his fight in the House on the 17th to get possession of the anonymous letter from Maryland; but President Hancock stuck to the view that it was a private communication, and, after considerable debate, Johnson's motion was defeated.

Congress also passed a resolution requesting the Maryland Council of Safety to seize Governor Eden.

The following letter presents the arguments advanced *pro* and *con* on the floor of the Congress: [2]

GENERAL JOHNSON TO THE COUNCIL OF SAFETY

Gent.

We moved yesterday in Congress, that the letter referred to by Mr Johnson, should be immediately transmitted to you that you might have an opportunity of vindicating your Honour against the malitious charges made by the writer, this produced a warm debate which lasted for several hours, we insisted (and were supported by several Gentlemen) that the letter containing the most severe reflections upon you as a publick Body ought not to be concealed; that it was absolutely necessary in the present state of our Affairs that the Dignity of the Executives of every province should be supported if properly conducted and if there rested a suspicion that any publick Body either from weakness or want of integrity omitted or refused to execute the Trust committed to them it ought to be made known to their constituents that the power might be placed in more safe Hands. That the exertions of the Letter Writer had already produced in part of the Council of Virginia distrust and suspicion of you: That we had the most convincing proofs upon all occasions of your integrity, Vigilance and Activity in the common cause: And therefore esteemed it our duty to insist that justice might be done, to your injured characters.

It was argued against the motion that the letter was confidential, that it had raised no suspicions in the congress of your zeal or integrity, because they had reposed the highest confidence in you, immediately afterwards by the recommendation sent by the return of the express. And that the mischief which would be produced by communicating the letters would be greater than any benefit which could be expected from it. And that the President was not obliged to produce the letter for the Congress to take order thereon, Although it had been read in the House.

Upon the question whether the President should be requested to lay the letter before congress five colonies voted in the neg^e three in the affirm^a and one divided. We conceived this treatment to you & our province to be cruel and ungenerous to the last degree, the obligation to secrecy expired yesterday and we immediately determined to give you such a state of this Transaction as our memories supply us with; and Mr Johnson committed to writing what passed on the first day.

We this morning waited on Mr Hancock to demand the letter, but he refused to see us, Thus the affair rests at present, & as we cannot delay communicating it to you longer, We have ordered an express immediately to set out for Annapolis and have not the least doubt but you will take the proper steps to vindicate your Honour against the foul Calumny of Mr Purviance who has dared to detract from your Patriotism & spirit. We are determined at all hazards to support you, and tho very sorry for the occasion hope you have complied with the recommendation of Congress, by securing Mr Eden and his papers. If he has conducted himself fairly an Examination will do him credit if otherwise we ought to know it and guard against his unfriendly endeavours. We shall write you by the Post and are Gen^t   Y^r most ob^t Ser^ts

	TH. JOHNSON, JUN^R.
Phil^a	T. STONE,
Thursday 18 April 1776.	R. ALEXANDER.

President Hancock immediately sent off to Annapolis the resolutions requesting the seizure of Governor Eden. The Massachusetts statesman attached a personal letter, in which he said the Congress relied on the diligence and zeal of the Council of Safety for the execution of the resolutions.

But the members of the Council of Safety were not in a hurry to arrest Governor Eden. They placed more confidence in General Johnson's opinion than in the advice of John Hancock and the resolutions of the Continental Congress. "We have," the Council assured the Marylanders at Philadelphia, "all the advantages we could have had, if we had committed him [Governor Eden] to the public Goal, and we are persuaded many more. Nobody can believe that we are courting the Governor at present: 'tis the Peace and Happiness of the Province we wish to preserve, and we are persuaded that it will be best done by keeping up the ostensible Form of our Chartered Constitution." At the same time the Council thanked General Johnson and his colleagues for their efforts—unsuccessful though they were—in this connection. "We feel for you;" was the word from home. "The insult offered by Mr. Hancock in not admitting you to his presence must have been grating."

Replying to President Hancock, President Jenifer declared the members of the Council were quite aware of the facts in the case and had taken proper measures. On April 23, General Johnson informed Mr. Jenifer that the Maryland deputies approved the conduct of the Council of Safety and were determined to support it. "The letter to the President," wrote General Johnson, "gave high offence to some of the very hot gentlemen. No Resolution is yet formed on it, but probably will today." [3]

It appears, however, that no further action was taken by Congress in this direction. Some of Governor Eden's correspondence was printed in the Philadelphia newspapers, causing considerable public resentment against the titular Maryland Executive; but General Johnson and his associates, knowing the kind of man Sir Robert Eden was, discredited the charges which the intercepted letters from England seemed to impute.

[3] XI *Maryland Archives*, 372.

Johnson was imbued, as he had been during the debate over Governor Dunmore, with the thought that the Government of Great Britain was fundamentally beneficent; that the Colonies should ever hold in mind the prospect of reconciliation with the Crown; but that he would be ready for war, if war was inevitable. Back in October, 1775, when the *forward* delegates advocated the resolution requesting Virginia to seize Lord Dunmore, Johnson cried on the floor of Congress: "I see less and less prospect of a reconciliation every day; but I would not render it impossible!" And still he clung to this idea. Nor was he alone in this view. As long as the commander-in-chief of Maryland's Militia held to this opinion, the other deputies from Maryland—with the exception of Chase—stood steadfast by his side. For example, as late as April 24, 1776, Delegate Stone, writing to President Jenifer, assured the folks at home that he hoped for reconciliation with the Crown. His views coincided with those of General Johnson. "I wish," said Stone, "to conduct affairs so that a just and honorable reconciliation should take place, or that we should be pretty unanimous in a resolution to fight it out for Independence. The proper way to effect this is not to move too quick. But then we must take care to do everything which is necessary for our security and defence, not suffer ourselves to be lulled or wheedled by any deceptions, declarations or givings out. You know my hearty wishes for peace upon terms of security and justice to America. But war, anything is preferable to a surrender of our rights." The Marylanders were patriotic, but they were also conservative.

The Maryland Convention was scheduled to meet again in May, and Johnson was now preparing once more to depart from Philadelphia before adjournment of Con-

gress. On the 25th of April, a message, signed by Johnson, Tilghman and Stone, was dispatched to the Council
of Safety, asking for the attendance of Mr. Rogers, in
order that, so the letter said, "as many of us as might be
should be at the Convention." They added: "We don't
think the Province ought to be left unrepresented here."

In the meantime, Purviance had been haled before the
Council of Safety. He acknowledged that the anonymous
letter criticizing the Maryland authorities contained some
of his sentiments but he swore he could not remember
writing it. "He prevaricated most abominably," thought
the Council, which gave him a reprimand and placed him
under bond to appear before the Provincial Convention.

The Convention, assembling at Annapolis May 8,
1776, received the formal complaint against Purviance and
decided to form a special committee to examine the documents relating to the controversy and to report back to the
Convention concerning the charges. Brigadier-General
Johnson, Deputy from Anne Arundel County, was one of
three members elected by ballot on this committee. His
associates were Robert Goldsborough of Dorchester
County and James Hollyday of Queen Anne's.

At the end of ten days, the committee reported that
Purviance's conduct had been reprehensible but recommended his discharge after a severe reprimand. In accordance with these recommendations, the Convention on
the 22nd of May resolved: "Justice would well warrant a
more exemplary punishment to be inflicted on the said
Samuel Purviance for his said misdoings; but that in consideration of his active zeal in the common cause, and in
expectation that he will hereafter conduct himself with
more respect to the public bodies necessarily entrusted with

power mediately or immediately by the people of this
province, and will be more attentive to propriety, this
Convention hath resolved, that the said Samuel Purviance
for his said conduct be censured and reprimanded, and that
Mr. President do from the chair censure and reprimand
him accordingly, and that he be thereupon discharged."
Thereupon Purviance was brought in before the bar of the
House and was given a public reprimand by the President
of the Convention.

Meanwhile Governor Eden had sworn upon his honor
that he had never tried to enflame the British Ministry,
but that he had always spoken of the members of the
American Congress as acting within the line of moderation.
On May 24, 1776, the Convention resolved that, although
Eden's correspondence did not appear to have been carried
on with hostile intent towards the Colonies, "it be signified
to the Governor that the public quiet and safety, in the
judgment of this Convention, require that he leave this
province and that he is at full liberty to depart peaceably
with his effects."   When it is remembered that the Continental Congress more than a month before had directed
the Council of Safety to seize Sir Robert Eden, the resolutions of the Maryland Convention *offering the Governor
permission* to leave the Province were a remarkable tribute
to Eden's popularity. The resolutions were adopted by a
vote of 36 to 19. Johnson was one of the members who
voted for them.

A committee was then appointed to present the Governor with a copy of the resolutions together with an address
of esteem. Johnson was named a member of the committee.

On May 25, 1776, Johnson was also named on a

committee to prepare a passport for the deposed Governor and to draft a communication on the subject to the Virginia Committee of Safety. When the authorities in the Old Dominion received word that the Governor of Maryland had been allowed to escape, contrary to the order of the Continental Congress, they were astounded. They felt that the intercepted letters from England, which found their way to Philadelphia, made Governor Eden *particips criminis* with Lord Dunmore; and they sent to Annapolis a remonstrance which expressed their indignation and disgust.

Sir Robert Eden's courtesy and hospitality, his charms of culture and refinement, had long ago won the affections of the people of his Province. Until an opportunity came when he could depart on one of Lord Dunmore's vessels, he was allowed to remain unmolested on parole. He was accompanied to the British frigate with every mark of respect by the most distinguished patriots of Maryland. The days of the Proprietary were over.

CHAPTER XV

RECONCILIATION VERSUS INDEPENDENCE

"It is true that Mr. Jay—as well as Mr. Dickinson and Mr. Johnson—contributed to retard many vigorous measures, and particularly the vote of Independence, until he left Congress, but I have reason to think he would have concurred in that vote when it was taken, if he had been there."
—*John Adams, Letter to Thomas Jefferson, September 17, 1823.*

"Many motions were made, and after tedious discussion, lost. . . . Mr. Richard Henry Lee, of Virginia, Mr. Sherman, of Connecticut, and Mr. Gadsden, of South Carolina, were always on my side, and Mr. Chase, of Maryland, when he did speak at all, was always powerful, and generally with us. Mr. Johnson, of Maryland, was the most frequent speaker from that State, and while he remained with us, was inclined to Mr. Dickinson for some time, but ere long he and all his State came cordially into our system."—*Adams, Works, II, 506.*

IT must have been a scene of strange emotions when Barrister Carroll, Johnson, Paca, Hollyday and Plater came into Sir Robert Eden's presence with the Resolutions and the Address—one paper ordering him to leave the Province; the other expressing the sincerest hope that he would, upon the restoration of peace, return to America to resume his duties as Governor of Maryland. This was less than six weeks before the Declaration of Independence! Yet the Convention still deplored the severance of connection between the United Colonies and the Mother Country and hoped for a happy reconciliation. "From the disposition your Excellency hath manifested to promote the real interests of both countries," Governor Eden was assured, "the Convention is induced to entertain the warmest hopes and expectations, that upon your arrival in England, you will represent the temper and principles of the people of Maryland, with the same candor you have hitherto shown, and that you will exert your endeavors to promote a reconciliation upon terms that may be secure and honorable both to Great Britain and America."

Nor were these words intended to cajole. They expressed the real and unquestioned sentiment of the Maryland Convention. Just a few days before—May 21, 1776—when Tilghman, Johnson, Alexander, Chase, Goldsborough, Paca, Stone and Rogers were reëlected to Congress, it was unanimously resolved—following the report of a committee headed by Mr. Johnson—that "the said Deputies are bound and directed to govern themselves by the instructions given to them by this Convention in its session of December last, in the same manner as if the said instructions were particularly repeated." The instructions of the December session, we recall, emphatically warned the eight Representatives to strive for *Reconciliation*, not for *Independence*, at Philadelphia. "We further instruct you," were the solemn words of the Convention, ordained January 12, 1776, "that you do not without the previous knowledge and approbation of the convention of this province, assent to any proposition to declare these colonies independent of the crown of Great Britain, nor to any proposition for making or entering into alliance with any foreign power, nor to any union or confederation of these colonies, which may necessarily lead to a separation from the mother country, unless in your judgments, or in the judgments of any four of you, or of a majority of the whole of you, if all shall be then attending in congress, it shall be thought absolutely necessary for the preservation of the liberties of the united colonies."

This being the sentiment in Maryland, we can now appreciate the attitude of Johnson in the Autumn of 1775, endeavoring as he was to represent the wishes of his constituents, when he warned the Continental Congress that if any step were taken to render Reconciliation impossible, the people of Maryland would "take it into their own hands and make concessions inconsistent with the rights of America." Lover of Liberty, implacable foe of Oppression, Mr. Johnson was nevertheless so deeply attached to the Common Law and British institutions that he was striving for Reconciliation long after the leaders in other parts of America were openly clamoring for Independence.

For some time the powerful leaders from New England had been advocating complete separation from the Mother Country. Aligned with them were such men as Lee, Jefferson and Wythe of Virginia, Benjamin Franklin of Pennsylvania, Rodney and McKean of Delaware, John Rutledge and Gadsden of South Carolina and Sergeant of New Jersey. Even from Maryland, bound as she was by the instructions of the Convention, the *advanced party* had moral, if not active, support in the person of Samuel Chase. Indeed, John Adams includes Mr. Chase amongst this group of thinkers.

Nevertheless, the *backward men*, chief among whom were Dickinson, Johnson and Jay, still entertained hopes that the olive branch would be brought across the Atlantic and the difficulties settled by a Reconciliation. R. R. Livingston and Duane of New York, Wilson, Willing and Morris of Pennsylvania, William Livingston of New Jersey, Braxton and Harrison of Virginia, Hooper of North Carolina, and Lynch, Middleton and Edward Rutledge of South Carolina were among the statesmen of this group. "Every important step," says Adams, "was opposed and carried by bare majorities, which obliged me to be almost constantly engaged in debate. I constantly insisted that we should be driven to the necessity of declaring independence from Great Britain."

Amid popular enthusiasm, stirred by the war drum and fife, it was none too easy to oppose, at this time, American Independence. But, so far, Johnson stood firm in the hope that the difficulties could be settled and that the friendly relations with the Crown would be resumed.

The last two weeks of May, 1776, were a busy period for Brigadier-General Johnson. In addition to the prominent part he played in handling the charges against Governor Eden, and in deciding the position of Maryland with reference to Independence, he was the dominant figure on the committee "to consider of the further means of defence necessary for this province." His influence was also potent in deciding the *situs* of powder mills and salt works. And, on the day before adjournment, when the Convention resolved "that a court of admiralty be erected, for the purpose of determining upon such captures and seizures of vessels as are or shall be made according to the late resolves of the continental congress upon that subject, and brought into this province," the senior Brigadier-General was made chairman of a committee of five "to devise a proper establishment for such court of admiralty." The jurisdiction of this tribunal, of course, was limited to the adjudication and condemnation of prizes; however, the Court of Admiralty, as conceived by Johnson immediately prior to the birth of the Nation, holds an interesting place in Maryland history.

The adjournment of the Convention, May 25, 1776,

enabled Johnson to enjoy a few weeks of much-needed rest and recuperation. Matthew Tilghman, Thomas Stone and John Rogers were in attendance at the sessions of Congress. So Johnson felt that he could afford to remain at home for a short time to attend to his private affairs. At the same time he would have a chance quietly to observe the sentiment of the people of Maryland with reference to the all-important subject of Independence.

It was during this period—June 7, 1776—that Richard Henry Lee offered the resolution in Congress that: *"The United Colonies are, and of right ought to be, free and independent states; that they are absolved from all allegiance to the British Crown; and that all political connection between them and Great Britain is, and ought to be, dissolved."* An exciting debate ensued. Finally, on June 10th, action was deferred until the first of July.

Delegates Tilghman, Stone and Rogers, who were then in Philadelphia, realized that the tide was rapidly mounting toward Independence and in a letter to the Council of Safety, dated June 11, recommended that the Convention be called together to consider the subject in the light of the new developments. "The proposition from the Delegates of Virginia to declare the Colonies independent," they declared, "was yesterday after much Debate postponed for three weeks then to be resumed, and a Committee is appointed to draw up a Declaration to prevent Loss of time in case the Congress should agree to the Proposition at the day fixed for resuming it. This postpone was made to give an opportunity to the Delegates from those Colonies, which had not as yet given Authority to adopt this decisive measure, to consult their constituents; it will be necessary that the Convention of Maryland should meet as soon as possible to give the explicit sense of the Province on this Point. And we hope you will accordingly exercise your Power of convening them at such Time as you think the members can be brought together. We wish to have the fair and uninfluenced sense of the People we have the Honour to represent in this most important and interesting affair and that it would be well if the Delegates to Convention were desired to endeavour to collect the opinion of the people at large in some manner or other previous to the meeting of Convention. We shall attend the Convention whenever it meets if it is thought proper we should do so. The approaching Harvest will perhaps render it very inconvenient to many Gentlemen to attend the Convention. This however must not be regarded when matters of such momentous Concern demand their deliberation." [1]

This communication from the Maryland representatives reaching Annapolis on the morning of June 14, the Council on the same day replied as follows: "We have already complied with almost every thing you requested, and we wish we had time to collect the fair and uninfluenced sense of our people on the most important point of Independence before the meeting of the Convention; but as the assembling of that body is already fixed on the 20th of this month, it will be impossible to make the necessary enquiry before that time. We presume the first business of the Convention will be regulating the movement of the militia, and that if necessary in the mean time the several committees of observation may be directed fairly to collect the sense of the Province on the subject of Independence, and make report thereof to the Convention. Any mode their Representatives may think proper to point out would be better relished by

[1] XI *Maryland Archives*, 478.

the people, than for us to put them into a violent ferment
in a way that might not be approved of—'tis a point of
great magnitude, and we think it's best, the shortness of
time considered, to leave it untouched until the meeting of
the Convention on thursday next. Mr. Paca no doubt is
with you before now, Messrs. Johnson and Goldsborough
still with their families we hear—we wish to have you all
down when the grand question is decided, we leave it however to yourselves to judge whether you can be spared from
Congress, and hope whatever is done will be generally agreed
to." [2]

Mr. Paca had, in fact, arrived in Philadelphia by that
time; and Matthew Tilghman had left in order to attend
the Convention at Annapolis.

When the deputies assembled on Friday, June 21,
Tilghman, Johnson, Chase and Goldsborough were among
those present. Mr. Tilghman was elected to the chair.

After the organization had been effected, a letter was
read from the President of Congress, containing resolutions
of the 1st, 3rd and 4th of June. The communication was
ordered to be referred to a committee "to report their opinion thereon." [3] Johnson, Hollyday, Chase, Goldsborough
and Plater were elected by ballot a committee for that purpose. On the 3rd of June, Congress had recommended the
raising of a Flying Camp—troops ready for rapid movement from place to place—and the Maryland Convention
on the 27th of June accepted the challenge by deciding to
furnish Maryland's quota of 3,400 men.

After the adoption of this resolution, the deputies
agreed that Brigadier-General Johnson should take com-

[2] XI *Maryland Archives,* 490.
[3] *Proceedings of Conventions,* 166.

mand of the troops. Following is the official minute of his selection: [4]

"The convention proceeded to the election of officers for the militia to be raised for the flying camp.

"Mr. Thomas Johnson, jr., was elected brigadier-general to command the said militia."

The time had now, at last, arrived when the Maryland statesmen realized that if they held back they would be practically alone in their opposition to Independence. Accordingly, on the 28th of June, 1776, the Convention completely reversed its stand in this connection. Unanimously the deputies resolved: [5]

"That the instructions given by the Convention of December last (and renewed by the Convention in May) to the deputies of this Colony in Congress, be recalled, and the restrictions therein contained removed; that the deputies of this Colony attending in Congress, or a majority of them, or any three or more of them, be authorized and empowered to concur with the other United Colonies, or a majority of them in declaring the United Colonies free and independent States, in forming such further compact and confederation between them, in making foreign alliances, and in adopting such other measures as shall be adjudged necessary for securing the liberties of America, and this Colony will hold itself bound by the resolutions of a majority of the United Colonies in the premises: provided, the sole and exclusive right of regulating the internal government and police of this Colony be reserved to the people thereof."

As Maryland's vote in favor of Independence was now assured, Brigadier-General Johnson decided not to return to Philadelphia immediately while his duties were growing so rapidly at Annapolis. As late as June 29, for example, he was made chairman of another committee "to examine

[4] *Proceedings of Conventions*, 174.
[5] *Proceedings of Conventions*, 176.

the accounts of the supervisors of salt-petre works and report thereon."

To serve simultaneously in Convention and Congress was not considered as any disadvantage, but to serve both in civil and military capacity at the same time was regarded by many as very objectionable. It seems that a resolution had slipped through on the 25th of June "making all militia officers ineligible to any future convention." A fight broke out on the first day of July to repeal this provision. General Johnson, although personally affected, did not hesitate to show his hand. He voted to repeal. Among others who voted with him were Charles Carroll of Carrollton and Charles Carroll, barrister. Chase desired the resolution to stand. A division was called, and it was found that the Johnson faction had succeeded in rescinding the resolution by a vote of 34 to 24. The Chase forces were still dissatisfied. They put the question in a slightly different form by moving that, if any field officer of the Militia should be elected a member of a Convention, his commission should thereupon become void. The two Carrolls again supported General Johnson. The motion was defeated— but by the narrower margin of 30 to 28.

And still Johnson's committee assignments continued. On the 2nd of July, he was selected (along with Hollyday, Chase, Goldsborough and Carroll, barrister) to consider a set of resolutions which had been received from the Virginia Convention.

Meanwhile, on the 1st of July, the question of Independence appeared again in the hall of Congress, following the polished report of Thomas Jefferson of Virginia. The formal Declaration was debated with great spirit on the 3rd, when it became evident that the work of the committee would be accepted. On the morning of the 4th, the discussion was resumed and that afternoon at 2 o'clock the immortal *Declaration of American Independence* was adopted unanimously. It proclaimed that all men are created equal; that all have a natural right to liberty and the pursuit of happiness; that human Governments are instituted for the sole purpose of securing the welfare of the people; that the people have a natural right to alter their Government whenever it becomes destructive of liberty; that the despotism of George III and his ministers had become destructive of liberty; that time and again the Colonies had humbly petitioned for a redress of grievances; that these petitions had all been spurned with derision and contempt; that the King's irrational tyranny over the American subjects could no longer be endured; that war was preferable to slavery; and that, therefore, the United Colonies of America are, and of right ought to be, free and independent States.

The crowds that thronged the streets of Philadelphia answered the signal from the belfry of the State House with shouts of exultation. Couriers bore the glad tidings throughout the land. But about the time the tidings were reaching Annapolis, the Convention, on Saturday morning, July 6th, adopted the *Declaration of the Delegates of Maryland*, declaring the separation of Maryland from Great Britain. In this paper [6] the members of the Convention, after referring to the unjust Acts of Parliament, declared:

"A war unjustly commenced hath been prosecuted against the United Colonies with cruelty, outrageous violence, and perfidy; slaves, savages, and foreign mercenaries have been meanly hired to rob a people of their property, liberties and lives; . . . their humble

[6] *Proceedings of Conventions,* 201.

and dutiful petitions for peace, liberty and safety, have been rejected with scorn. . . .

"Compelled by dire necessity, either to surrender our properties, liberties and lives, into the hands of a British king and parliament, or to use such means as will most probably secure to us and our posterity those invaluable blessings,

"We, the delegates of Maryland, in convention assembled, do declare that the king of Great Britain has violated his compact with this people, and that they owe no allegiance to him."

"For the truth of these assertions," they said in conclusion, "we appeal to that Almighty Being who is emphatically styled the searcher of hearts, and from whose omniscience nothing is concealed. Relying on His divine protection and affiance, and trusting to the justice of our cause, we exhort and conjure every virtuous citizen to join cordially in defence of our common rights, and in maintainance of the freedom of this and her sister colonies." Maryland had long been *backward*, due to her supreme desire to effect an honorable reconciliation with the Mother Country; but this paper, promulgated about the time the echoes of the Liberty Bell were reaching Annapolis, is one of the most memorable documents in the archives of the State.

On account of the force of circumstances, Thomas Johnson did not have the opportunity of voting for the Declaration of Independence at Philadelphia; but the part he played in securing the adoption of the Declaration at Annapolis shows that he, like Jay and Dickinson, to use the words of John Adams, "would have concurred in that vote when it was taken, if he had been there."

On the glorious 4th of July, 1776, Thomas Johnson was devoting his time to official duties at Annapolis. That he was attending the Maryland Convention on that day is shown by a roll call included in the proceedings of the session.[7] The question concerned the change of *per diem* of 14 shillings to each member of the Convention to 10 shillings and reasonable "itinerant charges." General Johnson voted against the change. Mr. Chase and the two Carrolls also voted in the negative. The motion was defeated.

Just before this question was put, the Convention proceeded to ballot for deputies to represent Maryland in Congress. Tilghman, Johnson, Paca, Chase, Stone, Charles Carroll of Carrollton and Alexander were duly elected for that purpose.

It was at this point that the Convention recommended that Mr. Johnson should serve as a member of Congress rather than as commander of the Maryland Flying Camp. This action was taken in the following resolutions: [8]

"*Resolved,* That the honorable Matthew Tilghman, esq., and Thomas Johnson, jr., William Paca, Samuel Chase, Thomas Stone, Charles Carroll of Carrollton, and Robert Alexander, esqrs., or a majority of them, or any three or more of them, be deputies to represent this colony in congress, in as full and ample manner as the deputies of this congress might have done under any appointment heretofore made, until the next convention shall make further order therein.

"Thereupon the convention considering the said Thomas Johnson, esq., cannot discharge the duty of brigadier of the forces to be raised in this province in consequence of the resolves of congress of the third day of June last, to which command the convention, from a confidence in his capacity and abilities to fill the same with advantage to the public cause, and honor to himself, had appointed him, and also execute the trust reposed in him as a deputy in congress for this province; and being of opinion, that it is of very great importance to the welfare of this province, that it should not be deprived

[7] *Proceedings of Conventions,* 190.
[8] *Proceedings of Conventions,* 189.

of the advice and assistance of the said Thomas Johnson in the public councils of the united colonies, and that his place can be supplied
with less inconvenience in the military than in the civil department,
therefore, *Resolved,* That a brigadier-general be elected by ballot
in the room of the said Thomas Johnson, esquire.

"The convention then proceeded to elect a brigadier-general in
the room of Thomas Johnson, esqr., and John Dent, esqr., was
elected by ballot to that office."

Despite the Convention's action on July 4, selecting
Mr. Dent leader of the Flying Camp, Mr. Johnson retained
his commission as Brigadier-General. Indeed, as we shall
see, Dent was before very long ousted from the service and
Johnson assumed active command of the Maryland Forces.

The session of the Convention was largely consumed on
July 5 by Mr. Chase, aided by Barrister Carroll, in an
attempt to stop the running of interest during the war. A
number of motions were offered, but each time Mr. Johnson
and Mr. Carroll of Carrollton voiced opposition. All of
the motions were defeated overwhelmingly.

After the Convention declared Maryland's independence, the deputies dispersed. Mr. Carroll of Carrollton and
Mr. Chase left soon after for Philadelphia and won immortal distinction by signing—together with Stone and
Paca—the American Declaration.

Once more Fate snatched laurels from the brow of
Johnson. Although authorized to return to Congress—and,
indeed, relieved of the command of the Flying Camp for
that express purpose—Johnson felt that it was his duty to
remain for a while in Maryland to assist with recruiting.
He felt that his services would be more valuable at
Frederick Town, in the important work of equipping the
Flying Camp, than at Philadelphia.

Thus, at the time that Carroll of Carrollton and Chase were, from Philadelphia, expressing their belief that the militia would "come in fast to compose the Flying Camp," the harvest being over, and the hope that they would "march with all possible expedition." [9] Johnson was finding from personal experience that the job of recruiting, drilling and equipping was infinitely more difficult than any one, unacquainted with the conditions, could appreciate.

It was at this time that Johnson heard that British ships had appeared in the Potomac. He sent the following letter to the Council of Safety explaining the situation in Western Maryland: [10]

GENERAL JOHNSON TO THE COUNCIL OF SAFETY

Fred. Town
22nd July 1776.

Gent.

In conversation with Mr Ringgold as he past through he told me that Genl Dent was collecting the Militia below to attack Lord Dunmore. I am apprehensive they will want arms for the purpose and that a good many of the men notwithstanding their Desire to go on the service may reluctantly leave their own neighbourhoods unhappily full of Negroes who might it is likely on any misfortune to our militia, become very dangerous. I have spoke with several here and it seems to be a general sentimt that we ought to assist & I believe though our Exertions are already as great as we can well make that for a short Expedition on this very interesting occasion we might soon collect a Battalion and borrow the Arms which would be wanting. If you who are acquainted with all circumstances think it necessary to have men from hence I shall most gladly execute any orders you may think proper to give for that purpose.

9 XII *Maryland Archives*, 130.
10 XII *Maryland Archives*, 92.

Mr Ringgold gave me your letter for my Brother James our furnace is not now in Blast.   I went out to him as soon as I got the Letter.   We have now by us a few potts of about the size you describe, a few Kettles & a few Dutch ovens of much the same contents, the covers we could lay by and of all sorts, make up perhaps 60 or upwards.   We shall have Bales made to them, and unless you have an opportunity of supplying the men with others more to your satisfaction, send them to Balt as soon as we can: the prices must depend on their sizes and the whole shall be so reasonable as to give Satisfaction.   But if you can be better provided please to advise me of it.   My Brother is getting his furnace into Blast with all Diligence and hopes to effect it within a fortnight.   You may then have any number of pots and Kettles that you please within a short time. We shall also attempt to cast such guns as are wanted but cannot contract for them in all Events because the metal may not suit, though we have every Reason to expect it will.   If we succeed in making good Guns the Public may have them del^d at Baltimore at 40 £ a Ton the Guns being proved at the works at the public Expense, the swivels at their common price, but I should be glad if you would ascertain the length & other Descriptions as the make of cannon carrying the same shot vary very much.   If any Body also will contract for a Certainty, I wish he should be preferred even at a greater price.

I am Gen^t with great respect

Your very obed^t Servt

TH. JOHNSON, JUN^R

It appears from this letter that General Johnson gave his time unstintingly to the myriad of details in the Military Department.   That he also kept in close touch with the officers and men of the various companies is likewise indicated by a letter he sent on the following day to the Council.   A Lieutenant in Captain Hardman's Company of Militia had been transferred by the Committee to the "Company of Riflemen now raising in this County," and General Johnson recommended "one Mr. Morris," who had

been serving under Captain Hardman temporarily, to fill
the vacancy with a permanent commission. "Morris is a
fine lively young fellow," Johnson declared, "has been
very serviceable in raising the men and I think, from what
I hear of him, will make a good officer." [11]

The Council of Safety expressed to General Johnson
great satisfaction that the Militia of Frederick County were
"so ready to turn out on the present occasion," but declared
that their services were not immediately required. "For
altho' there are many of the Enemy's ships in Potowmack,"
said the Council, "yet there are but few men in them; those
sickley and die fast."

In reply to Johnson's inquiries concerning supplies, the
Council said: "We have already contracted for a large
number of Camp Kettles of Iron and Copper, and expect to
procure some of Tin. If your brother's Iron is suitable for
casting Guns we could contract with you for 50 three-
pounders, 50 four-pounders, and 75 Swivels to carry one-
pound Ball. Captain Nicholson informs us that the length
of the Swivels is not material, and three and four-pounders
ought to be somewhat shorter than the common standard."

"Should we find it necessary," Johnson was assured, "we
will hereafter give orders for the march of a Battalion from
Frederick County."

These were the circumstances under which Mr. Johnson
—notwithstanding the recommendations of the Convention
—felt constrained, during the hot Summer months of 1776,
to remain in charge of military operations in Western
Maryland rather than to return to Philadelphia. On
account of his devotion to duty, he prevented himself from
signing the Declaration of Independence. And that is one

[11] XII *Maryland Archives,* 108.

of the reasons why the ablest and most influential member of Congress from Maryland during the days of the Revolution, the beloved friend of Washington, and an idol of the people, has been deprived of a high place of distinction among the patriots of American History.

CHAPTER XVI

FRAMING THE STATE CONSTITUTION

THE provisional régime, founded in 1775 under the guidance of Congressman Thomas Johnson, had been very successful. For nearly a year it had served its purpose well. It had assumed all the legislative, executive and judicial functions of the Province and had been administered with eminent justice. But, as every one knew, its machinery had been hastily improvised. And the time had now arrived when the Almighty ordained that Maryland should forge a Declaration of Rights and a State Constitution in the sacred fires of the American Revolution.

Accordingly, in the Maryland Declaration of Independence, adopted on the 6th of July, 1776, is to be found the following statement:

"We have also thought proper to call a new Convention, for the purpose of establishing a Government in this Colony."

Familiar with every sentence of the celebrated paper proclaiming Maryland's independence, Delegate Johnson was unquestionably aware of the plan "of establishing a Government in this Colony." Yet, while other leaders were marking time in those torrid days of late July, awaiting the momentous gathering, Johnson, as we have just seen, was taking advantage of the interim on the Maryland frontier, training and equipping the Flying Camp. Firm was he in the opinion that as the Royal troops were daily advancing in more formidable numbers, it was his duty—notwithstanding the official order relieving him of his command— to furnish General Washington additional troops with all possible expedition, regardless of any sacrifice to his civil obligations.

Nevertheless, it was, without question, a public duty of no little importance to send to the approaching Convention the ablest and most farsighted men in all the Colony. For, upon the result of their labors depended, to a large degree, the future welfare of the State. And, indeed, the people of Maryland realized this grave necessity. Behold, for instance, a few of the more notable nominees in Anne Arundel County—the stormy Samuel Chase! The erudite William Paca! The wealthy Charles Carroll of Carrolton! The gallant Thomas Johnson! What a brilliant array of candidates!

The election began on August 1, 1776. Now, elections (in those days as well as in more recent years) oftentimes produce unexpected results. This particular election was unusually surprising. Within twenty-four hours after the polls had opened, it became evident that several of the outstanding patriot leaders—men who had generally been able to command any office in the gift of the people, for the asking—would be defeated! The people in other sections of Maryland were amazed. They could scarcely believe it possible for anyone in Anne Arundel County to secure the preferment over such brilliant and popular statesmen as Paca, Carroll of Carrollton and Johnson.

Yet such was the fact. On the 2nd of August, the Council of Safety rushed to the Maryland Representatives at Philadelphia this burning message: "Yesterday our election for this County [Anne Arundel] began and is not yet ended. We are sorry to inform you that Messrs Johnson & Paca and Carroll of Car^{n} from present appearances will not be elected." [1] Mr. Chase, it seemed, would receive sufficient votes; but Rezin Hammond, Brice Thomas Beale Worthington and Charles Carroll, barrister, were likewise "greatly beyond any others on the Poll"—and Anne Arundel was entitled to only four seats in the Maryland Convention. The Council of Safety added that very few people from Elkridge or the lower part of the County had "as yet attended." There was not the slightest indication, however, that the result of the election would be different from the forecast. The early prediction of the Council of Safety was correct. Rezin Hammond, B. T. B. Worthington and Barrister Carroll were elected, together with Mr. Chase, to represent Anne Arundel County in the Maryland Constitutional Convention.

The defeat of Thomas Johnson at this crucial period, it is quite certain, gave him little concern. Indeed, according to one rather generally accepted tradition, he was unwilling to occupy a seat when bound, as he knew he would be, by the instructions adopted by the voters of Anne Arundel County. And in the writings of Gen. Bradley T. Johnson, of the Confederate Army, the defeat of Thomas Johnson on this occasion is ascribed to his "refusal to yield to some popular notion." However this may be, it is certain that on the eve of the election, the first Brigadier-General was devoting his time and his energies, as well as a considerable amount of his money, to his little army—and paying no attention to his personal ambition.

Yet, while it is probable that Mr. Johnson himself did

---

[1] XII *Maryland Archives,* 163.

not grieve over the result of the poll, his defeat was the cause of profound regret in all sections of the Colony. "I am sorry," were the words of Charles Grahame of Lower Marlborough, typical of the attitude of the people, "to hear that Mr. Johnson is dropped by Anne Arundel County. It would have given me pleasure to have served with him and as I have heard nothing of the City [Annapolis] Election am still in hopes of his being elected for that." [2]

The City of Annapolis and the City of Baltimore were entitled, like the several Counties of Maryland, to send delegates to the Constitutional Convention. Accordingly, all eyes now turned—as Mr. Grahame suggested—to Annapolis, to see if Johnson and Paca and Charles Carroll of Carrollton would be elected to represent the municipality. But so far as Johnson's election was concerned, they were disappointed. "We shall say nothing particular about the elections," wrote the Council of Safety under date of August 9, to the Maryland Deputies, "more than what relates to yourselves. S. Chase is in for Ann[l] [Anne Arundel], W. P. [William Paca] & Carrollton Carroll for Annapolis. T. J. [Thomas Johnson] & T. Stone are left out." [3]

So, when the historic Constitutional Convention of 1776 opened at Annapolis on the fourteenth of August, and after that stanch old veteran, Hon. Matthew Tilghman of Talbot County, was elected to the chair, the older delegates missed the open countenance with the large piercing eyes, so long familiar in the hall of the Convention.

It was not long, however, before a way was opened for Johnson to enter the door of the Convention. The first step

[2] XII *Maryland Archives,* 186.
[3] XII *Maryland Archives,* 191.

in this direction was a resolution adopted on Friday afternoon, August 16, declaring that any member of the House who accepted a commission in the Flying Camp would automatically vacate his seat. Then came the election of Delegate William Richardson, of Caroline County, as Colonel of the Eastern Shore Battalion of the Flying Camp. This was followed on Saturday morning by an order "that a delegate be elected for Caroline County in the room of Mr. William Richardson, whose seat is vacated by his acceptance of a Colonel's Commission in the Flying Camp." There has always been a tradition in Maryland that Colonel Richardson conveyed a tract of land in Caroline County, containing about 300 acres, to Thomas Johnson for the purpose of making the eminent Western Maryland statesman eligible for the vacant Eastern Shore seat. Did Mr. Johnson accept such a deed? How long, if at all, did he have possession of the property? These are questions that have never been satisfactorily answered. Suffice it to say, the news that he would, after all, become a member of the Constitutional Convention immediately spread like wildfire to all sections of the Colony. Within one week after Delegate Richardson automatically removed himself from the Convention by his acceptance of the Colonelcy, it became common gossip that "Tom" Johnson would secure virtually the unanimous support of Caroline County for the vacant seat. One of the evidences of this certainty is a letter written at that time by Joseph Nicholson, Jr., one of the Eastern Shore members of the Council of Safety, to Daniel of St. Thomas Jenifer. Writing from Queen Anne's County, August 23, Mr. Nicholson said: "I shall do my self the pleasure of waiting upon the Council next week, as soon as Mr. Johnson is elected for Caroline, which will undoubtedly be the case without opposition. I speak this from assurances made me by every man of interest and note in the County, every one of whom I have had personal interviews with." [4]

The special election in Caroline County was held on August 26th, and on Friday afternoon, August 30th—exactly two weeks, to the day, after William Richardson gave up his seat—the Committee of Elections reported that *"Thomas Johnson, esqr., is duly elected a delegate for Caroline county."* Then appears, in the Proceedings, the following brief, but significant, statement: *"Mr. Johnson appeared and took his seat in the House."*

Delegate Johnson had come to the Constitutional Convention by an unusual route. And although the committee had already been appointed "to prepare a declaration and charter of rights, and a plan of government agreeable to such rights as will best maintain peace and good order, and most effectually secure happiness and liberty to the people of this state," an opening was made, as if by the hand of Providence, for Mr. Johnson to become a member of this committee. Soon after the Convention opened, President Tilghman, Samuel Chase, William Paca, Charles Carroll of Carrollton, Charles Carroll, barrister, George Plater and Robert Goldsborough had been elected for the important task. But three days prior to Mr. Johnson's arrival, came a stirring development. Three members of the Convention—Samuel Chase, Carroll, barrister, and Worthington, all representing Anne Arundel County—resigned, declaring they had received "instructions from their constituents, enjoining them, in framing of a government for this state, implicitly to adhere to points in their opinion incompatible

[4] XII *Maryland Archives,* 234.

with good government and the public peace and happiness."
Mr. Johnson had just taken his seat when the Convention
proceeded to fill two places on the committee made vacant
by the resignation of Samuel Chase and Carroll, barrister.
Mr. Robert T. Hooe was one of the men chosen on the
committee. Mr. Johnson was the other.

While the work of drafting the organic law of the State
required diligent application, the members of the committee meanwhile continued to take part in the proceedings
on the floor of the House. Mr. Johnson, for example,
offered a plan to empower the Council of Safety "to purchase and store 30,000 bushels of salt in such of the islands
in the West Indies as they may think proper and by proper
opportunities to import the same into this state, to be sold
out on the public account." His proposal was adopted by
the Convention on the last day of August.

On the 6th of September, a plan was presented to divide
Frederick County into three different parts. Carroll of
Carrollton, Robert Goldsborough and Robert T. Hooe were
among those who favored postponement of the question;
but others, including Johnson and Paca, were in favor of
immediate action. When the question came to a vote, it
was decided to act at once. It was thereupon resolved that
after the first of October, 1776, all of Frederick County
west of South Mountain should be erected into a new
County to be known as *Washington;* the territory extending from the mouth of Rock Creek to the mouth of the
Monocacy River to be known as *Montgomery;* and the remaining, or central, portion to continue under the name of
Frederick.

The 7th of September marked the beginning of an
attempt to authorize Thomas Stone to represent Maryland

in the Continental Congress. Evidently intending to forestall any such action, Mr. William Fitzhugh of Calvert
County moved that no person should be eligible for Congress except a member of the Convention. Mr. Fitzhugh
warned the House that to depart from this custom might
"introduce and intrude on this community men unworthy of
confidence into the most important and highest trusts, dangerous to the safety and welfare of America, especially at
this critical conjuncture." When the previous question
was called, the majority—including Johnson, Goldsborough, Hooe, Paca and Carroll of Carrollton—voted
against it; and Mr. Fitzhugh's proposition was placed upon
the shelf. A motion was thereupon offered by Mr. Paca
that Mr. Stone be empowered "to represent this state in
congress, in as full and ample manner as the delegates heretofore appointed might or could do, until the said delegates
or any two or more of them shall attend, or this convention
make further order therein." The motion was supported
by Johnson, Goldsborough and Carroll. However, the
anti-Stone men won by a margin of 31 to 27, and for the
time being, the appointment was prevented; but, as we shall
see, Mr. Stone's friends succeeded a few days later in securing his appointment.

Before adjourning for the week, Mr. Johnson directed
the attention of the House to the necessity of curbing the
activities of non-associators. He moved the passage of a
resolution authorizing the appointment of a committee to
prepare and report resolutions "to prevent non-associators
from endangering the peace of this state." The Convention adopted his plan and selected five men to study the
situation. Mr. Johnson was placed at the head of the
committee.

On Tuesday, September 10th, after various matters of routine business were transacted, the committee chosen to draft the Constitution and Declaration of Rights made its report to the House. The proposed form of Government for the State was read, and in order that it could be thoroughly digested, was ordered to lie on the table. On the following morning, this question was raised: Should the draft be considered immediately or should it be deferred? Most of the leaders, among them Mr. Johnson, were in favor of deferring action "till Monday fortnight"—i. e., until September 30th. Thirteen members voted for immediate action, but the majority felt that adjournment for a few weeks would present an opportunity to ascertain the sentiment of the people.

On September 11, it was moved "That the deputies appointed to congress, and now attending this convention, or any three of them, immediately repair to congress, and in conjunction with Thomas Stone, esq., represent this state in such manner as is prescribed by the nomination and appointment heretofore made." Mr. Fitzhugh and a handful of others voted against the previous question; but the overwhelming majority—including Johnson, Carroll of Carrollton, Paca and Samuel Chase, who being members of Congress were directly affected by the motion—cast their votes for the motion and it was accordingly resolved in the affirmative. It is necessary at this juncture to explain that Mr. Chase, who had resigned from the Convention, was reëlected by his constituents; Brice T. B. Worthington was also sent back to the Convention; but the seat of Carroll, barrister, was filled by John Hall.

Johnson, Chase and Paca bade adieu to the members of the Convention on September 12th and, soon after, were on their way to Philadelphia. Mr. Carroll of Carrollton, it appears, remained in Annapolis until the adjournment of the Convention on September 17th.

*   *   *   *   *

At the Head of Elk, Johnson stopped for a brief visit at the home of Lt.-Col. Henry Hollingsworth. This is inferred from a letter, written September 28, in which the Lieutenant-Colonel, after assuring the Council of Safety that he had begun forging barrels "in earnest" (at the rate of one per day), promised that he would send to Annapolis several samples of muskets for inspection—"if locks could be had which Mr. Thomas Johnson informed me he thought might at Frederick." [5]

On arriving in Philadelphia, Mr. Johnson commenced a search for military supplies. His efforts were soon rewarded. Through the coöperation of Congressmen Willing and Morris, he succeeded in securing seventy-four casks of gunpowder. He ordered this supply to be shipped at once to Lt.-Col. Hollingsworth, with the request that he, in turn, forward it to its destination. The bill of lading for the shipment of powder to Philadelphia stipulated one-half the customary freight charge; but the owner of the vessel alleged an agreement with the shippers that the regular freight would be paid. Mr. Johnson demurred. In sending the bill of lading to Annapolis, he exhibits an insight into his character. At no time was he too busy to attend to the minutest details; he was exact and careful in all his dealings; he always bore in mind that he was a servant of the people and that he had to give strict accountability for his actions. Asking the Council of Safety if they had heard anything of the full rate, contrary to the

<hr/>

[5] XII *Maryland Archives,* 308.

terms of the bill of lading, Mr. Johnson took occasion to emphasize that the communication received from the shippers by Delegates Willing and Morris mentioned "nothing of the kind." [6]   The reply from Annapolis gave Johnson little satisfaction.   It requested him to pay whatever he thought was right.

During these stirring days, a nasty dispute arose between Captain Thomas Watkins and his men.   The captain was extremely unpopular with his company and his soldiers were leaving him.   Appearing before the Maryland members of Congress, he declared the discontent of his men was due to the lack of clothing and blankets.   Johnson, Paca, Chase and Stone listened patiently to the tale of woe; and finally ordered Captain Watkins to repair to Annapolis to lay his troubles before the Council of Safety.   On the 20th of September, the four Representatives sent a joint communication to the Council, giving their version of the dispute.   They explained that the Captain had only thirty-seven effective privates left in Philadelphia, and added, rather facetiously, that "indeed several of that number appear to us not really effective."

After telling of the scarcity of clothing in Philadelphia, the four Congressmen continued: "Lieut. Long goes to Worcester to endeavour to get the Deserters to return to their Duty under an Assurance which we have presumed to give that on their immediate return the past shall be forgiven.   Capt. Watkins and his men we are sorry to inform you are on very ill terms, the Capt has beat some of them, he says he had great cause.   They say he had none.   Some of the men have said nothing shall induce them to continue in the company under Capt Watkins.   We shall endeavour

[6] XII *Maryland Archives,* 291.

to keep the Remnant of the Company together under the care of the third Lieu^t until your Orders can interpose, for though an Inquiry seems to us to be necessary it cannot be had here; if the Independ^t companies should be regimented or even if the soldiers cloaths can be got, perhaps order may be restored in the company." The Congressmen, however, warned that Mr. Paca had heard Captain Watkins "is addicted to Drink and his appearance at several times we have seen him bespeaks it." [7]

Replying to the Representatives, the Council of Safety declared that Captain Watkins, before his departure from Maryland, had received £1,000 currency for pay and subsistence and that he had been furnished everything possible. "And to say the truth," said the Council, "we firmly believe that he renders himself incapable of taking proper care of his Company by drinking to excess. . . . His removal perhaps would be the best method of promoting the publick service."

Watkins was given abundant opportunity to make good. During October, he secured an order for 200 pounds to purchase arms and blankets and also 250 pounds for recruiting service. But his troubles evidently continued, for early in December he resigned his commission; and the members of the Council of Safety were only too glad to accept his resignation.

Having only two weeks, at this time, to remain in Philadelphia, Mr. Johnson and his companions from Maryland had little opportunity to participate in problems of National consequence. Nevertheless, on September 24th, Johnson was assigned to a committee of five "to devise ways and means for effectually providing the North-

[7] XII *Maryland Archives*, 291, 292.

ern Army with provisions and medicines, and supplying their other necessary wants."

*   *   *   *   *

The Maryland Constitutional Convention was scheduled to meet again on Monday, September 30th; and Messrs. Chase and Paca hurriedly slipped away from Philadelphia on Sunday, September 29th. The Convention adjourned from day to day until Wednesday, October 2, 1776, when both Mr. Chase and Mr. Paca appeared in the House.

Mr. Johnson did not appear in his seat until Monday, October 7. But, as soon as he did arrive, the Convention passed a special resolution adding him to the committee chosen the previous Friday to consider a communication from John Hancock, President of Congress. This communication explained that as the Continental Army, at Washington's request, was about to be reorganized, Maryland was requested to provide eight battalions in lieu of the Militia. The Convention, acting upon the advice of the committee, resolved that although the eight battalions required by Congress exceeded Maryland's just quota—being based on a calculation of white and black inhabitants, whereas the quotas of men to be raised by the several States ought to be in proportion to the number of white inhabitants —yet the State of Maryland, eager to support the liberties and independence of the United States, would use its utmost endeavors to raise the troops as soon as possible.

At this time, on the eve of the adoption of the Maryland Constitution, Mr. Johnson showed conclusively on a number of occasions how conscientious he was as a public servant. One of these occasions arose when a motion was made to pay each Deputy in Congress the sum of 10 pounds per week during actual attendance. Some one offered an amendment to insert *twelve pounds ten shillings* in place of *ten pounds.* Mr. Paca, Mr. Chase and Mr. Carroll of Carrollton found no scruples in voting for the amendment, Johnson, however, refrained from voting. By a margin of 33 to 28, the amendment was adopted and the salaries of the Congressmen were raised.

An effort was likewise made, as at the previous session, to set the allowance of members of the Convention at 10 shillings, besides the usual "itinerant charges," instead of 14 shillings per day. Mr. Johnson again opposed this change. A number of the members, including Mr. Worthington and Mr. Hooe, favored the motion; but it was defeated by a decisive majority.

Later on, Mr. Johnson, noticing that many of the members were somewhat irregular in their attendance, offered a motion, "That every member who asks for leave of absence shall give his reasons for asking such leave, and that they be entered on the journal." The House so resolved. From that time on, there were many cases of "bad state of health," and "sickness of family" as well as "particular private business" and "private affairs requiring attendance at home."

Conscientious public service, diligent attention to all appeals for succor, unflagging industry and self-sacrifice for the general good, made Thomas Johnson by this time not only the leading member of the Maryland Convention but perhaps the most popular man in the State. Although at this time a representative from the Eastern Shore, Mr. Johnson received, as no other Deputy, appeals for help from persons in all sections of Maryland. When, for example, a dispute arose between Marylanders and Vir-

ginians as to the right of operating a ferry between Georgetown and the Virginia shore of the Potomac, and a Maryland ferryman was arrested by a sheriff in the Old Dominion, in October, 1776, and "dragged to Fairfax Gaol in
Alexandria," the entire grievance was explained by Robert
Peter and Thomas Richardson in a letter to the Caroline
County Representative.[8]   The matter was duly presented
to the Convention by Mr. Johnson and later a careful investigation was made of the trouble.

Finally, all the matters extraneous to the absorbing
subject of the form of Government were laid aside, wherever possible; and on the 31st day of October, 1776, the
Constitutional Convention entered upon a consideration of
the report on the Declaration of Rights.

The first memorable fight made by Thomas Johnson on
the floor of the Convention was enacted on Saturday afternoon, November 2nd, in behalf of a number of religious
sects, to relieve them of the necessity of making an *oath*
through the medium of the *affirmation*.   He proposed to
do this by moving that the following Article be inserted in
the Declaration of Rights: [9]

*"That the manner of administering an oath to any person ought
to be such, as those of the religious persuasion, profession or denomination, of which such person is one, generally esteem the most effectual
confirmation by the attestation of the Divine Being.   And that the
people called Quakers, those called Dunkers, and those called
Menonists, holding it unlawful to take an oath on any occasion,
ought to be allowed to make their solemn affirmation in the manner
that Quakers have been heretofore allowed to affirm; and to be of the
same avail as an oath in all such cases as the affirmation of Quakers
hath been allowed and accepted within this State, instead of an oath,*

[8] XII *Maryland Archives*, 355.
[9] *Proceedings of Conventions*, 308.

And further, on such affirmation, warrants to search for stolen goods, or the apprehension or commitment of offenders, ought to be granted, or security for the peace awarded; and Quakers, Dunkers or Menonists ought also, on their solemn affirmation as aforesaid, to be admitted as witnesses in all criminal cases not capital."

After Mr. Johnson had moved the adoption of the aforegoing Article, Samuel Chase offered an amendment to strike out the concluding phrase: "and Quakers, Dunkers or Menonists ought also, on their solemn affirmation as aforesaid, to be admitted as witnesses in all criminal cases not capital." But the Chase amendment was turned down by a vote of 37 to 17.

Johnson's amendment was then ready for final action. When the question arose on the entire Article as submitted, it was adopted without a roll call. Concerning Thomas Johnson's effort in this connection, Gen. Bradley T. Johnson says:

"True to the traditions of his State and his family, he proposed and secured to be inserted in the Bill of Rights the article securing religious liberty to Quakers, Dunkers and 'the people called Menonists' by giving them the right to testify in courts of justice without taking oaths, but on their simple affirmation. This perpetual monument of Johnson's glory appeared as Article 36 of the original Declaration of Rights as agreed to on Sunday, November 3, 1776, and it has been retained in every Bill of Rights of Maryland from that day to this. It is the historical, logical sequence of Cecil Calvert's act to secure religious toleration in matters of opinion."

Article XXXIX of the present Declaration of Rights, using the words of Johnson, provides: "That the manner of administering the oath or affirmation to any person ought to be such as those of the religious persuasion, profession, or denomination, of which he is a member, generally esteem the most effectual confirmation by the attestation of the Divine Being."

The adoption of the Declaration of Rights was followed by a consideration of the Constitution, and in the week that followed, a number of amendments were offered to the proposed document. On Monday morning, November 4th, when the reading of the Form of Government, Article by Article, began, the first roll call occurred over the question of reducing the amount of property necessary as one of the qualifications of a voter from *thirty* to *five* pounds valuation in current money. Thomas Johnson voted against this reduction, as did Chase, Paca and Carroll of Carrollton. The motion was defeated.

The original draft of the Constitution proposed that all freemen qualified to vote for members of the House of Delegates should assemble in the Court House of each county on the first Monday of October, 1777, and on the same day in every year thereafter, and then and there elect, *viva voce*, four Delegates. Mr. Chase preferred to have the elections every third year. His suggestion, however, fell on deaf ears. Failing in this, Chase moved that the elections be held every other year: in this motion he was supported by Johnson, Chase, Paca and Carroll of Carrollton. But the original scheme of annual elections appealed to the majority of the members; and, by a majority of eight votes, Chase's second motion was defeated.

The State Senate was to be composed of fifteen members—nine from Western Maryland and six from the Eastern Shore. The Senators were not to be elected by direct vote of the people but by an Electoral College. This method was recommended by Charles Carroll of Carrollton. Writing to a friend in 1817, Mr. Carroll said: "I was one of the Committee that framed the Constitution of this State, and the mode of chusing the Senate was suggested by me; no objection was made to it in the Committee, as I remember, except by Mr. Johnson, who disliked the Senate's filling up the vacancies in their own body. I replied that if the mode of chusing Senators by Electors were deemed eligible, the filling up vacancies by that body was inevitable, as the Electors could not be convened to make choice of a Senator on every vacancy, and that the Senate acting under the sanction of an oath and *l'esprit de corps*, would insure the election of the fittest men for that station." On the floor of the House, no amendments were offered to the plan for constituting the Senate.

Likewise, there appeared no criticism of the plan of electing annually, by joint ballot of the two Houses of the Legislature, "a person of wisdom, experience, and virtue" for Governor of the State. The Governor was to be assisted by a Council of five members, likewise chosen by the two Houses of the Legislature.

Only one modification was proposed regarding the qualifications for Governor. The draft provided: "That no person unless above twenty-five years of age, a resident of this state above five years next preceding the election, and having in the state real and personal property above the value of five thousand pounds current money, one thousand pounds whereof at least to be of freehold estate, shall be eligible as governor." One of the deputies proposed, as an additional prerequisite, that the Governor should be "a native of the United States of America." Mr. Johnson opposed this amendment, as did Chase, Paca and Carroll; and it was rejected by a vote of 29 to 25.

Chase, Paca, Carroll and Johnson generally lined up

together on questions of policy; but Mr. Chase withdrew from the other three leaders when he proposed "That no delegate, senator, or member of the council, after he is qualified as such, shall hold any office of profit during the time for which he is elected." An overwhelming majority agreed with Mr. Chase, only thirteen deputies—among them Paca, Carroll and Johnson—opposing the restriction.

But the four distinguished leaders returned to the same fold, when Mr. Chase presented a motion "That a Justice of the Peace may be eligible as a Senator, Delegate, or Member of the Council, and may continue to act as a Justice of the Peace." This amendment was adopted by a large majority, and was incorporated in the Constitution.

Later, however, when Mr. Chase moved "That no field officer of the militia shall be eligible as a Senator, Delegate, or member of the Council," Johnson, Paca and Carroll again withdrew their support. Nevertheless, Mr. Chase's amendment was adopted by a vote of 26 to 25.

While these four distinguished members of Congress had great power in the Maryland Convention, their opinions did not, by any means, always prevail. Mr. Chase, for example, proposed that the Governor, with the advice of the Council, should have the power to appoint the sheriffs; and his idea was endorsed by Carroll and Johnson. Yet, only nine votes, all told, were recorded in favor of the amendment.

On the sixth of November, Mr. Fitzhugh moved "That lawyers' fees ought to be ascertained and limited by law." A very large majority, including the four members of Congress, opposed even the previous question, and the attack against the legal profession was immediately repulsed.

That afternoon, the Convention arrived at the Article,

which prescribed the oath necessary to be administered to every man before entering a public office in the State. Among other things, such person was required to swear that he would use his utmost endeavors to disclose all treasons, traitorous conspiracies or attempts which he knew to be against this State and the Government thereof. Mr. Johnson moved that, instead of the long and cumbersome oath prescribed in the original draft, the following be inserted: [10]

"I, A. B., do swear that I do not hold myself bound in allegiance to the King of Great Britain, and that I will be faithful and bear true allegiance to the State of Maryland."

Chase and Paca voted against the amendment, but Carroll of Carrollton supported it. By a vote of 29 to 26, Johnson's oath was ordered to be made a part of the Constitution.

While the renunciation of allegiance to the Crown has disappeared, the second clause of the oath proposed by Thomas Johnson in 1776, is still to be found in Article I, Section VI, of our present Constitution. To this day, every person elected or appointed to any office of profit or trust under the Constitution of Maryland or the laws made in pursuance thereof, before entering upon the duties of such office, must swear or affirm, in the simple language of Johnson, *"that I will be faithful and bear true allegiance to the State of Maryland."*

On the morning of Thursday, November 7th, Mr. Johnson was unusually active on the floor of the House. His first effort of the day was to repeal the Act passed in 1773 "for the more effectual preservation of the breed of

[10] *Proceedings of Conventions,* 341.

wild deer." The war, no doubt, had made meat increasingly scarce. At any rate, the House agreed with him and it was resolved that no further prosecutions should be made for any breach of the Act.

Following this, Mr. Johnson presented a resolution to remove all doubt concerning the jurisdiction of Justices of the Frederick County Court and Justices of the Peace, resulting from the division of Frederick County. This resolution was adopted, without a roll call.

Mr. Johnson also sponsored a motion to defer the poll to determine the site for a Court House and prison in Montgomery County until at least twenty days after the first meeting of the General Assembly. In this motion he met with strong opposition; but Chase, Paca and Carroll favored the postponement, and Johnson's motion was adopted.

The final constitutional question before the Convention was: Should every person who refused to subscribe to the Association be disqualified from holding any office of profit or trust in this State, unless by Act of the General Assembly? There were many, like Messrs. Chase and Paca, who believed that the non-associators should never be eligible to hold office in Maryland; but Johnson and Carroll of Carrollton took the opposing view, and, by a small majority, the proposed amendment was rejected.

Finally, on Friday, November 8th, 1776, the Delegates, "in free and full Convention assembled," agreed *in toto* to the Constitution and Form of Government.

Mr. Johnson was granted leave of absence on Saturday morning; and on Sunday morning, he was elected, along with Matthew Tilghman, William Paca, Thomas Stone, Samuel Chase, Charles Carroll, barrister, and Benjamin

Rumsey, to represent the State in Congress until the first of March, 1777.

That Sunday afternoon, the members of the Council of Safety were elected; and on the following day (November 11) the Constitutional Convention adjourned *sine die.*

The instrument promulgated as the organic law of Maryland reflected lasting honor upon the statesmen who drafted it. Dugald Stuart, the well-known Scotch philosopher, praised the document in glowing terms; and Alexander Hamilton, the noted American statesman, termed it the wisest of all the Constitutions adopted by the States following their separation from the Crown. Although never submitted to the people for ratification, the Constitution of 1776 proved to be eminently satisfactory; and remained, as amended from time to time, the fundamental law of Maryland from that day until 1851.

The times have changed. The members of the State Senate are no longer chosen by an Electoral College. The Governor is no longer appointed by the Legislature. Yet, a portion of the simple oath, recommended by Thomas Johnson during the American Revolution as a prerequisite for public office in Maryland, still remains in the Constitution of the State. And the words of Johnson, recognizing *affirmation* as the equivalent of an *oath*, continue in the Declaration of Rights to guide successive generations along the pathway of religious toleration.

CHAPTER XVII

OFF TO THE AID OF WASHINGTON

"This was the gloomiest period of the war. The campaign had been little else than a series of disasters and retreats. The enemy had gained possession of Rhode Island, Long Island, the city of New York, Staten Island, and nearly the whole of the Jerseys, and seemed on the point of extending their conquests into Pennsylvania. . . . In short, so great was the panic and so dark the prospect, that a general despondency pervaded the Continent."
—Sparks, *Life of George Washington*, 277.

"English writers are fond of insisting upon the alleged fact that America only won her freedom by the help of foreign nations. Such help was certainly most important, but, on the other hand, it must be remembered that during the first and vital years of the contest the Revolutionary colonists had to struggle unaided against the British, their mercenary German and Indian allies, Tories, and even French Canadians."
—Theodore Roosevelt, *Life of Gouverneur Morris*, 42.

"It appears to me that a strong reinforcement is now not only desirable, but necessary to keep our officers in their late course. I am anxious to contribute all I can to it, and from all that I can collect am persuaded if the militia would now generally and vigorously exert themselves we should have a fair chance of ruining the British army in the Jerseys."
—Thomas Johnson, *Letter from Philadelphia to the Maryland Council of Safety, January* 20, 1777.

WHILE engaged in framing the organic law for the State, the members of the Maryland Constitutional Convention frequently received alarming reports from the Continental Army. It was not long after he took his seat as a Delegate for Caroline County, August 30, 1776, that Thomas Johnson heard the news from Long Island—a severe blow to the American cause. Already the troops, beginning to show signs of discouragement, were anxious to return home as soon as their short terms of enlistment expired. Diseases were prevalent. There were many desertions. Indeed, only the consummate skill and constant exertion of George Washington saved the remnant of his forces from disintegration. After the disaster on Long Island, General Howe made a peace proposal to the American Congress; but the day of reconciliation had passed and Benjamin Franklin, in reply, explained some of the things the British could expect from the people of the new Continent. It was about this time— late September and early in October, 1776, during the recess of the Maryland Convention—that Thomas Johnson spent a few busy weeks in Congress. In Philadelphia, Mr. Johnson heard how the red coats, after landing on Manhattan had swarmed into the City of New York. The British were jubilant. But the Americans, tattered and torn, reduced by heavy losses, were despondent over the gloomy prospect of a winter campaign.

Cold weather was about to set in. Delegate Johnson, his patriotic ardor stimulated by the stirring scenes in Pennsylvania, emphasized in Annapolis the great need of reënforcing the Army. Rather than to serve in the Congress, Mr. Johnson felt it a supreme duty to return to the frontier, where supplies not only, but also the inspiring enthusiasm of a patriot leader, were greatly needed. Accordingly, on the 9th of November—the day following the adoption of the Maryland Constitution—Johnson obtained leave of absence from the Convention and threw himself into a winter of unremitting toil and hardship as the comrade of the Maryland recruits.

Still there came news of reverses in the North. Mr. Johnson received the distressing news with anxiety—but never lost hope. He heard how the Commander-in-Chief, apprehending a British drive toward the South, crossed the Hudson and established Fort Lee. Then came the fall of Fort Washington, resulting in a loss of several thousand men—another great disaster. This was followed by the evacuation of Fort Lee, leaving army supplies and artillery in the hands of the advancing hosts. "The reduction of Fort Washington and easy possession obtained of Fort Lee," wrote Samuel Chase from Philadelphia, "has greatly encouraged General Howe, and probably induced him to carry on the Campaign much longer then he would otherwise have done. There is great reason to believe his views extend to this city." [1]

Of the members of the Maryland delegation, Mr. Chase was one of the most faithful in attendance upon the sessions of Congress. So numerous were their duties at this critical time that the patriot leaders of Maryland had to be importuned to remain in Philadelphia. Mr. Paca and Mr. Rumsey were present occasionally. Mr. Stone was absent for a while on account of his wife's sickness. Matthew Tilghman was on duty in Congress early in December, for on December 3, he wrote a letter to the Council of Safety from Philadelphia; and in it he ventured the following information concerning the military situation: "By the best information our General could get, the enemy are between 6 and 7 thousand, his army now not more than 3 thousand. If any considerable reinforcements can be sent from thence, he intends to make a stand at Trenton in case the Enemy come forward. . . . Such is the present situation of our affairs. It is bad eno' but may be worse, a few days will determine and afford us either

[1] XII *Maryland Archives,* 482.

a small respite or greatly add to the distress and confusion of this place." [2]

Notwithstanding appalling disasters, the Maryland leaders were stanch. The Council of Safety wrote to the Maryland Delegates on December 6: "We received the letter wrote us by M[r] Matthew Tilghman, and are obliged to him for the intelligence; the prospect is not very agreeable but we hope Cornwallis will be repulsed. Sure 6 or 7000 men will never be able to penetrate through the Jerseys to Phil[a]. We cannot as yet believe it."

The Annapolis people who felt confident that the British Army would never be able to cross the Delaware probably did not realize the full extent of General Washington's predicament. Completely worn out and disheartened were the fighters who made the melancholy retreat from Newark to Elizabethtown—thence to New Brunswick—to Princeton—and finally to Trenton. Many of the boys, barefoot and bleeding, left stains of blood on the frozen ground. The British, meanwhile, pressed on with increased vigor. So spirited was their pursuit that the music of their bands frequently was heard by the rear lines of the retreating Americans. Philadelphia was thrown into a panic of excitement and terror. But on the 11th of December, Samuel Chase calmly announced in a letter to Baltimore: "The Congress will not quit this city but in the last extremity."

On the 12th, the Maryland Council of Safety wrote a message to Johnson—then at Frederick Town—urging him to proceed to Philadelphia to take his seat in Congress. The message follows: [3]

[2] XII *Maryland Archives,* 503.
[3] XII *Maryland Archives,* 524.

"*Sir.* By Letters lately received from our Delegates in Congress we are strongly desired to press your joining them as soon as you can with any degree of convenience. They say that Congress is very thin, and entreat your immediate attendance in which we join, and, wishing you a pleasant journey, are, &c.

Decr 12th 1776.
Thomas Johnson Esqr."

Johnson felt that it was now high time for him to comply with the expressed desire of the Convention and the Council of Safety that he return to Congress. He accordingly made plans to leave Frederick on the 17th of December. But the Congress itself, through a resolution adopted on the 9th of December, was the cause of a change in his plans. This resolution read as follows:

"*Resolved,* That expresses be immediately sent to the committees of the counties of Cecil, Baltimore, Harford, and Frederick, in Maryland, requesting that they apply, without delay, to the militia of their respective counties, and send forward, as fast as possible, for the defence of this city, and the reinforcement of General Washington's army, as many troops as possible, informing the said committees that some assistance, in the way of arms, may be furnished here, to provide such as have no arms to bring with them."

Colonel Thomas Ewing was chosen by President Hancock to hurry with all possible speed to Annapolis and notify the Maryland authorities of the action of Congress. The messenger, in a few days, arrived in Annapolis; and appearing before the Council of Safety, December 14, explained his mission. A courier, he said, was following him with an official copy of the resolution. No time was to be lost. The fate of America was hanging in the balance!

The Council of Safety immediately sent off the following message to Johnson—and a similar one to Brig.-Gen. Chamberlaine, Brig.-Gen. Buchanan and Colonel Charles Rumsey—explaining the critical situation:[4]

To Brigadier Gen¹ Johnson

Sir. We have certain information that Lord Howe has joined Lord Cornwallis, and that the main army of the Enemy is near the City of Philadelphia with intention to attack that important place. They are still on the East Side of Delaware. Assistance will be most wanted, and we request you will give the necessary orders to your Brigade to hold themselves in Readiness to march to Philadelphia. Col. Ewing tells us that a requisition has passed Congress for the militia of Baltimore, Harford, Frederick and Cecil, Counties to march and that he was desired by the President of that honorable Body to give us notice thereof, we wish not to loose a moment's Time. As soon as we hear further Intelligence, we will write you by express.

14ᵗʰ Decʳ 1776

On Monday, December 16, a messenger came riding into Frederick Town bearing the flaming message from the Council of Safety. Johnson forthwith answered it as follows:[5]

JOHNSON TO THE COUNCIL OF SAFETY

Fred. Town.
Gent.   16ᵗʰ Decʳ 1776.

Your letter of the 14ᵗʰ by Express came to me this moment 12 o'clock, and I shall not lose a minute in sending to the Col[onels] as you direct. I am afraid we shall be able to arm only a small pro-

---

[4] XII *Maryland Archives,* 529.
[5] XII *Maryland Archives,* 533.

portion of the men these parts having been much drained of arms, and those of the Flying Camp who have returned, having left their guns behind them. I am told no Field officers are yet appointed to the Battalion of which Wells was recommended to be Col⁰. If there's no capital objection I wish the commissions were sent.

I would not intrude advice but if no steps are already taken for the purpose, I wish to submit to your consideration whether it would not be well to remove our magazine further into the country, it appears to me that if our Enemies succeed against Philᵃ, our stock of powder may be an object.

I intended to have set out in the morning for Balt., but shall now wait till I hear from you, or am well informed of a considerable change in our affairs.

I am Gent.
Your most obed^t Servant
Th. Johnson, Junʀ.

The aforegoing opinion that if the British captured Philadelphia the stock of powder in Maryland would be an objective and the suggestion that it might "be well to remove our magazine further into the country"—this position shows conclusively that Johnson stood firmly by the side of the Father of his Country. While many patriotic and stanch Americans were losing courage in the midst of scenes of trial and discouragement, the Maryland statesman and the great Virginian never lost the faith. Washington, like Johnson, realized that in the event of further disaster the patriots would find shelter in the wilderness of the frontier, rather than surrender. Dr. Sparks says in this connection: "Whatever his [General Washington's] apprehensions may have been, no misgivings were manifest in his conduct or his counsels. From his letters, written at this time on the western bank of the Delaware, it does not appear that he yielded for a moment to a sense of immediate danger, or to a doubt of ultimate success. On the contrary, they breathe the same determined spirit, and are marked by the same confidence, calmness, and forethought, which distinguish them on all other occasions. When asked what he would do, if Philadelphia should be taken, he is reported to have said: 'We will retreat beyond the Susquehanna River; and thence, if necessary, to the Alleghany Mountains.' " [6]

On December 19, an express reached the Frederick County Committee, requesting the militia to march immediately in pursuance of the resolution of Congress, "for the defence of the City of Philadelphia, and the reinforcement of General Washington's army." As soon as the express reached Frederick Town, the Committee gathered together and decided unanimously to "send forward . . . as many troops as possible." That evening, in a letter to the Council, Mr. Johnson expressed the belief that "a very great proportion" of the militia would soon be on their way to Philadelphia. "Though," he interjected, "as you must imagine many of them are very illy provided for a winters campaign." He then entered a strong plea for needed supplies. "If you have," he said, "any stock of shoes, stockings or blankets that you can spare to be forwarded to York immediately and there sold to the men at moderate prices or sent after them it would be a great Relief." [7] The lack of clothing for the soldiers was one of the most serious problems that confronted Johnson.

Another question that concerned Johnson was the choice of a leader for the Flying Camp. In this connection it is appropriate to explain that John Dent had suc-

[6] Sparks, *Life of George Washington*, 278.
[7] XII *Maryland Archives*, 540.

ceeded Johnson as senior Brigadier-General, but when Lord Dunmore made his appearance during the Summer of 1776, the Maryland Council of Safety requested General Dent to proceed to the mouth of the Potomac and endeavor to prevent any invasion, with the understanding that he could, for a while, assume command in Southern Maryland without interfering with his duties as Brigadier-General of the Militia, inasmuch as the Flying Camp was not yet quite ready to march. A few days later, however, Major Thomas Price, who had been on the Eastern Shore, was ordered to take command in the Southern Counties in order to relieve General Dent. This angered the General, and on August 1 he returned his commission as Brigadier declaring that under the controlling power of the Council of Safety he was "resolved never more to act." Dent was obdurate. It was evident that the State needed another man to assume command of the Militia, and on August 16 Rezin Beall was chosen Brigadier-General. But again it was evident that the question of leadership was not finally settled. The trouble with Gen. Beall was the fact that he was hated by the soldiers. Indeed, the sentiment of the people, rapidly crystallizing throughout Western Maryland, both in and out of the military service, pointed conclusively to Thomas Johnson as the most satisfactory commander of the Maryland troops. Regardless of the action of the Convention, depriving him, as it did, of his commission, the soldiers, almost to a man, desired Johnson to lead them to the Headquarters of General Washington.

Johnson was at all times ready and willing to undertake what the majority of the people wanted him to do. He realized that it was a duty to guide his actions according to the Convention and the Council of Safety.

Nevertheless, he was also aware that he was not skilled, like Washington, in the science of warfare—indeed, had never had any military experience. He was in a quandary. After revolving the subject in his mind for some time, Johnson sent the following observations to the Council of Safety:

"I do not know whether it is intended that I should command the whole Militia or any part of them or not. If it is I think some special authority for that purpose will be necessary and I shall cheerfully execute it as well as I can, but in a matter of so much consequence I shall frankly give my opinion at every hazard that it is best not to let our militia go out under any provincial Brigadier. Genl Beall's commission I suppose has expired and if not, many of the Flying Camp speak of him so far from respectfully that you may be assured that many from here would but half obey him, and so far with all ill will. None of the rest of us have seen service and I fear we are not so competent nor will the men have the same confidence in either of us, as in one who has had experience. Genl Smallwood and several others I believe have but very small Brigades, but if any Gent. goes from here as Brigadier he must have a great stock of philosophy to give up his brigade to another tho' superior in abilities, and having nothing to do when he foresees the general however unjust imputations which will be thrown upon him. If these reasons appear to you in the same strength they do to me, I imagine our militia might be put under the immediate command of Smallwood by a request to Congress, or General Washington. I have seen a good many of the Flying Camp who speak well and some who speak ill of Smallwood."

On December 23, Johnson again pointed out the unpopularity of Rezin Beall. "I took the freedom," wrote Johnson, "to mention my sentiment that if Genl Beall's comm^n had not expired it would not do to give him the command of the militia: The prejudice is so strong against him that many of the officers say they will not go under him. As I hear this sentim^t is so general I think it my duty to mention it to you. I wish to be ascertained whether I am to go or not. I am heartily willing to exert myself, in the military line, if you think it may possibly promote the service." [8]

It was at this time that a supply of money was received from Congress for the equipment of the militia. But it seems that there never was a time when all the men were amply provided with supplies. Johnson knew that the soldiers—boys, most of them—would encounter hardship and suffering on the long, dreary march and in the campaign against the trained troops of George III. Time and again, in communications to the Council of Safety, Johnson emphasized the distressing lack of clothing. Said he, in one of his appeals: "If you can possibly supply shoes, stockings, Tents, or Blankets especially the last it may save a good many poor fellows; if you can spare any do hurry them to this place or Taney Town and advise us of it."

There was a third problem of immense proportions that Johnson faced on the eve of departure. It was the dispute over officers' commissions. This was one of the causes of delay in the expedition. Some time back, the Frederick County Committee had organized a battalion with Upton Sheredine Colonel, and David Steiner Lieutenant-Colonel. In explaining how the controversy arose, Mr. Johnson wrote as follows to the Council of Safety from Frederick Town: "It is said here the recommendation was sent to the Council of Safety and is lost. Afterwards, as it is said under the countenance of some of

[8] XII *Maryland Archives,* 543.

the Committee and after a very general agreement on time and place, and two or three weeks intervening, most of the officers and some of the men though from what I understand not a majority of the privates, met and voted for Field Officers to be recommended." At this meeting a new set of officers was chosen, headed by Colonel James Wells and Lieutenant-Colonel David Moore. Recommendations were forwarded to Annapolis "according to the vote." Then followed a dissension which threatened to split the little army into pieces.

Johnson endeavored to stand impartial between the two factions in order to prevent a breach. Said he: "I see neither set of Field Officers will entirely please the Battalion and yet if Field Officers are not appointed to that Batt. I fear little may be expected from it. I wish therefore commissions were immediately sent up." Only one objection was raised by him. This was against David Steiner as Lieutenant-Colonel. "Dav. Steiner," said Johnson, "is an infirm man and tho' enrolled never musters, so that there can be no use in appointing him a field off^r."

Against the officers chosen for the *Upper* Battalion, no objection appears to have arisen. However, while the recommendations for these officers had been sent to the Council of Safety, the commissions had not arrived in Frederick. "If the recommendation is before you and not very exceptionable," wrote Johnson in this connection, "I would wish the commissions were sent up; what few people may on any occasion be got from that quarter will tell for at least so many."

On Christmas eve, Mr. Johnson wrote: "I had no suspicion that the Militia Commissions in this and Washington County were in such disorder. . . . I went to the minits of the Committee and on a long search could only find five companies had been returned." [9] In order to expedite the work, Johnson asked the Council to give either the Committee or himself the permission to "get up commissions for all the Gent." who were entitled to them or at least to "fill up the Christian names" of those they were unable to supply.

Even at this late hour, the recruits at Frederick were in dire need of supplies. "I imagined from what passed in the Committee last night," Johnson continued in his letter, "they would have sent off an Express this morning to have known for a Certainty whether the Militia could have had any supply of blankets &c from the Council of Safety, but this morning on my several Times mentioning it the Gent. seemed disinclined to it, presuming you would not furnish them. They were never wanted more than by those, who now offer to turn out and I cannot forbear repeating my former request that if you possibly can, you will forward shoes, stockings and blankets especially the latter to Taney Town or this place."

Referring to the expedition, Johnson said: "The Committee as I wrote you resolved the militia ought to march and the Humor seems to be that all ought to march; it will if any thing general leave the Country rather too naked. I should have liked better that about one half was to march, but I do not know that it was possible to contrive it so."

As Johnson penned these words, there were many less courageous souls who admitted America's defeat. The British believed the war had practically come to an end.

[9] XII *Maryland Archives*, 550.

Lord Cornwallis was ready to leave for England. The Hessians were preparing to spend the holiday in drinking and carousals. But General Washington planned to cross the Delaware and strike the enemy at Trenton.

The dawn of Christmas morn—instead of heralding *"Peace on earth, good will towards men!"*—witnessed the Commander-in-Chief inaugurating his attack with utmost caution. And likewise Johnson was preparing to speed his recruits to the aid of Washington. Both Colonel Beatty's battalion and the battalion under Baker Johnson assembled on Christmas morning. The former made preparations to begin their expedition on December 28th; the latter on December 30th. The boys under James Johnson were also nearly ready.

Thomas Johnson, aroused by the critical situation along the Delaware, yearned for the command of the Flying Camp. He did not covet military honors, but he felt personally responsible for the speedy arrival of the Maryland boys in the camp of General Washington. "I believe," Johnson asserted on Christmas day, in a postscript to the Council of Safety, "if you think proper the Militia of this County will be pretty generally pleased at going under me. Therefore unless the Militia from any of the other Counties will be much dissatisfied I think you had better give me orders." Within twenty-four hours after this Christmas message, in which Johnson asked permission to lead the Maryland troops, General Washington had taken Trenton by surprise. Confidence in the Commander-in-Chief was restored. The report of the brilliant victory of Washington gave his countrymen new courage and determination to continue the struggle for American freedom.

On December 28, the Council of Safety sent Johnson

a reply concerning the three subjects in which he was so profoundly interested—namely: officers' commissions, army supplies, and the command of the militia.[10]

FIRSTLY, the Council enclosed commissions for the battalions of Colonels James Johnson, Upton Sheredine and Normand Bruce. Thomas Johnson was authorized to insert Christian names and, where the names of captains, lieutenants and ensigns were not known, he was empowered to "assure any of the Gentleman who may march, that we will send them forward so soon as you will be pleased to favor us with a list of names."

SECONDLY, with regard to the scarcity of supplies, the Council explained: "We are exceedingly desirous of forwarding the Service all we can, and should cheerfully have sent forward Blankets and stockings, but we have them not, nor can we get enough of Blankets for the Hospitals; we will send up five hundred or a thousand pair of shoes by the first waggon we can get to be left at Frederick Town and delivered to you, or in your absence to your order; unless you should write us that they had better be sent to Christiana Bridge, or the Head of Elk where we are of opinion the Troops might more readily get them. We expect to hear from you on that head as soon as possible: in the mean time we will order them to be packed up ready."

THIRDLY, the proper man to lead the recruits—this was left largely to Johnson's discretion. "As to the command," they said, "we would by no means be instrumental in disappointing your wishes on the occasion, and desire you would take the command unless some other be appointed by Congress, which we think not improbable, as

[10] XII *Maryland Archives,* 556.

S. Chase has wrote them on the subject; he was here and
saw your former Letter, and has requested Congress to
send up money. To tell you the truth we wish Congress
may appoint some other, and that you should take your
seat in that honorable body, where you may be of great
service at present. However if they do not appoint a
commander we leave it to your own judgment and discretion to march or not as you may think best for the public Service."

Before this reply from Annapolis had reached Frederick,
Johnson had grown quite impatient. News of Washington's victory at Trenton on Christmas night had not yet
reached Western Maryland, and Johnson could scarcely
control his consuming anxiety for the American cause.
"We have a very deep snow," he wrote to the Council
December 28th, "Upwards of 300 of Colo. Beatty's Batt.
begin their march in the morning. I wish they were better
provided. I am very desirous of hearing from your
Board." [11]

In view of the discouraging conditions under which the
Maryland lads ventured forth in the dead of winter, and
in view of their primitive training and equipment compared with the seasoned Royal soldiers and Hessians,
Johnson realized it was a herculean task to hold his regiment together. According to the late President Roosevelt, a lack of stamina existed amongst the Militia in the
Continental Army. "The Revolutionary troops," Mr.
Roosevelt declares,[12] "certainly fell short of the standard
reached by the volunteers who fought Shiloh and Gettys-
burg. . . . Throughout the Revolution the militia were

[11] XII *Maryland Archives*, 557, 558.
[12] Theodore Roosevelt, *Life of Gouverneur Morris*, 43, 44.

invariably leaving their posts at critical times; they would grow either homesick or dejected; and would then go home at the very crisis of the campaign; they did not begin to show the stubbornness and resolution 'to see the war through' so common among their descendants in the contending Federal and Confederate armies." While this criticism is largely true, yet it must be remembered that the militiamen fought under great hardships and at great disadvantage. Then, too, the service suffered greatly from lack of discipline and on account of the absence of that strong, central authority which now exists in the Government of the United States. Indeed, it is evident that many of the commissioned officers were as trifling as the private soldiers. Even James Lloyd Chamberlaine, honored with the rank of Brigadier-General, showed his lack of enthusiasm for the patriot cause—especially when contrasted with Johnson—when he resigned his commission on account of discouraging conditions on the Eastern Shore. "A sincere desire to render my country every service in my power," said General Chamberlaine, "induced me to accept of the enclosed commission, but finding myself disappointed that many of us rather disposed to quarrell with his neighbour than face the Enemy, that a general discontent prevails and unwillingness in the people to do any duty or even attend musters, and a disregard to any sort of order, several Battalions without field officers and others absolutely refusing to obey the commands of those appointed over them, has determined me to resign that Commission with which I was honored by the Convention and wish he that succeeds me may give general Satisfaction."

Similar conditions prevailed West of the Chesapeake.

Everywhere there was confusion. Everywhere there was delay. Resignations were numerous. The Winter was unusually severe and the men, eager as they were to preserve their liberty, were none too eager to leave their firesides for an expedition of hardship and suffering. Upton Sheredine, Colonel of the *Linganore* Battalion, was among those who rejected their field commissions. Johnson, on the other hand, although urged by Convention and by Council to return to Congress, preferred to march. He knew of no one at the time who could handle the volunteers more successfully than he could himself.

The decision was made. Johnson determined to command the expedition to the Headquarters of General Washington. "*I have appointed the Battalion to meet next Tuesday,*" Johnson wrote to the Council on the night of January 4, 1777, "*and shall attend it in my way to Philadelphia!*" [13]

Even at this late hour the troubles over commissions continued. Johnson explained: "It is really difficult to put things on a footing at such times that will please generally." The only way he would be able to forward to the Council "a list of such as will do," he said, was by actually accompanying the marching soldiers.

In the *Linganore* Battalion, the troubles concerning rank had reached such a point that Mr. Johnson made a special trip to meet the soldiers in that body in an effort to adjust their difficulties. On the 10th of January, upon his return to Frederick Town, General Johnson wrote as follows to the Council: "But few of the men and not quite half the officers attended; my journey was fruitless, though most of those who attended declare their willingness to

[13] XVI *Maryland Archives*, 14.

march, yet none of them will give up their pretensions.
. . . Of the officers and men who met me some were desirous that Wells should be first Colonel; about the same
number that Moore should be first Colonel, and about a
like number that declined expressing any inclination either
way, so that I do not know whose appointment would most
promote the public service, yet I think it necessary commissions should issue, and be sent to the chief Colonel, as
well for the command as field officers as soon as possible,
perhaps by so doing we may get some of them to
stir." [14]

Now that he had finally determined to march, the question that seemed to bother Johnson was: How many battalions am I authorized to command? "Disputes about
command," he declared, "will be destructive of all authority and order. I wished to know whether I was to
command all the Maryland Militia or only those of this
Brigade. Your silence on that head compels me to repeat
my request that you will send me something decisive on
that point." The Council decided to grant him power to
command the entire Flying Camp from the State. Under
date of January 10, 1777, the Council issued the following order: "Your commission gives you the right to command, and we are desirous you should take the command of
the whole Militia from this State in case you determine
to go under the requisition of Congress. We cannot be
more explicit. Your going or not we leave to your own
discretion." [15]

General Johnson was also solicitous that the militiamen should be properly armed. Several times he had writ-

[14] XVI *Maryland Archives,* 35–37.
[15] XVI *Maryland Archives,* 33.

ten to the Council of Safety regarding the serious short-
age of muskets. Failing to receive a satisfactory answer
in this regard, the Brigadier ordered his men—as they were
about to depart—to "take what good arms they could with
them," declaring they could "expect the deficiency would
be supplied out of those arms" which belonged to the
Maryland militia but which had been stopped at Philadelphia by the Board of War. While the Maryland lads
were mustering, Johnson importuned the Council of Safety
to send him an order for the necessary rifles. Here the
Council demurred. Did the muskets belong to the State
or to the Congress? Indeed, inasmuch as many of them
had been lost or exchanged for worse arms, it was a question whether the State ought to claim them or whether
she ought to hold Congress responsible for the deficiency.
The Congress, in making requision for the Flying Camp,
had promised arms and accordingly the Council of Safety
requested Johnson to apply for them upon his arrival in
Philadelphia. "We heartily wish you success in the military line," the Council assured General Johnson, "since it
seems to be your choice and would gladly gratify you in
every thing, but we apprehend it may involve this State
in a dispute about the arms. Should we give you an absolute order, it would be an evidence against us that we consider them as our own, which we think at present would be
a disadvantage to the State. Few or none of the good
arms we fear will be got at any rate, and we should be
extremely obliged to you to enquire into the affair and let
us know your opinion when you get to Philadelphia, what
arms that did belong to this State can now be got."

While the Council of Safety was framing this communication (January 10), Thomas Johnson was preparing to

set out on the following day for Philadelphia. Realizing the hazards that awaited him, Johnson, on the eve of departure, penned his final warning from Frederick Town. It follows: [16]

"From several unforseen delays, I judged it unnecessary to proceed on Wednesday. I shall go tomorrow. I cannot but repeat my request that you'd send 1000 pair of shoes to Philadelphia. Many poor fellows will want shoes by the time they get there, and I wish you'd give me a conditional credit for blankets, if to be got, for a good many march without 'em. If you have it in your power too to send us a skilful physician it will be well worth while, we are badly off, and the people who go from the little care taken of their countrymen, are very apprehensive of fatal sickness, indeed I fear that their scanty cloathing will subject them to severe pleurisies."

Finally, on January 11, 1777, the Maryland Brigadier-General set out from Frederick Town upon his perilous expedition to the battle-line in New Jersey. The tramp through the trackless wilderness and across icy streams was, in itself, sufficient to test the stoutest hearts; it was all the more severe on account of the lack of warm clothing. But the boys from Maryland were resolute, and, under Johnson's inspiring leadership, were eager to reach Philadelphia and from thence hasten to the camp of General Washington.

On the eve of Johnson's departure from Frederick Town, the Council of Safety forwarded 500 pairs of shoes to Philadelphia "to be sold out to the soldiers" under General Johnson's directions. After the Brigadier was well on his journey, the Council of Safety again assured him (January 17) that the consignment of shoes had been made. "We have some days ago," wrote the Council,

[16] XVI *Maryland Archives,* 36.

"sent forward five hundred pair of shoes to Philadelphia to be delivered to your order. They are in the course of stages and we hope will soon be there, they have been delivered Jesse Hollingsworth and the boat is returned to Annapolis a day or two ago; these are all we can spare. The Regulars are calling on us fast for shoes." [17]

Considering the distance to Philadelphia approximately 150 miles, and each day's march 8 or 10 miles, it required between two and three weeks for the members of the Flying Camp to reach the city. But the companies had set out from their places of mobilization at different times; they tramped along only as rapidly as their inclinations, and not their commanding officers, dictated; and for several weeks they came straggling into the City of Brotherly Love in groups of fifty or a hundred.

General Johnson, although delayed in starting from Frederick, reached the Schuylkill ahead of about half of his men. In less than ten days after he had left Frederick, the Brigadier-General had been in Philadelphia long enough to locate 700 of his men within the environs of the city.

Anxiously the Maryland commander awaited the remainder of his militia. "All Col. J. Johnson's Battalion that may be expected," the Brigadier-General reported on the 20th of January, "about 250 are here, part of Col⁰ Beatty's about 160, part of Col⁰ B. Johnson's, about 120, part of Col⁰ Bruce's about 150, and Col. Stull's I do not know the number are also here. The other parts may be soon expected, and the whole of them will from what I learn average about 250. Some of the Montgomery Militia I hear are on the way, what may be expected from

[17] XVI *Maryland Archives*, 56.

Col⁰ Smith's Battalion, or from Battalion Harford and Cecil I do not know, but suppose not much. A good many of the Cumberland Militia I hear are here and on their way and that the Philadelphia Militia and part of the Cumberland Militia now at Camp are coming away." While reporting that many of his own brigade had not yet arrived in Philadelphia, Johnson nevertheless declared that he intended to send off the battalions of James Johnson and Col. Beatty on the following day—February 21st —and the other battalions soon thereafter.

It is generally understood that Thomas Johnson commanded a force of about 1,800 men. Certain it is that he took with him all the recruits that he was able to collect. And even after they had decided to accompany him, he had to be alert lest none of them would leave his command. Before he left Frederick, he asked the Council of Safety: "Would it not be well that a few recruiting officers were ordered to attend us? I suspect if they do not, I shall have broils about our Militia enlisting as the quota of our neighbours which I must oppose." Subsequently, in Philadelphia, Johnson discovered, as he had feared, that many were being enticed into other commands. "Some of the Pennsylvania Officers," he said, "have as I expected inlisted a few of our Militia. Genˡ Gates and Lord Stirling, both now here, have concurred with me in stopping it; where we have found the men we have taken them back. I mention this that some of our officers may be ordered forward without delay, to inlist such as are desirous of entering into the service."

The shoes shipped to General Johnson from Annapolis arrived in course of time in Philadelphia. "You mention to me," Johnson wrote in regard to this consignment, "that Mr Hollingsworth would send 500 pair, he tells me in his letter that he has sent 1000, but I have not yet had the packages examined." Johnson also busied himself in investigating what action had been taken by the Board of War regarding the arms of the Maryland Flying Camp. In this connection, he wrote as follows: "I enquired on my coming here for the Flying Camp arms and accoutrements. I find what were fit for use were sold, and the rest I am told are sent to be repaired. Seeing your Sentiments, I shall receive none as belonging to our State, but it was much my wish to have got what good arms I could into my hands as a part of ours and to have carried them home, for presuming the Congress are not sufficiently supplied to return arms at present, I thought about 2000 stand would be better to us than almost any sum of money."

Johnson now heard of General Washington's stand at Trenton; how Lord Cornwallis had been outwitted at Princeton; and how the ragged Americans, under the guidance of their superb commander, were rapidly recovering the soil which had been overrun so recently by the British. On the subject of the general military situation, General Johnson's comment (in his message of January 20 to the Council of Safety) follows:

"It appears to me that a strong reinforcement [Flying Camp] is now not only desirable, but necessary to keep our officers in their late course. I am anxious to contribute all I can to it, and from all that I can collect am persuaded if the miliita would now generally and vigorously exert themselves we should have a fair chance of ruining the British army in the Jerseys." [18]

In dispatching the militiamen across the Delaware,

[18] XVI *Maryland Archives*, 63–65.

Thomas Johnson, who like General Washington became an exponent of a strong Central Government, recognized at this time—more than ten years before the adoption of the Constitution of the United States—the necessity for a Federal Union. Johnson saw that this necessity was especially urgent in time of war, when the Commander-in-Chief of the American Army needed reënforcements from all parts of the country, regardless of the Commonwealth from which they came. It is true, Johnson's Flying Camp—consisting entirely of Militia, *i. e.*, State troops —marched under the requisition of the Congress of the United States. And it is also to be remembered that there was no opportunity at this time—when the patriots were joined together by sheer necessity to repulse a common enemy—to discuss the Doctrine of State's Rights. But even in this critical epoch, Johnson could see plainly the indications of a friction, if not a jealousy, between the Government of the United States and the State. These indications appeared when the American Congress, after sending requisitions for Militia to the County Committees of Observation, neglected to correspond on this subject with the Council of Safety, which during the recess of the Convention was the sovereign power of Maryland. It would be incorrect, of course, to say that the members of the Council were insulted; for they were anxious to do everything in their power to aid the patriot cause; but it was an incident which pointed the way to two separate, coördinate authorities—the State and the future Nation. "So that we have always had doubts," was the simple observation of the Council, "how far it would be proper for us to interfere."

Thomas Johnson realized, in this hour of need, that

his best course was to pacify the Council of Safety—to send his regrets to Annapolis for the failure of Congress to confer with the Council regarding the State Militia. Johnson's logic was fine. He argued that the State had no power to send its Militia to engage in war beyond its borders; therefore, he contended, as soon as the inter-state expedition commenced, with the permission of the Council of Safety, the State's control over the Flying Camp virtually came to an end. "I know," he explained, "you had no authority to *order* the militia of Maryland to Pennsylvania or the Jerseys, and would expect your *permission* only, which I thought you gave when you ordered me to have the militia got in readiness to march on further order that not a moment's time might be lost. I have with the best intentions acted myself and pushed others to do what I thought best and shall be happy in contributing in any degree to save the Country from the devastations which would most certainly without extraordinary exertions have soon extended much further than the Jerseys."

On account of delay in arming the Flying Camp—a considerable portion of the Maryland arms and accoutrements had been delivered to the Pennsylvania Militia—Brigadier-General Johnson was able to send toward the scene of action only a very small portion of his men, properly armed, at one time. The first section to march forth from Philadelphia towards the camp of General Washington included James Johnson's battalion and a part of the battalions of Beatty and Bruce—in all, not more than a few hundred men. They crossed the Schuylkill on January 21, 1777.[19]

Meanwhile, on January 19, the Commander-in-Chief,

[19] XVI *Maryland Archives*, 68.

still apprehensive that the feeble condition of his troops might result in a great disaster, wrote as follows to President Hancock: "As militia must be our dependence, till we get the new army raised and properly arranged, I must entreat you to continue your endeavors with the States of Pennsylvania, Maryland and Virginia to turn out every man they possibly can." In compliance with General Washington's letter, the Congress on January 21 adopted a resolution urging the Maryland Council of Safety to request additional militia to march forward at once to reënforce the American Army. Upon receiving this request from Congress, the Council of Safety on the 25th ordered out the Militia of Harford, Baltimore and Cecil Counties and made requisitions for Anne Arundel, Prince George's, Queen Anne's and Kent. On the following day, the members of the Council forwarded a message to General Johnson, explaining their requisitions; and, while fearing that not as many would turn out as they desired, yet they promised to notify him from time to time "how the militia move forward." [20] "We intend," wrote the Council, "that you should have the command of the whole, as they get up to [Washington's] Camp or the neighbourhood thereof. . . . We shall be much pleased to have a line from you now and then to give us intelligence how affairs go in the Jerseys."

On the eve of his departure from the Capital of Pennsylvania, the Maryland Brigadier-General sent the following reply to Annapolis: [21]

[20] XVI *Maryland Archives*, 78.
[21] XVI *Maryland Archives*, 115.

GENERAL JOHNSON TO COUNCIL OF SAFETY

Philadelphia
Gent.   4ᵗʰ February 1777.

I this minute received yours of the 26ᵗʰ last. All this time has been spent in getting about 1000 men, officers included, fitted out for the Camp. I have not more than 180 yet to send forward except Smith's Battalion from Washington, which I hear is on the road. The delay has been as prejudicial as mutinying, many of our people, some whole companies have returned. I believe could we have got arms in a day or two we should have raised upwards of 1500 men. I have understood the Congress have some arms at Baltimore or Chester, and I think you had best get as many of them as you can for those of the militia who may march under the last requisition for you may depend if they stay here any time the same answer will prevail with them as with the Frederick militia. While I am writing this some officers call on me to let me know another company to about 6 or 8 privates have broken off. As many militia as possible ought to avoid calling here at all. The small Pox is very rife and every thing is prodigious dear. There can be no great dependence on equipments or supplies here; if those who come are partly fitted I think they had best proceed, for Genˡ Washington, to prevent a continuance of the shameful embezzlement of arms, has lately stopped all that belong to the Public, on the discharge of the Militia, so that he can as he says, partly supply those who go in. Some of our people have been 6 weeks and some 4 from home already not only inclined, but necessity will urge their return. I shall have difficulties on that head, for whatever you may hear of the great numbers with Genˡ. Washington he ought to be strengthened.

We have nothing very material from Camp. I am afraid we can expect no great things from New York. The Enemy are kept pretty close in the Jerseys. The war is carried on pretty much by small scouting parties on our side, and they often take some prisoners, 16 British were brought here on Sunday, taken within about a mile of Brunswick, as they were going out without arms to plunder. I am told the duty of the regulars is very severe from very frequent attacks on their pickets &c. Gen¹ Gates has sent off a fine regular Battalion (McCoys) this morning. Tomorrow he and I set out for the Camp.

I am Gent,
Your most obedient humble Servᵗ
TH. JOHNSON, JUNᴿ.

Setting out from Philadelphia in company with General Gates on February 5, 1777, Johnson soon afterwards reached the Delaware, a journey of about twenty-five miles, and then pushed with all possible haste towards the North. He received a message from the Council of Safety expressing genuine regret that he had met with so much delay in his march and containing the heartiest wishes for the ultimate success of his expedition. "We will endeavour," read the message from Annapolis,[22] "to prevent what militia march from this State to Camp in future calling at Philadelphia for the reasons you suggest, which appear to us weighty. If Congress have arms at Baltimore or Chester we doubt not their willingness to let the militia who are now on their way have them, and for this purpose we shall apply. We wish you all success and a safe return to your family."

After a final march of some thirty-five or forty miles beyond the Delaware, the Maryland recruits finally approached the scene of battle. The story is told that upon reaching the camp of the United States soldiers, Johnson rode straight to the Headquarters of General Washington. The Maryland Brigadier, small in stature, badly bespattered with mud, did not present a very pleasing appearance. He was stopped suddenly by an Irish sentinel, who announced that the Commander-in-Chief had given

---

[22] XVI *Maryland Archives,* 128.

orders that he should not be interrupted. But Johnson, after several months of preparation and a journey of several hundred miles, was not to be delayed in this fashion. He declared he wanted to see Washington without delay.

"Who are you?" demanded the sentinel.

The visitor told who he was and again demanded that he be granted admittance.

The Irishman, so the story goes, had never heard of Johnson; but the Maryland leader became so positive in his statements that the sentinel finally went to General Washington and asserted that a "little insignificant-looking man" insisted on seeing him.

"Who is he?" inquired Washington.

"He's a little red-headed man, Your Honor, and he says his name is Tom Johnson, and be damned to you and that he is bound to come in!"

"*Oh!*" exclaimed Washington. "*It is Johnson of Maryland! Admit him at once!*"

CHAPTER XVIII

FIRST TERM AS GOVERNOR

"I have the pleasure to congratulate you on being appointed to fill the most honorable and distinguished station in the gift of a free people to bestow. And having the utmost confidence that the affairs of the State now entrusted to your care, will meet with all the attention they require or deserve, it is with the highest satisfaction I address you on this important occasion."

*John Hancock, President of Congress,
to Governor Johnson,* April 2, 1777.

"The Campaign is therefore opening, and our present situation, weaker than when you left us, forces me to entreat your utmost attention to the raising and equipping the Continental Troops allotted to be raised in your State. . . . Let me therefore, in the most earnest terms, beg that they may be forwarded to the Army without loss of time."

General Washington to Governor Johnson, April 11, 1777.

"You may be assured that I have done and shall continue with pleasure to do every thing in my power to strengthen you."

Governor Johnson to General Washington, April 19, 1777.

O N February 5th, 1777—the day Thomas Johnson set out from Philadelphia with General Horatio Gates toward American Headquarters in New Jersey—the first State Legislature of Maryland convened in Annapolis. Members of the House of Delegates had been elected by direct vote of the people; members of the State Senate by Senatorial Electors. Mr. Johnson, while at Frederick Town, had been chosen a member of the Senate; but, centralizing all his energy on the Flying Camp, he declined the honor and Charles Grahame was chosen to take his place. Among the fifteen members of the first Maryland Senate were William Paca, Thomas Stone and Charles Carroll of

Carrollton, three of the signers of the Declaration of Independence. The venerable Matthew Tilghman, a statesman with long experience in the Continental Congress, added luster to the Upper House. Daniel of St. Thomas Jenifer, of Charles County, was chosen President of the Senate; and Nicholas Thomas, of Talbot County, Speaker of the House of Delegates.

One of the important duties imposed by the Constitution of 1776 upon the Legislature was the selection of the Governor. Accordingly, at the time the battalions of Western Maryland Militia were tramping through New Jersey on the way to the camp of General Washington, Senators and Delegates at Annapolis were solemnly deciding to urge the Maryland commander to assume the duties of Chief Executive of the State.

The Governor was elected by joint ballot of the two Houses of the Legislature on February 13, 1777. One complimentary vote was cast for Senator Tilghman, one for Senator Paca, and another for Senator George Plater. Nine votes were cast for Samuel Chase. All the remaining Assemblymen—a total of 40 out of 52 members— voted for Thomas Johnson. The overwhelming majority in favor of Johnson for Governor was an unquestioned tribute to his integrity, ability, and lofty patriotism.

The man had not sought the office; it had sought the man. "The yeomanry, in their own rude, rough-and-ready manner," says an author describing Maryland at the Revolution,[1] "reflected the same sort of personal independence of character and proud sense of individuality as the social aristocracy. No other colony of the thirteen, perhaps, with such a wealthy and trusted leader as Charles

[1] Scharf, *History of Maryland,* Vol. II, 103.

Carroll, of Carrollton, in the van of its public men, would have passed him by to choose sturdy Thomas Johnson, the man of the people, for its 'great war governor.' " Johnson was not elected Governor by direct vote of the people, but by the ballots of two score members of the Legislature; yet it is not to be denied that the selection of the sturdy "man of the people" for Revolutionary War Governor of Maryland was a preëminent satisfaction to the people of the State.

A joint letter of notification, prepared by President Jenifer, of the Senate, and Speaker Thomas, of the House, reached the Governor-elect on February 23, just ten days after the election. It can well be imagined that on the night of the arrival of the express and on the following day, Mr. Johnson—stationed then at Basking Ridge—deliberated over the new request and very probably discussed the subject with the Father of his Country.

Meanwhile, the loyal people in Maryland, anxious for a powerful leader at Annapolis, were concerned lest the Governor-elect might prefer to remain by the side of General Washington. They knew that Johnson was farsighted, talented and courageous, and had developed executive ability of a high order. He had already rendered public service of inestimable value through a period of two decades, and they felt that his unflinching courage and sound judgment were greatly needed during this most critical period.

Imagine, therefore, the rejoicing at the Maryland Capital on that March day in 1777, when the courier arrived from Basking Ridge! The Governor-elect's message of acceptance was as follows:[2]

[2] Original now in possession of the Maryland Historical Society, Baltimore, Md.

JOHNSON'S ACCEPTANCE OF THE GOVERNORSHIP

Basking Ridge, East Jersey,
25 Feby 1777.

Daniel of St. Thomas Jenifer Esqr
President of the Senate of Maryland.

Sir

The Evening before last I rec^d your and the Honble Speaker of the House of Delegates joint letter. I have the highest sense of the Honor done me by the General Assembly. I regard it as the strongest Testimony of my Country's approbation yet if my own wishes could have taken place the Choice would have fallen on some other person whose abilities might promise more General good. I can only promise that my utmost Endeavours shall be faithfully executed to promote the public Happiness and that I shall take on myself the important office with a confidence that the uprightness of my Intentions will insure to me the support and assistance of the Legislature & every good man.

The weather was so bad yesterday that I detained the Express. I have yet some little matters to adjust and propose to begin my journey tomorrow or at farthest the next day.

We have not had anything of Consequence since I have been here; we have almost daily skirmishes on the one side or the other in which the little advantages gained are generally, I believe I may say, universally in our Favor but regular Troops are much wanted. The Enemy had a reinforcement a few days ago from Rhode Island but I believe it is not very considerable.

I am Sir with the greatest Respect

Your most obed. Servant,
TH. JOHNSON, JUN^R.

It was not long after the receipt of his message of acceptance that Johnson himself arrived in Annapolis. Preparations were then begun for the inauguration, which was set for Friday, March 21, 1777.

When the historic day arrived, the people for many miles around about journeyed to the Maryland Capital to behold the ceremonies. First on the program was the stately parade, which formed at the Assembly House and proceeded through the winding streets in the following order:

High Sheriff, President Jenifer of the Senate, Members of the Senate, Hon. Thomas Johnson, Members of the Governor's Council, Sergeant-at-Arms bearing the Mace, Speaker Thomas of the House of Delegates, Members of the House of Delegates, Mayor of Annapolis and Recorder, Aldermen, Common Council, Military Officers, Gentlemen Strangers, Citizens.

Between noon and one o'clock, the procession ended at the State House, where a great crowd of spectators had gathered. There is no record of an inaugural address by the first Maryland Executive. In giving an account of the event, the Annapolis newspaper simply says: "Silence being commanded, the high Sheriff then proclaimed the Governor." [3]

Immediately after this brief and solemn pronouncement, three volleys from a firing squad served as a signal for the discharge of cannon as a salute to the first Governor of the State. Thirteen cannon were fired as a mark of honor for each of the thirteen States. Losing his way in the smoke in front of one of the cannon, just as it was fired, one of the soldiers was shot and mortally wounded— a sacrifice strangely ominous of the bloodshed that was to follow.

After the formal proclamation of Governor Johnson, State and City officials, military officers, visitors and local

[3] *Maryland Gazette,* March 27, 1777.

citizens again formed in line, and returned according to the same order in which they had come, except that immediately behind the High Sheriff were the Governor and members of his Council marching now in front of the members of the Senate.

At the conclusion of the parade, the marchers "repaired to the coffee-house, where an entertainment was provided, the field officers of the army and strangers then in town being all present." During this repast, the assembled guests drank the following toasts:

   I. Perpetual Union and Friendship between the States of America.
  II. The Freedom and Independence of the American States.
 III. The Prosperity of Maryland.
  IV. The Congress.
   V. General Washington and the American Army.
  VI. The American Navy.
 VII. The Arts and Sciences.
VIII. Agriculture.
  IX. Trade and Navigation.
   X. The Friends of Liberty throughout the World.
  XI. The memory of the brave Patriots who have fallen in the Cause of America.
 XII. General Lee and our Friends in Captivity.
XIII. Wisdom and Unanimity in the Councils of America, and undaunted Courage in Her Forces to execute Her Measures.

How happily chosen were these thirteen toasts! How deeply significant! How singularly prophetic!

That night the Capital presented a scene of unusual brilliance. "The festivities of the day," says James McSherry,[4] "were closed with a splendid ball; a renewal of the ancient and pleasant amusement, for which Annapolis, the Athens of the Colonies, had been so widely celebrated in the days of the Proprietary, but which had been solemnly discontinued in the dark hours of the opening struggle."

So, while the inauguration of the first Governor of the State of Maryland during the gloomy period of the American Revolution was accompanied by impressive formalities, yet the deep significance of the occasion could not restrain the great rejoicing in the hearts of the people of the State. The joy of the Maryland freemen on the day of Governor Johnson's inauguration has been set forth in the following eloquent language:[5] "Although the perils of a great war then environed the infant State, whose position peculiarly exposed her to invasion, though she had already borne, and knew she would be called on still to bear her full share of the toils, the dangers and the sufferings of the conflict; though the outlook was dark and growing darker, the people of Maryland never wavered in the confidence with which they clung to the cause of liberty; and in this installation of a Governor, not appointed by the proprietary nor the Crown, but elected by the representatives of the people, marking as it did the opening of a new era, was the occasion of rejoicing springing from a deeper source than the mere triumph of a party or the gratification of a popular desire."

But it was all too brief a day of rejoicing! Hardly had the echoes of the inaugural celebration died away before

[4] McSherry, *History of Maryland.*
[5] Scharf, *History of Maryland,* Vol. II, 287.

MARYLAND'S PORTRAIT OF THOMAS JOHNSON
This painting of the first Governor is in the Gallery of Governors in the
State House

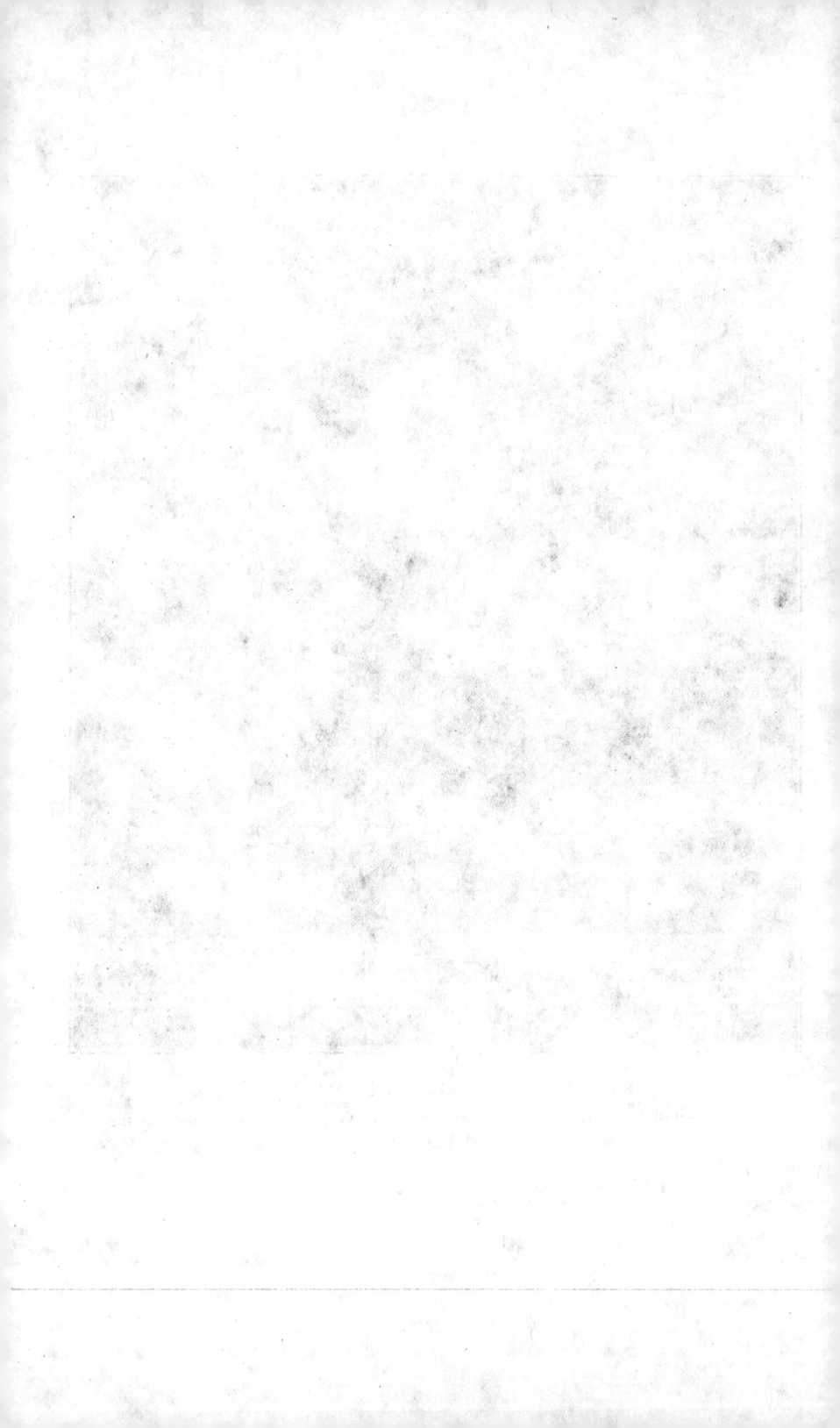

the resounding reverberations from the British guns were
heard in Maryland. Now came the days of hardship and
suffering. From the very beginning of his Administration,
Governor Johnson faced the problem of filling the State's
quota of Revolutionary soldiers. When information was
first brought to Congress by Major-General Greene from
the Commander-in-Chief that the British were preparing to
attack Philadelphia, Daniel Roberdeau, one of the members of the House, wrote as follows to Governor Johnson
on the day following his inauguration:

"Your Excellency's zeal and activity in the cause of these United
States gives us confidence in addressing you upon a critical emergency.
. . . We wish that the new Levies in your State may be forwarded
with the utmost expedition possible, so that they may either join our
troops already in the Jersies, or at least be at hand to arrest the
Enemy at the Delaware, in the supposed attempt to pass it." [6]

Soon after this, upon being warned by General Washington that Enemy troops had embarked from Staten
Island, Congress notified the Governor of Maryland that
General Howe was on his way South. President Hancock
sent Governor Johnson a copy of General Washington's
letter and also the resolution urging removal of public
stores to places of safety. In his letter to Governor Johnson, dated April 2, President Hancock said: "You will perceive from the inclosed copy of a letter from General
Washington that the information it contains is of the most
serious nature, and that our Enemies are meditating an
invasion of the State of Maryland. In this situation of
affairs, I am earnestly to request you will take such measures as will have a tendency to defeat their designs should

[6] XVI *Maryland Archives*, 187.

any attempts be made in consequence of this intelligence. The inclosed Resolve of Congress respecting the removal of the public stores to the places therein mentioned, I am to request you will pay the utmost attention to and give orders for removing the same as soon as possible." [7]

Governor Johnson lost no time in placing the letter before his Council. Under the provisions of the Constitution, the Governor's Council, or Cabinet, was to consist of five men, but some difficulty was met at first in securing five suitable men who were willing to serve. The first three to accept positions in the Council—John Rogers, Edward Lloyd and Josiah Polk—qualified in the Senate chamber in the presence of both Houses of the Assembly on March 20th; and, selecting Richard Ridgely as clerk, took over the unfinished business of the old Council of Safety. Complying with the recommendation of Congress, the Governor and Council ordered most of the powder in the magazines at Annapolis and Baltimore to be removed to Frederick Town. In a letter dated April 12th, the Council asked Major Benjamin Johnson to deposit the ammunition in the Market House until a special magazine could be constructed, and to employ a dozen men to guard it.

At the same time Governor Johnson redoubled his energies to enlist recruits. Numerous obstacles lay in his path. One cause of delay was the exasperating scarcity of supplies. From Chester Town, for example, the Governor received the report of Thomas Smyth, Jr., that Kent County recruits were without the barest necessities—clothes, blankets and provisions—and nearly all the soldiers were suffering from exposure.

[7] XVI *Maryland Archives*, 196.

It was at this time, and under such circumstances, that Governor Johnson received one of the most earnest entreaties ever written by the Father of his Country. Washington realized that the British were scheming to advance upon the American capital. His Continental forces were gradually weakening and he implored the Maryland Governor "in the most earnest terms" to expedite reënforcements to the Army. The General's letter is as follows:[8]

GENERAL WASHINGTON TO GOVERNOR JOHNSON

Headquarters, Morris Town,
11th April 1777

Govr Johnson
Sir:

The latest accounts received respecting the Enemy, (rendered probable by a variety of circumstances) inform us, that they are very busily engaged in fitting up their Transports at Amboy for the accomodation of Troops, that they have completed their Bridge, and are determined to make their first push at Philadelphia.

The Campaign is therefore opening, and our present situation, weaker than when you left us, forces me to entreat your utmost attention to the raising & equipping the Continental Troops allotted to be raised in your State. I have waited in painfull Expectation of a Reinforcement; such an one as would probably have ensured an happy Issue to any Attack I might have determined upon, and such as I had a right to expect, had the officers faithfully discharged their duty. But that time is past, and I must content myself with improving on the future Chances of War. Even this can not be done, unless the officers can be perswaded to abandon their comfortable Quarters and take the Field. Let me therefore, in the most earnest

[8] *Washington Manuscripts,* Library of Congress. XVI *Maryland Archives,* 207.

terms, beg that they may be forwarded to the Army without loss of time.

I have also to ask the favour of you, to transmit to me, a List of the Field Officers of your Battalions, and their Rank with the number of their respective Battalions.

I have the honour to be, with great Respect,

Y^r most obed^t Servt

Go WASHINGTON.

P.S. Since writing the above, I have the disagreeable information that Disputes still prevail in your State, about the rank of your officers, and that the recruiting service is exceedingly injured by them. Shall the general Cause be injured by such illtimed and ineffectual Jarrings among them? I have inclosed two Resolves of Congress,[9] warmly hoping that the knowledge of them may tend to an honourable and necessary accommodation. No settlement which they can make or submit to among themselves, will affect the army at large. I have long since determined to refer the adjusting of Rank to a Board of General Officers, which will proceed upon the business so soon as the Army collects and Circumstances will admit.

The appeal of General Washington was rushed to Annapolis with all possible speed, and in his response Governor Johnson reassured that he would do everything in his power to strengthen the Commander-in-Chief. Governor Johnson said:[10]

---

[9] One Resolution, adopted February 12, 1777, authorized General Washington to settle all disputes regarding rank of officers in the Army; the other, April 1, 1777, stipulated that rank should be determined by actual date of appointment, and not by antedated commission.

[10] *Washington Manuscripts*, Library of Congress, Vol. 45, page 5771.

GOVERNOR JOHNSON TO GENERAL WASHINGTON

"Annapolis
19th April 1777.

His Excellency
General Washington.

Sir.

Many Circumstances have unluckily concurred to retard the recruiting Service in this State amongst them Rank has not been the most inconsiderable; that Matter is at last so far accomodated that I hope for the Service of nearly all those Officers who shared in the Fatigue of the last Campaign. Inclosed is a List of our Field Officers with the Numbers of their Regiments and I expect in a few Days to forward a Roll of all the Officers of the seven Battalions; several Commissions have been filled up and delivered and I did not know of the Resolution of Congress of the 12th of February.

From Information received some part, I believe, of every Regiment except the second, has moved a part of that waits for a fair Wind only to embark here.

I exceedingly regret the slowness of our preparations and the loss of past Opportunities. You may be assured that I have done and shall continue with pleasure to do every Thing in my Power to strengthen you.

I am Sir with the greatest Respect,

Your most obed. Servt
TH. JOHNSON.

Accurate, concise and prompt, George Washington on April 26, immediately upon receiving the Governor's letter, returned from Morristown a brief message of acknowledgment. He declared that, with the exception of Colonel Price's, he had received no "Returns from any of the Colonels of the state of their Regiments" and added: "If

Gen¹ Smallwood is at Annapolis, be kind enough to desire him to collect them and transmit them to me as soon as possible." [11]

But the duties of the Governor and Council extended far beyond the work of raising the recruits. The Executive Power was really a State Council of Defense to enforce the Acts of the Maryland Legislature and to coöperate with other States and the Congress. For example, Johnson and his Council assumed charge of all prisoners of war within the boundaries of Maryland, subject to the orders of the Continental Commissary General of Prisoners. And, during the recess of the Legislature, the Governor and Council exercised control over the supply of arms and ammunition. When, in April, 1777, it was represented that nearly all the arms belonging to private people had been sent to the Flying Camp, and none had been returned, the General Assembly adopted a resolution requesting Congress to allow Maryland two thousand muskets on account of her "naked and dangerous situation." A copy of the resolution was forwarded to Congress by the Council, and Governor Johnson also wrote a personal letter to Mr. Hancock on the subject.

The correspondence and the Executive papers of Thomas Johnson show that he retained, like Washington, remarkable composure during the stirring days of the Revolution, a calm determination to do his best amid scenes of great excitement. Frequently there arose occasions which, but for the steadfast courage and sound judgment of the Governor, might have resulted in disaster. The high feeling that prevailed during Johnson's first Administration was manifested by a vicious assault on William God-

[11] XVI *Maryland Archives*, 231.

dard, editor of the *Maryland Journal*. Shortly before Governor Johnson's inauguration, there appeared in this journal a letter, signed *Tom Tell-Truth*, commending General Howe for his proposal to the United States and criticizing Congress for concealing the terms of peace. When Mr. Goddard refused to disclose who the author of the letter was, the *Whig Club*—a society organized in Baltimore by the most radical members of the old patriot Committees to oppose the Tories—ordered him to leave the State. The editor gave no sign of leaving, and on March 25 a band of armed men went to his residence, seized him, and dragged him out of his home into the street. Allowed to stay at home that night, Mr. Goddard immediately placed himself under the protection of the Baltimore guard and the next morning—five days after the Governor's inauguration—set out for Annapolis to register a complaint. The House of Delegates, realizing that the publisher had been subjected to high indignities, resolved:

"That every subject in this State is entitled to the benefit and protection of the laws and government thereof. That this House highly disapprove of any body of men assembling or exercising any of the powers of government without proper authority from the Constitution. That the proceedings of the persons in Baltimore Town, associated and styled the *Whig Club*, are a most daring infringement and manifest violation of the Constitution of this State, directly contrary to the Declaration of Rights, and tend in their consequences (unless timely checked) to the destruction of all regular government. That the Governor be requested to issue his Proclamation declaring all bodies of men associating together or meeting for the purpose of usurping any of the powers of government, and presuming to exercise any power over the persons or property of any subject of this State, or to carry into execution any of the laws thereof, unlawful assemblies, and requiring all such assemblies and meetings instantly to disperse. That the Governor be requested to

afford the said William Goddard the protection of the law of the
land, and to direct the Justices of Baltimore County to give him
every protection in their power against all violence or injury to his
person or property."

The Speaker of the House notified Governor Johnson
of the resolution and the Governor then issued his Proclamation against unlawful assemblies. It is the first Executive Proclamation in the history of the State. It follows:

BY HIS EXCELLENCY THOMAS JOHNSON, ESQ.,
GOVERNOR OF MARYLAND

A PROCLAMATION

WHEREAS, The honourable House of Delegates have unanimously requested me to issue my Proclamation, declaring all bodies
of men associating together, or meeting for the purpose of usurping
any of the powers of government, and presuming to exercise any
power over the persons or property of any subject of this State, or
to carry into execution any of the laws thereof, unlawful assemblies, and requiring all such assemblies and meetings instantly to disperse:

WHEREFORE, I have issued this, my Proclamation, hereby declaring all bodies of men associating together, or meeting for the
purpose of usurping any of the powers of government, and presuming to exercise any power over the persons or property of any subject of this State, or to carry into execution any of the laws thereof
on their own authority, unlawful assemblies. And I do hereby warn
and strictly charge and command all such assemblies and meetings
instantly to disperse, as they will answer the contrary at their peril:
And that due notice may be had of this, my Proclamation, and that
no person may pretend ignorance thereof, the several sheriffs within
this State are hereby commanded to cause the same to be made
public in their respective counties.

Given at Annapolis, this seventeenth day of April, seventeen hundred and seventy seven.

Th. Johnson.

By his Excellency's command,
R. Ridgely, Sec.

God save the state.

The Proclamation, characteristic of Johnson's style, presented no rhetorical display; but simply gave in cold facts the situation as stated by the House of Delegates. But the unequivocal stand against unlawful assemblies in the State at the very outset of Governor Johnson's Administration was a clear warning against any activities contrary to the authority of the Government. The Proclamation has been referred to as "the first vindication of the liberty of the press in Maryland." [12]

Following the Proclamation of Governor Johnson, little further trouble arose from the overzealous Whig. But now came the really alarming troubles with the Tory. In Somerset and Worcester Counties, and in Sussex County, Delaware, the anti-American feeling was especially strong. Patrick Henry, Governor of Virginia since July, 1776, had already called the attention of the newly-chosen Governor of Maryland to the lack of military protection on the peninsulas of Maryland and Virginia. In the event of invasion, both Governors agreed that it would be extremely difficult—even if at all possible—to transport troops across the Chesapeake in time to repel an attack of the Enemy. It was becoming increasingly apparent to Governor Johnson that an insurrection of the Tories on the Eastern Shore would render the State open to British invasion. General Smallwood believed, and so told the Governor, that the

[12] Scharf, *Chronicles of Baltimore,* 161.

upper part of Somerset County was the best place to station troops in order to prevent a congregation of the Tories.

In a letter to Congressman Robert Morris, Governor Johnson urged that one of the Continental regiments be allowed to remain on the Eastern Shore. The letter was referred to Benjamin Rumsey, Congressman from Maryland, who moved on the floor of the House that General Smallwood be ordered to station a Continental battalion "under the direction of the executive power of the State of Maryland." A spirited discussion followed, in which many of the members expressed an opinion that a special battalion might be raised and supported by Continental funds, but that none of the regiments already raised could be spared for use in Maryland. However, it was finally decided to refer the question to a committee for investigation; and on this committee were named Rumsey, Colonel Duer, Colonel Wilson, and Samuel Adams.

On April 19, 1777, the General Assembly of Maryland adopted a resolution urging Congress to leave one of the Maryland battalions temporarily in the State; and the Governor, through a letter to President Hancock, gave notice to Congress of this desire. "The Regiment being left for a time in this State," Governor Johnson explained, "may probably be the occasion of its filling the sooner, for a good many of our people are possessed with the humour of serving within, rather than out of, their own State." [13] It is a coincidence that on the same day the General Assembly passed its resolution, appropriate action was taken in Philadelphia to allow one of the Continental regiments to remain in Maryland. On April 19th, the Congress provided:

[13] XVI *Maryland Archives*, 222.

"That the Governor of the State of Maryland be authorized to detain the weakest Continental battalion raised in the State of Maryland, till a further order of Congress; and that it be recommended to the executive authority of the State of Maryland forthwith to embody 300 of the militia of the said State, and to the executive authority of the State of Delaware 100 of their militia, the said militia to cooperate with the battalion of Continental troops, to obey the officer commanding the same, and to continue in service so long as the joint executive authority of the States of Delaware and Maryland shall think necessary."

On receiving a copy of the Congressional resolutions, Governor Johnson ordered Colonel William Richardson's battalion to be detained for the time being on the Eastern Shore; and at the same time wrote to John Hancock: "It must give the Gentlemen of the Congress pleasure to see that they have anticipated the request of the General Assembly and made a provision fully adequate, as we judge, for the occasion."

However, on account of the rigid precautionary measures adopted by the Legislature and strict enforcement thereof by the Governor, the soldiers did not, after all, encounter a great amount of trouble in preventing an insurrection of British sympathizers on the Eastern Shore. By a Tory Act passed by the General Assembly, magistrates were granted "pretty extensive powers"; while the Governor's Council was given power to transport and imprison persons suspected of being "inimically disposed" toward the State. About fifty or sixty captured Tories had already been sent to Annapolis; but, according to Governor Johnson, most of these were "ignorant miserable people, and some who seemed rather to have been spectators than concurring." All prisoners with the slightest apparent disloyalty to the patriotic cause were kept in confinement; but "the wretched," Johnson assured Congress, "we have discharged, on taking the Oath of Fidelity."

Throughout the State a careful vigil was maintained. Persons regarded as Royal adherents were deprived of their muskets. On one occasion, a party of Tories congregated near Pipe Creek in Frederick County; but they were promptly dispersed by the Militia. Thanks to prompt and courageous action of the Governor and the soldiers who supported him, bloodshed was avoided. But ample precaution was still maintained; and when on May 1, 1777, General Schuyler informed Congress that about one hundred of Colonel Richardson's men had arrived in Philadelphia on their way to the Headquarters of General Washington, Congress authorized Governor Johnson to replace them on the Eastern Shore by detaining two of the weakest Maryland battalions remaining in the State.

As in this instance, Congress often communicated with the Governor and urged coöperation in the American cause. But, after all, the Congress at this day was little more than a clearing house for information. Without a Federal Executive corresponding to the President under the Constitution of the United States, the Congress during the American Revolution had to rely upon the Governors to carry many recommendations into effect.

So, Thomas Johnson acted virtually as the Commander-in-Chief of all classes of military forces as long as they remained within the borders of the State. The first General Assembly, before adjourning, made provision for recruiting the "Maryland Line"—Continental Infantry, distinguished from the Militia—and authorized the Governor, with the advice of the Council, to purchase provisions for all military troops in Maryland. Governor Johnson issued a special appeal to officers of the Militia to train and discipline their corps, and Clerk Ridgely of the Council accepted sealed bids for contracts to supply rations.

The Governor was likewise the Commander-in-Chief of the Maryland Navy—such as it was. Governor Patrick Henry of Virginia, hearing the British fleet was moving Southward, was keen for coöperation between Maryland and Virginia vessels in the Chesapeake and Potomac. "I join in sentiment with you," Governor Johnson wrote to the Virginia Executive, "as to the utility of stationing Gallies on the Eastern Shore; some of ours are designed for that service, but our utmost efforts have not yet been effectual to get any one completely fitted. We have three in the water, partly manned, and three others ready, or very nearly ready, to launch, but have not been able, as yet, to get a sufficiency of Cordage or Hands for the first three. The fitting out of the Gallies is an object of the first attention with us, will be prosecuted as such, and as soon as any of them are fit, they will be ordered below, where we shall be glad to hear some of yours are ready to act in concert with them." [14]

In trying to strengthen the "Navy," Governor Johnson confronted many exasperating obstacles such as he had encountered in recruiting the infantry. Writing again to Governor Henry on April 29th, he admitted that he had not succeeded in making much headway in this direction. One of the Galleys—"the forwardest of them"—said Governor Johnson, "is on the lower part of our Eastern Shore with intention to exercise the Hands she has and endeavour to get more." The ship *Defence*, said the Governor, was still at anchor in the harbor of Annapolis on account of lack of

[14] XVI *Maryland Archives*, 227.

hands. "She has now about 60 [hands]," Johnson added, "and wants at least as many more, we are using our utmost endeavours to get them, but the privateers and the high wages given by merchants, make it very difficult to get men of any sort."

But Thomas Johnson reassured Patrick Henry of Maryland's desire to coöperate with Virginia. "As soon as we can get any of our Row Gallies ready," said Johnson, "they will be ordered down, in such a situation that they may be easily collected to take the advantage of a calm and with orders to act in concert with yours; it is our idea that, in a calm, an attack might be decisive against a Man of War, and that if the Row Gallies should be worsted, they might almost certainly retreat. . . . We look on this State equally interested with yours, in the defence of the Bay, are heartily disposed to contribute to it, and are indeed sorry that it is not in our power, jointly with your State to effect it."

During May, June and July, while the people of Maryland were anxiously watching for the movements of the Enemy fleet, Governor Johnson was besieged with a multiplicity of duties. Food and supplies were becoming increasingly scarce. For a while Colonel Mordecai Gist made a diligent search for equipment in Baltimore and before leaving for camp notified Governor Johnson of the delay in receiving commissions. On a number of occasions Congressman Rumsey wrote to the Governor that the lack of commissions had caused much discontent among the Maryland officers. The Governor tried to expedite the commissions.

Meanwhile, there arose disputes which cast upon Governor Johnson duties of a judicial nature. One of these dis-

putes resulted from the practice of Captain James Nicholson of "impressing men into the Naval Service of the Continent." Most of the members of Congress objected to
the practice, contending that it was pernicious to the commercial interests of the country and a violation of the principles of civil liberty. Captain Nicholson—a Naval commander of ability, but an unyielding Whig—claimed that
unless he had the right to impress seamen he could not man
his frigate in the Philadelphia harbor. On April 25,
Nicholson wrote a letter which was so caustic in its terms
that Governor and Council and members of Congress were
alike deeply offended. Congress, refraining from any decision, referred the controversy to Governor Johnson. In
behalf of the Marine Committee, Representative Morris
sent a letter on May 1 to the Maryland Executive,[15] declaring that Captain Nicholson was "inflamed by the
violence of that species of Whiggism that savours more of
passion than true patriotism." The Governor was told in
plain words that Nicholson deserved to be dismissed, and
unless he apologized ought to be dismissed. The Council
realized that the controversy was an unfortunate one, because the Captain was an officer, whose discharge from the
service would mean a heavy loss to the Continent. It was
not long afterwards that Nicholson sent an apology, which
the Council accepted. But, as a matter of fact, Nicholson's
letter was not entirely satisfactory and Governor Johnson
so told the Marine Committee. The Governor and Council
determined that all impressed sailors should be discharged.

Another dispute brought before Governor Johnson during the Summer of 1777 was based upon complaint filed
against George Cook, another Captain in the Navy, by

[15] XVI *Maryland Archives*, 236.

Major Nathaniel Smith. Captain Cook had been sent by the Council on a mission to Baltimore, and on his arrival there ordered a number of Major Smith's men to guard some vessels at the wharf. The Major contended that Cook, a Naval officer, usurped authority in ordering the guards about. By way of explanation, two of Captain Cook's subordinate officers on the ship *Defence* testified before the Council that they had made a diligent search for Major Smith; but, unable to find him, asked the Sergeant to lend a few of his guards—a favor that was cheerfully granted. The Governor assured the Major that, unless further affidavits were presented, the inquiry would be ended, the Council feeling that Captain Cook executed his mission in all possible haste and had no intention of treating Major Smith with disrespect.

So Governor Johnson virtually became a "Court of last resort." And it is safe to say that his decisions were received with universal respect.

But of all the duties which Thomas Johnson was called upon to assume as Governor, doubtless the most gigantic was that of raising and equipping the recruits. Believing that the members of the Legislature could assist him in solving the perplexing problems connected with the raising of Maryland's quota, Governor Johnson determined towards the close of May to convene the General Assembly. In the House of Delegates some difficulty was found in securing a quorum, but the members finally came to order on June 16, 1777. The Legislature, aware of slowness of the enlisted men, authorized the Governor to issue a Proclamation calling on all recruits in the Continental battalions to appear for duty. His Proclamation follows:

BY HIS EXCELLENCY THOMAS JOHNSON, ESQ., GOVERNOR OF MARYLAND

A PROCLAMATION

WHEREAS, Many of the soldiers who enlisted in the late [16] Colonel Smallwood's battalion, and the independent companies, have not yet joined any of the regiments of Continental troops raising in this State, I have therefore thought fit, at the request of the General Assembly, to publish this my Proclamation, hereby requiring such of them as are on the Eastern Shore to appear on or before the last day of July next, at furthest, at any place where Col. Richardson's Regiment shall be; and such of them as shall be on the Western Shore, to appear on or before the last day of July next, at the City of Annapolis, or Baltimore, or Frederick Town, under the penalty of being treated as deserters; and do promise, to such who shall so appear, that they shall be indulged to enter for three years in any of the battalions raised by this State, and shall thereupon receive the Continental bounty, and other allowances. And that all persons concerned may have due notice of this, my Proclamation, the several sheriffs within this State are hereby commanded to make the same public in their respective counties.

GIVEN at Annapolis this thirtieth day of June, in the year of our Lord, one thousand seven hundred and seventy-seven.

TH. JOHNSON.

By his Excellency's command,

T. Johnson, jun., Sec.

GOD SAVE THE STATE.

Many of the Maryland soldiers, while ready at all times to defend their State from invasion, were none too eager to march away from their homes, leaving their families unprotected against the British, the Tories, and the Indians. Governor Johnson's ringing Proclamation showed

[16] Recent.

dauntless courage and a grim determination to secure every possible recruit for the Commander-in-Chief of the Continental Army.

It is true, there was a distinction between State Militia and Continental troops. Nevertheless, as long as the soldiers—State or Continental—camped within the borders of Maryland, they remained under the control of the Governor; whereas, after they left the State, they all fought for the same cause and all fought under the supreme direction of General Washington. A story is told of one regiment that assembled in Annapolis under orders to march to American Headquarters. On the eve of departure, the Colonel told Governor Johnson that the soldiers would not march further than Baltimore. Hearing this, and having little faith in the Colonel himself, Johnson ordered the entire regiment to be drawn up in the form of a hollow square on the campus of St. John's College. The Executive then marched straightway into the square and cried out in a loud voice:

"I understand, Colonel, that your men will not march further than Baltimore. I give you positive orders: If any man deserts you before you reach the Army, you are to follow him up and hang him—and I will be responsible for the act!"

Then pointing to a large shade tree on the College green, the Governor shouted to the commanding officer:

"And, mark you, Colonel! If *you* do not obey the order, I will hang *you* on that poplar tree!"

According to this narrative, the recalcitrant battalion on the following morning marched away from Annapolis and proceeded toward the Head of Elk without stopping in Baltimore. It has also been said that it was the only Maryland regiment that reached the Headquarters of General Washington without the loss of a single man.

It is not to be thought, however, that after the Maryland troops crossed the Pennsylvania line, Governor Johnson was relieved of further responsibility concerning them. On the contrary, he frequently received pathetic appeals for assistance not only from members of Congress but also from officers in the field. One letter, written by Colonel John Hoskins Stone on July 24th from "Crumb Pond below Peeks Kills," declared that, unless adequate supplies of clothing were received, the Maryland soldiers would suffer as severely as they did the Winter before.

Unfortunately clothing was scarce. In August, the Governor shipped a supply of jackets, shirts, overalls and shoes—enough for several hundred men—to the Maryland Congressmen at Philadelphia; but he plainly declared: "Very little more cloathing can be had from here."

But the Governor, ever diligent and resourceful, cast his eyes towards the South for a possible source of supplies. In Virginia he located some food and clothing. And it was not long before he extended his vision to foreign counties. To the Moale and the Havana he sent Captain Robert Conway to exchange a cargo of Maryland products for medicinal supplies. The Captain was given instructions to proceed first to the Moale, dispose of his cargo, and purchase Peruvian bark, Spanish flies and a quantity of salt; but if unable to make a satisfactory transaction there, to proceed to the Havana. He was also instructed by the Governor not to trade unless by permission of the authorities. "We are situated," the Governor of Maryland wrote to the Governor of the Havana, "in a country where drugs of various kinds are necessary and none more so, in some cases, than Flies, or in many, than Peruvian bark. Since our connection with England has ceased and our intercourse with Europe is interrupted and almost cut off by the British cruisers, we must enquire in other places for such essential articles as we have not amongst ourselves. . . . I hope the subjects of his most Catholic Majesty and those of the United States may be mutually benefitted by a generous and fair commerce and shall be happy if this incident should lead to an acquaintance and confidence between those in your Department and those over whom I have the honor to preside." [17]

So the Summer of 1777 wore on. It was a period of intense preparation. The Governor was constantly urging the men to arms. Fortunately for the patriots, the British were in no great hurry to strike. Sir William Howe did not finally leave in his brother's fleet until July, and it was not until the 30th of that month that the vessels reached the Capes of Delaware. Congressman Francis Lewis, a member of the Navy Board, was at that time in Baltimore; and to the Congressman Captain Nicholson on August 1 proposed the plan of sailing his frigate armed with 150 seamen to the Head of Elk and thence toward Philadelphia. Mr. Lewis endorsed the plan and notified Governor Johnson and the Navy Committee of the suggestion. To the Governor he wrote: "I thought it would be greatly for the service of the States at this critical juncture. I consulted Capt. Cook also for a reinforcement from his ship for the same service."

Suspecting the object of Lord Howe's cruise, General

[17] XVI *Maryland Archives,* 328.

Washington broke up camp and marched the patriots to the South. But Howe was also wary. Believing that the Americans would obstruct the Delaware to prevent the passage of his fleet, he changed his design and proceeded further down the coast.

In due time—on August 16, 1777—the British vessels arrived at the entrance of the Chesapeake! On up the Bay they sailed until early on Thursday morning, August 21, they appeared at the mouth of the Severn! In the fleet were counted 260 men-of-war and transports. Annapolis was terror-stricken!

Calmly facing the situation, Governor Johnson called the members of the Council together and sought their advice. The absorbing question was: Should an effort be made to defend the city? Major John Fulford, who was asked for an opinion, expressed the belief that the Capital could not be successfully defended by a handful of Militia against the trained troops of George III. And the Governor and Council realized that, in the event the British landed and made an attack, the people of Annapolis would soon be at their mercy. It was, therefore, decided to evacuate. Public stores and guns were hastily moved to places of security.

But, to the surprise and gratification of Annapolis, General Howe gave no indication of landing. Instead, the fleet continued on up the Bay; and, as the shades of night fell, Governor Johnson realized that the invaders were aiming to take Philadelphia. On the following morning, the Governor issued his Proclamation ordering the Western Maryland Militia to hasten toward the Susquehanna. His Proclamation follows:

BY HIS EXCELLENCY THOMAS JOHNSON, ESQ., GOVERNOR OF THE STATE OF MARYLAND

A PROCLAMATION

This State being now actually invaded by a formidable land and sea force, and the enemy, in all probability, designing to land somewhere near the head of this Bay, I have, in order to collect a body of militia to be ready to act with the Continental Army, which may soon be expected to meet the enemy, thought proper to issue this my Proclamation; hereby requiring and commanding the county lieutenants, the field and other proper officers of the militia of the Western Shore of this State, immediately to march at least two full companies of each battalion of the militia to the neighbourhood of Susquehanna river, in Cecil and Harford counties, where they shall receive orders.—To defend our liberties requires our exertions; our wives, our children, and our country, implore our assistance: Motives amply sufficient to arm every one who can be called a man.

Given at Annapolis this twenty-second day of August, in the year of our Lord, one thousand, seven hundred and seventy-seven.

TH. JOHNSON.

By his Excellency's command,
T. Johnson, Jun., Sec.
GOD SAVE THE STATE.

From the Eastern Shore word was received by the Governor that the Militia companies were collecting with a deep determination to give the invaders obstinate resistance. The trumpet-call to the Western Shore resounded across mountain and valley—and echoes of response came back from every section of the State.

In the meantime, patriot leaders stationed at various points along the upper Chesapeake kept the Governor ad-

vised of the progress of the British fleet. Major Nathaniel
Smith notified the Governor that the entire fleet, headed
by the Admiral's ship, appeared off Baltimore early Friday morning, August 22nd, weighed anchor and "stood up
the Bay." Major Smith assured that, if the red coats attempted to take the Fort at Whetstone, he would give them
the warmest "reception" possible. General Buchanan was
encouraging the Militia to assemble, and Captain Nicholson
was in readiness with his sturdy seamen. A short time afterwards, the British ships appeared at the mouth of the Gunpowder, and Benjamin Rumsey wrote to Governor Johnson
that two companies of soldiers had been ordered down to the
shore to prevent a landing, but admitted that there were
but five guns distributed among a total of forty men!

Congress now heard of the progress of the British fleet
in the Chesapeake and on August 22nd adopted a resolution authorizing the release of General William Smallwood and Colonel Mordecai Gist from Headquarters of
General Washington in order to allow them to arrange and
command the advancing Maryland troops. Washington
marched from Philadelphia on the 24th of August, and
establishing himself at Wilmington, Delaware, endeavored
to concentrate his forces to protect the American capital.

The British, continuing up the Chesapeake, advanced
as far as Turkey Point, on Elk River, and late on Sunday afternoon, August 24th, commenced to land on the
soil of Maryland. Altogether General Howe disembarked
upwards of 18,000 soldiers. But the Maryland patriots
remained calm, and in Annapolis the landing of the British was reported in the following unsensational manner:
"We are informed that the Enemy have landed a considerable body of men at Cecil court-house, which they

burnt, together with all the records and papers of that county, and that General Washington, with ten or twelve thousand regulars, is now at Christeen. Deserters say, that Howe's intention is for Philadelphia." [18]

Another Maryland leader who supplied Governor Johnson with much valuable information at the time of the British invasion was William Paca, who remained at Chester Town to expedite recruits from the Eastern Shore. Mr. Paca rendered a valuable service in securing supplies for the Militia. About the time General Howe was landing his men, Paca was sending to Governor Johnson an urgent appeal for supplies. The Governor received Paca's message at midnight. Fearing the British might attempt to interrupt all intercourse between the two Shores, Johnson dispatched a boat on a hurried trip across the Bay in order to reach the Eastern Shore before daybreak. Along with the supplies on the vessel, the Governor also sent an order authorizing the Treasurer of the Eastern Shore, with the approval of Mr. Paca or of Matthew Tilghman or of Robert Goldsborough, to appropriate any amounts deemed necessary for the support of the Militia.

The Council, which was now meeting with Governor Johnson in Baltimore since the evacuation of Annapolis, approved the Governor's action as an emergency measure. "We are of opinion," the Council wrote on August 31st to Tilghman and Goldsborough, "that strictly we cannot give to others a discretionary power to draw out the public money; but surely when every thing is at stake, the Treasurer will not be particular or ceremonious; he and we must rely on the equity of the Legislature; however if we have the power or may be thought to have it, the enclosed

[18] *Maryland Gazette,* August 28, 1777.

may satisfy the Treasurer." Some time later, Governor Johnson, feeling his responsibility to the representatives of the people, sent a message to the House of Delegates explaining that the apparent irregularity was due to the grave situation of affairs.

It soon became apparent that the British were not bent on molesting the inhabitants of Maryland to any special degree, but were aiming to take Philadelphia with all possible haste. But the Army of the Crown was large and skilled in warfare, and the Governor felt that it was expedient, while Enemy ships were yet in the Bay, to take every possible precaution in all sections of the State. Lieutenant Charles Beatty was directed to remove prisoners from Frederick Town to Sharpsburg. Major Benjamin Johnson was ordered to strengthen the guard over the public magazine at Frederick and to be "vigilant and attentive." The Governor himself was urged by Secretary Richard Peters, of the Board of War, to cause the Continental powder and stores at Baltimore to be moved in the direction of Carlisle, Pennsylvania.

Appeals were now coming frequently from the War Office, the Board of Treasury and other Departments of the United States Government. On one occasion the Governor was asked to lend a quantity of lead to the Board of War, on account of the great scarcity of this essential in the Continental magazines. Another request came from John Gibson, Auditor General of the Treasury, asking the Governor to dispose of tickets in the United States Lottery, authorized by Congress to help defray the enormous expenses of war.

But the task of raising Maryland's full quota of Continental troops and Militia, equipping them with clothing, arms and ammunition, supplying them with food, and moving them off as fast as possible to the Headquarters of General Washington—this was still the most important task of the Governor. Johnson continued firm in faith and hope, but he was at a loss to know what to do next to supply the troops preparing to meet the horde of British invaders. Finally the situation became so acute that it was necessary to resort to a plan almost equivalent to confiscation. Finding that the supply of muskets was insufficient to furnish the Militia on the way to the Susquehanna, Governor Johnson ordered the officers to take all arms wherever found and turn them over to the marching troops. The process was described by the Governor as "borrowing" and he assured that, in case of loss, the owners of the guns would be reimbursed. Meat was also scarce, and Governor Johnson authorized the purchase of cattle on credit. And in most cases a promise of Thomas Johnson was sufficient to secure any necessities—whether arms, food or clothing—even though the owners had no prospect of immediate payment.

The British troops, encountering no difficulty in landing on the banks of Elk River, soon found that they were going to meet much stouter resistance than they expected. The Maryland soldiers were few compared with the vast army of red coats, but, playing for time, they did all they could to keep the Enemy "amused." The Marylanders contented themselves with guerrilla, and it was in one of their skirmishes on August 28th that Henry Hollingsworth was wounded in the face at Gilpin's Bridge. His brother, Jesse Hollingsworth, stationed about four miles North of the British Headquarters, wrote to Governor Johnson that the Maryland "Light Horse" in their scouting parties had taken captive nearly one hundred British soldiers. The Maryland officers were stationing sentinels, the Governor was informed, at Susquehanna Ferry, Harford Town, and other places for the conveyance of news. Meanwhile, General Washington was rapidly concentrating his forces. He had already collected about eleven thousand American soldiers, although it was well known that the forces under Howe were superior in numbers as well as in training and equipment. However, selecting his ground carefully for a stubborn defensive, the American Commander hoped to beat back the foreign invaders and save the Capital. Naturally somewhat concerned over the critical situation, and hoping to make use of every possible advantage, Washington sent a hurried message on the first of September to Governor Johnson, then in Baltimore, inquiring whether it would not be possible to rush the Maryland war ships to the Head of Elk and surprise the British fleet from the rear.

Governor Johnson felt that the plan was not feasible. He said: [19]

GOVERNOR JOHNSON TO GENERAL WASHINGTON

Balt. 4 Sept 1777.

Dear Sir

I reced your Letter of the first Instant and was happy in having it in my power to converse with General Smallwood on the Contents of it. I see several vessels in the Harbour which I think might well be applied for the purpose you mention and believe I could get men who would at least endeavour to go through it but I am apprehensive it could not be conducted with success we have very

[19] *Washington Manuscripts,* Library of Congress.

little Tide it does not commonly exceed eighteen Inches, in the Bay about the Mouth of this River; and of course it is still less higher up, so that from that circumstance we could derive little or no advantage from hence to the Bay is at least 15 Miles added to the Distance from thence to Turkey Point it would require a South westerly wind of a pretty long continuance to carry a vessel from hence there and the Situation of the Enemy would most probably prevent it for from what I have been from Time to Time informed two or three Men of War constantly lay in the channel some Distance below the rest of the Fleet and yesterday and the Day before several Men of War have moved down against this and Annapolis— Genl Smallwood on the present view of Matters thinks with me that the Attempt would in all likelihood fail—yet Sir if you think that there's the least chance of success I will most cheerfully and industriously get Things prepared and throw out the idea of its being done with a view only to the River which would be the best pretence to mislead for it is impossible to effect it with^t its being known at all.

I hope you will excuse the Freedom with which I have objected against the Scheme and be assured that I rely so much more on your Judgm^t than my own in a Matter of this kind that if you think it proper to be prosecuted I shall expect success.

I am my dear Sir,

Your most obed^t Servt

TH. JOHNSON.

By this time, General Washington was growing impatient over the delay of reënforcements from the Eastern Shore of Maryland. Colonel Richardson had been trying to move the Militia toward the Susquehanna and William Paca had been giving valuable aid. But September came and still no recruits! Congress had sent down a large sum of money, but supplies were very scarce and there were many obstacles to surmount. In a letter to Governor Johnson, Mr. Paca explained that it was even becoming necessary to call upon the inhabitants to give up their clock and window weights in order to get a supply of lead.

Feeling that Colonel Richardson was perhaps not as aggressive as he might be, General Washington called on John Cadwalader, an alert and trustworthy officer, to take general command of the Eastern Shore forces. General Cadwalader received the request from the Commander-in-Chief on August 29th, and the next day set out for the Head of Sassafras.

General Washington then sent the following letter to Governor Johnson, urging Cadwalader's formal appointment as head of the Eastern Shore Militia: [20]

GENERAL WASHINGTON TO GOVERNOR JOHNSON

Wilmington, Septr 3, 1777.

Sir:

The late Resolution of Congress for sending Genl Smallwood and Colo. Gist from this Army to arrange and command the Militia of Maryland, now called to the Field, and the frequent applications I had, before the arrival of those Gent^n at this place, to send Officers to the Eastern Shore to take the command of the Militia assembling there, give me reason to believe, that the regulations, in this line, are not so good as either you or I wish them to be; and that there is a want of Officers in that part of the State, or at least of a Head, to conduct matters properly, and in the best manner that circumstances will admit.

Under this persuasion, if you have not already appointed a General Officer—or have no particular Gentleman in view for the purpose, I would beg leave to mention John Cadwalader, Esqre for your consideration. This Gentleman I know to be a judicious, valuable officer, and I have often regretted that he did not hold

[20] *Washington Manuscripts,* Library of Congress. XVI *Maryland Archives,* 360.

a high command in the Army of the States. If you should entertain the same opinion of him, and there is no Objection to appointing him, I am satisfied he would render essential services at the
Head of the Eastern Shore militia, if he will accept the command,
which I am inclined to think would be the case.

Before Col⁰ Gist went on this business on Monday, on account
of the applications I have mentioned, and not knowing who the
militia officers were on the Eastern Shore, I wrote to Mr. Cadwalader and requested his Good Offices and exertions in assembling
and arranging the militia, which, I find, have been employed with
great assiduity; and if arms could have been procured, that he would
have collected a respectable body of men. My interfering in this
matter was the result of necessity—I thought the situation of our
affairs required it, and I trust I shall have your excuse upon the
occasion. I would also observe, if Mr. Cadwalader is appointed,
Col⁰ Gist's services there may be dispensed with, and he may join
his Regiment again.

I sincerely congratulate you on our late success at the Northward in raising the siege of Fort Schuyler, and obliging the Enemy
to go off with great precipitation,—leaving their Tents, provisions
& ammunition, and with the loss of several prisoners & Deserters
& Four Royals.

I have the Honor to be, with great respect,
Sir,
Your most Obed^t Servt
G⁰ WASHINGTON.

George Washington's confidence in John Cadwalader
was well placed. A short time afterwards, when Major
General Thomas Conway was accused of intrigue to oust
General Washington and put General Gates in supreme
command of the American Army, General Cadwalader was a
faithful supporter of the Commander-in-Chief. On account
of unjust aspersions against Washington, General Cadwalader challenged General Conway to a duel. The duel

was fought and Conway was severely wounded. Later Conway left the country, never to return.

A few days after General Cadwalader's appointment, the Militia of the Eastern Shore was at last ready to set out for camp. The Tories were doing all they could to retard the work of recruiting the Militia: about eighty assembled with arms along the borders of Queen Anne's and Caroline Counties and they caused some little excitement, but they were promptly dispersed, and several were captured. Mr. Paca reported on the 6th of September to Governor Johnson that ten companies of Militia—three from Queen Anne's, two from Caroline, and five from Kent— had already mobilized at Chester Town and the recruits in Talbot and Dorchester Counties were likewise ready to march.

Governor Johnson now watched the defense of Philadelphia with great anxiety. He knew that Howe was preparing for a mighty movement against "the rebel Capital," as the British called Philadelphia; and he could hear General Washington, entrenched near Wilmington, appealing to the Militia to hurry on in order to strengthen him.

Occasionally bits of information were received in Baltimore from British prisoners and deserters. Two of these red coats, who gave themselves up to the Militia in Gunpowder Neck, were sent to Governor Johnson by Benjamin Rumsey, who felt they could furnish some important information. But from now on, most of the information concerning the campaign came from General Smallwood and Colonel Gist, as they proceeded from camp to camp on their way to join the main Army of General Washington.

On September 8th, General Smallwood reported that the British fleet lay at Sassafras, and that the Militia were preparing to cross the Susquehanna. The British were now cutting a road through the woods in an attempt to penetrate to the capital, and General Smallwood decided to harass their rear and endeavor to cut off any retreat to the Enemy fleet. Washington selected his line of defense on the left bank of the Brandywine and on September 11, 1777, the British made their memorable attack. The wing, under General Lafayette and Lord Stirling, although fighting with great valor, was crushed in by the forces under Cornwallis. At the battle of Brandywine, the "Maryland Line" shared the disasters of the day. The patriots retreated, Washington taking post at Germantown, a few miles from Philadelphia.

Shortly after this, Colonel Gist's forces and those under immediate command of General Smallwood united and then merged into the command of Washington. After the battle of Brandywine there followed several weeks of maneuvering, and finally on September 26, 1777, Howe, without opposition, entered Philadelphia. Upon Howe's approach, Congress adjourned to Lancaster and a few days later to York.

The main division of the British encamped at Germantown, and General Washington, entrenched about twenty miles from Philadelphia, decided to attempt to take Germantown by surprise. On the night of October 3rd, the Americans marched quietly toward Germantown and on the next morning began their attack. The Maryland troops, under Major John Eager Howard, served with distinction in the battle on that cold, foggy morning of October 4th. But the troops became bewildered in the dense

fog, and the confusion was so great that the plans of Washington were disarranged and a disorderly retreat followed.

The only complaint made to Governor Johnson of the
lack of valor at the battle of Germantown was registered
against Colonel William Hopper, who led one of the brigades under the command of Colonel Gist. In a communication to the Governor, Colonel Gist declared that, when
the Enemy's pickets commenced a scattering fire on the
Maryland columns, Hopper was suddenly attacked with
"qualms of sickness" that obliged him to leave his regiment.
With that exception, the Maryland officers went bravely
into the battle at Germantown. Writing from York a few
days later, Samuel Chase reported to Governor Johnson the
casualties among the commissioned officers.

But the gloom caused by the British invasion of Maryland and the capture of Philadelphia was greatly relieved
by the American successes in the North. General John
Burgoyne, who had organized a force of about ten thousand British veterans, Hessians, Canadians and Indians,
and had swept down from Canada with the hope of joining the main division of the British Army and cutting off
New England from the Middle and Southern States, was
met by stout resistance from the sturdy Americans in the
North. On the 14th of October, General Smallwood wrote
to Governor Johnson that if Fort Mifflin held out, General
Howe's situation would soon become as alarming and critical as that of Burgoyne. "The wretched situation the
Royal Northern Army must be in," said General Smallwood, "will lower the pride of the once pompous and boast-
ing Burgoyne which must afford a sensible pleasure to every
honest American."

The lines of General Gates gradually closed in around

Burgoyne, and on October 17th the whole army of Burgoyne, numbering between five and six thousand, surrendered at Saratoga. It was a great achievement, and as soon as General Burgoyne's invasion was brought to an end, a large portion of the victorious Army of the North was dispatched to the aid of Washington.

But the American situation, taken as a whole, was still discouraging. Fort Mifflin was captured by the British, and Fort Mercer, on the opposite side of the Delaware, was abandoned. But the surrender of Burgoyne gave relief and as the British gave no sign of leaving the American capital, the people of Maryland felt somewhat composed. The members of the Maryland Legislature felt that the Loan Office and Treasury could now be returned with safety to Annapolis, and on November 4th, 1777, the Council ordered the State's money, books and papers to be moved back to the Maryland capital.

This was the condition of affairs in America when Thomas Johnson concluded his first administration as Governor of Maryland. It was a brief period of less than eight months from his inauguration on the 21st of March to the end of his term on the 10th of November; but it was a period filled with big events—the suppression of Whigs and Tories in Maryland, the invasion of the State by General Howe, the defeat of General Washington at Brandywine, the capture of Philadelphia, the battle of Germantown, and the surrender of Burgoyne at Saratoga. But, during this tempestuous period, Governor Johnson guided the Ship of the State with remarkable zeal and courage.

CHAPTER XIX

SECOND TERM AS GOVERNOR

"There is one thing more to which I would take the liberty of solliciting your most serious and constant attention, to wit, the Cloathing of your Troops, and the procuring of every possible supply in your power for that end."   *Washington to Johnson, Valley Forge,* December 29, 1777.

"From this view of matters, and foreseeing the fatal and alarming consequences that will necessarily attend a dissolution or dispersion of the Army, I must take the liberty of solliciting your good Offices, and to request your exertions and to prevent as far as possible, so melancholy a catastrophe, by having forwarded to Camp all the provisions of the meat kind that may be in your power."
    Washington to Johnson, Valley Forge, February 16, 1778.

"I have to acknowledge the receipt of yours, some little time ago, informing me of the steps you had taken to procure us a supply of Provisions. I sincerely thank you, and hope I shall find the same readiness in you to assist us with carriages."
    Washington to Johnson, Valley Forge, March 21, 1778.

"From a number of concurring circumstances, there is reason to believe that the Enemy mean to evacuate Philadelphia. . . . I would, therefore, beg of you to embody and send forward five hundred of your Militia, equipped, and the most contiguous to the Head of Elk. . . . I rely upon your particular assistance on this critical occasion."
    Washington to Johnson, Valley Forge, May 17, 1778.

SINCE March 21, 1777—the day of the first triumphant inauguration at Annapolis—Thomas Johnson had been serving as Governor of Maryland in pursuance of Article LXI of the Constitution, which authorized the immediate election by the first General Assembly of a person to serve as Governor "for the residue of the year," *i. e.,* until the regular annual election in November. But while the first term as Governor lasted only seven months and a half, Johnson nevertheless had ample opportunity during this brief Administration to demonstrate his qualities—absolute fearlessness in the discharge of duty, sound judgment, keen foresight, a rare degree of executive ability, and unfaltering loyalty to the cause of American independence. Governor Johnson was now, without doubt, the most prominent man in Maryland. Indeed, so firm a place had he won in the affections of the people of the State that when Autumn came not a single man from such a brilliant array of statesmen as Chase, Paca and Tilghman, Plater, Jenifer and the Carrolls, was suggested as a candidate for Governor against him.

The members of the Legislature, assembling together again at Annapolis on the last day of October, failed to find in the early days of November a single Gubernatorial candidate in opposition to the incumbent. Article XXV of the Constitution, which provided for the election of the Governor on the second Monday of November, directed that the votes "be taken in each House respectively, deposited in a conference room; the boxes to be examined by a joint committee of both Houses, and the numbers severally reported." In accordance with the Constitutional directions, the members of the Senate and House of Delegates on the afternoon of Monday, November 10, proceeded to ballot for Governor. The election was manifestly nothing more than a formality. The joint committee—consisting of two members of the Senate and three from the House—after collecting the votes in both branches of the Assembly, retired to their conference room but returned shortly afterwards to their respective chambers with the report that Governor Johnson had been reëlected unanimously.

The Governor was formally notified of his reëlection

by a committee consisting of Senator Plater and Delegates Forbes and Kent. Johnson knew that he could not do otherwise than accept. In the midst of the war, with upwards of 20,000 British soldiers and Hessians occupying Philadelphia, he knew that it was his duty to carry on the work in which he had been engaged since his return from the side of General Washington in New Jersey. He, therefore, informed the notification committee that he would accept and qualify on the following morning for the full-year term.

Accordingly, on Tuesday morning, November 11, 1777, Johnson for the second time took the oath of office as Governor of Maryland. The installation ceremony was brief and without ostentation. The House Proceedings mention briefly that the Delegates, upon receiving word that the Governor was ready to be sworn in, left their seats, marched to the Senate Chamber, "saw His Excellency qualify in the presence of both Houses," and then returned. The second inauguration was marked by Johnsonian directness and simplicity.

The members of the Legislature now returned to the consideration of measures intended to aid in the prosecution of the war. The first need of the Government, as Governor Johnson saw it, was to prevent as far as possible disloyalty among the people. In order to help the Governor in keeping the activities of the Tories in check, the Legislature promptly passed a criminal statute imposing the death penalty upon any person found guilty of burning any Maryland or United States magazine or of destroying or delivering to the enemy any State or United States vessel.[1]

[1] *Laws of Maryland*, October 1777, Chapter I.

War always demands extraordinary powers in the hands of the Executive. And thus the Act enlarging the powers of the Governor and Council, passed shortly after Johnson's first inauguration, and continued at the June session of the Assembly, was reënacted.[2] "These extensive powers," writes James McSherry, "were placed, without hesitation, in the hands of Thomas Johnson, whose sterling patriotism and public virtue merited the confidence which was reposed in him. It was not abused." The broad war powers of Governor Johnson were continued in like manner at each successive session of the General Assembly.

Another law, imposing still further power in the hands of the Governor and Council, was passed by the Legislature upon receipt of letters from General Washington and General William Smallwood appealing for clothing for the Continental troops. Following the battle of Germantown, the American soldiers were led to White Marsh, about twelve miles from Philadelphia; and as the raw winds of November began to sweep through the camp, the scenes of want and suffering touched the hearts of the officers in command.

Worried over the distressing condition of the Maryland soldiers, Smallwood made a stirring appeal to General Washington, who decided to send Lieutenant Colonel Peter Adams, a Maryland officer, with a supply of money to buy up clothing under Governor Johnson's supervision. It was thus about the time of the second inauguration that Johnson received the following entreaty from the Commander-in-Chief: [3]

---

[2] *Laws of Maryland,* October 1777, Chapter II.
[3] *Washington Manuscripts,* Library of Congress, Vol. II, page 177.

GENERAL WASHINGTON TO GOVERNOR JOHNSON

Head Quarters Nov[r] 6th 1777.

D[r] Sir

The approaching season, and the scanty supplies of cloathing in public store, without an immediate prospect of their being increased, have induced me, to send Lt. Col[o] Adams of your State to procure, if possible a Quantity for the Troops which come from thence. The distress of the Army in this instance I am sorry to inform you, is now considerable, and it will become greater and greater every day, if some relief should not be had. Gen[l] Smallwood has addressed you on the subject and having pointed out the wants of your soldiery in a particular manner, it is unnecessary for me to make a minute detail of them. I shall therefore take the Liberty of referring you to his letter, and must entreat the interposition of your aid, to facilitate, as much as possible, the purpose and design of Col[o] Adams Commission. I do not know what supplies of Cloathing Maryland may have on hand; however, whatever they are, they can never be furnished with more propriety, than at the present juncture. Our wants extend to every species and to Blankets, but to the latter, and to shoes and stockings in a peculiar degree. Besides the necessaries, which I hope will be derived from the State, I have instructed Col[o] Adams to obtain all he possibly can by purchase from the inhabitants, in which I trust, he will have your countenance and warmest recommendation. These requisitions are not the result of choice but of painful necessity; and viewing them in this light, I am well assured, you will not only excuse them, but will readily afford every relief in your Power to give. Our calls are pressing, and equal to any the imagination can represent. If they can be answered and Troops can be properly provided in these instances, I should hope that we may be able to obtain some signal, if not some decisive advantages over the Enemy, by a winter's campaign; If not, we shall not be in a situation to attempt anything on a large and general scale. We are trying to make a collection here, and, under the authority of Congress, compulsory measures have been adopted, in some cases, to draw aid from the disaffected, where it could well be spared but not refused.

I congratulate you sincerely on our success in the surrender of
Gen¹ Burgoyne an event this, that reflects much honor upon our Arms.
I have nothing new to inform you of here, the repulse Count Dunnop
met with and the destruction of the two Ships of War, being the last
interesting occurrences.

I am Dʳ Sir

Your Most Obᵗ Servᵗ

G. WASHINGTON.

In sending to Governor Johnson the list of supplies
needed by the Maryland soldiers, General Smallwood declared that while all the Continental troops were in pathetic
need, the two brigades from Maryland were perhaps more
destitute than any in the Army.[4]

The entreaties in behalf of the Maryland Continentals
received prompt attention at Annapolis. Governor Johnson informed the members of the Legislature of the serious
situation and a law was speedily passed authorizing the
Governor and Council to appoint a special agent in each
County of the State to collect clothing for the Continental Army.[5] On the day Johnson qualified for his second
term, the Assembly rechose Thomas Sim Lee, Edward
Lloyd, Joseph Sim, John Rogers and Josiah Polk as members of the Council; but only two of them agreed to serve,
and these two—Lee and Lloyd—did not qualify until November 19, and did not meet with the Governor until November 20. The Assembly selected Daniel Carroll, James
Brice and William Hemsley to fill the three vacancies; and
when Hemsley declined, the Council appointed James
Hindman to take his place. On the 27th of November—
the day before Mr. Carroll qualified—the Governor and

[4] XVI *Maryland Archives,* 413.
[5] *Laws of Maryland,* October 1777, Chapter IV.

Messrs. Lee, Lloyd and Brice appointed eighteen Clothing Collectors and gave them directions to forward the supplies to Cambridge, Chester Town, Frederick, Baltimore, Annapolis or the Head of Elk. Each Collector was allowed his traveling expenses and a commission of 7½ per cent of the value of clothing bought, and to the vendor he was authorized to give a certificate for the proper amount of money payable by either of the Treasurers of the State.

To supplement the work of the Collectors, Governor Johnson continued his search for clothing South of the Potomac. He deplored the fact that the soldiers in the Maryland brigades were suffering from exposure; and, on hearing that some Virginia supplies were obtainable, deputized David Crawford, a citizen of Prince George's County, to purchase cloth, blankets, shoes, stockings and hats from merchants in the Old Dominion. "I hear there are some goods at Alexandria," the Governor wrote Mr. Crawford,[6] "and I know of no Body in the Public Service who I can, with Propriety, send to make a purchase. Supposing you have Time and not doubting your Inclination to serve the Public, I beg the Favour of you to go to Alexandria and, if you can, purchase coarse Woollens sufficient for 1000 Suits of Cloaths, any Number of Blanketts, 1000 Pair of Shoes & Stockings and Hats."

As December drew near, General Washington felt that his troops—worn out by a hard campaign and already suffering intensely for want of food and clothes—should, if possible, be spared the rigors of a winter campaign. Many different opinions were offered by his officers regarding the disposition of the Army; but, after listening to their dis-

[6] XVI *Maryland Archives*, 419.

cordant suggestions, he decided to establish his soldiers in Winter quarters at Valley Forge. Here—on the West bank of the Schuylkill, not more than 20 miles from Philadelphia—the Commander-in-Chief felt that his Army, though weakened by hunger and exposure, could at least keep a watch on the invaders and stand between them and a great extent of the country. The cold march of the troops to Valley Force was dreary and disheartening, blood from many frost-bitten feet marking their steps in the snow. Arriving on the site of the encampment on the seventeenth of December, the men had still to brave the wintry winds in the tents until trees could be cut down and the logs built into huts. Hunger and exposure added daily to the list of sick and within a few days after arrival in camp many of the famished soldiers were on the verge of mutiny.

Not hearing from General Washington for a number of weeks, Governor Johnson was unaware of the increasing scarcity of Continental supplies and the terrible hardships of the men at Valley Forge. Indeed, upon receiving in November a request from Congress to set aside a day for Thanksgiving, the Governor had issued a Proclamation calling upon the people of Maryland to observe the 18th of December "in all churches and congregations of Christians throughout this State, as a day of general and solemn Thanksgiving."

Johnson, therefore, was devoting his entire attention to problems within the State. One problem, for example, that confronted him at the close of the year 1777 was how to guard the growing number of British prisoners assigned to Maryland. Abraham Faw, who was the Clothing Collector for Frederick County, called the Governor's attention to the fact the British prison house at Frederick Town contained many captives of war and many more were expected, and contended that the guard was inadequate to protect the citizens of the town. The difficulty, Mr. Faw explained, was to secure men to serve as guards without offering a bounty. Governor Johnson did not doubt the necessity of having better protection at Frederick, where there was a large magazine, but at that time he had no authority from the State to grant bounties to recruits. However, after consulting with members of his Council, he decided it was proper in view of the emergency to advance a sum from the Treasury for the purpose of "defraying the expence of a Guard." So, while he himself had no authority without the action of the Legislature to offer bounties to the soldiers, the Governor presented Mr. Faw with 200 pounds to deliver to Colonel Charles Beatty, Lieutenant of Frederick County, and suggested that it might be quietly used to advance a month's pay to prospective recruits or in any other way to expedite the formation of the Guard. The Governor felt that it was highly necessary for the protection of Frederick to have at least sixty men in the guard and he so advised Colonel Beatty. "I am so well satisfied," said the Governor, "of the Necessity of a good Guard that, if the Men cannot be got without a small Bounty, that I think it will be better for the Inhabitants to advance it—I will give forty Dollars towards it myself." [7] The Governor also promised to place the matter before the General Assembly and urge the passage of a bounty law. But the efforts to raise the Frederick Guard met with little success, and nearly two months later it became necessary for the Governor and Council to order Colonel Beatty to call out a Company of the Militia to serve as Guard over the prisoners at Frederick.

On New Year's Eve Governor Johnson learned of the

[7] XVI *Maryland Archives*, 451.

organization of two companies of Artillery and he gave them orders to march to Wilmington.   In his message to General Smallwood regarding the Artillery, the Governor said: "I have given them Orders to march to Wilmington, rather than to the Valley Forge, presuming that if they should be less useful at Wilmington, or, if General Washington should chuse to have them with the Main Body, the Difference of the Distance will not be very great and you will be better able than myself to direct the route." [8]   The Maryland Artillery arrived in due time at the post at Wilmington, and the Governor's message was relayed by General Smallwood to the Commander-in-Chief.

It was not until early in the year 1778 that Governor Johnson received his first letter from General Washington after the establishment of the camp at Valley Forge.   The General declared that words failed to describe the great suffering of his soldiers.   Of a total of about 11,000 men, not less than 2,898, he told the Governor, were "unfit for duty, by reason of their being bare footed and otherwise naked."   Washington's letter follows: [9]

GENERAL WASHINGTON TO GOVERNOR JOHNSON

Head Quarters Valley Forge,
29th December 1777.

Sir:

Gen[l] Smallwood will, by this Conveyance, transmit you a Return of Seven of the Maryland Regiments.   The Eighth, which was composed of part of the German Battalion, and part of Rawlings' Regiment, is in the same situation in point of numbers.   By this you will discover how deficient—how exceedingly short they are of the complement of Men, which of right, according to the Establishment, they ought to have.

[8] *Ibid.,* 452.
[9] *Ibid.,* 448.

This information I have thought it my duty to lay before you, that it may have that attention which its importance demands, and in full hope, that the most early and vigorous measures will be adopted not only to make the Regiments more respectable, but compleat. The expediency and necessity of this procedure are too obvious to need argument. Should we have a respectable force, to commence an early Campaign, before the Enemy are reinforced, I trust we shall have an opportunity of striking a favorable and happy stroke. But if we should be obliged to defer it, it will not be easy to describe, with any degree of precision, what disagreeable consequences may result from it.

We may rest assured, that Britain will strain every nerve to send, from home and abroad, as early as possible, all the Troops it shall be in her power to raise or procure. Her views and schemes for subjugating these States, and bringing them under her despotic Rule, will be unceasing and unremitted. Nor should we, in my opinion, turn our expectations to, or have the least dependance on the intervention of a foreign War. Our wishes on this Head have been disappointed hitherto, and I do not know that we have a right to promise ourselves, from any intelligence that has been received, bearing the marks of authority, that there is any certain prospect of one. However, be this as it may, our reliance should be wholly upon our own Strength and exertions. If, in addition to these, there should be aid derived from a War between the Enemy and any of the European powers, our situation will be so much the better. If not, our efforts and exertions will have been the more necessary and indispensible. For my own part, I should be happy, if the Idea of a foreign rupture should be thrown entirely out of the scale of politics, that it may not have the least weight in our public measures. No bad effects could flow from it, but on the contrary, many of a salutary nature. At the same time, I do not mean that such an Idea ought to be discouraged among the people at large.

There is one thing more to which I would take the liberty of solliciting your most serious and constant attention, to wit, the Cloathing of your Troops, and the procuring of every possible supply in your power for that end. If the several States exert themselves in future in this instance, and I trust they will, I hope that the supplies they will be able to furnish, in aid of those which Congress may immediately import themselves, will be equal and competent to every demand. If they do not, I fear—I am satisfied that the troops will never be in a situation to answer the public expectation, and perform the duties required of them. No pains—no efforts on the part of the States can be too great for this purpose. It is not easy to give you a just and accurate Idea of the sufferings of the Army at large, and of the loss of Men on this account. Were they to be minutely detailed, your feelings would be wounded, and the relation would not be probably received without a degree of doubt and discredit. We had in Camp, on the 23ᵈ instant, by a Field Return then taken, not less than 2898 men unfit for duty, by reason of their being bare footed and otherwise naked. Besides this number, there are many others detained in hospitals, and crowded in farmers Houses for the same cause. I flatter myself the care and attention of the States will be directed in a most particular manner, to the supply of Shoes, Stockings and Blankets, as their expenditure, from the common operations and accidents of War, is far greater than that of any other article. In a word, the united and respective exertions of the States can not be too great—too vigorous in this interesting work, and we shall never have a fair and just prospect for success, till our Troops (Officers and Men) are better provided for than they are or have been.

We have taken post here for the Winter, as a place best calculated to cover the Country from the Ravages of the Enemy, and are busily employed in erecting Huts for the Troops. This circumstance renders it the more material, that the supplies should be greater and more immediate than if the men were in warm comfortable Houses.

Before I conclude, I would also add, that it will be essential to innoculate the Troops or Levies as fast as they are raised, that their earliest services may be had. Should this be postponed, the work will be to do, most probably, at an interesting and critical period, and when their aid may be more materially wanted.

I have the honor to be,

With the greatest Respect, Sir,

Your most obᵗ Servᵗ

Gᵒ WASHINGTON.

Washington's first message from Valley Forge to the Governor of Maryland contained a ringing appeal for Winter clothing. But supplies of blankets, trousers and shirts, stockings and shoes, and other warm apparel had already been gathered by the Clothing Collectors; and shipments were expedited in wagons to the camp of the Continental Army.

As the loads of clothing found their way to Valley Forge and were eagerly grabbed up by the shivering soldiers, appeals now rang out for something to eat. It was early in the year 1778 that Governor Johnson received his first information concerning the increasing scarcity of provisions. This news came from Horatio Gates, who had been chosen President of the Board of War at the time of the inception of the Conway Cabal late in 1777, and who while in the War Office with Thomas Mifflin was carrying on intrigue to drive George Washington from the supreme command of the Army. In his letter to Governor Johnson, Gates explained the great need of meat and other provisions for the use of the Continental soldiers. The Governor and Council issued orders deputizing persons to secure cattle, either by purchase or seizure, for the use of the Army.

Virtually every Continental request—whether it came from the Commander-in-Chief, the Congress or the Board of War—was given prompt attention by the Governor. Of course, there were instances when a request did not seem justifiable; and on such occasions Johnson did not hesitate to present his views in a frank and fearless manner. One instance of Johnson's firm refusal appeared early in 1778 in response to a request from Henry Laurens, President of Congress, to confiscate a cargo of salt in the Chesapeake.

President Laurens, the South Carolina Congressman who had been elevated to the chair in the Fall of 1777 upon the resignation of John Hancock, declared that a great scarcity of salt existed and urged Governor Johnson to seize the salt-laden ship that lay in the harbor of Baltimore. But just as George Washington refrained from seizing the property of farmers in Southern Pennsylvania even though for the use of the suffering soldiers fearing that such drastic action would precipitate dangerous disaffection, so Thomas Johnson preferred to acquire by contract rather than by confiscation, unless the owners of the property were inimically disposed toward the patriot cause. Governor Johnson felt that his first step was to investigate the ownership of the vessel and the cargo. Accordingly, in the middle of January, he made a trip to Baltimore in quest of first-hand information. In Baltimore the Executive found a large supply of salt offered for sale and he learned that additional cargoes were on the way to port. He, therefore, maintained that confiscation was unnecessary and inadvisable. In his reply to President Laurens, Johnson declared that, if Congress desired a supply of salt, he could purchase possibly 2,000 bushels for the use of the Continent; and added that he would have made a purchase from State funds if the condition of the Treasury of Maryland had not been unable to bear the expenditure. "But a seizure," Johnson maintained, "will certainly determine People to stop what they can and prove only highly prejudicial to the Inhabitants of this State, but prevent Congress from being supplied at so cheap a Rate on the whole, with any large Quantity at the Places by much the most convenient for Carriage." [10] The promptness with which Governor John-

10 XVI *Maryland Archives*, 469.

son had made his investigation of the salt supply at Baltimore and the frank manner in which he had reported to President Laurens won the praise of Congress. "Congress is extremely sorry," Congressman John Henry, Jr., wrote to Governor Johnson a few days later, "the Salt could not be procured; at the same Time they highly approve of your Excellency's Conduct, and desired the President to return you and the Council the Thanks of Congress for your respect and attention to their resolve." The supply of salt found by Governor Johnson in the Bay was gladly accepted.

There were also times when the Governor of Maryland found it necessary to oppose schemes advanced by the Board of War. One of these occasions occurred early in 1778 when General Gates presented a plan to transport Southern supplies by water. It seems that Congress adopted a plan in January to promote the carriage of provisions to the Continental Army; and Maryland was asked by the War Office to coöperate by forwarding supplies from Virginia and North Carolina by water. The State of Maryland owned at that time a number of galleys, but Governor Johnson took the position that water carriage would be too unreliable. British men-of-war were still hovering about and the Enemy were growing more venturesome. Only a short time before one of Maryland's tobacco ships had been captured in the Potomac. And the Governor felt that, if the British learned of the transportation of supplies to Valley Forge by water, men-of-war would promptly be rushed to the scene and there would be trouble in the Chesapeake! Johnson, therefore, informed General Gates that Maryland could not carry out the scheme of the Board of War.

Meanwhile Congress, continuing to hear of the distressing condition of the Continental Commissary Department, directed the Board of War to make an investigation of the great deficiencies; and General Gates sent out circulars to Governor Johnson and other Executives on February 10 inquiring if there existed any "Languor in the Department." A radical change in system was also discussed by Congress, upon Washington's earnest solicitation, in the hope of preventing a recurrence of such alarming conditions in the future.

Congress appointed a committee to proceed to Valley Forge and confer with the Commander-in-Chief regarding the conditions of the Army and recommend a method of rehabilitation. When the committee arrived at Valley Forge, Washington laid before them in great detail the defects of previous arrangements and outlined plans for a new and improved system. For weeks the Congressmen remained in camp trying to secure data for their report. They found that the meat supply was particularly inadequate. Washington told them how he had so frequently relied on Governor Johnson. The committee decided to send a communication to Johnson telling him that the very existence of the Continental Army depended upon prompt receipt of food supplies from Maryland. The communication was dated February 16 and was signed by Francis Dana, John Harvie, Nathaniel Folsom and Gouverneur Morris. "We have the Honor," they said,[11] "to compose a Committee of Congress appointed to confer with the General upon the Affairs of the Army and with him to concert measures for opening the Campaign with Vigor and Activity. During the Progress of this important Business the critical situa-

[11] XVI *Maryland Archives,* 503.

tion of the Army on the score of Provisions hath filled our minds with Apprehension and Alarm. Fed by daily supplies and even those uncertain we have to fear a total Want. Some Brigades have not tasted Flesh in four Days and the Evil great as it is seems rather to increase than diminish. The Commissaries inform us that they have not only met with great Difficulties in purchasing Provisions in your State but that they cannot even transport what they have purchased for the want of Waggons and the like. Whether these apologies are justly founded we will not presume to say but this is certain that upon an early Transportation of large Quantities of Provisions to this Camp from the State you preside over the very Existence of our Army depends. Let us then intreat you Sir to exert the full Influence of your Abilities to forward such supplies as may have been already bought up and also to obtain by such measures as you may think most adequate to that Purpose as much as can be spared by the Inhabitants from their own particular Consumption."

Washington sent a personal letter to the Governor and enclosed the appeal from the committee. The General's letter follows: [12]

GENERAL WASHINGTON TO GOVERNOR JOHNSON

Camp, Valley Forge
Feb^ry 16th 1778.

Sir

I do myself the honor of transmitting you this inclosed Letter from a Committee of Congress now here. These Gentlemen have represented the distress of the Army for want of Provision so fully, and in so just a light, that I shall forbear to trouble you with many

[12] *Ibid.,* 501.

observations upon the subject. I shall only add, if the picture they have drawn is imperfect, it is because the colouring is not sufficiently strong. It does not exceed our real situation, nor will it be easy to give you an adequate idea of it.

The only public stores of the meat kind that I can hear of in your State, lie at the Head of Elk. I have sent an active Officer there today, and I hope with the assistance of Mr Hollingsworth, who resides there, that in the course of a few days they will be transported to Camp: But, should this be the case, the quantity is so small that it will afford but a very short and temporary relief. Nor can I find from the most minute inquiry, that the Magazines of this kind, when drawn together and aided by the Supplies of Cattle the Commissary expects to get, will be more than sufficient to support the Army longer than this month. After [that] our prospect of support from him seems to be at an end, or at least it will be extremely precarious.

From this view of matters, and foreseeing the fatal and alarming consequences that will necessarily attend a dissolution or dispersion of the Army, I must take the liberty of solliciting your good Offices, and to request your exertions and to prevent as far as possible, so melancholy a catastrophe, by having forwarded to Camp all the provisions of the meat kind that may be in your power. I know not what resources Maryland may have in this instance, but perhaps thro your means and influence, we may derive no inconsiderable supplies. Not to mention our distresses during the active part of the last Campaign, and that our operations were then much retarded. This is the second time in the present year, that we have been on the verge of a dissolution on this account.

I am sensible, Sir, I have addressed you upon a Subject out of your province. But I am assured, your zeal for the service and wishes to promote it, where possible, will indulge me with an apology, especially when I add that my application is the result of the most painful and pressing necessity.

I have the Honor to be

With great esteem & regard

Sir

Your most Obed^t Servant

G^o WASHINGTON.

Governor Johnson, in his reply, did not discuss the statement of the Congressmen that great difficulties had been encountered in Maryland in the work of buying and transporting provisions, except to offer the suggestion that the embarrassments of the Commissaries "proceeded rather from the want of a preconcerted plan and timely orders for the purchase than any other cause." The Governor had received a similar appeal from the Board of War just a few days before, and he had advised General Gates of the possibility of securing large quantities of herring at the head of the Chesapeake, upwards of 5,000 barrels of salted shad "of the large, white kind" at the fisheries along the Potomac, and, with the help of the General Assembly which was about to reconvene, a large supply of pork and other meats which had been engrossed by "some avaricious people" in Baltimore. And likewise, in replying to the chieftain at Valley Forge, Governor Johnson, while not mentioning specifically the fish and the meat, expressed the confident belief that all provisions that Maryland could offer would be collected and forwarded promptly to the Army. Following is Johnson's letter to Washington:[13]

GOVERNOR JOHNSON TO GENERAL WASHINGTON

Annapolis 22ᵈ Febry 1778.

Sir.

I this Moment received your Letter of the 16ᵗʰ Instant with its Inclosure. I have within a few Days past received Letters on the same Subject from the Board of War and also from Members of the Congress from this State—the first Intimation or indeed Apprehension I had of any Difficulty in your Supplies of provisions was about the tenth of January and every Assistance which I thought

---

[13] *Washington Manuscripts,* Library of Congress.

could be given by the Executive power of this State was immediately given—the Embarrassments of the Gentlemen in the Purchasing Department I believe have proceeded rather from the want of a preconcerted plan and timely orders for the purchase than any other cause however Sir as Things are circumstanced we must now look forwards for the Remedy. I am glad Henry Hollingsworth is employed and shall in a few Days send some provisions to him. The Assembly is to sit in a few Days and I have no doubt but what can be spared from this State will be collected and forwarded. I hope Virginia and Maryland can and will yet supply the Army if they can be fed for a little while with what is in the neighborhood—With the greatest Respect and Esteem—

I have the Honor to be

Your Excellencys

Most obed^t hble Servt

TH. JOHNSON.

Again the minds of Washington and Johnson were moving in the same direction. Before the Governor had recommended "a preconcerted plan and timely orders for the purchase" to prevent a recurrence of such dreadful conditions as then existed at Valley Forge, the Commander-in-Chief had already begun to look for a remedy. There in the wilderness, as the winds of Winter whistled in the camp, the American General was preparing his Address to the people of Pennsylvania, New Jersey, Maryland, Delaware and Virginia, asking them to drive their cattle to the Continental Army in the following Summer. In this Address from his snow-bound encampment, Washington assured the people not only that they would receive "a bountiful price" for their cattle, but also that in complying with his request they would render "a most essential service to the illustrious cause of their country."

In sending a copy of the appeal to the Governor of

Maryland, Washington requested that it be given publicity in the newspapers of the State. "For reasons that will be obvious to you," [14] he suggested to the Governor, "it is thought the publication of the inclosed Address may answer valuable ends; and I beg leave to submit to you, whether it may not serve to increase its effect, if it were ushered into the Papers of your State with a recommendatory line from yourself. If you should suppose there will be any impropriety in this, you will be pleased notwithstanding to commit the Address itself to the Printer."

As the month of February, 1778, drew to a close, the situation began to brighten at Valley Forge. In all parts of Maryland quantities of provisions were being collected for the use of the famished soldiers. In a letter to Governor Johnson, dated February 23, General Gates admitted that the Commissary General, in the purchase of supplies, had "injured rather than promoted the business," and sent the thanks of the Board of War for the splendid coöperation of the Executive. "We are happy in perceiving," declared Gates in his letter to Johnson, [15] "that your Excellency and the Honorable Council are making those exertions for its [the Army's] assistance this Board expected from your known zeal and patriotism."

Already the opposing forces were looking forward to the next campaign. The British having organized two troops of light horse, the Americans were anxious to recruit several corps of cavalry in order to meet the Enemy on equal terms; and it was about the first of March when Maryland and adjoining States were asked by the committee at Valley Forge to raise their quotas of horses and

[14] XVI *Maryland Archives,* 512.
[15] *Ibid.,* 518.

saddles. "The number estimated for the State of Maryland," Congressman Francis Dana told the Governor,[16] "is three hundred and fifty, which we believe will not appear by any means too large for the Resources of your State which has with a laudable care cultivated a valuable breed of Horses for a long time past. We doubt not but on this occasion your Excellency and the Gentlemen of the Legislature will favor us with a continuance of those Exertions the beneficial Effects of which we have already experienced."

At this time the British troops in Philadelphia and in the vicinity of New York numbered about 35,000; while the total strength of the American Army—including nearly twelve thousand disheartened men at Valley Forge—was barely 15,000. As the Enemy continued to grow more formidable, Congress resolved that the Continental Army should be increased to 40,000 men, in addition to the artillery and cavalry. And, accordingly, Governor Johnson was asked to raise in Maryland nearly 3,000 additional soldiers.

It is needless to say that Johnson did all he could to supply the new demand for recruits. In the Western part of the State—where Johnson himself had served in 1776 as Brigadier-General and had raised several thousand men —Otho Holland Williams, a brilliant young officer, was placed in command. Entering the service as Lieutenant, and promoted to the rank of Major after his march to Boston, Williams was wounded at Fort Washington and held captive for more than a year until he was exchanged for a British officer. On March 6, 1778, Williams, still under the age of thirty, but now a Colonel, assured Governor

[16] *Ibid.*, 522.

Johnson [17] that he desired to march to Headquarters as soon as possible but declared the Army "had better be reinforced by a Regiment without a Colonel, than by a Colonel without a Regiment."

Claiming that he had been able to locate scarcely more than a hundred men, Colonel Williams, in his letter to the Governor, said: "The laws for recruiting and equipping men in this State (of themselves deficient) I find very badly executed, and I could wish it in my power to afford some assistance, which I cannot possibly do until I am instructed where to get cash and how to subsist the recruits till they are equipped and fit for duty."

The request from Congress to supplement the Continental forces was presented by Governor Johnson to the General Assembly, which reconvened on March 17; and a bill entitled "An Act to procure troops for the American Army," was promptly introduced. In its preamble, the bill declared that Congress called for "the most vigorous exertions to bring a powerful Army into the field the ensuing campaign" and added that the coöperation of Maryland towards this end was the "indispensable duty of this State." The Act was passed—but all that it did was to authorize the Governor and Council "to continue the recruiting service in the most effectual manner."[18] And so, the problem of raising the quota was simply handed back to the Executive.

Meanwhile, the Legislature was also considering a bill to expedite the purchase of meat and on March 20 adopted a resolution asking Congress for one hundred thousand dollars for the purchase of provisions in the State. The Gov-

[17] Scharf, *Chronicles of Baltimore.*
[18] *Laws of Maryland,* March 1778, Chapter V.

ernor and Council notified President Laurens and the Maryland members of Congress of the Assembly's request, and shortly afterwards an assurance came from Congressman James Forbes that the money would be provided. Before this, however—March 23—the Legislature passed an Act authorizing the Governor and Council to appoint a Purchasing Agent in each County of the State to buy up "fat cattle, salted beef, pork, and bacon" for the Continental Army.[19] Two days later eighteen Agents were appointed.

While the Legislature was considering the plan to facilitate the purchase of meat, General Washington heard that clothing had been collected in immense quantities throughout Maryland and was ready for shipment to Valley Forge. The next task that confronted the Commander-in-Chief was to find Army wagons sufficient to haul the supplies from the Maryland border to the Winter encampment. He accordingly asked Governor Johnson to provide for the transportation through Southern Pennsylvania.

In his request to the Governor, Washington said: [20]

GENERAL WASHINGTON TO GOVERNOR JOHNSON

Head Quarters 21st March, 1778.

Sir

I do myself the honour .to inclose you a representation, made to me by Mr. Chaloner, Dep'y Commissary of Purchases, upon the difficulty under your present law, of procuring Waggons to bring the public stores of Provision collected at the Head of Elk and Middle Town in your State. The State of Pennsylvania has been already exceedingly harrassed in providing teams, as we have drawn our Horses and Waggons almost totally from them since the commencement of this dispute.

[19] *Laws of Maryland,* March 1778, Chapter I.
[20] *Washington Manuscripts,* Library of Congress.

I would therefore wish, that you would lay this matter before your Legislature and endeavour to procure an amendment to the law, whereby a mode may be fallen upon to obtain a sufficient number of Waggons to bring forward the stores at the places above mentioned and in the neighborhood of them. Governor Livingston lately did us the favour to procure a law of the State of Jersey vesting him and the Council with powers to impress any number of Waggons, to supply the Army in cases of great emergency, and I assure you, that it is truly the case now. If we do not establish magazines in camp and near it before our Reinforcements arrive, it will be impossible to subsist our force when collected.

I have to acknowledge the receipt of yours, some little time ago, informing me of the steps you had taken to procure us a supply of Provision. I sincerely thank you, and hope I shall find the same readiness in you to assist us with Carriages. As one of the Gentlemen in the Commissary Department will wait upon you with this, he will inform you of the number wanting at present.

I have the honour to be with great respect and Regard

Your Excelly's Most Ob[t] Serv[t]
G[o] WASHINGTON.

The work of *transporting* supplies, however, was far less difficult than *securing* them. And Governor Johnson believed that, no matter how large was the quantity of stores ready to be hauled to camp, it was unwise to discontinue the search for further supplies. Samuel Hughes, a member of the Legislature, was authorized to proceed to New Orleans, by way of the Ohio and the Mississippi, in quest of clothing and arms. In a letter to the Governor of New Orleans,[21] March 23rd, the Governor of Maryland expressed the hope that, on account of the interruption of commerce with Europe, "a mutually beneficial intercourse might take place between the Subjects of his most Catholic

[21] XVI *Maryland Archives,* 548.

Majesty and those of the States of America," and gave assurance that any contract entered into by Mr. Hughes would be "acknowledged and made good by this State, with a due sense of the obligation."

The Maryland Council also appointed Joshua Johnson —a brother of the Governor—as agent to purchase merchandise in France, Holland and Spain. The Governor's brother had also been recommended on the floor of Congress by Forbes, of Maryland, for appointment as commercial agent of the United States, but Congress decided to delegate the power of selecting the agents to the American Commissioners in France—Benjamin Franklin, Silas Deane, and Arthur Lee.

As April, 1778, drew near, the Tories were assembling again on the Eastern Shore; and, fearing that they might cause even more trouble and delay in military preparations than they had caused during his first Administration one year before, Governor Johnson on April 6th sent a stirring Message to the Legislature recommending that martial law be proclaimed in Somerset County. The Governor's Message follows: [22]

Gentlemen of the General Assembly:

From the Letters received from Worcester and Somerset Counties, which I have laid before you and the Conversations I have had with People from thence as well as from the Insurrections some Time since, I am apprehensive that unless decisive Measures are speedily taken the Balance in Somerset County will be in Favor of our Enemies and Toryism. If that should be the Case and our Friends are left under Apprehension of suffering instantly all the Cruelties which brutal Rage can inflict—and the Enemies of their Country fear nothing but a slow Prosecution for the atrocious Villanies, enter-

[22] XXI *Maryland Archives,* 11.

taining at the same Time the Hope that their Guilt may be shielded by the Forms incident to the Proceedings of Courts—Men's Minds will be influenced by the immediate Evil and the Consequent Influence will probably extend much to the Prejudice of the State.

I cannot therefore but entreat your Advice and Assistance in a Matter which appears to me of so great Magnitude and submit to your Consideration whether it will not be well, immediately to order one hundred or one hundred and fifty of the Militia from some of the other Counties, into Somerset to do Duty there 'til a sufficient Regular Force can be raised for that Service and to proclaim Martial Law in Somerset County and erect a Court Martial competent to the Trial of Spies, Piracies and such of our own People as may be taken in Arms, with a Power of ordering the Execution of the Guilty without waiting for the Assent of any other Authority.

Upon receipt of the Message from the Governor, the Legislature promptly enacted a measure intended to quell the Tories' activities. According to the terms of the Act,[23] the Governor and Council were authorized not only to call out the Militia of Somerset and Caroline Counties and any other Counties that might be "disaffected," but also, whenever necessary, to use the Maryland war ships to cut off communication in the Chesapeake between the Tories and the Enemy. The Act also provided for a Court-martial, with legal authority to disarm any person who failed to take the Oath of Allegiance to the State.

The Legislature also passed a statute authorizing the arrest of any person considered dangerous by the Executive.[24] This Act not only gave the Governor power to cause arrest on suspicion, but also denied to the prisoner the right of *habeas corpus*. The Act declared in its preamble that "in times of imminent danger it is necessary for the safety

---

[23] *Laws of Maryland*, March 1778, Chapter VIII.
[24] *Laws of Maryland*, March 1778, Chapter XIII.

and protection of the State that extraordinary powers be vested in the Governor and Council, and it is at all times necessary that a proper respect and regard be paid to the supreme Executive authority." On one occasion, a man named John Lawrence, who claimed to be a citizen of the State of Pennsylvania, was asked to take the Oath of Allegiance. The man not only refused to do so but also made open threats of violence against Governor Johnson. At a mass meeting, called at Annapolis to discuss the case, the citizens decided that Lawrence would have to leave the City. The war powers of the Governor, however, were not greater than the powers usually given to Executives in times of imminent peril in American History. When Vallandingham, the Copperhead leader in the Civil War, was tried by Court-martial, he contended that he was arrested without due process of law and without warrant from any judicial officer; but his sentence to close confinement during the continuance of the war was approved by General Burnside. President Lincoln's Proclamation of September 24, 1862, declared that all person interfering with the progress of the war or giving aid and comfort to the Rebels should be subject to Court-martial; and the judge of the United States District Court refused to release Vallandingham in *habeas corpus* proceedings, declaring that "the power of the President undoubtedly implies the right to arrest persons who hinder the military operations of the United States."

And so, the patriots in Maryland seemed to have little trouble in keeping the anti-American sentiment in check. The uprisings of the Tories were confined mostly to the peninsula. In the month of April, 1778, Congress received from General Smallwood, stationed at Wilmington, the news of an insurrection in Delaware; and Charles Carroll

of Carrollton, one of the members of Congress, was asked
to notify Governor Johnson regarding the situation. In a
letter from York, April 21,[25] Mr. Carroll requested the
Governor to call out 300 Maryland militiamen to protect
the stores along the Chesapeake.

Johnson did as requested. Likewise he tried to comply
with a number of other requests that came in rapid succession from the members of Congress. Samuel Chase told
how General Howe had sent out from Philadelphia a cart
load of hand-bills, aimed to deceive the American people
by inducing them to relax their efforts "with a prospect of
peace"; and requested Governor Johnson to disclose the
Enemy's scheme by a statement in the newspapers in order
to "remove the baneful effects it may have on the credulous
and weak among the people." [26] Carroll of Carrollton urged
the Governor to "employ some ingenious writer to combat
and expose the perfidiousness of our Enemies," and to rouse
the people from lethargy.[27] Governor Johnson received
copies of the two bills in Parliament, and Lord North's
speech concerning them, offering reconciliation to the
United States; and the Governor undoubtedly agreed with
the opinion of Mr. Carroll that the Administration at London had begun "to see the impracticability of reducing these
States, or of retaining them when reduced, in such a state
of subordination as to be useful to Great Britain," and that
the enlargement of the Continental Army for the ensuing
campaign would hasten the day of Independence.[28] From
Paca, Jenifer, Plater and Henry came a request for five
pieces of heavy cannon to aid General Washington in the

[25] XXI *Maryland Archives*, 49.
[26] *Ibid.*, 44.
[27] *Ibid.*, 49.
[28] *Ibid.*, 55.

defense of North River.[29] And from Richard Henry Lee,
Thomas McKean and William Duer, members of a special
committee of Congress, came a request to use the utmost
vigilance to prevent the Tories on the Eastern Shore from
escaping on board British ships.[30] The Governor and Council replied that the Militia had been powerless to prevent
the desertions on account of the lack of armed vessels, and
asked Congress for a supply of seamen to man the Maryland galleys.[31] Virtually every letter from York, whether
depressing or cheering, contained a plea for succor. In one
letter, dated the third of May,[32] Samuel Chase, after declaring that the Treaties with France, by acknowledging the
independence of the United States, had given the new Government a rank among the Nations of the world, and after
exhorting the patriots to be grateful to God for "this sin-
gular unmerited mark of His favour and protection," in
the same breath requested the Governor to continue his exertions in support of the war and especially to speed up the
campaign for loans of money to the Continent.

As the Spring advanced, conditions continued still further to improve at Valley Forge. The loads of clothing
and victuals were received with delight by the needy soldiers, and Washington, who had breathed the spirit of patience into his soldiers, now enthused them with the desire
to enter upon a new campaign. But when a Council of
War was held on May 8th, it was decided to wait until the
plans of the Enemy were more obvious before taking the
field. "To take the city [Philadelphia] by storm," says
Dr. Sparks, "was impracticable without a vastly superior

[29] Ibid., 74.
[30] Ibid., 89.
[31] Ibid., 106.
[32] Ibid., 64.

force; and equally so to carry it by siege or blockade, strongly fortified as it was by nature and artificial works, and by vessels of war. Militia might be called out, but it was uncertain in what numbers; and, however numerous, they could not be depended on for such an enterprise. In every view of the subject, therefore, weighty objections presented themselves against any scheme of offensive operations." Accordingly, in view of the hazardous situation of the stores along the Chesapeake Bay, General Washington requested Governor Johnson to allow the Maryland Militia to remain for the time being in Maryland. In his communication to Johnson at this time, the Commander-in-Chief said: [33]

GENERAL WASHINGTON TO GOVERNOR JOHNSON

Head Qu^{rs} Valley Forge
11th May, 1778.

Dr Sir

I was some little time past empowered by Congress to call for 5000 Militia from the States of Jersey, Pennsylvania and Maryland. This Resolve was, I believe, occasioned by a report, which has proved groundless, that the Enemy intended suddenly to evacuate Rhode Island, to draw part of their force from New York, and attack this Army, before its expected reinforcements arrived. Finding no immediate occasion for the Militia, I forbore to make the requisitions, except in a very small degree from Jersey and Pennsylvania.

I know it is a very favourite scheme with many not acquainted with the situation of our Magazines and the deranged state of the two capital departments of Commissary and Qu^r Mr Genl which have not yet resumed a proper tone, to draw together a great body of Militia in addition to our Continental force and make an attack upon the Enemy in Philadelphia. However much a meas-

[33] *Washington Manuscripts,* Library of Congress.

ure of this kind is to be wished two capital obstacles render it totally ineligible at present, the want of Provisions (or means of transportation) and the uncertainty, both with respect to time & numbers, of obtaining the Recruits for the Continental Regiments. The new Commissary General is exerting himself, and I hope with the generous aids which the States are giving him, that when grass fed cattle come in, we shall be able to victual a very considerable force, should a fair opportunity offer of making a capital Blow against the Enemy. But till these happen, you will plainly perceive, that it would be fruitless to call out the Militia; it would be consumptive of Public Stores, and disheartening to the People; who, finding nothing done upon their first tour of duty, would perhaps come out very unwillingly when there is real occasion for their services. Abstracted from all these, is a consideration of equal, if not greater magnitude, which is the immense loss suffered by drawing out the farmer and tradesman until the moment of necessity arrives.

I would therefore wish you to hold up an idea that the Services of the Militia may probably be wanted and endeavour to have a plan digested, by which a given number may be drawn and armed, accoutred and ready for the field, upon the shortest possible notice. Something upon the plan of the minute Battalions and Companies formed at the commencement of this war, might answer the end.

I need not point out to you the many advantages that will result from having the Continental Battalions completed and I therefore hope that you will persevere until yours are filled either by recruits or drafts.

I have the honour to be
Sir Your Most Ob^t Ser^t
G^o Washington.

Within a few days, however, there appeared an entirely new aspect of the situation. From intelligence communicated by spies and from various indications, it was suspected that the British were preparing to leave Philadelphia. The Treaties signed at Paris by the three American Commissioners were regarded at London as a declaration of war by France; and the British Ministry saw the necessity of causing a change in the plans of warfare in America. France, prepared for hostilities, dispatched a fleet across the Atlantic with the view of blockading the British squadron in the Delaware.

General Washington, wishing to be strengthened by the regular forces at Wilmington, requested Governor Johnson to relieve General Smallwood by sending forward 500 additional militiamen to guard the stores at Head of Elk. Washington's letter to the Governor follows:[34]

GENERAL WASHINGTON TO GOVERNOR JOHNSON

Head Quarters, Valley Forge,
17th May, 1778.

My Dear Sir

From a number of concurring circumstances, there is reason to believe that the Enemy mean to evacuate Philadelphia.

It is necessary, therefore, to draw together as great a force as can be provided for, with the utmost expedition. But as several of our out-posts covering Magazines and the like, cannot be recalled without a body of Militia to act in their room, I am obliged to request of the neighboring States a reinforcement for this and other purposes. The requisition of Congress extends to 5000 Militia from the Jerseys, Pennsylvania and Maryland.

A large compact body of regulars are wanted, and several valuable intentions to be attended to at the same time. General Smallwood, who lays at Wilmington, covers a quantity of stores at the Head of Elk. If he is withdrawn, the Enemy may destroy our Magazine at that place.

I would imagine that five hundred Militia of your State would be sufficient security, and proper restraint upon the Enemy on that quarter. I would, therefore, beg of you to embody and send forward five hundred of your Militia, equipped, and the most contiguous to the Head of Elk. You may probably find it most convenient to send them by Companies.

The most expeditious way is certainly the best, and the sooner

[34] David Ridgely, *Annals of Annapolis*, 263.

they get to the Head of Elk, the sooner shall I have it in my power to recall the garrison from Wilmington, and complete such a body of Continental troops as may enable me to act according to conjunctures.

I rely upon your particular assistance on this critical occasion, and am,

Dear Sir, with Respect and esteem,

Your Ob^t and very humble Ser^t

G^o WASHINGTON.

When the emergency call for Militia reached Annapolis on May 20, the Governor, with the consent of the Council, ordered out eleven companies, advising the County Lieutenants that Washington had urged compliance with the requisition "with great earnestness" and with reasons "important and decisive." [35] The hope was expressed that the soldiers would march to the Head of Elk "with cheerfulness and alertness," and assurance was given that the guard duty would be of short duration. In order to prevent the possibility of delay, the Governor also ordered Colonel Charles Rumsey, the Cecil County Lieutenant, to collect for the same service an entire battalion, to be discharged "Company after Company, as the other Militia arrive." [36] The Governor's reply to Washington: [37]

GOVERNOR JOHNSON TO GENERAL WASHINGTON

Annapolis 20th May 1778.

Dr Sir

I received your Letter of the 17th within these few Hours. We had before ordered about 300 Militia, as Guards to the Stores at & in the Neighbourhood of the Head of Elk. In Consequence of your

---

[35] XXI *Maryland Archives,* 99.
[36] *Ibid.,* 100.
[37] *Ibid.,* 101.

Letter, Orders are already gone to the Lieuten^t of Cecil to call out a Battalion of that County on the same Service, for three Companies from Baltimore and two from each of the Counties of Kent, Cecil, Queen Ann's & Harford, the Cecil Battalion to be discharged as the Companies arrive. The Orders are larger than your requisition, to prevent any Inconveniencies from the whole Number not being so prompt as desirable. Two Field Pieces such as we have with thirty two Matrosses are also ordered.

Col^o Rumsey of Cecil is directed, as soon as he has 400 Men, to advise Genl Smallwood by Express, who is requested to forward Information to you, to enable you to give such Orders as you may judge proper. I hope the Orders from hence will be executed with Alacrity and your Intentions take Place.

I am Dr Sir

With the greatest Respect, &^{ca}

TH. JOHNSON.

Before the close of May, the Commander-in-Chief had reasons to believe that the British were planning to leave for New York. In a letter to Washington, dated on the 22nd of May, Governor Johnson stated that many Maryland people had asked for permission to enter Philadelphia, but that the Council had refused to recommend such passports except for three women. "We were not satisfied," wrote Johnson,[38] "of the propriety of frequently suffering People to go in especially those who wanted to return again and are unwilling to put the rejection of their Importunities on you; but the Earnestness with which some sollicit and it's being said that such Favors are frequently granted at Head Quarters makes us desirous of knowing whether you think proper that such Applications, when we have no particular suspicions, should be promoted by us and to whom we shall refer then ultimately." It was in reply to

[38] *Washington Manuscripts,* Library of Congress.

this inquiry that the Commander-in-Chief predicted the Continental Army would soon again be in possession of Philadelphia.

Washington sent the desired advice to Johnson on May 29th. "Satisfied that an intercourse with Philadelphia," was the reply from Valley Forge,[39] "would be productive of great disadvantages, I have endeavoured to prevent it, as far as I could; and have not in any instance granted passports for that purpose, but where the parties applying have been recommended, either by some public body or by Gentlemen in whom I had entire confidence; and where the objects of the applications have been materially interesting. Those whom you or the Council shall think proper to recommend, will always meet with a ready indulgence on my part; being convinced, that requests, not founded in necessity or on circumstances of an interesting nature will not be countenanced. The permits must be obtained at Head Quarters, as the situation of the Army might make it expedient on some occasions, to defer granting them for a short time. From the present appearance of things, I flatter myself, we shall not be obliged to use these restrictions much longer, and that we shall be in full possession of the City. Every information leads to this hope, and it is generally imagined that New York, in case of an evacuation will be the first place of rendezvous of the Enemy now in this quarter."

Washington's predictions were correct. The British Ministry had resolved to order a sudden descent upon some of the French possessions in the West Indies; and to aid in executing this project, Sir Henry Clinton, who succeeded Sir William Howe in command of His Majesty's forces, was

[39] XXI *Maryland Archives,* 115.

ordered to send a large detachment of his forces to the South. Clinton, however, decided to mobilize his forces at New York; and as Admiral Howe had already sailed out of the Delaware, Sir Henry prepared to march with the main body of his army through New Jersey. The British finally evacuated Philadelphia on the morning of the 18th of June. Washington followed the Enemy and on June 28th overtook them at Monmouth. It was here, after the blunder of General Lee, that the Maryland troops checked the advance of the red coats and enabled Washington to recover the advantage.

And so, Maryland, during Governor Johnson's second Administration, played a large part in saving Washington's Army from disaster—holding it together at Valley Forge with shipments of clothing and food, until relief came from France in the Spring of 1778.

Furthermore, in response to the call from Congress, the State furnished considerably more than 3,000 regular troops during the year 1778. In addition, many recruits were raised at this time in Maryland for "Pulaski's Legion."

Indeed, at times it was felt that Maryland was doing more than her share. When Lieut.-Col. Samuel Smith arrived in York, in June, 1778, he presented to the Maryland Delegates in Congress a message from the Governor and Council, complaining that the Maryland troops in the Regular Army had received practically no clothing from the Continental Commissary Department. "We have struggled all in our power," wrote the Council,[40] "but are tired of being taken in for a large share of the public expense, which is enhanced too by the Continental officers overbidding us, and providing separately for our own. We request

[40] XXI *Maryland Archives,* 120.

you to obtain an order of the Board of War on the Commissary of Cloathing for 1000 suits of Cloaths, 2000 shirts and 1500 blankets." Carroll of Carrollton and Plater, who referred the complaint to the Board of War, expressed the opinion that the soldiers would never again be exposed to the same distress they had hitherto suffered from want of clothing.[41] And Mr. Chase reported to Governor Johnson from Philadelphia in July as follows: "I do not believe our Army will want Cloathing this year, it appears by the Returns of the Clothier General, that we now have sufficient for 22,000 men." [42]

However, in September, as cool weather began to creep on, Johnson received messages from the Maryland officers that they were unable to secure clothing and blankets from the Continental stores. And so, the Governor and Council, on September 17th, once more wrote to the Maryland members of Congress demanding that the boys from Maryland be given their proper proportion of supplies. "It is high time," wrote Johnson and his Council,[43] "that those, who were clad here in Linen, had cloth and that they all had Blanketts. We yesterday purchased two hundred Blanketts and have about four hundred suits of Cloaths nearly made up, which we shall send to the Maryland Troops, unless you can get them immediately furnished and shall purchase, at any time what further may be necessary, for Policy and Humanity bid us not to rely longer on the Cloathier General, and we shall charge the Cost, let it be what it will, to the Continent."

As General Washington continued to push toward the North in pursuit of the British, the Governor of Maryland

41 *Ibid.,* 126.
42 *Ibid.,* 155.
43 XXI *Maryland Archives,* 206.

had less opportunity to keep in close communication with the Army. However, the General and the Governor tried at all times to keep in touch with each other, as far as the circumstances of war and slow transportation would permit. Their views seemed always to coincide. On August 12th, 1778, Johnson sent a message to Washington, recommending the reënlistment of the "nine months' men"; and several weeks later the Governor received a reply from the General that he approved the plan and had, in fact, suggested the plan to Congress. This message, penned at White Plains, follows: [44]

GENERAL WASHINGTON TO GOVERNOR JOHNSON

Head Quarters, White Plains
29th Augt 1778.

Sir

I am honoured with yours of the 12th instant. I very highly approve of the determination of your Council, to reinlist the nine month's men at this period; if it is left undone, until the time of their service is near expiring, it will be almost impossible to re-engage them. I some time ago, pointed out to Congress the expediency of adopting this measure but as yet have not received their Answer. The Money supplied by the Board of Treasury to the Pay Master General, is barely sufficient to pay the Monthly Abstracts of the Army, and to defray other contingent expenses; I therefore have it not in my power to advance the State Bounty of 40 dollars, out of the Military Chest: Indeed, I should not be authorized to advance it, without the special order of Congress, did the State of the Chest allow it.

I have the honour, &c.,

Go Washington.

General Smallwood labored under the impression for a

[44] *Washington Manuscripts,* Library of Congress.

time that the sum of eight thousand dollars advanced by General Washington was intended to pay the State Bounty of forty dollars to the "nine months' men," but instructions were received later that the money was to be used entirely for Continental Bounties. Accordingly, Smallwood wrote from a camp on October 24th that money was greatly needed to induce reënlistments. "I should be glad of your direction," wrote Smallwood to Governor Johnson,[45] respecting the Inlistment of the nine months men, how far I might engage, and at what time their State Bounty and Cloathing could be delivered, and whether the Officer inlisting them is to receive the allowance of sixteen dollars for each as limited by the late Act of Assembly."

The General Assembly had met in June, but the session was not of great importance. The House of Delegates had adjourned until October 3rd, and the Senate until the first Monday in November. Governor Johnson issued a Proclamation calling both Houses to meet on October 19th.

[45] XXI *Maryland Archives,* 223.

CHAPTER XX

THIRD TERM AS GOVERNOR

"You will hear I am in my way to Georgia; give me leave to take my farewell, and in the mean time to beg for the continuation of your kindness for my Legion. . . . The Capt. Segond who stay behind, is desired to return you a thousand thanks, and let you know all the chagrin, and sorrow I had of having not the honour to see your Excellency."
—*Count Pulaski, Farewell Message to Johnson, April* 10, 1779.

"Cet arrangement est une nouvelle preuve que cet Etat donne de son attachement à l'Alliance et de son zèle pour tout ce qui peut interresser la Cause Commune ainsi que le bonheur et le salut des sujets respectifs. Une conduite semblable ne peut que fortifier de plus en plus la parfaite confiance que toute la conduite de l'Etat dont 'Votre Excellence est le Chef a déjà inspirée à sa Majesté et j'ose m'en rendre le garant auprès de vous."
—*Conrad Alexandre Gérard, French Ambassador at Philadelphia, to Johnson, August* 21, 1779.

"The prudence, assiduity, firmness and integrity with which you have discharged, in times the most critical, the duties of your late important station, have a just claim to our warm acknowledgments and sincerest thanks."
—*Legislature's Address of Thanks to Johnson, November,* 1779.

WHEN the Maryland Legislature reconvened in October, 1778, it became apparent that Thomas Johnson would again receive the unanimous call of the State to continue as Chief Executive. On the 9th of November, Mr. Johnson was reëlected without opposition: and, for the third time accepting the office as a sacred trust, qualified at a joint meeting of the Senate and House of Delegates. On the following day, the members of the Governor's Council—James Brice, Daniel Carroll, Edward Lloyd, James Hindman and Thomas Sim Lee—were reëlected by the General Assembly.

During his third term as Governor, Johnson continued

to receive from the Commander-in-Chief frequent appeals for help. The first of these appeals was an urgent call for 500 men to guard the Convention Troops in their march through the State of Maryland. It appears that Congress, while ratifying the Convention of Saratoga, refused for certain reasons to allow the men who served under General Burgoyne to return to Europe; and General Washington made arrangements to keep them in the South until Congress authorized an exchange. The British captives were taken as far as North River by an escort of Connecticut Militia, to Delaware by Continental soldiers, and to the border of Maryland by Pennsylvania Militia. On November 18, 1778, General Washington—stationed at Fredericksburg, about thirty miles from West Point—sent a request to the Board of War to provide for an adequate guard in Northampton, Berks, Lancaster and York Counties, in Pennsylvania; and to make "the like requisition to Govr Johnson of Maryland for an escort of Militia and supply of Waggons thro the County of Frederick in that State." [1]

Hoping to locate the prisoners in a secure place before the arrival of severest Winter weather, General Washington requested the Board of War to expedite the journey as much as possible. "I could wish," said the Commander-in-Chief, "that no time may be lost in giving the orders lest there should be some unnecessary delay on the Road at this advanced Season." However, the requisition from the War Office did not reach Annapolis until the 4th of December; and Governor Johnson feared that the Convention Troops would reach the Maryland line before the Militia was ready. The Governor forthwith notified Colonels Charles Beatty and Normand Bruce to collect *posthaste* 500 men

[1] XXI *Maryland Archives*, 254.

to guard the marching prisoners.[2] An immediate order was also sent to Baltimore for a shipment to Frederick of muskets, bayonets and cartridges. In this way the Governor quickly started the military machinery in operation, and Burgoyne's men were safely guarded in their journey from Pennsylvania to the Potomac.

In the meanwhile, Sir Henry Clinton had dispatched about two thousand troops to the extreme South—here the patriots were weak and the Tories strong—and on the 29th of December they commenced the conquest of Georgia. After two years of warfare in the North, the British had accomplished practically nothing. And when the people of Maryland on the 30th of December, in accordance with a Proclamation of Governor Johnson, observed "a day of public Thanksgiving and Praise," [3] they realized that while the States were struggling against tremendous odds, yet the positions of the opposing forces at the close of 1778 were virtually the same as in 1776.

Inasmuch as General Clinton remained with the greater portion of his Army in New York, General Washington established Headquarters at Middlebrook, on the West side of the Hudson, and prepared for a Winter of vigil. Quartered with Washington were seven brigades: the remainder of his troops were stationed in a line of small cantonments around New York and were thus prepared to reënforce each other in the event of a sudden incursion of the Enemy. During the cold, gloomy days of January and February, 1779, Governor Johnson received very little intelligence from the Commander-in-Chief. It was a period of idleness in the opposing camps. The French forces under Count D'Estaing had sailed to the West Indies and it was

[2] *Ibid.,* 258.
[3] *Ibid.,* 266.

impossible for General Washington, without a fleet, to attack New York; while Clinton did not dare to attack the Continentals in their strong positions.

When the month of March arrived, General Washington was still watching every movement of the Enemy. In the following letter to Governor Johnson—an example of the extreme caution maintained throughout the stay at Middlebrook—Washington broke his silence at Winter quarters: [4]

GENERAL WASHINGTON TO GOVERNOR JOHNSON

Head Qu^{rs} Middle Brook
1st March 1779

Dr Sir

Sir Henry Clinton, in order to supply the British prisoners at Fort Frederick and Winchester with necessaries and money, has twice requested a passport for a vessel to go with the same to the port of Baltimore. As it is necessary the Prisoners should be supplied, I have granted permission to a Schooner to proceed to Hampton Roads, where the Cargo is to be received into some of the Bay craft, and sent to Alexandria or George Town under the conduct and escort of our own People, and from thence to its place of destination.

I refused the passport to Baltimore, especially as it was twice pressed upon me, as that port did not appear to be the nearest to Frederick's Fort and Winchester, and as it might be made use of for the purpose of exploring a navigation with which they may be in some measure unacquainted.

I have been thus particular, lest under colour of hard weather the vessel should run towards Baltimore.

I have the Honor to be
Your Excellency's most obed^t Servant
G^o WASHINGTON.

The Legislature convened again in March and, on account of the great scarcity of money, authorized the Governor and Council to dispose of any galleys the State had been unable to man. On receiving this authority, Johnson offered to sell the unmanned vessels to the Commonwealth of Virginia, explaining to Governor Patrick Henry that, for the sake of protection in the Chesapeake, Maryland preferred to have the galleys owned by Virginia rather than by private individuals.[5] Authority was also given to the Governor and Council to sell any supplies that were not needed by the Militia: and accordingly a large part of the powder stored at Frederick was offered to Congress for the use of the Continental Army.

At the March session, the Assembly also passed an Act empowering General Washington to settle the disputes of officers concerning their rank in the Maryland Line. In order to assist him in settling the controversies, Washington appointed a committee to make recommendations in this respect. On the 8th of April, the General sent the following report to the Maryland Governor regarding the subject: "I have, agreeable to the powers vested in me, appointed a Board of General Officers to take into consideration and report to me the rank of the Maryland Line. I do not imagine that it will be possible to give general satisfaction, but I am convinced that the Gentlemen who have the Business in hand will pay the strictest attention to the claims of all parties, and give the most disinterested decision. Whatever that decision may be, I hope it may be considered by the State as definitive, and that they will not in future pay any regard to the importunities of those

[5] XXI *Maryland Archives,* 381.

who may be discontented with the arrangement which is about to be made." [6]

At the same time, the Legislature also took occasion to recommend to General Washington that the portion of the German Battalion belonging to the State of Maryland be united with the remnants of Colonel Moses Rawlings's Rifle Corps and incorporated into an individual Maryland regiment. Washington demurred. He pointed out that the German Battalion, in point of fact, had always been "wholly attached to the State of Maryland and considered as her Regiment." The Rifle Corps had dwindled to about seventy-five men; but Congress agreed with General Washington that, unless the remnants were commanded by Colonel Rawlings as a separate unit, surpassing difficulties would result—"particularly in regard to reconciling the ranks of the officers." Washington expressed a "very high opinion of the merits" of Colonel Rawlings and his officers, but he believed it was impracticable to introduce them into the Line. "In short," Washington explained to the Governor, "the difficulties attending the measures recommended are more than can be conceived, and I am convinced by experience that it cannot be carried into execution without totally deranging the German Regiment."

After receiving this information from Middlebrook, Johnson did not undertake to meddle any further into the arrangement of the Army. "I am sincerely sorry," the Governor replied to the Commander on April 23rd, "that we are so often obliged to take up your attention in the very disagreeable Business of adjusting claims and Difficulties amongst our Quota of Troops. I am apprehensive that any

[6] George Washington, *Varick Transcripts*, Library of Congress, Vol. III, p. 32; XXI *Maryland Archives*, 339.

Settlement of Rank will still leave much Dissatisfaction amongst our Officers but I believe our Assembly will never touch the Subject again." [7]

A short time later, General Washington informed the Governor that the arrangement of the Maryland Line had at last been fixed "after a variety of attempts, and much time and labour spent by several Boards of Officers." [8] It should be said, however, in this connection that while the Board of General Officers succeeded in settling a number of puzzling disputes, Washington never undertook to commission any man who had never received an appointment from the Governor. "Filling up Vacancies," the Governor and Council notified Congress, "is a work not the most agreeable to us, but we cannot with Propriety give up that Part of the Civil Power of this State." [9] The Maryland officials were assured, however, that after a brief period in 1778—when a committee from Congress was helping the Commander-in-Chief to reduce the number of commissioned officers—the States resumed their power of appointment. That Washington made no effort to usurp authority in this direction is shown by the fact that he refrained from giving the rank of Lieutenant to four worthy Maryland soldiers —"Gentlemen of merit and well entitled from every consideration to these promotions"—until he had received the sanction of Governor Johnson.

Early in April—when the disputes of rank in the Maryland Line were referred to the Board of General Officers— General Washingon, hearing of Maryland's offer to assist further with the work of raising recruits for the Continental

---

[7] *Papers of George Washington,* Library of Congress.
[8] George Washington, *Varick Transcripts,* Library of Congress, Vol. III, p. 76; XXI *Maryland Archives,* 430.
[9] XXI *Maryland Archives,* 422.

forces, sent off a corps of officers with orders to apply to Governor Johnson for instructions and money. In this connection, the Commander-in-Chief had but one suggestion to make: namely, that the Governor should order the recruiting officers "in the most express manner" not to enlist any British deserter. "These people," Washington declared, "not only debauch our other troops, but are sure to desert again to the Enemy upon the appearance of an offer of pardon, or any the least encouragement, and more than probable carry others with them." [10]

In due time, the recruiting corps, with the drums and fifes, arrived in Annapolis and reported at the offices of the Governor. It can well be imagined that the vigorous Executive, following Washington's request, gave to all the recruiting officers a stern warning that any recruit, if found to be a British deserter, would be summarily dismissed from the American service, and that in such an event the bounty would have to be returned. Most of the officers requested Governor Johnson to allow them extra funds, to cover their expenses while engaged in recruiting in the State. The Governor explained that the State had made no provision in this respect other than the allowance of sixteen dollars for each recruit. He promised, however, that if they would keep an accurate account of their expenditures, he would endeavor to secure a reimbursement for them at the next session of the General Assembly. [11] Johnson reported to General Washington on April 23rd: "Most of the Maryland Officers sent hither on the Recruiting Service have since been with me and received the money they desired." [12]

[10] XXI *Maryland Archives*, 340.
[11] *Ibid.*, 485.
[12] *Papers of George Washington*, Library of Congress.

Among those who returned to Maryland at this time in search of recruits was Colonel Rawlings; and before setting out from Annapolis in the direction of Fort Frederick, he made a request for an extra amount of money to buy provisions for his officers. In this particular case, the Council, regarding the Rifle Corps as a part of Maryland's quota in the Continental Army, advanced the money and charged it to the Continent.

Brigadier-General Casimir Pulaski was also anxious at this time to augment his forces. The corps, which he had organized after distinguishing himself at Brandywine and Germantown, was ordered to Georgia; and fearing that he would lose some of his men by sickness and desertion during the course of the journey, the young Polish nobleman made application at Annapolis on April 10th for permission to secure recruits in the State. So courteously had he been received in Maryland and so grateful was he for the aid of Governor Johnson that he was eager to call his corps the "Maryland Legion."

On learning that Mr. Johnson was out of town, Count Pulaski directed one of his captains—the Chevalier De Segond de la Plaine—to remain in Maryland for a short time to try to secure additional men; and, after leaving a personal message of farewell for Governor Johnson, hurried on his way to Georgia. "You will hear," Pulaski wrote before setting out from Annapolis, "I am in my way to Georgia; give me leave to take my farewell, and in the mean time to beg for the continuation of your kindness for my Legion. I left a Request to the Council on that purpose. I flatter myself you will favour me with the influence you have among the Gentlemen of that Board. The Capt.

Segond who stay behind, is desired to return you thousand thanks, and let you know all the chagrin and sorrow I had of having not the honour to see your Excellency." [13]

However, when Captain De Segond applied shortly afterwards for the permission to recruit, the Governor and Council informed him that the Legislature, in order to fill the quota of Continental troops, had passed an Act prohibiting further enlistments in the State except for the regular Maryland battalions. Upon being informed of this Act of Assembly, the Chevalier decided to leave without delay for the South. But the Chevalier and the final contingent of Pulaski's soldiers, as they sailed down the Chesapeake early in May, 1779, retained none but the kindest feelings for the Governor and the people of Maryland. And Mr. Johnson performed his final service for the Legion when, at Captain De Segond's request, he urged the Governor of Virginia to provide the soldiers with necessary supplies while on their way to Georgia. [14] Under Brigadier-General Pulaski, the Legion won distinction in the Southern theater of war; but Fate prevented the young nobleman from ever returning to the soil of Maryland, for when the Legion joined with the forces of General Benjamin Lincoln and Count D'Estaing in the unsuccessful attempt to retake Savannah, Pulaski was mortally wounded.

While the British were overrunning Georgia, Sir Henry Clinton, still beleaguered in New York, was sending out detachments by sea with instructions to burn and plunder along the coast. Having met with little success in honorable warfare, the British were descending to methods of

[13] XXI *Maryland Archives,* 341.
[14] *Ibid.,* 370.

brutality and pillage. It was during his second Administration that Governor Johnson heard the appalling news of the Wyoming massacre, and, at the time of his third election, the tragedy at Cherry Valley. It was also about this time that the Governor received word of the expeditions of plunder along the coast of Connecticut, and doubtless he suspected that the British were doing everything in their power to break the spirit of the Americans.

While the warfare of the British, aided by the savage Indians, had degenerated into "a series of marauding expeditions unworthy of civilized soldiers," [15] the spirit of the Americans, if anything, was strengthened. Surely in Maryland the Governor found less trouble from the Tories in 1779 than he did in 1777 and 1778. The only internal disturbance of any consequence in the State during Johnson's third Administration—and similar troubles broke out in Philadelphia and other parts of the country—came from a limited number of people who maintained that a number of rich men had engrossed large quantities of grain and were charging exorbitant prices. Mr. Johnson did not approve of profiteering. Those in affluence, said he, ought to be "influenced by the dictates of Humanity," and should not "drive the necessitous to despair." On the contrary, the Governor, discounting the reports, refused to view the threats of violence with alarm. The Courts, he thought, were "fully sufficient to punish the past" and "a little moderation in those who have to spare" would prevent any irregularity in the future.[16] However, in order that there would be no excuse for any further disturbance of the peace, the Governor, with the advice of the Council, issued a

---

[15] Fiske, *The American Revolution*, Vol. II, 109.
[16] XXI *Maryland Archives*, 384.

Proclamation on May 11, 1779, warning all persons in the State against "raising or joining in any riotous assembly or proceeding" and giving notice that by "such unwarrantable conduct" they subjected themselves to the full penalty of the law.

General Clinton was also disappointed in the hope that his marauding expeditions along the coast would be of military value. He hoped that General Washington would send out detachments to protect defenseless towns along the coast, and thus scatter and weaken the Continental forces. But the American Commander foresaw that it was his duty to keep his Army united and to maintain his vigil around New York. He applied to Congress for heavy cannon for the further defense of North River, and Congress in turn appealed to Governor Johnson for as many cannon as the State was able to spare in the emergency. The Legislature had never granted authority to the Governor and Council to dispose of cannon belonging to the State, but in view of the urgent call from Congress, Johnson recommended that ten of the "eighteen-pounders" be delivered at once to the Commander-in-Chief. When the Legislature reconvened, the Governor told frankly why the cannon had been sent out of the State, asked for approval of his action, and explained that if the Legislature preferred not to sell the cannon to the Continent, they would be promptly returned to the State.[17]

Meanwhile, Sir Henry Clinton, not content with his plunder along the shores of Connecticut and New Jersey, determined to send out another detachment to destroy property and terrorize the inhabitants in another section of the country; and a force of approximately 2,500 British

[17] *Ibid.,* 490.

and Hessians embarked at New York, May 5th, on the new expedition. When news reached United States Headquarters that the vessels—about 25 square-rigged men-of-war and a number of sloops and schooners—had set sail and were steering in a Southern direction, General Washington suspected that they were headed for a point some distance down the coast—perhaps as far South as the Chesapeake.

General Washington immediately apprised Congress of the new movement of the Enemy, and the members of Congress decided to warn the States which were in apparent danger of attack. The note of warning to Maryland—signed by John Jay, President of the Congress—was received by Governor Johnson on Sunday, May 16th, 1779. Like lightning from a peaceful sky, the message startled old Annapolis from her Sabbath tranquillity. Quick as a flash, Johnson laid his plans for defense. He knew that the State was in imminent peril and he asked his Council to hold a special Sunday meeting. Once before—upwards of two years ago—the British had sailed up the Chesapeake; but, so eager were they at that time to press on towards Philadelphia, that they did not disembark until they reached Elk River; and Annapolis and Baltimore were unmolested. But how well did the Governor and Council remember the day when Admiral Howe's fleet appeared in view; how weak and defenseless they felt when confronted by the soldiers of the King; and how it was decided to make no effort to defend the Capital! But the plan of warfare had been changed. The Governor now feared that the British would sail up the Chesapeake, disembark at the Severn, burn the State House, and then proceed to Baltimore. Thousands of Maryland soldiers were in New Jersey with General Washington: the only home defense was the Maryland Militia. Without waiting for morning, Johnson, with the sanction of the Council, issued orders to General Andrew Buchanan, of Baltimore County, and Colonel Richard Dallam, of Harford County, to assemble the Militia and to be ready to march at a moment's warning.[18]

On Monday morning, news reached the Governor that the Enemy, instead of proceeding up the Bay, had landed at Portsmouth, Virginia. It was now feared that the invaders would make depredations along the shores of Southern Maryland; and a part of the Anne Arundel Militia was requested to remain at home to defend the plantations along the water, and the remainder was ordered to Annapolis. The Governor also notified the Militia of Calvert, Charles and St. Mary's and the Counties of the Eastern Shore to be prepared for any emergency.[19] Even the Frederick Militia —located 50 miles away, and the only protection of the frontier against the Indians—was ordered to be in readiness to reënforce General Buchanan.

As a further precaution, Governor Johnson ordered the records of the State to be removed from Annapolis to places of greater security. The money and papers of the Continental Loan Office, the Treasury, and the Office for Emitting Bills of Credit were stored at the home of Mr. Henry Ridgely at Elk Ridge; while the other records—those of the Courts, the Commissaries, the Land Office, the Auditor General, and the Council—were taken to Upper Marlboro.

Upon landing in Virginia, the British acted "with cruelties worthy of a mediaeval freebooter." [20]   In describing the destruction of Portsmouth and Norfolk by the British

[18] *Ibid.*, 394.
[19] *Ibid.*, 397.
[20] Fiske, *The American Revolution*, Vol. II, 110.

marauders, John Fiske says: "Every house was burned to the ground, many unarmed citizens were murdered, and delicate ladies were abandoned to the diabolical passions of a brutal soldiery." The reports that came from Virginia spread consternation in Annapolis. Mr. Johnson could scarcely believe they were true. After destroying property to a vast amount and terrifying the people in Virginia, it was reported that a band of Hessians and Tories, commanded by General Knyphausen, and supplemented by Negroes, were heading Northward.

Governor Johnson decided to turn to Congress for help. "It is conjectured in Virginia," he wrote Congress, "that they design to visit this Place [Annapolis] and Baltimore as soon as the work is done or they are drove off in Virginia. We imagine the Head of Elk is as much an Object as either Baltimore or Annapolis." [21] Pointing to the large quantity of Continental stores at the Head of Elk, the Governor continued: "In our situation, where nothing is wanted in all probability to secure us against 2500 men but Arms, we cannot but remember how we stripped ourselves of our Arms for the Support of the Common Cause and the little Attention that has been paid to our Request to return them; it may be too late for this Occasion or perhaps not. If it is possible to get a Return of our Arms or any of them, *pray do so and send them to the Head of Elk with all Expedition.*" At that time the only muskets to be found in Philadelphia were in poor condition, and Congress ordered the Board of War to repair about six hundred and rush them to the Head of Elk.

It was also decided by the Governor and Council to request General Washington to give to Mordecai Gist, now

[21] XXI *Maryland Archives,* 405.

Brigadier-General, a temporary release from the Continental Army to enable him to take command of the Maryland Militia during the emergency. "Could not Gen¹ Gist be spared from Camp?" the Governor inquired. "Our Militia have Confidence in him, he would be very useful. He would lie in his own Neighborhood, acquainted with every Man and every Foot of Ground, if you can, send him to us." On Sunday morning, May 23, a Continental rider sped away from Philadelphia in the direction of Headquarters in New Jersey; he carried the petition from the Governor and also a recommendation from the Maryland Congressmen that Brigadier-General Gist be allowed to return to Maryland—together with any other officers and troops that could be spared from the Continental Army.

After two days of travel on his horse in New Jersey, the messenger arrived on Monday night at the Headquarters of General Washington. At that time, the Commander-in-Chief was in need of the services of Brigadier-General Gist; but the great Virginian, mindful of the many important services rendered by Johnson in support of the Continental Army, decided to grant his request. "In compliance with the wishes of His Excellency the Governor, which you have been pleased to communicate," Washington replied on May 25th,[22] "I have requested General Gist to repair to Maryland as soon as he can, tho his service with the Army is now material, and from the train of Intelligence I have received from New York for some days past, it may become still more essential. I am sorry that I cannot spare any officers besides him. And as to a detachment of troops, I have to lament with you, that the circumstances of the Army will not admit of any; and what is yet more

[22] *Ibid.*, 419.

painful, they would not—even if events (in the Chesapeake) of a more pressing nature than any that have arisen,
were to take place—if the Enemy should continue their
present force at New York and its dependencies."

Washington ordered Gist to "proceed forthwith to Baltimore, apply to the Governor and concert with him the
measures necessary to be taken on the occasion." [23] Reaching
Baltimore on June 1st, the Brigadier-General sent to Annapolis an express announcing that he was at the disposal of
the Executive. He ventured a recommendation—endorsed
by General Washington—that beacons be erected on prominent heights throughout the State to serve as signals of
alarm. But General Buchanan had already provided for
signals around the countryside to aid in collecting the Militia in the event of attack. On the following morning, Gist,
in another letter to the Governor, pointed to the defenseless situation of Baltimore and recommended that a certain
number of Militia be retained to garrison the post, so that
the civil population would not be helpless if the British
arrived. But, as Johnson informed him, the force assigned
to Baltimore was all that could be kept there under the
circumstances.

Then came a joyous surprise! The message from Governor Patrick Henry—the British had left the Chesapeake!

Naturally, the tidings from Virginia brought great relief to the people of Maryland. Immediately—June 3,
1779—Governor Johnson and his Council ordered the discharge of the Militia. Likewise, Brigadier-General Gist
was permitted to return to the Headquarters of General
Washington. "We are very much obliged by your promptitude to repair hither on this occasion," Gist was advised

[23] *Ibid.*, 426.

by the Governor and Council, "and are very glad that you are so soon at liberty to return."[24]

And, so, the marauders decided to sail back to New York without attempting to plunder the soil of Maryland. And it was well for them that they did. For the people of Maryland, under the stirring leadership of Governor Johnson, were thoroughly aroused and ready to repel the invaders from the State.

An indication of the tense excitement that prevailed in the Chesapeake at the time the Maryland Militia awaited the Enemy is shown by an incident which led to a stirring complaint from the Government of France. While the Marylanders were alert for the slightest warning, two merchant vessels flying the French flag appeared in the Bay. At first the ships were supposed to be British men-of-war. After they approached the fort and were preparing to dock at Baltimore, a Maryland galley, trailing close behind, fired on one of the vessels and killed a French sailor. The French were incensed—and justly so. The Captain of the French ship, immediately upon landing ashore, apprised the Chevalier d'Anmours, Consul of France at Baltimore, of the outrage.

The Chevalier d'Anmours had been fulfilling ambassadorial as well as consular duties. Earlier in the Spring, when a French soldier, who held the rank of Captain in a Continental regiment, was arrested for fighting with a hostler, the Consul appealed to Governor Johnson to order a release so that the officer could return to the Army of the United States, explaining at the same time that the Frenchman had been insulted "in the most provoking manner" by the hostler, attacked by a large crowd and then sent to

---

[24] XXI *Maryland Archives*, 440.

jail. But this occurrence appeared insignificant when compared with the unjustifiable killing of a Frenchman. The late affair, M. d'Anmours believed, was not only a serious crime in itself but also a flagrant offense against the French Nation. Asking for redress on behalf of the Government of France, the Consul sent the following message on June 8, 1779, to the Governor of Maryland:

"A killed man whose head was carried away by the shot, is but an aggravation of the offense offered to his most Christian Majesty's service and flag, for which I ask satisfaction which I expect as well from your Justice as from the atrocity of the fact considered in itself. At my request the Commanding officer (for the Captain was not on board at that time) was immediately apprehended and sent to Jail. He pleaded the want of a salute which he required from her. In supposing even that this salute was due by his Majesty's subjects to *ships of war,* which I can never acknowledge till I have orders to do so, yet it could not be understood to *ships armed by merchants.* I repeat it, Sir. Your Justice, the Laws of Nations of which this is a capital breach, the sincerity of the Alliance that unites France and America, makes me hope for a satisfaction, which his most Christian Majesty has a right to expect, not only from all these motives; but also from the magnanimity with which the Americans are treated when in the ports of France." [25]

On June 10, 1779, Governor Johnson discussed the complaint with the members of his Council and returned the following reply:

"The galley belonging to this State is fitted out, in great part, at the expence of it and for the sole purpose of protecting the trade to and from this Bay, the efforts of the merchants in Baltimore were in aid of ours; the principal officers were, by our permission, proposed by them and approved and commissioned by us, as the officers of this State: they were so on the former cruise.

[25] *Ibid.,* 447.

"No instructions have been given by this Government for the conduct of its officers or subjects, towards the *ships of war* of his most Christian Majesty, or the *private ships* of his subjects; these facts, Sir, being generally known, the necessary inference must be, as the truth really is, that any such event as you complain of, was as unexpected to us as yourself, so that nothing of this accident can possibly be imputed to the Government. Considering this fact simply in the light you view it—as an unjustifiable firing of a *private vessel* on a *private vessel* of the subjects of his most Christian Majesty, and, if it was added, that it was done with the intention of insult and injury —nothing in our power remains undone since the officer who commanded on board, is committed to Jail and is in a course of legal prosecution.

"Whether the *private ships* of either Nation are to make any acknowledgment of respect to the *ships of war* of the other, on their occasionally meeting with each other in the parts of the other Power, is a matter out of our way to determine on; if at all, we imagine that between Independent Powers, they ought to be mutual, not acknowledgments of superiority but of respect only. The Supreme Powers, of the two Nations, we apprehend, are only competent to regulate where it may be demanded and, if it might tend in any degree to promote the Common Interests of the two Countries, we wish it done.

"It has hitherto been our constant endeavour to promote and confirm a good understanding between the two Countries and we flatter ourselves, that you'll do us the justice to believe we shall cheerfully embrace every opportunity to evince with what sincerity we wish to continue the harmony and extend the confidence now happily subsisting." [26]

In his expression of this opinion Governor Johnson was straightforward and firm. He openly admitted that the Maryland vessel was a regularly commissioned war ship of the State, but he unhesitatingly took the position that the Government of Maryland was free from any hostile

[26] *Ibid.*, 449.

intent towards France and therefore no wrongdoing could be charged against the State.

There is no question that Governor Johnson's statement of foreign policy is fundamentally sound. Dr. John H. Latané makes the following comment in this connection:

"The status of American state navies during the Revolution may have been somewhat uncertain, and the French vessel may have resented being examined, if she was signalled to for this purpose, by what she regarded as a merchant ship. There is no doubt now—and there was no question at that time—of the right of a war ship to stop and examine a foreign merchant vessel either on the high seas or within the territorial waters of the war vessel. Although it is not so stated, I presume that the Maryland vessel signalled to the French vessel for the purpose of examining her papers before firing the fatal shot. If, on the other hand, the shot was fired without warning, it was an unpardonable breach of all the recognized methods of procedure. In either case, the Governor of Maryland did all that could be expected of him when he officially repudiated the act, and the Government of Maryland did all that could reasonably be expected of it in committing the officer who commanded the ship to jail and instituting legal proceedings against him."

While the Governor's letter to Consul d'Anmours was plain and uncompromising, containing no apology from the State, yet the reply is softened in some degree by the concluding paragraph, which pleads for a continuation of friendly relations between France and America. And such a feeling was, of course, the sincere hope of Governor Johnson. At this very time, when the same Consul sought the release of a French subject, who had been acquitted of murder but who was still confined for the fees of prosecution— at that time a person indicted for a crime was held for costs even though acquitted—the Governor agreed to order the prisoner's release to prevent the possibility of any "uneasiness" between the two countries.

Another instance of Governor Johnson's effort at this time to coöperate with France is seen in his offer to assist in preventing the desertion of sailors from French merchant vessels. After receiving their salaries, many of these sailors took "French leave" at Baltimore and stole away, either to Philadelphia or to the South. The Consul asked the Governor to order all French sailors to be held at the ferries unless proper passports could be shown. Johnson, in reply, explained that the Legislature had not given him any such Executive power; and that the Government could neither command nor prohibit where the General Laws were deficient. However, the Governor and Council, anxious to prevent further violations of contracts, *requested* the ferry-keepers at Patapsco and Susquehanna to allow no French sailors to pass the ferries until after the closest examination, explaining that while the requests were not compulsory it was hoped they would "not be altogether without effect."

So, the frank and able manner in which Thomas Johnson dealt with international questions made him, in the end, popular both with his own countrymen and with the representatives of foreign Powers. That Johnson's treatment of international problems was approved and appreciated at home is attested by the fact that later on, as we shall see, he was urged by George Washington, as President of the United States, to accept the portfolio of Secretary of State.

And that Johnson's foreign policy was accepted with entire satisfaction by France is shown by the signed statement of Conrad Alexandre Gérard, Ambassador from France. M. Gérard had taken part in the negotiations of

the Treaties of Alliance and Commerce and, at the time
of the arrival of Count D'Estaing, had come as the first
duly accredited plenipotentiary of France to the United
States. After the Legislature forbade the exportation of
foodstuffs unless by authority of the Governor and Council, Ambassador Gérard, upon asking his Excellency for
permission to export a supply of salted meat and flour from
Maryland to the Martinique, included the following complimentary statement:

"This arrangement is a new proof which this State gives of her
attachment to the Alliance and of her zeal for all which can interest
the Common Cause; as, for instance, the happiness and the safety
of their respective subjects. A like behavior can only fortify more
and more the perfect confidence which the entire conduct of the
State, of which your Excellency is the Chief, has already inspired in
his Majesty, and I dare surrender myself as guarantor in your
behalf." [27]

In the meantime—while Governor Johnson was preparing for the marauders and in other ways grappling with
problems at home—General Washington was still entrenched at Middlebrook, watching every movement of
General Clinton with infinite patience and fortitude. The
American Commander-in-Chief, judging from the debates
in Parliament, felt that the British would send additional
troops to prosecute the war, thus giving the Enemy a superiority very dangerous to the safety of America. Moreover, while the British were strengthening, the Americans
were weakening. To Governor Johnson and other State
Executives, General Washington pointed out "the rapid
decline of our currency, the general temper of the times,

[27] *Ibid.*, 500.

the disaffection of a great part of the people, the lethargy that overspreads the rest, the increasing danger to the Southern States." All in all, Washington felt that the situation of affairs was "peculiarly critical." He believed it his duty to urge the several States to make "immediate and decisive exertions" to strengthen the Continental Army. "Our battalions," declared Washington, "are exceedingly reduced, not only from the natural decay incident to the best composed armies; but from the expiration of the term of service for which a large proportion of the men were engaged. . . . Not far short of one third of our whole force must be detached on a service undertaken by the direction of Congress and essential in itself. I shall only say of what remains, that when it is compared with the force of the Enemy now actually at New York and Rhode Island— with the addition of the succours, they will in all probability receive from England—at the lowest computation it will be found to justify very serious apprehensions and to demand the zealous attention of the different Legislatures." [28]

Clothing was another great need in the American Army. And at the time of his appeal for reënforcements Washington also urged the appointment of the State Clothier, as recommended by Congress. "I know not," said Washington, "what instructions may have been given relative to these appointments; but, if the matter now rests with the particular States, I take the liberty to press their execution without loss of time. The Service suffers amazingly from the disorder in this Department, and the regulations for it

[28] George Washington, *Varick Transcripts*, Library of Congress, Vol. III, p. 72; XXI *Maryland Archives*, 411.

cannot be too soon carried into effect." Johnson, however, had already complied with the request of Congress by appointing John Randall the Clothier for Maryland.

The Maryland Legislature had adjourned for the Summer; but, in view of the urgent appeal of the Commander-in-Chief for reënforcements and for a further supply of clothing, Governor Johnson felt that it was necessary to hold a special session. During June, however, the farmers of Maryland were busy with harvest; and so, while proclaiming that on account of "affairs of high importance and concern," a meeting of the General Assembly was required "as soon as well may be," [29] the Governor suggested that the session convene on the 15th of July.

Late in June, Mr. Johnson made a hurried trip to Frederick, where he ascertained the supply of clothing, provisions and ammunition, secured first-hand information regarding the wheat crop and inquired about the strength of the Militia. It was one of the few occasions when Mr. Johnson was away from Annapolis during his service of nearly three years as Governor.

Hastening back to the Capital about the first of July, the Governor resumed his daily sessions with the Council. On July 9, 1779, notice was sent to General Washington that a call had been issued for the Assembly. "We have to regret," the Governor and Council lamented to the Commander-in-Chief, "that Congress did not earlier make their Requisition on the States to fill up their Quotas of Troops and that Cloathing was not—we suppose could not be—sent with the Recruiting Officers." [30]

29 XXI *Maryland Archives,* 457.
30 *Ibid.,* 469.

It was not until July 22nd that the Legislature was able to secure a quorum. But when it did convene it speedily enacted measures in aid of the Common Cause. One Act was passed to prevent more effectually the practice of forestalling and engrossing within the State. Another Act prohibited the exportation of foodstuffs—"wheat, flour, rye, Indian corn, rice, bread, beef, pork, bacon, live stock, peas, beans, oats and other victual." Another authorized the Governor and Council to appoint subscription agents throughout the State to borrow twenty millions of dollars on the faith of the United States, in furtherance of the requisition of Congress dated June 29th. And still another authorized the Governor and Council, by means of heavier taxation, to pay 4,680,000 dollars more into the Continental Treasury. These and other measures were passed rather expeditiously, for after three weeks the members were ready to adjourn and return to their homes.

The reorganization in the Clothing Department and the appointment of State Clothiers failed to produce the results expected by General Washington. In August, the Commander-in-Chief—stationed now at West Point—sent out another circular to the several States, asserting that the supplies from the Clothiers would probably "fall far short" and pleading for further exertions in this direction. "From the best information I have been able to obtain," predicted the Commander-in-Chief, "I fear there is but too much reason to apprehend, that unless the respective States interpose with their exertions, our supplies of this essential article [clothing] will be very deficient; and that the Troops may again experience on this account, a part of those distresses, which were so severely and injuriously felt in past stages of the war, and which a regard to the interests of the States as well as to the duties of Humanity should prevent, if it be practicable." [31]

Still another urgent appeal from General Washington, which came to Annapolis during Governor Johnson's third Administration, was an appeal for flour. Early in the Spring of 1779, Johnson made an effort to ascertain the quantity of flour expected from the State of Maryland; and Gouverneur Morris, who had been delegated by Congress to superintend the Commissary and Quartermaster Departments, replied that about 10,000 barrels were desired. Through the Maryland members of Congress, Governor Johnson secured 500,000 dollars—all that could be spared by the Continent at that time—and an order for an additional sum of 800,000 dollars for the purpose. [32] And immediately the work of buying flour for the Army went forward in Maryland with unusual dispatch.

So eager, indeed, were the purchasers to secure results that in some instances they paid entirely too much for the flour. But the Maryland Governor, hoping above all else to secure the necessary quantity, explained to Congressman Morris why the price had increased. One of the purchasers in the whirlwind campaign found that he had bought flour that was already in Philadelphia; this led to sharp accusations. Suspicions of graft were also cast upon Colonel Henry Hollingsworth, Deputy Quartermaster General at the Head of Elk, and his brother, who was acting as one of the purchasing agents. Governor Johnson was too busy to harbor suspicions. He expressed regret to Colonel Hollingsworth that "any man should be brought into difficulties by his promptitude to serve the public" and he gave

[31] George Washington, *Varick Transcripts,* Library of Congress, Vol. III, p. 118; XXI *Maryland Archives,* 504.
[32] XXI *Maryland Archives,* 338.

the Colonel permission to use any of his [the Governor's] letters to clear up the suspicion. "You are as welcome as justifiable in making use of any thing from me," wrote the Governor, "to clear up the Truth and serve the purposes of Justice; I shall take the same freedom, whenever necessary, with any letters in my power, without thinking I do amiss." [33]

During July and August, 1779, the work of purchasing flour in Maryland progressed more quietly. In August, Colonel Ephraim Blaine was appointed Deputy Commissary General for the Middle Department of the Army, and he in turn appointed Assistant Deputy Commissaries in Maryland, with the sanction of the Governor. On September 7th, Governor Johnson received another circular from General Washington, telling of alarming apprehensions by reason of the want of flour for the American troops and entreating extraordinary exertions for a supply.[34] On the following day, the Governor and Council issued orders for the Assistant Deputy Commissaries to proceed with their work, regardless of whether orders had already been received from Colonel Blaine. In the event Colonel Blaine demanded an explanation, the Council declared that the Executive order would excuse them. "If not," said the Council, "we dare say General Washington's letter will." [35]

Colonel Blaine arrived in Annapolis on September 9th and conferred with the Governor and Council. After his visit, the following report was sent to General Washington regarding the situation: "We have no State Magazine and

[33] *Ibid.*, 434.
[34] George Washington, *Varick Transcripts,* Library of Congress, Vol. III, p. 124.
[35] XXI *Maryland Archives,* 516.

in a great part of our country the crop has been very bad, however we hope that enough may be soon got for the temporary subsistance of the Army." [36]

Finally, in October, 1779, as discouragement grew greater among the patriots at West Point, General Washington once more sent out from Headquarters an appeal to expedite all remaining supplies of flour. The appeal was forwarded from Philadelphia to Governor Johnson by John Jay, President of Congress. "The wheat of Maryland being in more forwardness for grinding than any other," wrote the Commander-in-Chief to President Jay, "I could wish that Governor Johnson may be requested to push the purchases within that State. The Commissary General gives the fullest encouragement on the score of beef, but of flour he continues to express his fears." [37]

Governor Johnson's third term was now rapidly drawing to a close. And Johnson knew that his third term was to be his last. For the Constitution of Maryland provided: "That the Governor shall not continue in that office longer than three years successively." [38] Before the end of Summer, Johnson was already awaiting, with a considerable measure of relief, the day of his retirement and a much-needed rest. In August, for illustration, when it appeared expedient to give the Governor power to remove incompetent officers in the Militia, Johnson offered to secure this authority for his successor. "As I am circumstanced I may do it with propriety," he said, "and therefore intend to represent to the Assembly at the next session, the necessity, as it appears to me, of giving the *future* Governor and

[36] *Ibid.*, 520.
[37] *Ibid.*, 548.
[38] Constitution of 1776, Article XXXI.

Council a power of issuing new commissions, where the public service might be promoted by it." [39]

During the months of September and October, 1779, Mr. Johnson continued, however, faithfully at his post. He gave directions to the Annapolis Company of Matrosses, commanded by Captain Edward Gale, to march to the Headquarters of General Washington; [40] from General Smallwood and General Gist he secured detailed information regarding the troops in the two Maryland brigades; [41] he called the Militia together again to guard the British prisoners ordered by the Board of War from Philadelphia to Fort Frederick; [42] worked indefatigably until the close of his Administration to secure further supplies of flour; [43] and continued to coöperate whole-heartedly with Mr. Randall, the State Clothier, to secure additional supplies for the Continental Army. [44]

As Winter approached, bringing again to mind the terrible sufferings at Valley Forge, the Governor and his Council took every means possible promptly to obtain adequate supplies—waistcoats, overalls, hats, shoes, stockings and blankets. The State, for example, owned a supply of leather sufficient to make upwards of 6,000 pairs of shoes; and it was hoped to have about 3,000 pairs ready for shipment by Christmas. In order to expedite the work, General Smallwood was requested to release a dozen shoemakers from his brigade so they could make shoes in Maryland all during the Winter for the troops. [45]

Near the close of his Administration, Governor Johnson received from Major-General Frederick William Au-

[39] XXI *Maryland Archives*, 504.
[40] *Ibid.*, 527.
[41] *Ibid.*, 532.
[42] *Ibid.*, 520.
[43] *Ibid.*, 564.
[44] *Ibid.*, 556.
[45] *Ibid.*, 536.

gustus Henry Ferdinand von Steuben a letter urging the further strengthening of the Maryland regiments. On being appointed Major-General, Baron von Steuben had established a system of discipline for the American troops which was of great value to the Army. In his message to the Governor, the German baron pointed to the weakened condition of the Maryland troops and showed the wisdom of beginning at once to appeal for recruits for the campaign of 1780. General von Steuben also promised that if the Governor would select a rendezvous, officers would be sent from Headquarters to exercise and train the recruits throughout the Winter.[46]

But, after nearly three years of faithful application to the duties of Chief Executive, Mr. Johnson was now ready to turn the work of the office over to the incoming Governor. On November 8, 1779, the General Assembly, prohibited by Constitutional restriction from reëlecting Governor Johnson, selected Thomas Sim Lee as the second Governor of Maryland. Mr. Johnson was now prepared to move to Frederick, where his brothers had engaged in business on an extensive scale, and where he could rest—for a while, at least—many miles away from the exciting scenes around the State House.

The country was still in a critical condition. But just as Governor Johnson was ready to relinquish his official duties at Annapolis and step down to private life, he was given a modicum of relief by Congressman Jenifer, who wrote from Philadelphia [47] that some of the Indian tribes of the Six Nations had decided to stop their outrages on the frontier and were suing for peace; that Stony Point

[46] *Ibid.*, 536.
[47] *Ibid.*, 566.

and Verplanck's Point, situated on opposite sides of the Hudson, had been evacuated by the British; and that the forces of Count D'Estaing, in coöperation with the patriots under General Lincoln, were making a valiant effort to recapture Savannah.

CHAPTER **XXI**

A YEAR IN RETIREMENT

"Relying on this, your ruling passion, the love of your country, we have the best founded hope that you will not suffer to remain long inactive, in the retirement of private life, those abilities which have often been so serviceable to the State, and of which it never, than at the present time, stood in greater need."

—Address of Legislature to Johnson, November, 1779.

"I hope whether I remain in the calm walk of private life—the most agreeable to my own inclination—or should fill a public station, I shall continue to the last, to wish and endeavour to promote her [my country's] happiness and prosperity."

—Johnson's Reply to the Legislature, February, 1780.

THROUGHOUT his exciting Administration as Governor of Maryland—perhaps even as he marched his soldiers to the camp of General Washington in New Jersey—Thomas Johnson yearned for the day when he might live under his own roof in tranquillity, free from the cares of state, and enjoy more leisure with his wife and growing children. Ever since the time of his marriage to Ann Jennings in 1766, he had been called upon by the people to take the lead in important positions; and now after fourteen stormy years, during which he served as Assemblyman, member of the Continental Congress, Brigadier-General of the Maryland Militia, and Governor, he was eager for a period of rest.

And so, even before the selection of his successor, Governor Johnson had cleaned his desk, had delivered to the Legislature the official papers which still remained in his

possession, and was eagerly awaiting the hour of his retirement. Fortunately he did not have long to wait. On
November 12, 1779, Governor Lee was installed; and now,
at last, Johnson was a private citizen.

His official duties completed, Mr. Johnson left at once
for Frederick County, where he had already decided to make
his permanent home. Impressed, as he was, with its vast
resources, he had come to regard Frederick County, where
he had an interest in thousands of acres, as his home, even
though he had been compelled to reside in Annapolis during
his tenure as Governor.

Moreover, the remarkable enterprise of the county seat,
Frederick Town, fired Johnson's energy and ambition. By
the time of the Revolution, this bustling inland town had
grown to a place of about 2,000 inhabitants. According
to one traveler of the day, these people "abounded in provisions and all the necessaries of life."[1] Comparing it
with other American settlements, the visitor declared:
"Frederick Town is not so large as Alexandria but more
considerable than Williamsburg or Annapolis."

The rich natural resources of Frederick County had
much to do with the prosperity of the county seat. "The
land around Frederick Town," the same observing visitor
declared, "is heavy, strong and rich, well calculated for
wheat, with which it abounds, this being as plentiful a
country as any in the world." But the character of the
inhabitants contributed greatly to its growth. While the
population included a few hardy families of English
blood and a number of Irish settlers, the great majority
were Germans, whose characteristic industry and thrift had

---

[1] Smith, *A Tour of the United States of America*, published in London
in 1784; Williams, *History of Frederick County*, 93.

produced "almost every kind of manufacture as well as a considerable share of trade." It was not long before Frederick ranked, next to Baltimore, as the leading town in the State, and one of the most important centers of business in America.

It was in this thriving region that Thomas Johnson cast his lot. He had already been admitted to the Frederick County Bar; and he hoped that it would be possible at the end of the war to devote his attention to both law and business. Accustomed, however, to culture and refinement, Mr. Johnson did not spend much of his time with the German immigrants, who had little fondness for social activities, and very few of whom were able to speak the English language.

He accordingly erected a magnificent Colonial mansion about four miles North of Frederick. This estate, located about midway between the Pennsylvania boundary line and the Potomac, was called "Richfield." It was on this farm, some years later, that Winfield Scott Schley, the hero of Santiago, was born.

But such a man as Thomas Johnson was not destined for seclusion. With remarkable fidelity, he had fulfilled important duties under the most trying circumstances; and the Maryland Legislature, in a Joint Address of Thanks, expressed the hope that he would not suffer his abilities "to remain long inactive in the retirement of private life."

The Legislature's Address, stating in glowing terms Maryland's profound appreciation of Johnson's public services, is a notable document in the annals of the State. First proposed, November 10, 1779, in the Senate, the actual work of framing the Address was delegated to a special committee of six—Senators Matthew Tilghman, Charles

Carroll of Carrollton and William Paca; and Delegates John Hall, John Henry and Peregrine Lethrbury. Upon being submitted to the two Houses by the joint committee, the draft was with unanimity adopted on November 20th. The Address follows:[2]

THE ADDRESS OF THE GENERAL ASSEMBLY

To Thomas Johnson, Esquire,
Late Governor of the State of Maryland.

Sir,

The prudence, assiduity, firmness, and integrity, with which you have discharged, in times the most critical, the duties of your late important station, have a just claim to our warm acknowledgments and sincerest thanks.

While dissipation and avarice have too generally prevailed, your conduct, Sir, has afforded a conspicuous example of unwearied attention and close application to the public welfare, and of disinterestedness, in foregoing those profits your known industry, knowledge of business, and of your profession, could not have failed of securing.

We approve and admire that consistency of conduct and uniformity of character, which distinguish a life, devoted, from a very early period, to the true interests of your country, steadily and invariably pursued through a variety of important trusts; and relying on this, your ruling passion, the love of your country, we have the best founded hope that you will not suffer to remain long inactive, in the retirement of private life, those abilities which have often been so serviceable to the State, and of which it never, than at the present time, stood in greater need.

The Address was signed by Daniel of St. Thomas Jenifer, President of the Senate, and Josias Beall, Speaker of the House, and forwarded to Johnson on November 22nd.

---

[2] *Votes and Proceedings of the Senate,* November Session, 1779, p. 6.

"We are happy," wrote the President and Speaker, "in the opportunity offered us by the General Assembly of Maryland of transmitting you their thanks for the public whilst supreme magistrate of this State: a testimony conveying the highest honor which can be conferred by a free people."

The Joint Address was more than a felicitous testimony of the love and esteem of the people: it was an appeal to Johnson to continue in the public service. A more specific request followed within thirty days. The Legislature selected him on December 22, 1779, as one of six men to represent the State of Maryland in Congress. The other members-elect of the Maryland delegation were: George Plater, John Hall, Edward Lloyd, James Forbes and John Hanson.[3]

Needless to say, Johnson's heart was touched by the Address of the Assembly and his election to Congress. He appreciated the "very ample and honourable testimony" as the very highest reward that could be given him by his State. But the Winter of 1779–1780—one of the most terrible in the history of America—was now sweeping the Atlantic seaboard; the channels of trade were closed; military operations were largely suspended; and Johnson, besides wishing to enjoy for a short time the companionship of his wife and children, also felt that he could be of considerably greater service in directing the manufacture of military supplies in Western Maryland than by leaving immediately for Philadelphia.

A call having been issued for the General Assembly to reconvene in March, 1780, Mr. Johnson, on February 23rd, wrote a brief reply to the Address of Thanks and a declina-

[3] *Votes and Proceedings of the Senate,* November Session, 1779, p. 29.

tion of the seat in Congress. His reply, which was read to
the members of the Legislature in March, follows: [4]

LETTER TO THE ASSEMBLY

To The Honourable General Assembly

Gentlemen,

I cannot flatter myself but that in appointing me to some of the
important trusts with which my country has honoured me, she has
over rated my abilities; they have been faithfully exerted to their
extent with a view to her good, nor am I conscious of having preferred, in any instance, a particular to the general interest: and I
hope whether I remain in the calm walk of private life—the most
agreeable to my own inclination—or should fill a public station, I
shall continue to the last, to wish and endeavour to promote her
happiness and prosperity. The favourable light in which you have
been pleased to accept my endeavours for the public service, is the
most noble and pleasing reward you could bestow; and I return you
my sincerest thanks for the very ample and honourable testimony you
have given of my conduct as a man and a magistrate: it highly
gratifies my ambition in handing me down as approved of by you
and deserving well of posterity.

TH. JOHNSON.

But even while enjoying a deserved respite from exacting official duties, Mr. Johnson retained a keen interest in
public affairs. When, for example, a man named Wall
was released from imprisonment on bail—a step that did
not please the former Governor—Johnson took it upon himself as a private citizen to urge Governor Lee to order the
man's imprisonment. "If you and the Council should think
proper to commit Wall," said Johnson, "I think it ought

[4] *Votes and Proceedings of the Senate,* March Session, 1779, p. 47; *Votes
and Proceedings of the House of Delegates,* p. 95.

to be to some other prison than this, and as it appears to me it will be a very ill consequence and example that this man should be suffered to go at large in our State." [5]

But perhaps the most of Johnson's restless energy during the year 1780 was directed to the management of the properties in which he and three of his brothers—James, Baker and Roger—were jointly interested. Governor Johnson had six brothers, but James, Baker and Roger were by far the most prosperous. It has also been said that they were of a much higher order of intellect and character than the Governor's other three brothers. According to one member of the family,[6] James had "a stormy mind, but finest resolution"; Baker was "popular in manners, a kind and hospitable friend"; and Roger was "domestic and retired, economical and temperate"; whereas, in striking contrast, Benjamin was "a good, easy man, a poor manager, with little mind"; Joshua "a weak, vain man, fond of great people, and impoverished by an ambitious and extravagant wife"; and Dr. John Johnson "extremely indolent, self-opinionated, and had as little of manhood as he had of his profession." Regardless of whether these descriptions of Benjamin, Joshua and John are to be accepted as accurate or not, there is no doubt that James, Baker and Roger were unusually successful, rising by pluck and self-reliance to places of commanding leadership in the Western section of the State.

Before the war, the Johnsons disposed of their entire interest in the iron furnaces West of South Mountain to Lancelot Jacques and his nephew, Denton; and James Johnson, who was four years younger than Thomas, estab-

[5] XLIII *Maryland Archives,* 428.
[6] James Johnson, Jr., son of James and Margaret Skinner Johnson, letter written in 1842.

lished furnaces nearer Frederick Town, and took as his partners the Governor and the younger brothers, Baker and Roger, who were still in their twenties. Throughout his career as Governor, Thomas Johnson retained his interest in the firm, the Land Records showing that during his third term a tract of about a hundred acres of woodland was purchased jointly by the partners. Later, during the period of the Governor's retirement, the four brothers acquired an additional tract of thirty acres.[7] And in the years that followed hundreds of acres more were added to their holdings.

Outstanding among the enterprises of the Johnson brothers was the famous Catoctin Furnace, built in 1774 on the 7,000-acre tract patented in 1770 to Thomas Johnson and Leonard Calvert.[8] From the hematite ore dug from this tract were cast cannon and tons of bombshells, which were sent to the American Army and proved to be of great value in the prosecution of the war.

The enterprises of the Johnsons were very successful financially; but the brothers never allowed their business interests to interfere with their devotion to the American cause. Throughout the Revolution, they gave liberally of their time and their money; and all the brothers—save Joshua, who was located in Europe—held commissions as field officers in the Maryland Line. In the Spring of 1780, the ex-Governor accepted from the State an allowance of 3,750 pounds, granted him as special compensation by the Legislature,[9] but there is a tradition that he used a considerable portion of his personal fortune to equip recruits for the Army, and the expenditure of his own funds largely

---

[7] *Land Records of Frederick County*, Liber W. R. No. 2, folio 684. August 16, 1780.
[8] Scharf, *History of Western Maryland*, Vol. I, p. 629.
[9] XLIII *Maryland Archives*, 113.

exceeded the salaries paid him by the State. One example of the patriotic interest of Thomas, James, Baker and Roger Johnson is shown, during the Summer of 1780, by their joint loan to the State of the sum of of 10,000 dollars.[10]

While Thomas Johnson was recovering his strength "in the calm walk of private life," General Washington was likewise resting, and gathering his energies for future campaigns. There were no military engagements in the North, except several attacks along the coast of New Jersey by General Knyphausen, the leader of the marauders, who had been left in charge of New York by Sir Henry Clinton. The development which brought the greatest cheer to Johnson and other American patriots was the arrival in the Summer of 1780 of five thousand soldiers from France, commanded by Count Rochambeau; but the forces under General Washington were in such a deplorable condition that they were unable to give the allies any immediate coöperation.

And while Washington and Rochambeau were laying their plans for the future, the reports from the South cast a profound depression over the country. The British had completely overrun the Carolinas, and the American reverses left the patriots in a condition from which it was feared they would not soon, if ever, recover. After the battle of Camden, in which General Gates was overwhelmingly defeated, the renowned Nathaniel Greene was recommended by Washington as commander of the patriot forces in the South. The appointment was pleasing to the leaders in Maryland; and the Legislature was quick to comply with one of Major-General Greene's requisitions, by resolving on the first day of December, 1780, that the State should fur-

10 XLIII *Maryland Archives*, 520.

nish sixty dragoon horses for Major Lee's Legion "with the utmost dispatch." [11]

When the Northern Army and the French went into Winter quarters at the close of the year, General Washington established his Headquarters at New Windsor. It was while stationed here, in December, 1780, that the Commander-in-Chief again turned to Johnson for assistance. It was a very unique appeal—a request from the supreme American commander to a private citizen, to aid the commander of the Southern Army in deciding a serious charge preferred against a military officer. General Washington desired to have the complaint fully investigated; he wanted the accused, Captain Eggleston, to be given a fair trial; and he directed that the accused be severely punished if found to be guilty.

"Mrs. Bainbridge, the wife of Peter Bainbridge," Washington explained in his letter directed to Frederick Town, "has laid before me some papers respecting the proceedings of Capt Eggleston of Col^o Lee's Legion on the case of their son Peter Bainbridge, which carry the face of a most extraordinary and unwarrantable kind of conduct. But as it is impossible to decide *ex parte*, I have, by the inclosed, referred the matter to Major General Greene commanding the Southern Army and I shall be much obliged to you to procure authenticated copies of the inclosed papers or any others that you may find necessary and transmit them to General Greene with my letter."

[11] *Votes and Proceedings of the House of Delegates,* October Session, 1780, p. 41.

Chapter XXII

IN THE LEGISLATURE — CONFEDERATION AND THE WEST

"That on the soundest policy, to secure the peace, safety, and happiness of the United States, the fertile and extensive Western country should in due season be laid out in convenient districts, and free independent governments established therein; and that those new States should be received on terms of equality into the Union. . . . That by acceding to the Confederation, this State doth not relinquish or intend to relinquish any right or interest she hath, in common with the other United States, to the back country."
— *Resolutions, Maryland House of Delegates,* January 20, 1781.

"The present appears to us to be a seasonable time to shew, that as our claim was better founded in justice than the exclusive claims of others—having supported it with firmness till a disposition is shewn of candidly considering it—we chuse rather to rely on the justice of the Confederated States, than by an overperseverance incur the censure of obstinacy."
— *Message to the Senate, reported by Johnson,* January 29, 1781.

"It was Maryland that, by leading the way toward the creation of a National domain, laid the corner stone of our Federal Union."
— *Fiske, Critical Period of American History,* 195.

GENERAL WASHINGTON's letter, asking Mr. Johnson to secure affidavits for the use of Court-martial, had been directed to Frederick Town: for it was supposed in the Winter encampment at New Windsor that the ex-Governor was still in retirement. It appears, however, that he had already been induced to leave home and reënter public life.

Toward the close of November, 1780, Johnson was offered two positions—a seat in Congress and a seat in the Maryland Legislature. Down at Annapolis, the Assembly leaders were expecting him to accept the seat in Congress. They had done all they could to send an able delegation to Philadelphia: they reduced the size of the delegation from six to four members, and agreed to provide a liberal allowance in order to "induce gentlemen of abilities and business to accept the trust."[1] The balloting, November 17th, resulted in the election of Johnson, Charles Carroll of Carrollton, Daniel of St. Thomas Jenifer, and John Hanson, as the delegates to represent the State of Maryland.

As late as December 1st, it was still being hoped that these four men would accept the trust: for, when the question of quorum for the Maryland delegation was brought up for consideration at this time, the names of Johnson, Carroll, Jenifer, and Hanson were particularly mentioned as the members-elect.

On the following morning, however, Johnson created a surprise by appearing in the State House and offering to qualify as a member of the Legislature. He announced that he had been elected to the House of Delegates by the voters of Frederick County.[2] That he declined the seat in Congress, but consented to serve in the Legislature, was by no means extraordinary. A number of other statesmen had followed the same course. Matthew Tilghman, who asked to be excused from Congress on account of "his age and other circumstances," was serving in the Upper House at Annapolis. Thomas Stone declared he could not serve at Philadelphia, on account of "the situation of his family and affairs," but he found that he was able to serve in the Senate, and for a short while also in the House of Delegates. Carroll of Carrollton, who had been elected to Congress,

[1] *Votes and Proceedings of the House of Delegates,* October Session, 1780, p. 24.
[2] *Ibid.,* p. 42.

also accepted a Senate seat at Annapolis. Samuel Chase, Brice T. B. Worthington, John Hall, and John Henry were among the other leaders of experience and ability who were sitting in the General Assembly. Perhaps one reason why the leading statesmen of the day were none too eager to serve in Philadelphia during "the inchoate period of confederation" was because the Congress had no organic authority, no real power of efficient action; the sovereignty surrendered to it by the several States was undefined in nature and extent; it was able to conduct affairs by sufferance only; its legislation was liable to be disregarded at any time by one or more of the Legislatures.

It is possible also that the patriot leaders, notably Johnson, Tilghman, Chase, Carroll, and Stone—were able to discern that problems of great importance were now confronting the Legislature. Did Thomas Johnson return to Annapolis simply to expedite measures intended to aid in the prosecution of the war, or was he interested in securing the passage of a law for confiscation of British property? Or was his chief concern the Articles of Confederation? Whatever the reason that drew him from retirement, the fact remains that he was entering a momentous session.

When ex-Governor Johnson took his seat in the Lower House on the 2nd day of December, 1780, the lawmakers had already been in session slightly more than a month. But Johnson's late appearance was not the result of tardiness. He was chosen at a special election to take the place of Normand Bruce, one of the Delegates-elect, who refused to serve.

With characteristic enthusiasm, the ex-Governor, refreshened by a year of private life, eagerly jumped into the whirl of legislation. It is not surprising to read in the

Journal that he was put to work—to draft a bill to encourage the manufacture and importation of salt—before Allen Quynn, Chairman of the Committee of Elections and Privileges, had a chance to report upon the new Delegate's credentials.

Johnson's assignments in the House of Delegates brought him in touch with a multiplicity of subjects. He analyzed the resolves of Congress and communications from General Washington; he prepared instructions for the Maryland delegates in Congress; he drafted a message to the Assemblies of Pennsylvania, Delaware, and Virginia, regarding a continuation of embargo on provisions; prepared a bill to prohibit exportation of corn, wheat and fresh provisions; formulated arrangements for the accommodation of the Convention Troops at Frederick; and recommended a measure authorizing the Trustees of the Poor of Frederick County to rent out the poorhouse and to apply the income towards the paupers' support; he considered ways and means of obtaining a loan in Europe; brought in a bill to adjust accounts of Maryland soldiers in the service of the United States; a bill to secure the quota of recruits; a bill to encourage the importation of clothing for the Army; a bill to raise supplies for the year 1781 pursuant to the request of the Commander-in-Chief; and a bill "for the defence and security of the State."

In the midst of these deliberations relating to the prosecution of the war, there came up the inevitable question of the *quantum* of salaries for public officials. On the 15th of December, Johnson was named on a committee to recommend the salaries for the Governor and other officials of the State. On the following day, the committee reported that the financial condition of the State had been taken into consideration together with "the spirit of our Constitution, which directs that salaries shall be liberal though not profuse." The salary recommendations were freely discussed on the floor of the House and voted on *seriatim*.

One of the most important measures before the Legislature at this session was the bill to confiscate British property. The plan had been suggested on a number of previous occasions, but no definite action had ever been taken. Finally, on December 20, 1780, the Legislature undertook to solve the problem "upon principles consistent with justice and the Law of Nations."

A joint committee was formed, and Delegate Johnson was named one of the conferees on the part of the House. Among the others on the committee were Matthew Tilghman and Carroll of Carrollton, from the Senate; and Samuel Chase and Thomas Stone, representing the House. The committee—consisting of four Senators and seven Delegates—deliberated many days on the subject. They realized that the proposed step meant drastic action against the British sympathizers; but they felt that, as the British had seized considerable property of American citizens, it was equally fair to confiscate British property in this State. Then, too, Maryland had a special grievance. She had invested in the stock of the Bank of England prior to the Revolution; and the Bank, acting on the advice of officers of the Crown, had refused to pay the dividends accruing for the use of the State since the outbreak of hostilities.

The bill reported favorably by the joint committee was entitled "An Act to seize, confiscate, and appropriate, all British property within this State." Its stirring preamble declared that Great Britain was waging an unjust war against America; that the British Army and Navy had

"committed various outrages on the persons, and devastations on the property, of the people of these United States,
contrary to the practice of civilised Nations, and the present usage of war"; and that the cruel treatment accorded
to American prisoners and civilians violated the "obligations of compacts" and the "rights of humanity."

When the bill came up for a vote in the House on
January 26, 1781, there appeared all sorts of conflicting
opinions regarding it. Many amendments were offered;
but they were strenuously opposed by Johnson and others
who had taken part in the preparation of the bill. One
Delegate, for example, proposed that those persons, whose
property had been taken or destroyed by the British, should
be reimbursed entirely from alien property; but the proposition was overwhelmingly defeated. The bill was finally
passed by the House by a vote of twenty to nineteen.

When the bill arrived in the Senate, it was altered in
a number of material respects; and with the alterations it
was returned on January 29th. The House, greatly disappointed, selected Delegate Johnson as chairman of a
committee to frame a message deploring the action of the
Senate. On January 30, 1781, Mr. Johnson reported the
message requesting the Senate to recede from its amendments. The Senate replied on the following day that it
would not recede. So far as debts were concerned, the
Senate admitted that citizens of Maryland ought to refrain
from making payments to subjects of the Crown, but declared it advisable to refer the question of confiscation of
debts to a future session rather than to jeopardize the bill.

And so, the Confiscation Act provided that all property
belonging to British subjects—debts only excepted—should

be seized and confiscated for the use of the State; and Maryland creditors of British subjects were to be indemnified
out of the confiscated property of individual debtors, *so far
as the debtors were solvent.* The people were also urged to
make no payments to subjects of Great Britain.[3]

The Maryland Confiscation Act of 1781 is an interesting measure in itself, but it is interesting also because of the
fact that ten years later Thomas Johnson, then an Associate
Justice of the United States Supreme Court, was one of
the jurists who sat at Richmond in the great case of the
British Debts, in which Patrick Henry showed his profound
mastery of constitutional law and John Marshall first won
his reputation as a commanding figure at the American bar.

But, while the struggle to enact the Confiscation Act
was exciting, the question of greatest National importance
in the Legislature at this session was whether Maryland
should ratify the Articles of Confederation.

The formulation of the plan of confederation, and the
ratification thereof by the States, had been a slow process.
Prior to the Declaration of Independence, a committee had
been appointed to devise such a plan; the committee reported a month later; but more than a year passed before
the members of Congress themselves were ready for a vote.
One of the chief causes of delay in ratification was the
dispute over title to the vast territory that stretched to the
Mississippi and the Great Lakes—popularly known as the
Western lands. The controversy arose in 1776, when Congress recommended bounties of land for recruits. Maryland, having no land West of the Alleghany Mountains,
took the position that the back country, if secured by the

[3] *Laws of Maryland, October Session,* 1780, Chapter XLV.

blood and treasure of all, ought to belong to the United States as "a common stock, to be parcelled out by Congress into free, convenient, and independent governments."

One month before Congress agreed upon the Articles of Confederation, it was moved that Congress should have exclusive authority to determine the Western boundaries and to lay out the territory beyond said boundaries into separate and independent States.[4] Maryland was the only State to support the motion; but in it was suggested the American policy of "political expansion under the sovereign control of Congress, which ultimately prevailed and constituted, upon grounds of necessity, a truly National Republic." [5]

Nevertheless, at the time of the adoption of the Articles of Confederation by Congress, November 15, 1777, seven of the States—Massachusetts, Connecticut, New York, Virginia, North Carolina, South Carolina and Georgia— still asserted their claims to the Western lands. Indeed, these States maintained originally that their land extended as far as the Pacific; but, since Louisiana had been transferred to Spain by the Paris Treaty of 1763, they did not claim any further than the Mississippi River.

Virginia—the largest of the States, with a population three times that of New York, and nearly double that of Pennsylvania—was particularly extravagant in her claims. She maintained that under her Charter of 1609—restricted only by the Treaty of 1763—the territory of the Old Dominion extended as far as Lake Superior. Thus her claim conflicted with the claims of Massachusetts, Connecticut and New York.

[4] *Journals of Congress,* Vol. II, 290.
[5] Herbert B. Adams, *Maryland's Influence upon Land Cessions to the United States,* Johns Hopkins University Studies, Series III, 23.

Throughout his Administration as Governor of Maryland, Thomas Johnson denied that Virginia had valid title to such a great extent of territory. Governor Johnson took the view that Virginia had no *title by charter*, as the Charter had been revoked in 1624; no *title by conquest*, for the reason that before the Revolution the people of Virginia were British subjects and all territory taken from the Indians inured to the Crown; and no *title by possession*, because the Northwest had not actually been occupied by citizens of Virginia.

Johnson and other patriot leaders in Maryland were alarmed at the pretentious claims of the larger States—particularly Virginia. It was feared that, if such claims were conceded, the larger States in the course of time would develop to such an extent that they would overwhelm the smaller States.

However, in the month of July, 1778, ten of the States, including New Hampshire, Rhode Island and Pennsylvania—these three were unable to claim title to the Northwest, since their boundaries were fixed by the Crown—ratified the Articles of Confederation. The only States that still refused to join were New Jersey, Delaware and Maryland.

New Jersey ratified in November, 1778. Delaware acceded with a mild protest in February, 1779. Neither State accomplished anything "towards breaking down the selfish claims of the larger States and placing the Confederation upon a National basis." [6]

Maryland was left to fight the battle alone. Governor Johnson had not yet used his influence to urge his State to enter the Confederation. His devotion to the patriot cause

[6] *Ibid.*, p. 24.

was unquestioned. And, after his vivid experience in the Continental Congress and as Governor, he understood the importance of establishing a confederation of the States. That some kind of union was needed had been apparent ever since the Congress was first called together on account of the imminent peril of the country. But Johnson, a profound constitutional lawyer, believed that the placing of the States as far as possible upon an equality in the Union was of greater importance than the ratification of a document, which at best provided but a very loose association of the States. And so, Maryland steadily refused to subscribe to the Confederation until she was assured that the claims to the Western lands were surrendered and the vast region West of the Alleghanies would become the common property of the United States. After Delaware, the twelfth State, had ratified the Articles of Confederation, the Maryland Legislature plainly warned the State's delegates in Congress against signing the Articles until the claims were surrendered. These instructions—read in Congress in May, 1779, during Johnson's third term as Governor—constitute "one of the most important documents in our early constitutional history." [7]

Time and again the question came up for discussion in Congress and throughout America—until finally in February, 1780, the State of New York agreed to relinquish all her claims to the Western lands. Six more months passed; and on the 6th of September, 1780, the Maryland plan of a National domain found positive support in Congress through the passage of a resolution, recommending that all States claiming Western possessions should make a general cession thereof to the United States. Again, on the 10th

[7] *Ibid.*

of October, Congress gave assurance to the claimants that ceded territory would be formed into distinct, republican States, which would become members of the Union and have the same rights of sovereignty as the original States.[8]

Several more months passed—and during these closing days of 1780 Thomas Johnson and other leaders in Maryland were eagerly waiting for the decision of Virginia. Finally, on January 2, 1781, Virginia agreed to yield! With the proviso that she be allowed to hold jurisdiction over Kentucky—a region actually explored and settled— Virginia offered to surrender completely her claim to the entire territory Northwest of the Ohio.

Mr. Johnson, while busily engaged in framing the Confiscation bill and other measures in the Maryland Legislature, was stirred by the important news from Virginia. He believed that Maryland's contention was now assured—that the great Western territory would be surrendered to Congress in trust for all the States. He, therefore, declared that Maryland should no longer hesitate to enter the Confederation.

On January 20, 1781, the question of ratification of the Articles of Confederation was the special order of the day in the Maryland House of Delegates. Mr. Johnson enthusiastically threw his influence in favor of ratification. Before the question was finally put, Johnson and other members who were eager for immediate accession diplomatically paved the way for action by offering resolutions, pointing out Maryland's interest "in the soil and government" of the Western lands and declaring that this extensive territory should be laid out "in due season" into independent States. Manifestly, to this proposition there

[8] *Journals of Congress,* Vol. III, 535.

could be no objection.   Such had been the Maryland theory
for several years.   The resolutions were as follows: [9]

"*Resolved,* That this House, on the most deliberate consideration,
are of opinion that this State is highly interested with the other
United States, both in justice and policy, in the soil and government
of the back country.

"That on the plainest principles of justice, any profits arising
from the sale of the back lands, ought to be a common stock, to be
applied by Congress towards the expences of the war; and that on
the soundest policy, to secure the peace, safety, and happiness of the
United States, the fertile and extensive Western country should in due
season be laid out in convenient districts, and free independent governments established therein; and that those new States should be received on terms of equality into the Union.

"*Resolved,* That this State hath, from the commencement of the
war, strenuously exerted herself in the common cause, and that if
no formal Confederation was to take place, it is the fixed determination of this State to continue her exertions to the utmost, agreeable
to the faith pledged in the Union."

After the introductory resolutions were adopted, the
members of the House were then asked to ratify the Articles
of Confederation.   The resolutions calling for ratification
by Maryland follow:

"*But Because* it is said that the common enemy are encouraged to
hope that the Union may be dissolved, unless this State confederates,
and therefore prosecutes the war, in expectation of an event so dis-
graceful to America, and our friends and illustrious ally are impressed with an idea, that the common cause would be promoted by
this State formally acceding to the Confederation; from an earnest
desire to conciliate the affection of the Sister States, to convince our
illustrious ally of an unalterable resolution to support the independence of the United States and the alliance with his Most Chris-

[9] *Votes and Proceedings of the House of Delegates,* October Session,
1780, p. 94.

tian Majesty, and to destroy for ever any apprehension of our friends or hope in our enemies, of this State being again united to Great Britain,

"*This House Resolve,* That this State now accede to the Confederation, and that the delegates appointed to represent this State in Congress, or any two or more of them, be authorised and directed, on behalf of this State, to subscribe and ratify the Articles of Confederation.

"*But this House Declare,* That by acceding to the Confederation, this State doth not relinquish or intend to relinquish any right or interest she hath, in common with the other United States, to the back country, but now claim the same as fully as was done by the Legislature of this State in their declaration, which stands entered on the Journals of Congress; *and also Declare,* that no article or clause in the said Confederacy can or ought to bind this or any other State, to guarantee the jurisdiction of any State over the said back lands or the inhabitants thereof, relying on the justice of the several States hereafter as to the claim aforesaid made by this State."

The resolutions were adopted in the House by the overwhelming majority of thirty-three to seven. In order to carry the resolutions into effect as promptly as possible, the suggestion was then made that the Legislature enact a bill directing the Maryland members of Congress to subscribe to the Articles of Confederation; and five members were appointed to draft the bill. Johnson was made chairman of the committee. Samuel Chase, who had voted with Johnson in favor of the resolutions, was also named on the committee.

On January 27, 1781, Johnson, as the committee chairman, brought in the bill, intended to place the Legislature upon record in favor of ratification.[10] Then followed in rapid succession the first and second readings, by special

[10] *Ibid.,* p. 102.

order, and the passage of the bill in the House by a vote of thirty to eight.

On the following morning—it was Sunday: but the Assemblymen felt that their work was work of necessity— the ratification bill was considered in the Senate. In this chamber the sentiment regarding the subject was more evenly divided. Four Senators—Carroll of Carrollton, Thomas Stone, George Plater and John Henry—voted for the bill; while four others of smaller reputation—William Hindman, Samuel Hughes, Richard Barnes and William Hemsley—voted against it. The tie was broken by President Jenifer, who voted in the negative.[11]

But the Senate's vote against Maryland's accession to the Confederation was not destined to be final. Delegate Johnson believed that the Senate had made a profound mistake. On that same Sabbath afternoon, the eminent Frederick County Delegate was chosen, together with Chase and Fitzhugh, to prepare a message to the Senate, asking for a reconsideration. And on Monday morning, January 29th, the Delegate from Frederick, offering the report of the committee, presented a Message, stating frankly why the House of Delegates was returning the bill to the Senate.

In his Message, Johnson pointed out the need of determining the powers of Congress. He knew how deplorable the loose system of Government had been; and he felt that some positive National authority was an urgent need of the United States. While the "firm league of friendship" failed to provide for a President or a Federal Court, Johnson argued that the settling of the powers of Congress "on a known and permanent basis," would improve the Executive Department. But he emphasized par-

11 *Votes and Proceedings of the Senate,* October Session, 1780, p. 38.

ticularly the importance of the psychological effect of favorable action. He felt that ratification would "spread confidence among the States" and be of material assistance in securing "the independence, peace and happiness of America."

Of course, Johnson understood why the ratification bill had been defeated in the Senate. The negative vote was undoubtedly due to apprehensions that still existed with respect to the Western lands. In this connection, Johnson ventured the following argument: [12]

"How far the United States may now be benefited by the Western country as a common fund, is impossible to determine; but it does not appear probable, that this State's still refusing to confederate can be a means of securing or improving it as a fund: on the contrary, where the free and independent will of many is to be consulted, giving up something of opinion of each is necessary to conciliate an agreement of all in one point. The present appears to us to be a seasonable time to shew, that as our claim was better founded in justice than the exclusive claims of others—having supported it with firmness till a disposition is shewn of candidly considering it—we chuse rather to rely on the justice of the Confederated States, than by an overperseverance incur the censure of obstinacy."

Johnson also shrewdly referred to ratification as a step of political expediency. Frankly he referred to the profound significance of the Maryland Senate's vote—it alone was necessary to make the Confederation effective throughout the United States—and suggested that the consequences would be wholly out of the control of the State.

The members of the Senate were impressed by Johnson's logic. They saw how the future of America depended upon their vote. They admitted an association of some

[12] *Votes and Proceedings of the House of Delegates,* October Session, 1780, p. 106.

kind was favored by every friend of the United States. And while they were still apprehensive that accession to the Confederation would injure Maryland's claim concerning the Western lands, they decided to rely upon "the justice and disposition of Congress hereafter for the establishment of our claim." Therefore, in order to "gratify the earnest desire" of the House of Delegates, the Senate promptly acquiesced by approving the bill for ratification.[13]

When the bill was returned to the House, January 30th, with the affirmative vote of the Senate, a committee was named, with Delegate Johnson as chairman, to prepare instructions for the Maryland members of Congress regarding the formal signature of the Articles of Confederation. On the second of February, Johnson presented the instructions, setting forth the motives that influenced the Maryland Legislature to ratify the Confederation. The ex-Governor reiterated herein the sentiment of Maryland in regard to the Western lands—i. e., that the selfish claims of the larger States were "unjust and injurious to the general welfare"—but declared that immediate accession by Maryland, in the opinion of the Legislature, "would be acceptable to our illustrious ally, give satisfaction to his Catholic Majesty, and probably be the means of negotiating loans in Europe."

Pursuant to the request of the Legislature, Congressmen Daniel Carroll and John Hanson signed the Articles of Confederation, which, now having the assent of all the States, went into effect on March 1, 1781. The old Congress now adjourned, and on the following morning the Congress convened under the new Government.

[13] *Ibid.*, p. 109.

Thomas Johnson had rendered an important service—similar to that in 1776, when he induced Maryland to vote for the Declaration of Independence. His course in 1781, in favor of ratification of the Articles of Confederation, was well taken, for his assurance that the Western lands would eventually be parcelled by Congress into independent States was destined to prevail. After years of discussion, Virginia withdrew her proviso with respect to Kentucky and in 1784 made her cession to the Confederation absolute. The other claimant States—Massachusetts, Connecticut, South Carolina, North Carolina and Georgia —also surrendered all their claims. Thus the Western lands became the "common stock" of the American Nation.

Maryland is entitled to great credit for her resolute protest against the avaricious claims to the great Northwest. While the acquisition of this extensive territory was important in itself, it was still more important because it set in motion a train of events of far-reaching consequences, which were never contemplated in the Articles of Confederation. It prepared the minds of the American people for the Convention of 1787, which adopted the Constitution of the United States.

In referring to the protests of the smaller States, John Fiske says: "But of these protesting States it was only Maryland that fairly rose to the occasion, and suggested an idea which seemed startling at first, but from which mighty and unforseen consequences were soon to follow." [14]

It is true, Maryland's inflexible refusal to ratify the Articles of Confederation until the year 1781 was regarded by many people as unfriendly to the Common Cause. Her

[14] Fiske, *Critical Period of American History*, p. 192.

grim determination to hold aloof aroused "fierce indignation" at the time. "Some hot-heads," says Fiske,[15] "were even heard to say that if Maryland should persist any longer in her refusal to join the Confederation, she ought to be summarily divided up between the neighboring States, and her name erased from the map."

But if we trace the consequences of the resolute attitude of the State, we find "it was Maryland that, by leading the way toward the creation of a National domain, laid the corner stone of our Federal Union."

[15] *Ibid.,* p. 195.

CHAPTER XXIII

AMERICA VICTORIOUS — RETURN TO PRIVATE LIFE

"I cannot conclude without expressing my warmest wishes for the prosperity of a State which has ever stood among the foremost in her support of the Common Cause."
—*General Washington to the Maryland Legislature,* November 23, 1781.

THE Maryland Legislature, which had adjourned shortly after Johnson's fight for the Articles of Confederation, reconvened in the Spring of 1781. As the scene of war—first in the North and later in the far South—was shifting toward the Chesapeake Bay, it was felt advisable to provide further means of defense. Early in the year, General Lafayette, arriving in Maryland to act in concert with the French fleet, found the Chesapeake occupied by a British squadron and advanced his troops only as far as Annapolis; but, returning to the Head of Elk, received fresh instructions from General Washington to proceed against the Enemy. Finally, on May 22, 1781—the day before the Legislature assembled in Annapolis—it was decided by the Commander-in-Chief, after a conference with Rochambeau and other officers, to undertake an expedition in Virginia.

When the roll was called in the General Assembly on May 23rd, Delegate Johnson of Frederick County was in his seat in the House.[1] He heard how British marauders had lately been plundering along the shores of the Chesa-

[1] *Votes and Proceedings of the House of Delegates,* May 1781, p. 123.

peake and its tributaries. And he eagerly went to work to shape legislation to insure greater security for the State. He was delegated to prepare measures to prevent correspondence with the Enemy and to punish marauders, spies and deserters; to emit bills of credit; to dispose of confiscated property; and to strengthen the law enacted "for the better security of the Government."

Delegate Johnson was also asked to adjust accounts of Maryland troops in the service of the United States; to consider remonstrances from officers in the Maryland Line; to inquire into the revenue raised by taxation for the year 1781; to ascertain the quantity of clothing necessary for the men in the Southern Army; to frame instructions for the members of Congress; and to recommend amendments to the Maryland Constitution.[2]

When the Legislature adjourned *sine die*, June 27th, after being in session scarcely more than a month, Johnson returned home to direct his attention to his iron furnaces and other interests. He realized that his most important patriotic duty now—since the arrival of thousands of French soldiers and sailors to aid the American cause—was no longer to scour the countryside for additional recruits, but to manufacture munitions. And so, in the Summer of 1781, when the combined forces of United States soldiers and French allies were mobilizing South of the Potomac, the Johnson brothers were firing their furnaces with supreme exertion to cast cannon and shells. It has been said that the Johnsons at this time made at least one hundred tons of cannon balls for the use of the Allied Army.

October, 1781, brought the news of the crowning triumph

[2] *Ibid.,* 124 to 178.

—the surrender of Cornwallis! It was such a decisive victory that it virtually assured American Independence and brought relief and unbounded joy throughout the States. The inhabitants at Frederick felt a special thrill of delight when large numbers of the British prisoners—among the 7,000 soldiers entrapped by General Washington—were driven into the Barracks in the Southern end of the town. Thus, soon after the great capitulation, it became Johnson's opportunity to see near his own home hundreds, if not thousands, of the captured soldiers of George III.

Shortly after the victory at Yorktown, Mr. Johnson was reëlected to the Maryland Legislature. It appears that John Hanson, one of the Delegates-elect in Frederick County, had declined the seat; and Johnson was chosen at a special election to fill the vacancy. But as the end of the war was now assured, the ex-Governor felt that he could ask to be relieved from further legislative service without shirking his patriotic duty. He notified the Legislature to this effect; and his letter of declination, read to the members of the House on December 11th, was immediately accepted.[3]

Shortly before Johnson declined to serve again in the Legislature, Annapolis was honored by a visit of General Washington. It was unfortunate that the former Governor, who had so frequently received and fulfilled the requisitions of the Commander-in-Chief, was not a member of the Legislature at this happy moment. In a message, adopted November 22nd, the members of the Legislature declared the State would be indebted to him forever for his services from the time of the passage of the Delaware "in a wintry and tempestuous night" to the day of the

3 *Ibid.*, November 1781, p. 30.

glorious success at Yorktown—"an event which reflects the highest honour upon your Excellency, adds lustre to the Allied arms, and affords a rational ground of belief, that under the favour of Divine Providence, the freedom, independence and happiness of America will shortly be established upon the surest foundation." [4]

In his reply, General Washington did not mention the name of Governor Johnson; but he cited the "ready attention" which his appeals received in Maryland during the Revolution. After giving credit for much of the success at Yorktown to Count de Rochambeau and Count de Grasse, and cautioning the people not to relax their exertions lest the Enemy might yet have a chance to recover, the General feelingly said: "I cannot conclude without expressing my warmest wishes for the prosperity of a State which has ever stood among the foremost in her support of the Common Cause. I confess myself under particular obligations for the ready attention which I have experienced to those requisitions which, in the course of my duty, I have occasionally been under the necessity of making." [5]

As General Washington had expected, the embers of war burned for a long time after Cornwallis's surrender. Early in 1782, the Commander-in-Chief entrenched himself at Newburgh, to resume his watch upon New York; and it was not until August that Sir Guy Carleton, who had superseded Clinton at the head of the British forces in America, informed Washington that Great Britain would concede American Independence at the peace negotiations in France. Even then Washington did not cease his vigilance, but established his forces in Winter encampment.

[4] *Ibid.*, p. 8.
[5] *Ibid.*, p. 9.

During the monotonous days of 1782—while doing his best to keep his discontented soldiers from mutiny—Washington began to ponder over a plan of Nationalism. He feared that if the Union dissolved the Revolution, with all its sacrifices of blood and treasure, might prove to be a curse, rather than a blessing, to mankind. And so at the beginning of the year 1783, while still entrenched at Newburgh, he commenced his campaign for a strong Central Government—a campaign that he was still to be waging five years later when he appealed to Thomas Johnson to influence Maryland to ratify the Federal Constitution.

"I am decided in my opinion," Washington wrote to Governor Harrison of Virginia, under date of March 4, 1783, "that if the powers of Congress are not enlarged and made competent to all general purposes, the blood which has been spilt, the expense that has been incurred, and the distresses which have been felt, will avail nothing; and that the bond which holds us together, already too weak, will soon be broken; when anarchy and confusion will prevail." [6]

And to Lafayette, who had returned to France shortly after the victory at Yorktown, Washington wrote on April 5th: "The honor, power, and true interest of this country must be measured by a Continental scale. To form a new Constitution that will give consistency, stability, and dignity to the Union and sufficient powers to the great council of the Nation for general purposes, is a duty incumbent upon every man who wishes well to his country." [7]

Toward the close of March, Congress heard from Lafayette that a provisional Treaty of Peace had been

[6] Maxwell, *Virginia Historical Register*, VI, 36.
[7] Sparks, VIII, 412.

signed between Great Britain and the United States; but it was not until the 11th of April that official confirmation was received from the American Commissioners that Independence of the States was formally acknowledged. Congress then issued a proclamation for the cessation of hostilities; and on April 19, 1783—exactly eight years after the first blood was shed at Lexington—General Washington proclaimed the end of the war.

In June, upon issuing his last official communication to the Governor of each State, the Commander-in-Chief found another opportunity to make a plea for Nationalism. Declaring it was within the power of the people themselves "to establish or ruin their National character forever," Washington stated the four principles which he considered essential for the very existence of the Nation—an indissoluble Union of the States; a sacred regard for public justice; a proper military establishment in time of peace; and a sacrifice of private advantages and local prejudices for the public good. "It is indispensable to the happiness of the individual States," he declared, "that there should be lodged somewhere a supreme power to regulate and govern the general concerns of the Confederated Republic, without which the Union cannot be of long duration, and everything must very rapidly tend to anarchy and confusion." [8]

The General's letter to the Governors was referred to the Legislatures and soon found its way through the press to all parts of the country. Among others, the Maryland newspapers discussed he plan of revising the Articles of Confederation; [9] and therefore by this time—even if not

[8] Sparks, VIII, 439.
[9] *Maryland Gazette*, July 11, 1783.

GEORGE WASHINGTON

From a portrait by Rembrandt Peale. John Marshall and others declared
this was the most faithful likeness of the first President

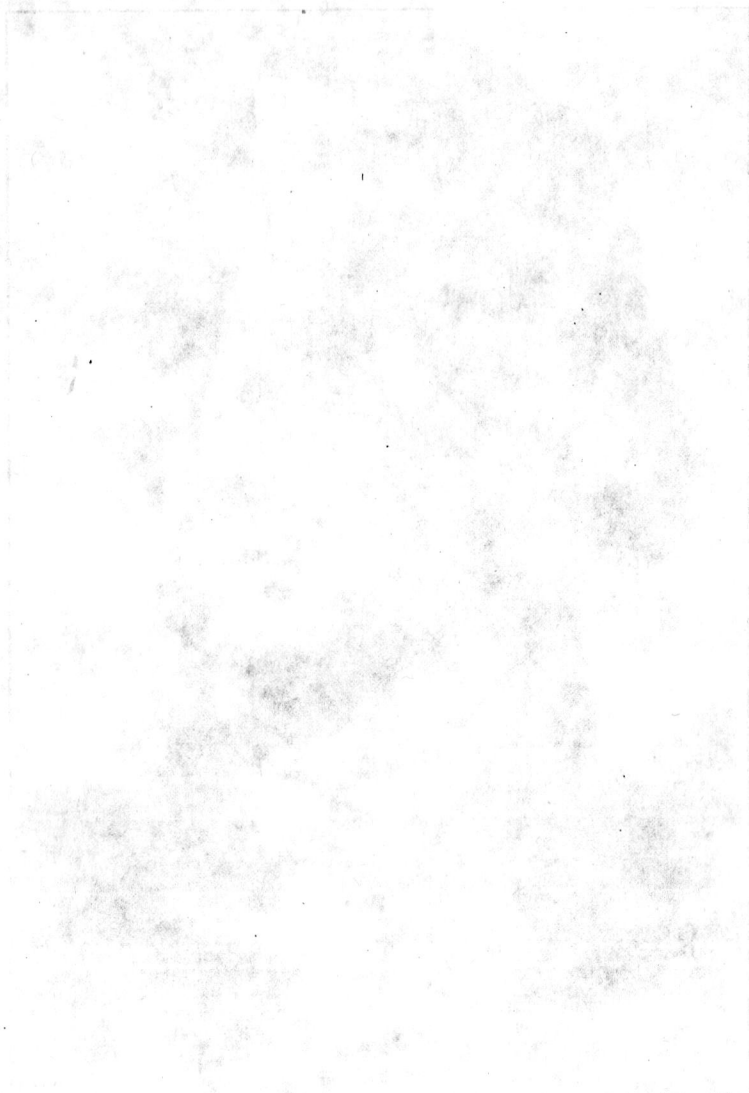

before—Johnson was thoroughly familiar with Washington's attitude upon the subject. The Maryland statesman was not enthused, like young Alexander Hamilton and other leaders in the North, over the form of Government; but at all events, when the time arrived to act upon the question of ratification of the Constitution, Johnson did not hesitate to support the "novel system."

After the final Treaty of Peace was signed at Paris, September 3, 1783, Washington never lost an opportunity to plead for an increase in Federal power. Even in his Farewell Address to the Army, he undertook to send forth "every one of his fellow soldiers as an apostle of Union under a new Constitution." [10] In this Address, on the 2nd of November, Washington said: "Although the General has so frequently given it as his opinion in the most public and explicit manner, that, unless the principles of the Federal Government were properly supported, and the powers of the Union increased, the honor, dignity, and justice of the Nation would be lost forever; yet he cannot help leaving it as his last injunction to every officer and every soldier to add his best endeavours toward effecting these great purposes, on which our very existence as a Nation so materially depends." [11]

General Washington realized that the Government, under the Articles of Confederation, was already on the verge of collapse. The country was in a deplorable condition. Commerce had been paralyzed. The Congress was without power to raise revenue by taxation. Many of the soldiers were enraged because they had to return home in destitution. Many people saw no alternative but monarchy

[10] Bancroft, *History of the Formation of the Constitution*, p. 106.
[11] Sparks, VIII, 495.

—with Washington as King. But never did the lofty patriotism of Washington shine with greater splendor than at the termination of the war. Giving solemn farewell to his fellow officers on December 4th, he made plans to deliver back to Congress his commission as Commander-in-Chief, and to return to private life. Congress was then in session in Annapolis. Since the Articles of Confederation had failed to designate a permanent seat of Government, the Congress had decided to meet alternately in New Jersey and Maryland; and in November, 1783, after lengthy sessions in Princeton, the lawmakers had assembled in Annapolis.

Johnson's earnest desire to remain in private life, in order to devote his entire attention to law and business, explains why he was not a member of Congress at this time. For within a month after Washington had proclaimed the end of the war, Johnson was strongly urged to accept a seat in Congress. At that time there were two vacancies in the Maryland delegation; and Johnson and James McHenry were chosen by the Legislature on May 12th to fill the vacant seats.[12] One reason for Johnson's election was the fact that it was believed he could exert powerful influence to induce Congress to lay out immediately "the common estate on the Western frontier of the United States"—the territory in which Maryland had always been so vitally interested. Johnson, one of the leading figures instrumental in saving this extensive region as a National domain, was thoroughly familiar with the subject; and, together with Dr. McHenry, Thomas Sim Lee and Daniel Carroll, the other members of the Maryland delegation, he was requested by the Legislature, in a resolution adopted

[12] *Votes and Proceedings of the Senate*, April 1783, p. 11.

May 31st, to urge the prompt opening of a Land Office, where creditors of the Government could receive warrants for land in lieu of money.[13] But preferring to remain in private life, Johnson declined the seat in Congress.[14] However, on November 26th—just four days after his letter of declination was read in the Legislature—his name was again placed in nomination; but, in view of his desire to remain at home, he was not elected. Later, on the 8th of December, after it was decided to add two additional members to the delegation, Johnson again was nominated, but again the Legislature refrained from electing him.[15]

Arriving on December 19th in Annapolis, Washington took the opportunity to impress upon members of Legislature and members of Congress the importance of establishing a stronger National Government. The members of the Legislature, in their reply, December 22nd, thanked the Commander-in-Chief for showing them how "to value, preserve, and improve that Liberty" which his services had secured under the smiles of Providence; but gave an evasive assurance when they said: "If the powers given to Congress by the Confederation should be found incompetent to the purposes of the Union, our constituents will readily consent to enlarge them."

At noon on December 23, 1783, the members of Congress and a crowd of visitors assembled in the Senate chamber of the Maryland State House—the same room in which Thomas Johnson had qualified as Governor during the war—to witness the resignation of Washington as the Commander-in-Chief of the Army. In describing how Washington now displayed the same quiet diffidence that he showed

13 Ibid., p. 52.
14 Ibid., November 1783, p. 3.
15 Ibid., p. 14.

at Philadelphia in 1775 at the time of his appointment, Woodrow Wilson says: "And then, standing before the Congress at Annapolis to resign his commission, he added the crowning touch of simplicity to his just repute as a man beyond others noble and sincere. . . . The plaudits that had but just now filled his ears at every stage of his long journey from New York seemed utterly forgotten; he seemed not to know how his fellow countrymen had made of him an idol and a hero; his simplicity was once again his authentic badge of genuineness." [16]

After referring to the justice of the American cause, the support of Congress and his countrymen, and the aid of Divine Providence, Washington said: "Having now finished the work assigned me, I retire from the great theatre of action and, bidding an affectionate farewell to this august body, under whose orders I have so long acted, I here offer my commission, and take my leave of all the employments of public life." Brief and simple as it was, Washington's address has been classed by Theodore Roosevelt and Henry Cabot Lodge as "one of the two most memorable speeches ever made in the United States" and "also memorable for its meaning and spirit among all speeches ever made by men." [17]

Thomas Mifflin, who had conspired with Gates during the Winter of Valley Forge to undermine the confidence of the people in General Washington, was now the President of Congress. It was Mifflin's duty to reply. "You retire," he said, "from the theatre of action with the blessings of your fellow citizens, but the glory of your virtues will not terminate with your military command; it will continue to

[16] Woodrow Wilson, *George Washington*, p. 226-7.
[17] Roosevelt and Lodge, *Hero Tales from American History*, Chapter I, p. 7.

animate remotest ages." He joined with Washington in beseeching God so to direct the people of the United States that they would accept the opportunity of becoming "a happy and respectable Nation."

On the following morning the marvelous Virginian, who had commanded the patriot forces for eight years and a half, departed from Annapolis as a private citizen and on Christmas eve entered the threshold of Mount Vernon. Like Thomas Johnson—lawyer, land owner and manufacturer —who preferred to return after his service as Governor to "the calm walk of private life," so George Washington— gentleman planter—declared his intention of spending the remainder of his days in "the practice of the domestic virtues."

CHAPTER XXIV

REVIVING THE RIVER PROJECT

"If the superintendence of this work would be only a dignified amusement to you, what a monument of your retirement would follow that of
your public life!"
            —*Thomas Jefferson to George Washington*, March 15, 1784.
"It appears to me, that the interest and policy of Maryland are proportionably concerned with those of Virginia, to remove obstructions, and
to invite the trade of the Western country into the channel you have mentioned . . . and I wish, if it should fall in your way, that you would
discourse with Mr. Thomas Johnson, formerly Governor of Maryland, on
this subject."
            —*Washington to Jefferson*, March 29, 1784.

PRIOR to the outbreak of the Revolution, Colonel George
Washington and Thomas Johnson, Esquire, were leading advocates of the scheme to extend navigation of the
Potomac River; but during the eight dreadful years that
followed, the project was altogether forgotten. With the
dawn of peace, General Washington and Governor Johnson took the view that development of inland navigation,
desired for *commercial* purposes during the days of the
Colonies, was now also of *political* importance—indeed,
essential for National solidarity, if not for the very preservation of the Union.

After proclaiming the end of the war, General Washington left his camp at Newburgh for a tour of the Mohawk
Valley to explore the possibilities of transportation. On
this trip, the Commander-in-Chief foresaw the profound
importance of navigation in the development of the United
States.

While General Washington was inspecting the region around the Great Lakes, two of Johnson's friends, Normand Bruce and Charles Beatty, were investigating for the State of Maryland the practicability of opening the Potomac River for navigation. Undoubtedly Johnson was pleased with the report—filed a month before Washington arrived in Annapolis to resign his commission—stating that the construction of approximately five miles of canal would probably afford navigation for light vessels as far as Fort Cumberland.[1]

By this time, other American statesmen were beginning to recognize the importance of inland transportation. While American sovereignty was carried as far as the Mississippi by the Treaty of 1783, it was evident that, if no means of communication were established, the people beyond the mountains would trade at New Orleans and perhaps ultimately drift apart from the Union. Therefore, the belief was growing that it was vitally necessary for the growth and prosperity of the Nation to establish communication through the gateways in the mountain-walls by means of locks, sluices around impassable falls and rapids, and portage roads where canalization was impossible.

Among those who became interested in the project was Thomas Jefferson, who served as Governor of Virginia following the Administration of Patrick Henry, and who was now a member of Congress. Like Washington, Jefferson stood for a possession of the great West not by military rule, as exercised by Great Britain and France, but by a commercial link that would be a blessing to all America. Hearing that the people of New York were considering a Northern route to the West, the Virginia Congressman

1 *Votes and Proceedings of the House of Delegates,* November 1783, p. 13.

urged Washington to take the lead in developing the Potomac route to the West, declaring that this route would "pour into our lap the whole commerce of the Western world." [2]

Washington replied that he heartily favored the project—indeed, he had promoted the idea, with the aid of Thomas Johnson, a decade before—and while agreeing that time should not be lost in getting the project under way, suggested that the former Governor of Virginia confer with the former Governor of Maryland regarding the plan. In his letter of March 29, 1784, Washington answered Jefferson as follows: [3]

"More than ten years ago, I was struck with the importance of it and, despairing of any aids from the public, I became a principal mover of a bill to empower a number of subscribers to undertake at their own expense the extension of the navigation from tide water to Will's Creek, about 150 miles. To get this business in motion, I was obliged to comprehend James River, in order to remove the jealousies, which arose from the attempt to extend the navigation of the Potomac. The plan was in a tolerably good train, when I set out for Cambridge in 1775, and would have been in an excellent way, had it not been for the difficulties, which were met with in the Maryland Assembly from the opposition which was given by the Baltimore merchants, who were alarmed at the consequence of water transportation to Georgetown of the produce which usually came to their markets by land. The local interest of that place, joined to the short-sighted politics or contracted views of another part of that Assembly, gave Mr. Thomas Johnson, who was a warm promoter of the scheme on the North side of the Potomac, a great deal of trouble. . . . It appears to me, that the interest and policy of Maryland are proportionably concerned with those of Virginia, to remove obstructions, and to invite the trade of the Western country into the channel you have mentioned. You will have frequent opportunities of learning

---

[2] *Letters to Washington*, IV, p. 62.
[3] *Sparks*, Vol. IX, p. 31.

the sentiments of the principal characters of that State, respecting this matter; and I wish, if it should fall in your way, that you would discourse with Mr. Thomas Johnson, formerly Governor of Maryland, on this subject."

In May, 1784, however, Jefferson retired from Congress; and having been selected at this time to assist Benjamin Franklin and John Adams in the negotiation of commercial treaties with European countries, he set sail for France early in July, and consequently was unable to coöperate with Washington and Johnson in connection with the Potomac project.

Hearing that certain portions of his land were being occupied by squatters and even offered for sale by thieving land agents, Washington decided to make a journey across the Alleghanies to familiarize himself with his possessions in the West: at the same time he could investigate "the nearest and best communication between the Eastern and Western waters."

Starting out September 1, 1784, Washington arrived on September 5th at the village of Bath—now called Berkeley Springs—where James Rumsey showed him a model of a boat intended to operate without sail against the current of a stream. The ingenious machinist, who had been born in Maryland scarcely more than forty years before, gave a demonstration of the boat; and so delighted was Washington that he gave the inventor a certificate of commendation. "I have seen," wrote Washington, on September 7th, "the model of Mr. Rumsey's boat, constructed to work against the stream; examined the powers by which it acts; have been the eyewitness to an actual experiment in running water of some rapidity; and give it as my opinion (although I had but little faith before) that he has discovered the art of working boats by mechanism and small manual assistance against rapid currents; that the discovery is of vast importance, that it may be of the greatest usefulness in our inland navigation, and if it succeeds (of which I have no doubt) that the value of it is greatly enhanced by the simplicity of the works which, when seen and explained, may be executed by the most common mechanic." [4]

Observe that Washington, in the aforegoing testimonial, did not use the word *steam!* Indeed, three years later, as we shall see, Washington is frank to tell Johnson that the use of steam was not contemplated by Rumsey as a part of his original plan in 1784, but was regarded by Washington merely "as the ebullition of his [Rumsey's] genius." However, the mechanical boat, crude as it was, served to deepen Washington's interest in the proposal of connecting the East and the West.

During the month of September, Washington was "deep in the wilderness, riding close upon seven hundred miles through the forested mountains, and along the remote courses of the long rivers that ran into the Mississippi." [5] During his long tour of the wilderness, Washington took particular pleasure in inspecting Johnson's land in the Glades of the Youghiogheny River, writing in his Diary on September 26th: "Part of these Glades is the property of Govr Johnson of Maryland who has settled two or three families of Palatines upon them." [6]

Before nightfall of October 4, 1784, Washington returned to Mount Vernon, more than ever convinced of the great value of opening the channel of the Potomac to navigation. He believed that it was practicable to reach the

[4] Williams, *History of Frederick County, Maryland,* Vol. I, p. 338.
[5] Woodrow Wilson, *George Washington,* p. 242.
[6] Hulbert, *Washington and the West,* p. 69.

Lakes by the following route: (1) ascend the South Branch of the Potomac; (2) cross a portage road to Cheat River; (3) descend to the Monongahela; (4) ascend the West Fork of the Monongahela; (5) cross a portage to Little Kanawha; (6) descend to the Ohio; (7) ascend to the mouth of the Muskingum; (8) ascend the Muskingum to a portage; (9) cross portage to the Cuyahoga; (10) descend to Lake Erie. It was a visionary proposal: and its espousal "by so sane a man as Washington is a graphic commentary on the pioneer American commercial problem." [7]

On October 10th, Washington sent to Governor Harrison, for the use of the Virginia Assembly, an exhaustive report of the Western journey. And five days later, Washington solicited the aid of Johnson in securing the passage of the Potomac measure at Annapolis. Washington's letter follows: [8]

GEORGE WASHINGTON TO THOMAS JOHNSON

Mount Vernon,
Oct. 15, 1784.

Dear Sir,

On a supposition that you are now at Annapolis, the petition of the Potowmack Company is enclosed to your care. A duplicate has been forwarded to the Assembly of this State, the fate of which I have not yet heard, but entertain no doubt of its favourable reception; as there are many auspicious proofs of liberality and justice already exhibited in the proceedings of the present session. I hope the same spirit will mark the proceedings of yours.

The want of energy in the Federal government—the pulling of one State and party of States against another, and the commotion amongst the Eastern people have sunk our National character much

[7] *Ibid.*, p. 124.
[8] Williams, *History of Frederick County, Maryland*, Vol. I, p. 105; Bacon-Foster, *Records of Columbia Historical Society*, Vol. XV, p. 134.

below par; and have brought our politics and credit to the brink of a precipice. A step or two further must plunge us into a Sea of Troubles, perhaps anarchy and confusion. I trust that a proper sense of justice and unanimity in those States which have not drunk so deep of the cup of folly may yet relieve our affairs, but no time is to be lost in essaying them.

I have written to no Gentleman in your Assembly respecting the Potowmack business but yourself. The justice of the cause and your management of it will insure success.

With great Regard and Respect,
I am, Dear Sir,
Your most obedient, humble serv't,

Go WASHINGTON.

Mr. Johnson, however, was now in private life; and he forwarded the petition to the Legislature which convened in November, 1784.

At an enthusiastic meeting in Alexandria on November 15th, attended by leading men from both sides of the Potomac, propaganda in behalf of inland navigation was set in motion. But it seemed that the provisions of the proposed Act were not altogether satisfactory to both Maryland and Virginia; and Washington suggested to James Madison, then a promising young member of the Virginia Assembly, that commissioners should be appointed by the two Legislatures to confer in regard to the measure. The suggestion was promptly adopted; and Washington, General Horatio Gates and Colonel Blackburn were named as commissioners for Virginia. Gates and Blackburn, however, gave no assistance, and Washington, meeting a committee from the Maryland Legislature at Annapolis on December 22, 1784, worked far into the night during the Yuletide season in shaping a measure that might prove to be satisfactory to both States.

The report of the conference recommended the adoption

of an identical Act, authorizing the formation of the Potomac Company (then generally written Patowmack) as a body corporate to undertake the work of making the Potomac River navigable. The corporation was given the power of *eminent domain* and perpetual authority to charge tolls on the Potomac River, provided that navigation was extended to Fort Cumberland within three years after the formation of the Company.[9]

The Charter was passed at Annapolis with only nine dissenting votes; and at Richmond, on January 5, 1785, without opposition. Thus the Potomac Company became a corporation. The prompt passage of the Charter shows the characteristic enthusiasm and the powerful influence of Johnson in Maryland and Washington in Virginia.

The subscription books were opened in February at Annapolis, Frederick and Georgetown; and at Richmond, Alexandria and Winchester. While the people had been impoverished by the War for Independence, the wealthier men on both sides of the Potomac purchased the stock when they heard that the corporation was endorsed by such men as General Washington and Governor Johnson. Among the Marylanders who purchased stock in the Company were members of the best families in the State, including many of the relatives and personal friends of Governor Johnson. Among the Virginians who subscribed was John Marshall, who voted for the charter in the House of Delegates at Richmond. "Thus early," it has been pointed out by Senator Beveridge, "did Marshall's ideas on the nature of a legislative franchise to a corporation acquire the vitality of property interest and personal experience."[10]

The first meeting of stockholders in the Potomac Com-

[9] *Laws of Maryland*, November 1784, Chapter XXXIII.
[10] Albert J. Beveridge, *The Life of John Marshall*, Vol. I, p. 218.

pany was held at Alexandria on May 17, 1785. About sixty subscribers put in their appearance. George Washington was present; but Thomas Johnson, although genuinely interested in the Company and the purchaser of a large block of its stock, did not attend, being prevented from making the trip to Alexandria by important business and professional duties. However, he gave a proxy to his personal friend, Abraham Faw, of Frederick.

Following a mid-day banquet, Washington called the meeting to order. Briefly he told of the political and commercial significance of the project and predicted ultimate reimbursement to the stockholders. It was announced that of the total issue of 500 shares of stock—offered at 100 pounds Sterling per share—approximately 400 shares of stock had already been sold. This indicated a fund of forty thousand pounds—upwards of one hundred and eighty thousand dollars—with which to commence the colossal task.

Daniel Carroll, of Maryland, who was chosen temporary chairman, next appointed a committee to examine the proxies. Then it was discovered that the proxy certificate signed by Governor Johnson—although an eminent lawyer, later to become Associate Justice of the Supreme Court—was disallowed. Johnson's proxy was one of those held defective on account of having only one witness; but most of the other proxies held by Mr. Faw—including those of Thomas Johnson's brother, Baker, and former Governor Thomas Sim Lee—were allowed to vote.

But while a legal technicality deprived Governor Johnson of a vote at the election of officers, he was honored —after Washington was elected President of the Company —by being chosen one of the members of the Board of

Directors. The other Directors (all elected to serve until August, 1786) were: Thomas Sim Lee, of Maryland; and George Gilpin and John Fitzgerald, of Virginia.

On the day after the organization meeting, Washington sent Johnson a letter, notifying him of his election to the directorate and inquiring if he could attend a meeting of the Board at an early date. Johnson accepted. His reply follows:[11]

THOMAS JOHNSON TO GEORGE WASHINGTON

Fredk 21 May 1785

Sir

I shall forward your Letter of the 18 Inst to Mr. Lee. I have no opportunity of consulting him as to the place or Hour of Meeting: as it can make very little Difference to him or me and Alexandria will be most convenient to you and the other Gent. I propose to meet there at 10 Oclock and shall write Mr. Lee accordingly—I much wished to have been at the Meeting the 17th if I could have attended. I should have endeavoured to excuse myself being under promise to attend at Williamsburgh next Month in the Federal Court and having a private Interest to adjust with the Company at the Great Falls I now agree to act as a Director imagining that the Great Falls will not be an immediate Object but if I am mistaken in that or my attenda at Williamsburgh will in any degree delay the Execution of the work I shall chearfully make Room for some Body else who can attend and act with propriety.

I am Sir
With great Truth & Respect,
Your most obedt Servant,

THs JOHNSON.

Johnson was kept busy, during the early days of commercial reconstruction, with business and legal affairs; but

[11] *The Papers of George Washington,* Library of Congress.

the project of inland navigation was near his heart; and moreover his service on the directorate of the corporation promised to give him an opportunity to come in close touch with Washington, whom he so fondly admired.

Johnson attended the first meeting of the Board of Directors at Alexandria on May 30, 1785. At this meeting it was decided to request subscribers to pay in their first installments on or before July 15, in order that actual operations could begin the first of August. Washington was jubilant on the 25th of July, when he wrote to Lafayette regarding the sale of stock and the election of Johnson, Lee, Gilpin and Fitzgerald to help "conduct the undertaking."

On Monday, August 1, 1785, Johnson met Washington and the other Directors at Georgetown, where they held the first annual meeting of the Board. They decided to make a personal inspection of the channel as far as the Shenandoah.

Accompanied by James Rumsey, whom they appointed superintendent, and Richardson Stuart, his assistant, the President and Directors started out on their survey on the morning of August 2nd. Having provided themselves with canoes, they paddled on the following day from Seneca Falls to the Great Falls. "The canoe or pirogue, in which General Washington and a party of friends made the first survey of the Potomac to ascertain the practicability of a navigation above tide-water," says G. W. P. Custis, [12] "was hollowed out of a large poplar tree under the direction of General Johnson, of Frederick County, Maryland. This humble bark was placed upon a wagon, hauled into the stream, and there received its honored freight. . . . At night-fall, it was usual for the party to land and seek

[12] Custis, *Recollections and Private Memoirs of the Life and Character of Washington.*

quarters of some of the planters or farmers who lived near the banks of the river, in all the pride and comfort of old-fashioned kindliness and hospitality."

On August 4th, Superintendent Rumsey started nine men to work; and on the 5th, the President and Directors started out again, after directing Rumsey to meet them on the following evening at Harper's Ferry. They decided to go by way of Frederick Town, so that Washington could spend a night with Johnson's family. In his Diary, Washington records the fact that he reached Frederick on Friday evening and lodged that night at the home of Governor Johnson. "In the Evening," says the Diary,[13] "the Bells Rang, and Guns were fired; and a Committee waited upon me by order of the Gentlemen of the Town to request that I w^d stay next day and partake of a publick dinner which the Town were desirous of giving me—But as arrangements had been made, and the time for examining the Shennondoah Falls, previous to the day fixed for receiving labourers into pay, was short I found it most expedient to decline the honor."

Unostentatious was the appearance of Washington in Frederick. And his entertainment by Johnson, hospitable but unceremonious, accorded with the desire of both for simplicity. After an early breakfast at Johnson's home on the morning of August 6th, they proceeded on their journey to Harper's Ferry. Ex-Governor Lee, whose home was located near the Gap, joined the party late in the day and at twilight Washington and the Directors held a meeting at one of the most picturesque spots of the Potomac.

Up at sunrise Sunday morning, the party made a further examination of the channel and inspected the gut through which they hoped to conduct the navigation. The prospect

[13] W. S. Baker, *Washington After the Revolution*, pp. 34 and 35.

appeared rosy; and President Washington, Director Johnson and their associates left for their homes with high hopes for the success of the Potomac Company and eventual transportation to the Lakes.

But the troubles of the Company were just about to begin. First came the labor problem. Superintendent Rumsey soon found that he was unable to employ more than about seventy men, and even these were very unreliable, many of them disorderly. Rumsey took up the problem with Johnson and Lee, who decided it would be advantageous to obtain a number of Negro slaves for the enterprise. Johnson wrote Washington a letter, maintaining that Negro labor would be more valuable than that of "common white hirelings." [14]

At the next meeting of the President and Directors, held in Georgetown October 17, 1785, the labor question was thoroughly discussed, and it was decided to hire Negroes at the annual wage of twenty pounds, Virginia currency, with clothing and rations.

At the conclusion of the business session, Washington accompanied the Directors on another inspection of the river. And as the Autumn twilight came while on their way to the Great Falls, the members of the party paired off in search of shelter for the night. "Dispersing for the convenience of obtaining Quarters," says Washington in his Diary, "Govr Johnson and I went to Mr. Bryan Fairfax." And so, cheered by the same glowing fireside in a comfortable Virginia home, the two bosom friends spent the night together, dreaming of the day when the mountains would be conquered and the great wilderness beyond transformed into a land of thriving civilization.

---

[14] *Records of the Columbia Historical Society,* Vol. XV, p. 160.

CHAPTER XXV

LAWMAKER AGAIN—THE RISE OF
NATIONALISM

"And [God] hath determined the times before appointed, and the bounds
of their [all nations'] habitation."—*The Acts, XVII, 26.*

"From Thee all human actions take their springs,
The rise of empires, and the fall of kings!"
—*Samuel Boyse.*

"Yet I doubt not thro' the ages
one increasing purpose runs,
And the thoughts of men are widen'd
with the process of the suns."
—*Alfred Tennyson.*

DURING a period of five years, following the adoption
of the Articles of Confederation, Mr. Johnson was repeatedly urged to return to public life. On December 4,
1784, he was chosen by the Legislature to serve as one of
Maryland's representatives in Congress;[1] but he promptly
sent back to Annapolis his declination. He did accept,
however, under date of February 27, 1785, an appointment
from Congress as Judge on a special Court to hear and determine a dispute between the State of Massachusetts and
the State of New York.[2]

In the meantime—on January 19, 1785—Johnson was
honored by the Legislature with another commission—to

[1] *Votes and Proceedings of the House of Delegates,* November 1784, p.
27.

[2] *Journals of the American Congress* (1774-1788), Volume IV, December
24, 1784, p. 460; *acceptance,* p. 487.

attend a conference between Maryland and Virginia for the discussion of the jurisdiction and navigation of the Potomac and Pocomoke Rivers and that part of the Chesapeake Bay lying within the limits of Virginia. It appears that Virginia had ceded to Maryland entire jurisdiction over the Potomac, reserving to herself only the right of free navigation; but the arrangement had proved to be unsatisfactory to Virginia. Congressman Jefferson, among those who favored a conference to insure harmony between the two States, explained to Mr. Madison that "the cession of the back lands" had put Maryland in "good humor" and offered "an apt crisis for negotiations."[3] Pleased with the idea, young Madison put a measure through the Virginia Assembly calling for the appointment of commissioners for the purpose; and Madison, Edmund Randolph, George Mason and Alexander Henderson were named to represent the Commonwealth. The Maryland Legislature, accepting the suggestion, appointed Thomas Johnson, Samuel Chase, Thomas Stone and Daniel of St. Thomas Jenifer.[4]

Johnson's interest in commerce—especially in connection with the Potomac project—was well known; and the members of the Legislature believed he could be induced to attend the conference. But he did not find it convenient to appear in Alexandria at the appointed time in March, 1785. Nor did Madison and Randolph attend. But the other commissioners, accepting an invitation to meet at Washington's home, negotiated there a Compact providing that the Potomac and the Pocomoke and the waters of the Chesapeake within the limits of Virginia should be a common highway and that no toll or duty should ever be im-

[3] Bancroft, *History of the Formation of the Constitution*, p. 113.
[4] *Votes and Proceedings of the House of Delegates*, November 1784, p. 113.

posed by Virginia upon any vessel sailing through the Capes of the Chesapeake to or from the State of Maryland.

The Maryland Legislature, in addition to ratifying the Mount Vernon Compact, recommended that commissioners from Maryland and Virginia should meet again to discuss interstate trade regulations—if possible, adopt a uniform system of duties and a uniform currency—and also invite representatives from Pennsylvania and Delaware to the conference. When this recommendation reached Richmond, Mr. Madison, an ardent advocate of a more perfect Union, was quick to take advantage of the opportunity of urging a Convention to discuss the whole subject of interstate commerce. If four States could participate in a friendly discussion of the subject, why could not all the thirteen? And in accordance with this idea, the Virginia Assembly, in January, 1786, favored a Convention of all the States to examine the situation of trade in the United States and "to consider how far a uniform system in their commercial regulations may be necessary to their common interest and their permanent harmony."

Perhaps not a soul in America dreamed how the plan to discuss commercial regulations would be an important step in the rise of Nationalism. Even Madison himself declared to James Monroe that the Convention might not amount to much, but was "better than nothing" and might "lead to better consequences than at first occur." In due time, a letter was issued by the Governor of Virginia to the several States, inviting them to select commissioners to attend a Convention at Annapolis on the first Monday of September, 1786.

Ex-Governor Johnson—although he had declined a seat in Congress and had failed to attend the conference at

Mount Vernon—was nominated in the House of Delegates on February 20, 1786, as one of the commissioners to represent Maryland in discussions concerning trade regulations. However, he was not among the five elected, doubtless due to his known desire to remain in retirement. But, on March 8th, after it was proposed to select two additional commissioners to attend the Convention of all the States— in accordance with the plan suggested by Virginia—Johnson was placed in nomination again to represent Maryland at the gathering.[5]

Now came an unexpected situation. A number of the members of the Senate became afraid that the proposed Convention "may be misunderstood or misrepresented in Europe, give umbrage to Congress, and disquiet the citizens of the United States, who may be thereby led erroneously to suspect that the great council of this country wants either the will or the wisdom to digest a proper uniform plan for the regulations of their commerce." The Senate, therefore, refused to ballot for commissioners!

The action of the Senate on the eve of adjournment was a great surprise—especially to Virginia. Since the adoption of the Declaration of Independence, Maryland had not been regarded as one of the "reluctant States." While she was the last State to ratify the Articles of Confederation, her delay in behalf of the Northwest as the common property of the United States had served as the foundation for the rise of Nationalism. Moreover, she had been complying with requests of Congress with a fair degree of promptness. And as Daniel Carroll pointed out, in a letter to Madison on March 13, 1786, the refusal of the Maryland

[5] *Votes and Proceedings of the House of Delegates,* November 1785, p. 185.

Senate to sanction the appointment of commissioners to the Convention of States was due to "an over-caution in behalf of the Union" rather than "opposition to a stronger Union." The attitude of the Maryland Senators—that the proposed Convention might "have a tendency to weaken the authority of Congress on which the Union and consequently the liberty and safety of all the States depend"—was ludicrous. As a matter of fact, even if "the spirit of the Confederation" required that all matters of general interest to America should be considered first in Congress, "sound policy" did not require such deference. Instead of guaranteeing the liberty and safety of the United States, the Confederation, as Washington stated to Johnson in 1784, had "brought our politics and credit to the brink of a precipice."

At all events, Johnson was not given the opportunity to decide whether to accept a seat in the Convention of 1786. But he was not especially concerned over the attitude of the State. Perhaps he felt that the critical condition of the country was due to the people themselves: that the country needed the homely virtues—honesty and patient endeavor—rather than the further enactment of laws. Johnson did not possess the enthusiasm of Washington, Hamilton and Madison concerning the form of Government. A business man by preference and a public man by necessity, he felt that hard work was needed for the reconstruction of the Nation and he was willing to leave the discussions of National policy to other men who had more leisure time at their disposal.

In the midst of the political discussions dealing with the proposed Convention in 1786, Johnson was devoting his attention to his varied private interests. He took considerable delight in the Iron Works which he owned in connection with his brothers, James, Baker and Roger.   Their Catoctin Furnace, located on the slope of Catoctin Mountain some miles North of Frederick Town, had become one of the most successful business enterprises in the country. Yet the workmanship in casting was still primitive and crude: there was much still to be learned.   Governor Johnson himself admits that the effort to forge at the Catoctin Iron Works some of the machinery for Rumsey's steamboat was a failure.   Following the meeting of the President and Directors of the Potomac Company in October, 1785, Mr. Rumsey disclosed the fact that he was relying on steam as the motive power for his boat, and asked Johnson if he would have the cylinders cast at the Furnace.   Johnson agreed to help the young inventor: but "the attempt did not succeed" and it became necessary to make the "copper cylinders in Frederick Town some time after." [6]   Thus, little, if any, of the machinery in the first steamboat was made by the Johnson Brothers at Catoctin Furnace, the boiler and the pumps and pipes having been made in Baltimore and other parts at the Antietam Iron Works.

But despite the crudeness of the workmanship, the enterprises of the Johnson brothers grew to tremendous proportions.   Continuing to expand their business, the four brothers built a furnace along Rocky Run, where they believed they could secure a quantity of valuable iron ore. Needing a large supply of firewood, they petitioned the Legislature to allow them to acquire the timberland on Sugar Loaf Mountain from the State.   They alleged that very little of the land was fit for cultivation and they agreed to pay a nominal price for it.   On March 9, 1786, the Senate

[6] *Exhibit, Public Document 189,* 27th Congress, 7th Session.

voted them an option until the first of September to purchase any part of the several thousand acres of vacant land on the rocky spur at the price of 1 shilling and 8 pence per acre.[7] In the House of Delegates the measure met with opposition and finally was voted down. Its rejection by the Lower House was a profound disappointment to the members of the Senate, who believed that it was the duty of the State to show appreciation of the magnanimous service rendered by Governor Johnson and his brothers during the Revolution. In plain terms, the Senators asked the Delegates to reconsider their action. Said the Senate: "The price to be paid for the land on the Sugar Loaf Mountain is certainly its worth, the object for which it is desired to be bought ought to be encouraged, and the persons who solicit to be purchasers have a just claim to the attention of the Legislature to their reasonable requests."[8] Accordingly, the question was brought up again in the House. But it is evident that personal jealousies had entered into the fight. Abraham Faw, of Frederick County, intimate friend of Governor Johnson, voted for reconsideration; while John Beatty, also of Frederick, voted against it. Among the others who turned a deaf ear to the Senate's appeal was the hot-tempered Michael Taney, of Calvert County, whose nine-year old son, Roger Brooke Taney, was destined to find Thomas Johnson one of his most helpful friends at Frederick in the early part of the nineteenth century. Despite the fact that such influential leaders as Samuel Chase and Thomas Stone, Signers of the Declaration of Independence, voted in accordance with the Senate's request, the motion was lost by a vote of 19 to 23.

[7] *Votes and Proceedings of the Senate,* November 1785, p. 80.
[8] *Votes and Proceedings of the House of Delegates,* November 1785, p. 196.

Undiscouraged by the refusal of the Legislature to allow them to buy the land on the Sugar Loaf, the enterprising brothers continued to purchase thousands of acres of wooded land in other sections. One of the large acquisitions of Governor Johnson about this time was a tract of 2,000 acres of land in Washington County, called "Thomas and Ann," secured by a patent from the State.[9]

In addition to his private business, Mr. Johnson continued to devote a considerable portion of his time during 1786 to the work of the Potomac Company. He attended a meeting of the President and Directors of the Company at the Great Falls on March 1, 1786; and he also conferred with Washington again on the 3rd of July.[10]

At the annual meeting of stockholders of the Potomac Company in Alexandria on August 7, 1786, when the first report of the Board of Directors was submitted by President Washington, it was clear that the corporation had not been making the degree of progress anticipated. Not only had the officers met with delay on account of troubles with laborers, but their work had been retarded considerably both in 1785 and in 1786 by the extraordinary amount of rainfall and the high waters that submerged the banks of the river. It was accordingly decided to authorize the President and Directors to petition the Legislatures of Maryland and Virginia for additional time in which to complete the work.

Washington agreed to use his influence to secure an amendment to the Charter at Richmond, while Johnson was to work for a similar enactment at Annapolis. It is very likely that the vital importance of such a measure was

[9] *Maryland Land Office, Liber* I. C. No. C, folio 6. December 6, 1786.
[10] *The Diaries of George Washington,* edited by John C. Fitzpatrick, Vol. II.

largely responsible for Johnson's decision to return to the Maryland Legislature. After declining a seat in the State Senate, offered him by the Electoral College in September,[11] he was elected to the House of Delegates. He immediately accepted.

After being in almost complete retirement from public life for more than five years, Mr. Johnson found that he was somewhat out of harmony with things around the State House when he took his seat as a Delegate from Frederick County in November, 1786. Conditions had greatly changed since he had last served in the Legislature. There were no war measures to be considered: but the grave problems that faced the State during this critical period of American history called for a high order of statesmanship. There were many new politicians in Annapolis. But one of the men who had long been a familiar figure at the Capital, who now claimed a seat in the House as a Delegate from Anne Arundel County, was the stormy Samuel Chase. Even now the validity of Chase's election was in dispute, it being claimed that he could not legally serve inasmuch as he was not an actual resident of Anne Arundel County at the time of the election. Delegate Johnson, who was a member of the Elections Committee, took this view; while the other members of the Frederick County Delegation— Abraham Faw, Mountjoy Bayly, and Peter Mantz—voted in favor of the validity of the election. It appears that Chase was seated by a comfortable majority.[12]

In the early days of the State, the legislators were not bound by blocs or cliques. These were the days when, regardless of friendships, men voted their own personal con-

[11] *Votes and Proceedings of the Senate,* November 1786, p. 3.
[12] *Votes and Proceedings of the House of Delegates,* November 1786, p. 1.

victions. During this session of the Legislature, Johnson showed his conservative temperament when he favored a *per diem* of 14 shillings and "the like sum for itinerant charges" for each member of the House of Delegates; whereas the allowance was set at 17 shillings, 6 pence, half penny, and "the like sum for itinerant charges." He again showed that he was not an extremist when he helped to defeat a scheme to impose a fine upon every able-bodied Delegate who failed to appear in the House by nine o'clock in the morning. Likewise he opposed an unsuccessful effort to increase the fee of jurors and witnesses attending the General Court.

While Delegate Johnson's time was largely consumed during this session in the consideration of innumerable complaints, claims growing out of the War of the Revolution, and applications for relief, he was also asked to give his attention to a number of legislative matters of general interest. He was appointed to draft bills to provide for the more effectual administration of justice in the County Courts; to provide for the performance of contracts made prior to the Revolution; to mark and bound lands; to establish the law relating to apprentices; and to repeal a portion of the Act for the security of the Government; and to regulate the Militia of the State. He was also called on to draft a referendum bill to determine whether the Harford County Court House and Jail should be removed to Havre de Grace; a bill to erect a town at Fort Cumberland; and a bill to erect a town at the mouth of Conococheague Creek.

At this early day the controversy over slavery was just beginning to assert itself. Already in force in Maryland was a law to prevent the manumission of disabled and superannuated slaves as well as the manumission of slaves by will. The Legislature was now asked to decide whether this Act should be continued. Mr. Johnson—the owner of many slaves during his lifetime—voted to continue it. As happened on many other occasions, his colleague, Abraham Faw, took the opposite view; but the vote to continue was carried by an overwhelming majority.

But probably the measure in which Delegate Johnson was most profoundly interested at this session was the bill to amend the Charter of the Potomac Company. After considering the Company's petition—this alleged that the corporation had entered upon its work within the time specified by the Charter and had prosecuted its work with unremitting assiduity—the House, on November 21, 1786, selected Delegates Johnson, Chase and Faw to draft a bill to carry out the wishes of the Company.[13] Under the careful guidance of Delegate Johnson, the Act was passed allowing the Potomac Company an extension of time until November 17, 1790, to complete the work of extending navigation to Fort Cumberland; provided a similar law was enacted by the Assembly of Virginia.[14]

On December 7, 1786, Mr. Johnson forwarded a copy of the Act of Mount Vernon. In this connection he said:[15]

THOMAS JOHNSON TO GEORGE WASHINGTON

Annapolis, 7 Dec. 1786.

Sir

I am now able to inclose you a copy of the Potomack Bill passed both Houses of our Assembly without any Opposition if there should

[13] *Votes and Proceedings of the House of Delegates,* November 1786, pp. 5 and 7.
[14] *Laws of Maryland,* November 1786, Chapter II.
[15] *The Papers of George Washington,* Manuscript Division, Library of Congress.

have any Deviation been made by the Virginia Assembly from the Application we made I believe I can readily obtain a correspondent Alteration here if it should be necessary.

It has occurred to me that Mr. Smith on being furnished with a little pine plank and a Joiner might in a few Days have a Model made of the Locks for the Great Falls so as to exhibit the actual Effect in Miniature. I profess it would give me Satisfaction, as well perhaps as some degree of pleasure to the other Gent [lemen] and might possibly render even Smith's Ideas more correct on the Subject by showing in Time a defect, if there is any, in his plan.

The Winter is so unpromising that I expect we shall be very still till the Spring but if agreeable to the Gent [lemen] of Virg^a it is to Mr. Lee I wish Brindley to assist and advise on the Survey and Tract at the Little Falls from what Col^o Gilpin said I think we may expect Brindley indisposed to assist us and what would be liberal for his Trouble may be very usefully laid out.

The necessary Demands of Congress, our own poverty and want of Spirit, the Distractions to the Eastward and our Rage for paper money make my Time pass away here heavily enough—I am afraid I shall learn in the latter part of my Life that Americans are not so good as I thought them a Lesson much against my Will.

I am my dear Sir,
With great Truth and affection,
Your most obed^t serv^t

TH. JOHNSON.

In the meantime, Johnson and the other members of the Legislature had heard echoes of the Convention which had been held in Annapolis in September. Due largely to public indifference to things of National importance, only five States were represented—New York, New Jersey, Pennsylvania, Delaware, and Virginia—and the deputies who assembled in the Maryland Capital refrained from taking any final action relative to interstate regulations, but adopted an Address to the States—drafted by Alexander Hamilton and softened to suit the wishes of Edmund Ran-

dolph—setting forth the defects in the Articles of Confederation, the dangers that threatened the life of the Nation, and the imperative need for reorganization of the system of Government. The Address called upon the States to
send deputies to another Convention, "to take into consideration the situation of the United States, to devise such
further provisions as shall appear to them necessary to render the Constitution of the Federal Government adequate
to the exigencies of the Union." And so, early in December, 1786—about the time of the passage of the amendment
of the Charter of the Potomac Company—the Maryland
Legislature received the communication from the Governor
of Virginia recommending that deputies be chosen to attend
a Convention at Philadelphia on the second Monday in
May, 1787.

While not very deeply concerned in matters of political
policy, Mr. Johnson favored the proposal; and, on December 21, 1786, the House of Delegates adopted it without
opposition. On the same day, the Senate acquiesced, declaring that the plan appeared "to be of the utmost importance, and most likely, with the least delay, to vest in the
Federal Government those powers which are so necessary
to give strength and stability to the Union." [16] At the
same time, the Senate proposed a joint conference of the
two Houses to fix the powers of the deputies from Maryland. The House, accepting the proposal, named Johnson
as one of the conferees. The others chosen by the House
were: Samuel Chase, William Paca, John H. Stone, and
Robert Wright. The conferees representing the Senate
were: Thomas Stone, Charles Carroll of Carrollton, and

[16] *Votes and Proceedings of the House of Delegates,* November 1786,
p. 36.

William Hemsley. The joint committee held meetings during the Christmas season; and on New Year's Day of 1787 Chairman Johnson presented to the House the Conference Report, which recommended that the deputies in the Convention be clothed with ample authority to represent the State.[17]

Although both Houses had adopted the Conference Report, the Legislature adjourned *sine die* on January 20, 1787, without naming the deputies to the Constitutional Convention. This neglect, in the rush of legislative activity at the close of the session, gave Johnson little concern. Indeed, he had obtained leave of absence from the Assembly on the 16th, so anxious was he to return home; but a number of official duties kept him at Annapolis until the close of the session. And he was extremely happy when he found that the Amendment of the Charter of the Potomac Company was among the Acts approved by the Executive; and he could now return home with a light heart to his favorite endeavors in Frederick County.

The Spring session of the Legislature, convening on April 18, 1787, and lasting about five weeks, presented a final opportunity to select deputies to the Constitutional Convention. Delegate Johnson arrived on the 19th, and on the 20th the House of Delegates proceeded to nominate candidates for deputies. Johnson himself was a logical man to represent the State as one of the deputies. He had acquired experience and reputation in the Continental Congress, had been the leading figure in Maryland during the Revolution, was an able lawyer, and was popular. And, indeed, he was importuned by his friends to attend the Convention. But, having work to do, in connection with his

[17] *Ibid.,* p. 48.

private interests, and as a member of the Board of Directors of the Potomac Company, and knowing that service in the Convention would probably necessitate his residing in Philadelphia for a number of months, he asked to be excused. The House, therefore, omitted his name in making its nominations. On the following day (April 21, 1787) the Senate replied that the appointment of deputies to attend the Convention was "a matter of the highest importance to the Union" and announced that it wished to make some additional nominations: one of these was the name of Thomas Johnson. On April 23rd, the House explained that Johnson's name had been suggested in the House but it was omitted at his own request.[18] Thereupon the Legislature selected Charles Carroll of Carrollton, Thomas Sim Lee, Thomas Stone, Robert H. Harrison, and Dr. James McHenry.

Delegate Johnson's duties at the Spring session of the Legislature dealt mostly with questions of law and finance. On May 2nd, he was named chairman of a committee [19] to examine and report upon the Edition of Laws, which had been ordered compiled in 1784. Samuel Chase and Alexander C. Hanson had been designated to edit the work; but it is said that Hanson did the actual work, which required several years for completion. The Code contained Acts of Assembly under the Proprietary Government, Resolves of the Convention, the Maryland Constitution, the Articles of Confederation, and Acts of the State Legislature—all familiar ground to Governor Johnson.

At this session of the Legislature Johnson also served as chairman of a committee to make a thorough survey of

[18] *Ibid.,* April 1787, p. 116.
[19] *Ibid.,* p. 136.

the condition of the State Treasury and to report a plan for raising the necessary revenues for the State. He was also named on a joint committee of the House and Senate to consider ways and means of affording relief for insolvent debtors, deserving men who on account of the extraordinary conditions of the country were unable to sell their properties without a heavy sacrifice. He was chosen to consider applications from two natives of Ireland for naturalization as citizens of Maryland. He was called upon to frame a measure to prohibit the importation of slaves into the State. And he had a part in framing laws dealing with taxation, highway improvements, and other matters of public concern. The confidence of the Legislature in Johnson's ability in fiscal affairs was shown before final adjournment on May 20, 1787, when he was named, together with Governor Smallwood and Charles Carroll of Carrollton, to fix the terms upon which the Agent of the State should compromise with the Stock Trustees in the recovery of the Bank stock claimed by Maryland and also to expend all money arising therefrom in the manner that appeared to them most beneficial to the State.

In the meantime, it was found that Dr. McHenry was the only one of the five deputies-elect who consented to attend the Convention at Philadelphia. Attorney-General Luther Martin, Daniel of St. Thomas Jenifer, Daniel Carroll and John Francis Mercer were then chosen to fill the vacancies.

Thomas Johnson, therefore, deprived himself of the honor of signing the Constitution of the United States, just as he had deprived himself of the honor of signing the Declaration of Independence. But, after all, through the victory in saving the Western lands as the common property of the United States and his coöperation with Washington in the Potomac River project, Johnson played an important part in the rise of Nationalism. This is indicated by Woodrow Wilson, who gives the following explanation of the origin of the Federal Constitution: [20]

"It was not merely the hopeless confusion and sinister signs of anarchy which abounded in their own affairs . . . that brought the States at last to attempt a better union and set up a real government for the whole country. It was the inevitable continental outlook of affairs as well; if nothing more, the sheer necessity to grow and touch their neighbors at close quarters. . . . Everybody knows that it was a conference between delegates from Maryland and Virginia about Washington's favorite scheme of joining the upper waters of the Potomac with the upper waters of the streams which made their way to the Mississippi—a conference held at his suggestion and at his house—that led to the convening of that larger conference at Annapolis, which called for the appointment of the body that met at Philadelphia and framed the Constitution under which he was to become the first President of the United States."

Wilson's statement, so far as it refers to the Mount Vernon Conference of 1785, is misleading—for the subject of discussion at this Conference was not the scheme of extending navigation across the Alleghany Mountains, but the question of jurisdiction over the Chesapeake Bay and the Potomac and Pocomoke Rivers. But, at all events, it is certainly true that the organization of the Potomac Com-

[20] Woodrow Wilson, *The Making of the Nation*, Atlantic Monthly, July 1897, p. 7.

pany in 1785 exerted a powerful influence in producing the "continental outlook of affairs" that led the way to the adoption of the Constitution.

Behold Thomas Johnson as a promoter of commerce, an advocate of internal improvement, a dreamer of territorial expansion!

Had he not become, like George Washington, a National statesman without aiming to be one?

CHAPTER XXVI

A FRIEND OF THE FEDERAL CONSTITUTION

"So far as the sentiments of Maryland, with respect to the proposed Constitution, have come to my knowledge, they are strongly in favor of it. . . . Mr. Carroll of Carrollton, and Mr. Thos. Johnson, are declared friends to it."
—*George Washington to James Madison*, November 5, 1787.

"I shall think myself with America in general greatly indebted to the [members of the Federal] Convention and possibly we may confess it when it may be too late to avail ourselves of their Moderation and Wisdom."
—*Thomas Johnson to George Washington*, December 11, 1787.

ALTHOUGH he had asked to be excused from attending the sessions of the Constitutional Convention at Philadelphia, Mr. Johnson was not opposed in any way to the new plan of Federal Government. Indeed, his conservative temperament, his fondness for system and order, his vivid experience with a weak Confederation—as well as his great admiration for General Washington, who had laid down his sword to take up his pen for Nationalism—all placed Johnson naturally on the side of the proposed Constitution.

The War Governor knew that Washington had presided over the deliberations of the great Convention. And he also knew that such men as Benjamin Franklin, James Wilson, John Dickinson, Roger Sherman, and John Rutledge—outstanding leaders with whom he had served more than a decade before in the Continental Congress—had done the best they could to devise a system of Government that would promote the welfare of the Nation. The Articles of Confederation had been falling to pieces: and Johnson took the view of General Washington and Doctor Franklin that while the Constitution was not perfect in every respect—Washington himself admitted that it was a compromise "tinctured with some real though not radical defects"—it was the best Constitution that could be obtained under the circumstances; and at all events it was the final hope of saving the Union from dissolution.

Furthermore, Johnson was well pleased with the novel scheme of separate Federal and State sovereignties, giving, however, ample powers to Congress, including the power to regulate commerce with foreign Nations and among the several States. And, inasmuch as Maryland was one of the smaller States, he was particularly pleased with Article I, Section 3, which gave equality of representation in the United States Senate. All in all, he was delighted with the work of the framers.

And so, while Johnson had appeared to be indifferent to the form of Government prior to 1787, his interest in the Federal Plan was now waxing stronger. Washington, crying out to the leaders in despair to save the Union from chaos, had already begun his campaign for ratification; and Johnson, who had responded so promptly to his appeals for help during the Revolution, now determined to strengthen his hand in the crucial battle for Nationalism. Congress having submitted the proposed Constitution to the several States, Johnson agreed to serve again in the Maryland House of Delegates, the people's forum, where he could try to strengthen public sentiment in favor of ratification.

During the Summer of 1787, the Federal plan was warmly debated in the press and around the countryside of Maryland; and, as Autumn approached, it became evident that the plan would be an important issue at the elections in all sections of the State. At the same time it was also becoming apparent that the financial and commercial interests of Baltimore—as in Philadelphia and other growing centers of industry—would throw their influence in favor of a more stable Government. Yet, the largest vote in Baltimore for the House of Delegates was received by Samuel Chase, who while regarded at first as friendly to "an increase of the powers of Congress," was soon to sponsor *conditional ratification*, which was to be employed as the strategy of the Anti-Federalists. Nevertheless, the sentiment among the people appeared to be so "strong and general" in favor of the Constitution that it was believed Chase would be bound to vote for its ratification even if elected to a State Convention.[1]

And so, although two of Maryland's delegates to the Philadelphia Convention—Attorney-General Luther Martin and Attorney John Francis Mercer—had left their seats thoroughly disgusted with the Federal plan, and although it was evident that a determined opposition would be made against ratification, the Father of his Country was greatly cheered when he heard that Governor Johnson had joined the camp of the Federalists. On November 5, 1787, the great Virginian advised Madison regarding the sentiment for ratification North of the Potomac. "So far," declared Washington, "as the sentiments of Maryland, with respect to the proposed Constitution, have come to my knowledge, they are strongly in favor of it; but as this is the day on which the Assembly of that State ought to meet, I will say nothing in anticipation of the opinion of it. Mr. Carroll

[1] *Daniel Carroll to James Madison,* October 28, 1787.

of Carrollton, and Mr. Thos. Johnson, are declared friends
to it." [2]

While the 5th of November was the proper day for the
opening of the Legislature, the House was unable to secure
a quorum until the 14th. Thomas Johnson and Abraham
Faw, of Frederick County, were in their places when the
House convened. The other two members of the Frederick
County Delegation—ex-Governor Thomas Sim Lee and
Richard Potts, a young lawyer who had accompanied Johnson on his expedition to New Jersey in the early part of the
Revolution—were absent. And although the House received a report on November 19th from the Elections Committee—Delegate Allen Quynn, of Annapolis, was again
chairman of this Committee and Delegate Johnson one of
the members—that Johnson, Faw, Lee and Potts had been
duly elected Delegates for Frederick County,[3] it does not
appear that Potts and Lee were present at any time during
the session.

Once more Delegate Johnson was called on to assist in
preparing a great many important measures. Among the
more important were bills to secure the payment of imposts
and duties imposed by law; to raise the supplies for the
current year; to pay the salaries of officials and the other
expenses of the State; to provide for the continuance of
civil suits in the General and County Courts; and to amend
the jurisdiction of the High Court of Chancery.

Johnson also served with Charles Carroll of Carrollton,
who was now a member of the State Senate, in making an

---

[2] *The Writings of George Washington* (edited by W. C. Ford), Vol.
XI, p. 182. Original letter in the New York Public Library, New York
City.
[3] *Votes and Proceedings of the House of Delegates*, November 1787,
p. 4.

investigation of a loan of 270,000 florins procured in Holland in 1782, when Matthew Ridley, Agent of the State of Maryland, contracted with Messrs. Nicholas and Jacob Vanstaphorst, merchants of Amsterdam, for the delivery of tobacco within the State. Delegate Johnson and Senator Carroll admitted in their report that the money was obtained from individuals in Holland on the credit of the State, but held that the loan had no connection with the contract and the claim of the Messrs. Vanstaphorst for damages was unreasonable and unjust. Johnson was made chairman of a committee to prepare a measure in pursuance of the report; and a bill was passed repealing the Act respecting the loan passed at the November session of 1785.[4]

Another assignment that was given to Johnson at this session of the Legislature was to consider a petition from John Fitch for the exclusive right to build and navigate steamboats in Maryland. Mr. Johnson was chairman of the committee, the other members being Gabriel Duvall of the City of Annapolis, James Carroll of Anne Arundel, Jeremiah Nicholls of Kent, and George Dent of Charles.[5]

Who had been the first American to catch the vision of the steamboat? John Fitch or James Rumsey? This was the question the committee was called upon to decide. Of course, Johnson knew that Rumsey had been experimenting with the principle of steam propulsion as early as 1785, because the inventor had asked him to manufacture copper cylinders for the steamboat in the Fall of that year.[6]

Fitch, who was a native of Connecticut in the 45th year of his age, had been conducting his experiments at Phila-

[4] *Laws of Maryland,* November 1787, Chapter XXXIII.
[5] *Votes and Proceedings of the House of Delegates,* November 1787, page 3. Committee appointed on November 15, 1787.
[6] *Exhibit to Public Document,* 189, 27th Congress, 7th Session.

delphia and had demonstrated his steamboat on the Delaware to members of the Constitutional Convention in
August, 1787. Fitch now represented that the idea of propelling boats by steam "first struck him" in April, 1785.
Johnson thereupon undertook to ascertain when Rumsey
first thought of the idea. In the hope of securing definite
information on the subject, Johnson sent the following letter of inquiry to Washington: [7]

THOMAS JOHNSON TO GEORGE WASHINGTON

Annapolis 16 November 1787.

Sir.

I happen to be one of a Committee to report on the petition
of Mr. John Fitch of Pennsylvania for an exclusive Privilege in
this State, similar to what he has obtained in Virginia and several
others, to propel vessells through the water by the Force of Steam
Engines. I have found a necessity to mention to the Committee
a Conversation I had with Mr. Rumsey in the Month of October,
I think, in 1785 on the principle he expected to effect his boat
Navigation when he told me that he was to gain his first power
by Steam. It was so different from what I conjectured and had
been led some how to believe that I remarked he had treated you
with indelicacy by exhibiting his Model and Experiment before you
on a false principle and obtaining your Certificate. He told me
that although he exhibited on a different principle to prevent his
being traced he mentioned and explained to you alone that he relied on the Force of Steam to gain his first power. I remarked
that it was well he did since there might be no other way of protecting his exclusive Right but by recurring to you. In the present
Situation of the Committee and with the strongest Desire to do
Justice between Mr. Rumsey and Mr. Fitch the Committee request,
if that is consistent with your Situation, that you will be pleased to

[7] *The Papers of George Washington,* Library of Congress, Manuscript
Division.

inform me by a Line whether Mr. Rumsey disclosed to you any Idea of gaining his first power by Steam as he asserted to me or not.
I am Sir with great Respect
Your most obedient and most humble Servant,
TH. JOHNSON.

Washington replied that while the use of steam was not a part of Rumsey's original plan, nevertheless Rumsey conceived the idea of steam propulsion before it was conceived by Fitch. Washington's reply follows: [8]

GEORGE WASHINGTON TO THOMAS JOHNSON

Mount Vernon, 22 November, 1787.

Sir

The letter with which you have been pleased to honor me, dated the 16th inst, came to my hand the day before yesterday. By tomorrow's Post this answer will be forwarded to you.

Mr. Rumsey has given you an uncandid account of his explanation to me of the principle on which his Boat was to be propelled against stream. At the time he exhibited his model and obtained Certificate, I have no reason to believe that the use of steam was contemplated by him, sure I am it was not mentioned; and equally certain I am, that it would not apply to the project he *then* had in view; the first communication of which was made to me in September, 1784 (at the Springs in Berkley). The Novr. following, being in Richmond, I met Mr. Rumsey there who was at that time applying to the Assembly for an exclusive Act. He then spoke of the effect of Steam and the conviction he was under of the usefulness of its application for inland Navigation; but I did not then conceive, nor have I done so at any moment since, that it was suggested as a part of his original plan, but rather as the ebullition of his genius.

It is proper, however, for me to add that some time *after this*

[8] *George Washington Letter Book,* Library of Congress, Manuscript Division.

Mr. Fitch called upon me on his way to Richmond and explaining his scheme, wanted a letter from me, introductory of it to the Assembly of this State the giving of which I declined; and went on to inform him, that tho' I was bound not to disclose the principles of Mr. Rumsey's discovery, I could venture to assure him that the thought of applying steam for the purpose he mentioned was not original, but had been mentioned to me by Mr. Rumsey—this I thought myself obliged to say, that whichever (if either) of them was the dicoverer might derive the benefit of the invention. To the best of my recollection of what passed between Mr. Rumsey and me, the foregoing is an impartial recital.

Permit me to ask you, my good Sir, if a letter which I wrote to you during the sitting of your last Assembly, enclosing one from Mr. Wm Wilson to me, concerning the confiscated property of (I think) Maj^r Dunlap & Co of Glasgow ever reached your hands— and if it did, whether any thing was, or can be done in that business. As an Executor of the Will of Col^o Thomas Colvill it behooves me to know precisely what is to be expected from that matter as a large sum is due from that Company to his Estate and I am the more anxious to do it immediately as Mr. Wilson who is concerned in the House of Dunlap & Co is about to leave the country.

With great esteem and regard,

I am, Sir

Y^r most Obed^t H^{ble} Servant,

G^o WASHINGTON

Johnson's committee also received an affidavit of a reliable witness to the effect that Rumsey declared as early as the month of March, 1784, "that a boat might be constructed to work by steam, and that he intended to give it a trial." Rumsey's public demonstration, it is to be admitted, was delayed until December 3, 1787; but his steamboat had been ready in March when a rise in the Potomac, pending the making of repairs to the boiler, brought down a mass of débris which tore the craft from its moorings and badly damaged it. The committee felt that, as Rumsey had conceived the idea of steam propulsion as early as 1784, even if not before, whereas Fitch did not conceive the idea until 1785, according to his own admission, therefore it would not be proper to grant Fitch's petition and ignore Rumsey, a native of Maryland. On December 18, Johnson accordingly wrote to Rumsey from Annapolis that Fitch's application had been rejected. "I esteem myself," wrote Johnson,[9] "no ways competent to decide on philosophical or mechanical principles, but if you can simplify the steam engine, render it cheap, and apply its powers to raise water in great quantities, for the purposes of agriculture and water-works of all kinds, or apply the powers more immediately, as has been much the conversation between us at times, every man may easily perceive a vast field of improvement will thereby be opened, which I most sincerely wish you may largely reap the good fruits of."

Governor Johnson's hope that Rumsey would be rewarded was never fulfilled. After securing help from Doctor Franklin and others in Philadelphia, Rumsey went to England where he constructed a new steamboat; but just as he was ready for an exhibition on the Thames the craft was levied upon for debt. Later, when about to deliver a lecture to raise some needed cash, he was stricken ill; and on the night before Christmas, in 1792—when Mr. Johnson was serving as Associate Justice of the United States Supreme Court—the unfortunate inventor died in poverty. But his name will never die. For the correspondence between George Washington and Thomas Johnson regarding the invention had luckily been preserved; and in the year 1839 Congress adopted a resolution requesting President

[9] Exhibit to Public Document 189, 27th Congress, 7th Session.

Van Buren to present to James Rumsey, Jr., the only surviving child, a suitable gold medal "commemorative of his father's services and high agency in giving to the world the benefits of the steamboat." Thus the Government of the United States has officially approved the report presented by Thomas Johnson to the Maryland Legislature in 1787, holding that James Rumsey was the first American who found a method of successfully propelling a vessel by the use of steam.

It was on the 23rd of November, 1787, that the Maryland House of Delegates commenced its consideration of the Federal Constitution. On that day Delegate Johnson presented to Speaker Thomas C. Deye a communication from the Governor of Virginia enclosing resolutions of the Virginia Assembly on the subject.[10]

After the message from Virginia was read to the members of the House, it was moved that all the Maryland deputies to the Federal Convention—Mr. Jenifer, Dr. McHenry, and Daniel Carroll, the three who had signed their names to the instrument, as well as the recalcitrants, Attorney-General Martin and Attorney Mercer—should be requested to appear in the House on the 29th of the month to give an account of "the proceedings of the said Convention." Samuel Chase supported this suggestion. And many friends of the Constitution—among them Faw of Frederick—voted with him. Johnson voted against it. It is supposed that he felt the speeches were unnecessary and a waste of time. However, the motion was carried by a vote of 28 to 22. As a matter of fact, there did exist very little necessity for oral reports at this time, because immediately

[10] *Votes and Proceedings of the House of Delegates*, November 1787, p. 9.

afterwards the House resolved without opposition that the proceedings of the Federal Convention, as transmitted by Congress, should be submitted to a Convention of the people of the State "for their full and free investigation and decision.[11]

On November 24th, Mr. Chase was excused from attendance, as was also his colleague from Baltimore, David McMechen; and the Federalist members of the House— perhaps taking advantage of Chase's absence [12]—determined to make arrangements for the holding of a State Convention without waiting to hear from the members of the Federal Convention. Accordingly, on November 26th the Lower House proceeded to arrange special elections for delegates to the proposed Convention. A motion was made that the elections should be held throughout the State on the first Monday in April, 1788. Many of the more ardent Federalists in the Legislature, realizing that prompt action in arranging for a State Convention would give the enemies of the Federal Constitution less opportunity to strengthen their defense, were favorable to having the elections not later than January. Johnson could see no valid reason for delaying the elections until April and he voted against the motion. But it was carried by the narrow majority of one vote—24 to 23. The date of the elections having been settled, it was then decided without objection that the members of the Convention should meet in Annapolis on Monday, April 21, 1788.[13]

On the following day—November 27, 1787—a slight change was made in the House resolutions. The amend-

---

[11] *Ibid.*, p. 10.

[12] Mr. McMechen appeared in the House on November 29th; but Mr. Chase was absent until December 5th.

[13] *Ibid.*, p. 13.

ment provided in effect that the approval of the Federal
Constitution by a *majority* of the delegates in the Maryland Convention was sufficient to assure ratification thereof
by the State. The Frederick County legislators differed in
their opinion of the amendment: Mr. Faw being for it and
Mr. Johnson against it. Perhaps the ex-Governor felt this
was a question the members of the Convention should be
allowed to decide for themselves. However, the amendment was adopted by a vote of 28 to 21.

After the adoption of the amendment, Delegate Johnson was designated to present the resolutions regarding the
proposed State Convention to the Senate; and he promptly
delivered the House resolutions to President Plater on the
27th of November, 1787.[14]

Meanwhile, the members of the Senate had voted to
hold the elections in Maryland on the third Wednesday
in January so that the State Convention could be held early
in March. The language of the Senate resolution was
plainly Federalist in tone, for while the Lower House
recommended a Convention for "full and free investigation
and decision" the Upper House voted for a Convention for
"assent and ratification." [15]

On the 29th and 30th, the members of the Legislature
heard the reports from the deputies to the Philadelphia
Convention. The three Marylanders who had signed the
Constitution, while accustomed to public life, were not
lawyers, nor did they possess any outstanding ability in
oratory or debate. Daniel of St. Thomas Jenifer was a
capitalist and man of affairs, 54 years of age; Dr. McHenry

---

[14] *Votes and Proceedings of the House of Delegates*, November 1787,
p. 14; *Votes and Proceedings of the Senate*, November 1787, p. 6.
[15] *Votes and Proceedings of the Senate*, November 1787, p. 5.

was only 34 years old; while Daniel Carroll, a farmer, was scarcely over 31.

In comparison with these three friends of the Federal Constitution, Luther Martin was a powerful figure. A brilliant graduate of Princeton, a forceful orator, a lawyer of ability and Attorney-General of Maryland for nine years, Martin was now approaching at 43 the zenith of his career. While it does not appear from the House Records that Mr. Mercer—the 28-year-old lawyer who also opposed the Federal Constitution at Philadelphia—was present in the House of Delegates, the Attorney-General was fully prepared to make his vehement arraignment of the members of the Federal Convention. He declared that as soon as he took his seat at Philadelphia he saw that the selfish aggrandizement of the several States—particularly, Massachusetts, Pennsylvania and Virginia—appeared to be sought after more than the general welfare of America. He feared not only that the large States might increase their power over the smaller ones, but also that the National Government might interfere with those Anglo-Saxon rights for which the Colonists gave their lives and fortunes during the American Revolution. And therefore, he said, he opposed the Constitution "in every stage of its progression." But realizing that his arguments were "fruitless and unavailing," he left the Convention along with several other members before the Constitution was completed. "So destructive," declared Martin in conclusion, "do I consider the present System [the Constitution] to the happiness of my Country, I would cheerfully sacrifice that share of property with which Heaven has blessed a life of industry; I would reduce myself to indigence and poverty; and those who are dearer to me than my own existence I would entrust to the care and protection of that Providence which has so kindly protected me—if on those terms only could I procure my Country to reject those chains which are forged for it." [16]

But the mighty Martin was unable to stem the tide of Nationalism. Johnson and other influential Federalists in the Maryland Legislature were too well acquainted with George Washington to believe that he was conspiring to increase the power of Virginia and to "subvert the liberties of the United States."

Powerful as he was as lawyer and orator, Martin was sadly incorrect in his opinion of the Federal Constitution. And in his peroration he unwittingly painted a picture of his own future, for some years later the Legislature imposed a tax of five dollars per annum upon every lawyer in the State to keep him from destitution.

Finally, on the 1st of December, 1787, the Senate took under consideration the House resolutions calling for the elections in April. The Senators still preferred to have the elections in January in order to expedite the ratification of the Constitution; but they realized that it was more prudent to adopt the House resolutions than "run the hazard of protracting the session" by adhering to their own resolutions. So they decided to accede to the wishes of the members of the Lower House to hold the elections as well as the Convention in April, 1788. [17]

Thus the machinery was complete in Maryland for the consideration of the Federal Constitution. The State Printer was ordered to print two thousand copies of the proposed Constitution together with the Legislature's reso-

[16] Jonathan Elliot, *Debates in the Several State Conventions, on the Adoption of the Federal Constitution*, Vol. I, page 344.
[17] *Votes and Proceedings of the Senate*, November, 1787, page 7.

lutions while the Printer at Frederick was directed to print in German three hundred copies of the same for distribution in the State.

The news that Maryland was planning to defer consideration of the Federal Constitution until April, 1788, was somewhat disconcerting to the Federalists in other parts of the United States. Writing from New York under date of December 9, 1787, James Madison advised Thomas Jefferson, who was now serving as American Minister in France, that the Federalists continued to be sanguine that the new plan would be ratified by the States although opposition was rapidly growing in Virginia and Maryland. "The Constitution proposed by the late Convention," said Mr. Madison,[18] "engrosses almost the whole political attention of America. . . . Virginia has set the example of opening a door for amendments, if the Convention there should chuse to propose them. Maryland has copied it. . . . A more formidable opposition is likely to be made in Maryland than was at first conjectured. Mr. Mercer, it seems, who was a member of the Convention, though his attendance was but for a short time, is become an auxiliary to Chase. Johnson, the Carrolls, Govr Lee, and most of the other characters of weight, are on the other side."

Meanwhile, the annual meeting of the stockholders of the Potomac Company was held in November, having been postponed several months while Washington, who was President of the Company, was in Philadelphia. It was shown at the meeting that scarcely more than ten thousand pounds Sterling had been paid into the Company by the stockholders, and it was accordingly decided to ask the States of Virginia and Maryland for legislation that would

[18] *The Writings of James Madison* (edited by Hunt), Vol. V, page 62.

enable the Company expeditiously to compel the delinquent stock subscribers to pay in the balance of their subscriptions. Prompt action in this direction was taken by the Virginia Assembly. Shortly after the measure was adopted at Richmond, Washington appealed to former Governors Thomas Johnson and Thomas Sim Lee—both were still serving as Directors of the Potomac Company—to urge the adoption of a similar measure at Annapolis. Washington's communication to them follows: [19]

GEORGE WASHINGTON TO JOHNSON AND LEE

Mount Vernon, December 9th 1787.

Sirs,

Presuming that Colo Fitzgerald according to his promise has communicated to you the vote of the Potomack Co passed at the last general Meeting, held at George Town, and the measures consequent of it, taken by the Directors, I shall trouble you with no more than the result which you will find in the enclosed authenticated Act of the Assembly of this State.

It is scarcely necessary to observe to you, Gentlemen, that unless a similar one is obtained from your Assembly, during its present Session that the work of Navigation will soon be at a stand. You know what steps have been taken, and how ineffectually, to collect the Dividends from the tardy members. The others think it hard to be further called on . . . until the arrearages are paid up.

To recover these will be a work of immense time under the existing law.

You know best under what form to bring this matter before your Assembly. If by way of Petition you will please to have one drawn, and if it is necessary the name of the President should be affixed thereto I hereby authorize you to give it my signature. With great esteem

I am Gentlemen

Yr Most Obedt & Very Hble Servant,

Go WASHINGTON.

[19] *George Washington Letter Book,* Library of Congress, Manuscript Division.

Ex-Governor Lee, although legally entitled to serve as a member of the Frederick County delegation, had not been attending the session of the Legislature; and Johnson, in compliance with Washington's request, at once asked the House on December 11th for permission to bring in a bill giving to the Potomac Company a speedier remedy against delinquent subscribers. The House acquiesced and asked him to prepare the measure.[20] In advising Washington to this effect, Johnson sets forth his views in regard to the Federal Constitution. He says:[21]

THOMAS JOHNSON TO GEORGE WASHINGTON

Annapolis 11 December 1787.

Sir.

Your Favor of the 9th directed to Mr. Lee and myself and it's Inclosure came to Hand today very opportunely. The Gentlemen of the Assembly purpose to rise next Saturday and preparatory to it resolved in the Morning to receive no new Business after this day. This Circumstance precluded all Formality and Mr. Lee being absent I moved for Leave to bring in a Bill under the same Title as the Act passed in Virginia. Leave was granted and I expect there will be no Opposition in any Stage of it. I think at present to make a small Deviation by giving the President and Directors their choice to prosecute in the County Courts, which will generally be speedier, or in the General Court.

Our Affairs are so embarrassed with a diversity of paper Money and paper Securities a sparing Imposition and an infamous Collection and payment or rather non-payment of Taxes that Mr. Hartshorn's repeated Application to our Treasury have proved fruitless nor can I say when there will be Money in Hand to answer the 300 £ Sterl. due. Some of our Debts are so pressing that a good

---

[20] *Votes and Proceedings of the House of Delegates,* November, 1787, page 36.

[21] *The Papers of George Washington,* Library of Congress, Manuscript Division.

many of us Delegates feel very uneasy and I yet hope a serious Attempt for an immediate provision for them and that the Potomack Demand may be included. The present circumstances with respect to the future Seat of Congress, in my Opinion call for vigorous Exertions to perfect the Navig[ation] of Potomack speedily and it is truly mortifying to see so little prospect of being supplied with the essential Means. Surely 5 or 600 Miles of inland Navigation added to the Central Situation and other Advantages would decide in favor of Potomack for the permanent Seat of Congress.

Col⁰ Fitzgerald wrote Mr. Lee and myself to mention the Time we could meet at Shennadoah to enquire into Complaints against Mr. Steward.[22] In his Absence I could only write him that I would attend at any Time that might be agreeable to you and the other Gent[lemen] after my Return home which will probably be the last of next week. I wish Sir your Convenience to be consulted and that it may be convenient and agreeable to you to make my House in your way. Very little Notice of the Time to meet will be sufficient for me and I dare say for Mr. Lee.

*   *   *   *   *   *   *

The Levon [leaven] of your State is working in ours. The scale of power which I always suggested would be the most difficult to settle between the great and small States, as such, was in my Opinion very properly adjusted. Any necessary Guards for personal Liberty is the common Interest of all the citizens of America and if it is imagined that a defined power which does not comprehend the Interference with personal Right needs negative Declarations I presume such may be added by the Federal Legislature with equal Efficacy and more propriety than might have been done by the Convention. Strongly and long impressed with an Idea that no Governmᵗ can make a people happy unless they very generally entertain an Opinion that it is good in Form and well administered I am much disposed to give up a good deal in the form the least essential part. But those who are clamourous [the enemies of the Constitution] seem to me to be really more afraid of being restrained

---

[22] Richardson Stuart, who had been chosen in 1785 by the President and Directors of the Potomac Company as assistant to Superintendent Rumsey. Mr. Stuart was a Baltimore manufacturer.

from doing what they ought not to do and being compelled to do what they ought to do than of being obliged to do what there is no moral Obligation on them to do. I believe there is no American of Observation, Reflection and Candour but will acknowledge Man unhappily needs more Government than he imagined.

I flatter myself that the plan recommended [the Federal Constitution] will be adopted in twelve of the thirteen States without conditions *sine qua non* but let the event be as it may I shall think myself with America in general greatly indebted to the Convention and possibly we may confess it when it may be too late to avail ourselves of their Moderation and Wisdom. You will pardon me my good Sir the Effusions which I cannot restrain when on this Subject and believe me to be

With very great respect
Your most obedt Servt

TH. JOHNSON.

Johnson's prompt action in paving the way for the passage of the new law for the Potomac Company was characteristic of him. Indeed, Washington would have been surprised if his appeal had been met with anything but an immediate response. Johnson presented the draft of the bill to the House on December 13th; and, although the Legislature adjourned *sine die* on the 17th, the measure was ready in ample time for Executive approval.[23] The correspondence is but another illustration of how Washington relied on Johnson in time of peace as well as in war.

Nor was there anything remarkable about the philosophical concepts which were embodied by Johnson in the above letter to Mount Vernon. Up to the present time in his life, Johnson had been too busy, too practical, to give much thought to generalizations; but now, at 55, he was

[23] *Votes and Proceedings of the House of Delegates,* November, 1787, pages 41 and 48; *Laws of Maryland,* November, 1787, Chapter XXV.

approaching that age in life when he was beginning to reflect and philosophize. But, even so, the two platitudes
which he included in his reply were in no respect extraordinary. Indeed, they were the common thought of the day.

The first idea—*"No Governm^t can make a people
happy unless they very generally entertain an Opinion that
it is good in Form and well administered"*—had been expressed by Benjamin Franklin in his memorable address at
the close of the Constitutional Convention at Philadelphia
on September 17, 1787, when he urged the members of the
Convention to sign the Constitution. "There is no *form*
of Government," said the venerable patriot in the address,
read for him by Mr. Wilson, "but what may be a blessing
to the people *if well administered.* . . . Much of the
strength and efficiency of any Government in procuring and
securing happiness to the people, depends on *opinion,* on
the general opinion of the goodness of the Government;
as well as the wisdom and integrity of its governors." It
is known that Doctor Franklin sent copies of the address in
his own handwriting to several of his friends, and one of
these soon found its way into print.[24] It is, therefore, possible that Johnson, even though he had been "strongly and
long impressed" with the idea, was prompted to pen the
words to Washington by the address of the Philadelphia
philosopher. It is also possible that both Franklin and
Johnson had been impressed by the lines written by Alexander Pope in 1732 in the *Essay on Man:*

> "For forms of government, let fools contest;
> Whate'er is best administered, is best."

[24] *The Records of the Federal Convention* (Max Farrand), Vol. II, page
641, note.

At all events, the thought expressed by Franklin and Johnson is rather commonplace. In all ages, statesmen and scholars have declared that the success of any Government depends upon the people themselves. Edmund Burke declared: "There never was long a corrupt Government of a virtuous people." Disraeli said: "We put too much faith in systems, and look too little to men." Samuel Smiles wrote in one of his books: "Indeed, all experience serves to prove that the worth and strength of a State depend far less upon the form of its institutions than upon the character of its men." President Roosevelt declared: "I do not care if you had the most perfect laws that could be devised by the wit of man or the wit of angels, they would not amount to anything if the average man was not a pretty decent fellow." Henry Van Dyke, theologian, diplomat and man of letters, says in one of his essays: "Every possible form of Government has been tried, and found both good and bad. They would all be intolerable but for the quiet people who trust in the Lord and do good." And in a treatise on the Constitution of the United States, W. W. Willoughby says: "In every State the very existence of its Government, the extent of its powers, and the manner of their exercise, is ultimately dependent upon the acquiescence of the people."

Likewise, the second platitude in Johnson's reply to Washington—*"Man unhappily needs more Government than he imagined"*—was in no sense unusual or surprising. Washington himself avowed: "Mankind, when left to themselves, are unfit for their own Government." John Jay declared mournfully: "The mass of men are neither wise nor good." Young John Marshall said: "I fear that these have truth on their side who say that Man is incapable of governing himself." The same view was taken by Hamilton, Madison, and other outstanding friends of the Federal Constitution. It was natural that Johnson accepted the view of the Federalists, because he had believed for a number of years that the people themselves were largely responsible for the country's desperate condition under the Articles of Confederation.

However, the letter sent by Johnson from Annapolis to Mount Vernon in December, 1787, shows his prophetic vision. Already—this was less than two months after the adjournment of the Federal Convention—the farsighted Maryland statesman was not only giving assurance that the State would vote for unconditional ratification of the Constitution, but was also looking forward to the day when the Capital of the Nation would be located permanently along the Potomac.

CHAPTER XXVII

THE FIGHT FOR RATIFICATION

"An adjournment (if attempted) of your Convention to a later period than the decision of the question in this State, will be tantamount to the rejection of the Constitution."

—*Washingon to Johnson, April 20, 1788.*

"The body [members of the Maryland Convention] . . . have ratified the new Constitution. A thorn this in the sides of the leaders of opposition in this State."

—*Washirtgton to James Madison, May 2, 1788.*

"I have not at any moment, despaired of this State's acceptance of the new Constitution and less since the ratification of Maryland by so large and decided a majority."

—*Washington to Gouverneur Morris, May 2, 1788.*

IN the Spring of 1788 it became evident that Maryland would be an important battle ground of the proposed Federal Constitution. In five States where the Federalists were prompt to act—Delaware, Pennsylvania, New Jersey, Georgia, and Connecticut—the new plan of Government had been ratified promptly after very little discussion. The real clash commenced in Massachusetts, the sixth State, where only by winning over John Hancock, President of the Convention, to the side of the Constitution by inducements of political rewards were the Federalists able to secure favorable action by the narrow margin of 187 to 168.

It now became known that the Anti-Federalists were scheming to postpone action in Maryland until after Patrick Henry, Richard Henry Lee and other leaders had set up their opposition in Virginia. As early as the 10th of February, 1788, Daniel Carroll, one of the signers of the Constitution, prophesied, in a letter to Madison, that the plan of the Anti-Federalists did not extend so far as to obtain a rejection of the proposed Constitution by the Maryland Convention but to attempt to secure an adjournment until the Convention of Virginia had made a decision.[1] And on the 19th of February, Mr. Madison informed Thomas Jefferson of the report that Maryland would be one of the ratifying States. "Mr. Chase and a few others," wrote Madison, "will raise a considerable opposition. . . . But the weight of personal influence is on the side of the Constitution, and the present expectation is that the Opposition will be outnumbered by a great majority."[2]

In the meanwhile the New Hampshire Convention had convened. In this State the Anti-Federalists had circulated propaganda to the effect that the Federal plan would strengthen the power of men of wealth and influence and imperil the rights of the masses. A large number of the delegates to the Convention had been instructed to vote against the Constitution and the Federalists were quite glad, after a week of deliberation, to secure an adjournment until June, thus deferring final action until after the delegates could consult further with their constituents.

As the news of the postponement in New Hampshire traveled Southward, the Federalists grew more apprehensive about the fate of the new Constitution. The Anti-Federal sentiment was growing stronger. Ratification was favored by the educated classes and the leaders of commerce and capital; it was opposed by those who feared that

[1] *The Papers of James Madison*, Library of Congress, Vol. XV, page 73.
[2] *Ibid*, Vol. I, page 378.

a strong Central Government would endanger the liberty of the people. Now was a crucial time in American history. Ratification by the Conventions of nine States was requisite for the establishment of the proposed Constitution. The result appeared to be in doubt in New York, Virginia and South Carolina. Rhode Island and North Carolina plainly opposed the new form of Government. All eyes turned to Maryland.

The elections for delegates to the State Convention on the first Monday in April, 1788, showed that the sentiment in Maryland was unmistakably favorable to the Federal Constitution. It is true, there were contests between the Federalists and the Anti-Federalists in nearly all sections of the State; but the Federal victory was very decisive. The Federalists carried the Cities of Annapolis and Baltimore as well as fifteen of the Counties; whereas the Anti-Federalists were successful in but three Counties—Anne Arundel, Baltimore and Harford.

In Frederick County, the local members of the House of Delegates—Thomas Johnson, Abraham Faw, Thomas Sim Lee, and Richard Potts, all of whom were friends of the new Constitution—were nominated as the Federalist candidates for the Convention. They were unopposed, and all four accepted seats in the Convention.

While it soon became known that the Federalists would have an overwhelming majority in the Convention, it was not forgotten that the Minority included several men of commanding ability who would not hesitate to throw every obstacle possible in the path of ratification. Among the twelve men who were preparing to attack the Constitution were Samuel Chase, John Francis Mercer, and Jeremiah Townley Chase, of Anne Arundel; and Attorney-General

Luther Martin, William Paca, and William Pinkney, of Harford.

On Monday morning, April 21, 1788—the day named for the opening of the Convention—while neither Samuel Chase, the leader of the Anne Arundel delegation, nor any of the Anti-Federalists from Baltimore and Hartford Counties, had yet arrived, most of the friends of the Constitution —including Johnson and Faw, of Frederick—were ready for immediate action.

From the beginning, Judge Alexander Contee Hanson, a brilliant jurist of Annapolis, assumed leadership of the Federal forces. Hanson [3] had been serving as a Judge of the General Court since 1778, and compiled the Maryland Code of Laws, which Johnson had been asked by the Legislature to approve in the Spring of 1787. After the adoption of the Constitution at Philadelphia, Judge Hanson had published, under the *nom de plume* of "Aristides," an able paper commending the Federal plan.

Early Monday morning—before the Convention organized—the friends of the Constitution held a caucus, where they pledged to stand firm for prompt ratification. According to Judge Hanson, [4] the members of the Majority agreed as follows: "That they and their constituents had enjoyed abundant leisure and opportunity for considering the proposed system of a federal government; that it was not probable, any new lights could be thrown on the subject; that (even if it were) the main question had already, in effect, been decided by the people, in their respective counties; that, as each delegate was under a sacred obliga-

---

[3] Alexander Contee Hanson, son of John Hanson, served as private secretary for General Washington during part of the Revolution.
[4] Alexander Contee Hanson, *Narrative of the Proceedings in Convention*, Letter to James Madison, June 2, 1788, *Madison Papers*, Vol. XV, page 123.

tion to vote, conformably to the sentiments of his constituents, they ought to complete that single transaction for which they were convened, as speedily as was consistent with decorum."

Thus Johnson, elected as a Federalist, was virtually bound to support prompt and unconditional ratification.

In addition to this, the ex-Governor received a stirring letter on the subject from the chieftain at Mount Vernon. Aware of the equal balance of the parties in the Old Dominion—warned by Madison that "the difference between even a *postponement* and *adoption* in Maryland" might possibly give a fatal advantage to the foes of the Constitution in Virginia [5]—and knowing that the members of the Opposition in Virginia were intriguing for a Southern Confederacy of slave-holding States, Washington frankly declared that the action of the Maryland Convention would decide the battle in Virginia. If the delegates at Annapolis failed to act promptly, the forces of Anti-Federalism in Virginia would be given encouragement in their fight to overthrow the work of the framers. Prompt action would virtually determine whether the American people would establish the new Republic! The warning from Mount Vernon, penned on the eve of the Maryland Convention, follows: [6]

GEORGE WASHINGTON TO THOMAS JOHNSON

Mount Vernon, April 20, 1788.

Dear Sir,

As well from report, as from the ideas expressed in your letter to me in December last, I am led to conclude that you are disposed

---

[5] *Madison Papers,* Vol. I, page 384.

[6] *George Washington Letter Book,* Library of Congress, Manuscript Division. Original in possession of Maryland Historical Society, Baltimore, Md.

(circumstanced as our public affairs are at present) to ratify the Constitution which has been submitted by the general Convention to the People; and under this impression, I take the liberty of expressing a *single* sentiment on the occasion.

It is, that an adjournment (if attempted), of your Convention to a later period than the decision of the question in this State, will be tantamount to the rejection of the Constitution. I have good ground for this opinion—and am told it is *the blow* which the leading characters of the Opposition in the next States have meditated if it shall be found that a direct attack is not likely to succeed in yours. If this be true, it cannot be too much deprecated, & guarded against.

The postponement in New Hampshire, altho' made without any reference to the Convention of this State, & altogether from the local circumstances of its own, is ascribed by the Opposition *here* to complaisance towards Virginia; and great use is made of it. An event similar to this in Maryland, would have the worst tendency imaginable, for indecision there would have considerable influence upon South Carolina, the only other State which is to precede Virginia, and submits the question almost wholly to the determination of the latter. The *pride* of the State is already touched upon this string, & will be strained much higher if there is an opening for it.

The sentiments of Kentucky are not yet known here. Independent of these, the parties with us, from the known, or presumed opinions of the members, are pretty equally balanced. The one in favor of the Constitution preponderates at present—but a small matter cast into the opposite scale may make it the heaviest.

If in suggesting this matter, I have exceeded the proper limit, my motives must excuse me—I have but one public wish remaining—It is, that in *peace* and *retirement,* I may see this Country rescued from the danger which is pending, & rise into respectability maugre the Intrigues of its public & private enemies. With very great esteem & regard

I am, Dear Sir,
Y^r Most Obed^t H^{ble} Ser^t,
G^o WASHINGTON.

Most of the members of the Maryland Convention were very stanch Federalists, anxious for prompt ratification,

Mount Vernon April 20. 1788.

Dear Sir,

As well from report, as from the ideas expressed in your letter to me in December last I am led to conclude that you are disposed (circumstanced as our public affairs are at present) to ratify the Constitution which has been submitted by the general Convention to the People; and under this impression I take the liberty of expressing a single sentiment on the occasion. —

It is, that an adjournment (if attempted), of your Convention to a later period than the decision of the question in this State, will be tantamount to the rejection of the Constitution. — I have good ground for this opinion — and am told it is the view which the leading characters of the opposition in your State have — — — — it shall be found that a direct attack is not likely to succeed in yours. — If this be true, it cannot be too much deprecated, & guarded against. —

The postponement in New Hampshire altho' made without any reference to the Convention of this State & altogether from the local circumstances of its own; is ascribed by the opposition here to complaisance towards Virginia; and great use is made of it. — An event similar to this in Maryland, would have the worst tendency imaginable; for indecision is — — — have considerable influence upon South Carolina, the only other State which is to precede Virginia, and submits the question almost wholly to the determination of the latter. — The pride of the State is already touched upon this string, & will be strained much higher if there is an opening for it. —

The sentiments of Kentucky are not yet known here. — Independent of these, the parties with

and did not need the appeal of Washington. Of the 76 delegates in the Convention, four were eligible to sit for each of the 18 Counties of the State; two for the City of Annapolis; and two for the City of Baltimore.[7] Only three Counties were represented by Anti-Federalists. The Federalists were in undisputed control of the Convention. However, Johnson was glad to show Washington's letter to a number of the delegates in the Convention, as he later declared, in order "to strengthen the Friends of the new Constitution and expedite its adoption."

Quite as a coincidence, Dr. James McHenry, a member from Baltimore, had already written to Washington to inquire what Washington thought would be the consequence of an adjournment of the Maryland Convention, and the Virginian gave his opinion exactly as he had already given it to Johnson—that postponement would result in the defeat of the Constitution.

The Convention organized by unanimously selecting George Plater, of St. Mary's County, as President. A committee, with Johnson as chairman, was then appointed to examine the returns of elections. The other members of the committee were: Faw of Frederick, Jeremiah Townley Chase of Anne Arundel, Richard Barnes of St. Mary's, and John Done of Worcester.[8] Then, after resolving to sit from nine in the morning until three in the afternoon each day, the Convention adjourned until Tuesday morning.

On the second day, April 22nd, when ex-Governor Lee and Mr. Potts put in their appearance, Mr. Johnson, as chairman of the Committee of Elections, brought in a report

---

[7] All qualified except two Federalists, who failed to appear on account of sickness.

[8] *Documentary History of the Constitution*, (Department of State) Vol. II, page 99.

naming those who were entitled to sit in the Convention.[9] Although the validity of some of the elections had been questioned—in Baltimore bitter charges had been made by the Anti-Federalists that Dr. McHenry and his running mate had received fraudulent votes—the report of Chairman Johnson was accepted without dispute. A set of rules of procedure, including the provision that all sessions should be public, was also adopted.

On Wednesday, the third day, the proposed Constitution was read the first time, after which it was resolved (pursuant to the action of the Federal caucus) that the Convention would "not enter into any resolution upon any particular part of the proposed plan of Federal Government." The Federalists felt that the crisis in the country's affairs was too grave to justify a tedious consideration of the Constitution section by section. But it was clearly understood that on the general question of ratification, following the second reading of the Constitution, when the subject was open to debate, every member would be given the opportunity to speak as often as he desired.

On Thursday morning, April 24th, Samuel Chase appeared for the first time in the Convention. It was apparent to all that Mr. Chase, able and influential as he was, would find it utterly impossible to secure enough votes to overthrow the Constitution; but, while heavily outnumbered, the enemies of the new form of Government were seeking delay by placing obstructions in the way of ratification, figuring that if New Hampshire, Massachusetts or New York rejected the Constitution, delay on the part of Maryland would operate as ultimate defeat of the new Government. So Chase began his attack, con-

[9] *Ibid,* page 100.

with us, from the known, or presumed opinions of the members, are pretty equally balanced—The one in favor of the constitution preponderates at present—but a small matter cast into the opposite scale may make it the heaviest.—

In surveying this matter, I have exceeded the proper limit, my motive must excuse me—I have but one public wish remaining—It is, that in peace and retirement, I may see this Country rescued from the danger which is pending, & rise into respectability maugre the intrigues of its public & private enemies. —With very great esteem & regard

I am, Dear Sir
Y.r Most Obed.t & H.ble Serv.t
G.o Washington

Tho.s Johnson Esq.r

WASHINGTON'S APPEAL TO JOHNSON FOR RATIFICATION OF
THE CONSTITUTION (*Page 2*)

tending that the proposed Constitution would establish a Central Government that would imperil the liberty of the people. After presenting a part of his objections, Chase took his seat, declaring that he was exhausted and that he would resume his argument on the following day.[10] The Convention then waited for some other member of the Minority to arise, but there was silence; and, after waiting a reasonable time, it was decided to adjourn for dinner and reassemble in the afternoon "to prevent further procrastination, and to have the business concluded immediately, in case the Minority should not proceed with their objections."

When the delegates reassembled Thursday afternoon, William Paca, former Governor of Maryland, had arrived. Attorney-General Luther Martin and John Love had also arrived from Harford, while young William Pinkney—later to become one of the most prominent lawyers in the United States—had arrived on Wednesday. Taking the floor, Mr. Paca declared that he had "a variety of objections" to the Federal Constitution. But he explained that, as he had just arrived, he was not yet ready to lay his amendments before the Convention, and accordingly asked permission to prepare his propositions and present them in the morning for the consideration of the members. Paca stated that under an expectation of obtaining the amendments he might vote for the ratification of the Constitution, but he wished them to be considered before the vote of ratification, because he imagined that after the vote the delegates would not remain a sufficient length of time for due consideration.

Mr. Johnson then took the floor. There was a hush about the room as he addressed the chair, not only because

[10] Hanson, *Narrative of the Proceedings in Convention*, page 124.

he was the revered War Governor and the acknowledged leader of the State but also because he was the spokesman for Washington. It was but natural that the first Governor wished to extend a courtesy to the third Governor. And accordingly, in his usual brief but impressive manner, Johnson expressed the opinion that Paca's request was "candid and reasonable" and accordingly recommended that the indulgence should be allowed by the Convention. In order to defer action on the main question, Johnson then moved an adjournment until the morning. Adjournment immediately followed. However, no other assurance by the House had been given to ex-Governor Paca. Nor, according to Judge Hanson, could any assurance have been *implied* from the adoption of Johnson's motion to adjourn.[11]

On the morning of the fifth day, when Paca was ready to present his amendments to the Convention, a member from each of eleven Counties and from the two Cities arose one after the other and declared that "he and his colleagues were under an obligation to vote for the Government." The position was taken by the Majority that they had "no authority to propose in behalf of their constituents that which their constituents had never considered, and concerning which their constituents could of course have given no direction."

While he was trying to explain his position, Paca was interrupted by George Gale, of Somerset County, who had been absent on the preceding afternoon, and who argued that Paca was out of order. Indeed, technically, he was; for the question was whether the Convention should assent to and ratify the proposed Constitution. Paca remonstrated against the alleged indecency of treatment accorded him

[11] *Ibid.*

after he had obtained permission, so he claimed, to present his amendments to the House. The point of order was sustained; Paca was not allowed to read his amendments.

So the Federalists spent the whole week "either in waiting for absent members of the minority, or in the most patient attention to objections, which were familiar to almost every auditor." There had been no undue haste. A number of times the Federalists were challenged to answer the objections to the Constitution; but the Federalists defended their silence by declaring that they were instructed to vote for the Constitution, while the Minority were instructed to vote against it, and it was not probable that any arguments could change their minds at that late period. The enemies of the Constitution were simply allowed to tire themselves out. They talked, while the friends of the Constitution listened.

Finally, on the afternoon of Saturday, April 26, 1788, the Majority called for the question, namely, *Does this Convention assent to and ratify the proposed Constitution?* The oratorical talents of the Anti-Federalists had been "amply displayed"; they had been heard "with candid and profound attention"; and the Federalists believed that it was their duty now to act without any further delay in accordance with the voice of the people. The question was decided in favor of the affirmative by a vote of 63 to 11. Thus, by a large majority, Maryland ratified the Federal Constitution. She was the seventh State to ratify it.

Johnson and his colleagues from Frederick County voted for adoption. The votes of the men from Anne Arundel, Baltimore and Harford Counties—except Paca who voted with the Federalists—were cast in the negative.

After it was decided to sign a certificate of ratification

on Monday, Paca again asked for consideration of his propositions, explaining that he had voted for ratification of the Constitution with the expectation that his amendments would be considered. In order to gratify Paca, the Convention allowed him at last to read them. Some of the Federalists took the view that as private citizens they could make certain recommendations to the people without proposing them in their official capacity. Judge Hanson did not relish this novel distinction; he felt that as long as the Convention was in session the members could not be considered as acting in a private capacity and that, if any of the individual members wished to propose amendments, such amendments could and should be endorsed after the dissolution of the Convention. "For our part," said Judge Hanson, "we were so far from thinking amendments either necessary to perfect the system or proper on the principle of accommodation, that we regretted the embarrassment into which the Convention was thrown." The Judge was apprehensive that the enemies of the Federal Government in other States would construe the Maryland Convention's action to indicate that the new Constitution was extremely defective and needed amendments. However, after several of the delegates spoke favorably of the amendments, the Convention in a spirit of fairness decided to consider the amendments—simply as recommendations to the people and not as any authoritative decision. A resolution was offered to authorize a committee "to take into consideration and report to this House on Monday morning next, a draught of such amendments and alterations, as may be thought necessary in the proposed Constitution for the United States, to be recommended to the consideration of the people of this State, if approved by this Convention."

Johnson favored the resolution. He was one of those "amiable Federalists" who hoped the plan of recommending amendments to the people would put an end to further opposition in the State.[12] The Convention, not seeing the entanglement into which it was falling, adopted the resolution by a vote of 66 to 7.

Former Governor Paca was named chairman of the Committee of Thirteen. Of the other members, nine were Federalists and three Anti-Federalists. The Federalist members were: ex-Governor Johnson, ex-Governor Lee, and Richard Potts, of Frederick County; James and William Tilghman, George Gale and Robert Goldsborough, from the Eastern Shore; Doctor McHenry, of Baltimore; and Judge Hanson of Annapolis. Samuel Chase, Jeremiah Townley Chase and John Francis Mercer, of Anne Arundel, represented the Opposition.

On Saturday evening, the Federal members of the Committee held a conference to determine what course they should take. Judge Hanson felt that in trying "to gratify and conciliate a few men opposed to the general sense of the State" the members of the Convention had been led into a very disagreeable situation; but he maintained that if they would simply explain and construe the Constitution without undertaking to alter the provisions, the Convention might perhaps be "extricated from its embarrassment."

On Sunday morning, April 27th, the Committee of Thirteen began consideration of Paca's reservations; and on Monday the members of the committee voted in favor of the following thirteen reservations: (1) Congress shall have no powers except those expressly delegated by the Constitu-

---

[12] Bernard C. Steiner, *Maryland's Adoption of the Federal Constitution*, American Historical Review, Vol. V, No. 2, page 213.

tion; (2) trial by jury shall be allowed in all criminal cases, but denying appeals from matters of fact; (3) State and Federal Courts shall have concurrent jurisdiction in matters *ex contractu;* (4) the jurisdiction of inferior Federal Courts shall be limited to cases involving a certain minimum amount; (5) State and inferior Federal Courts shall have concurrent jurisdiction in matters *ex delicto*, and any plaintiff suing a non-resident for damages shall be entitled to a trial by jury in the State where the alleged wrong was committed; (6) no Federal Court shall acquire jurisdiction by collusion; (7) no Federal judge shall be allowed to receive the profits of any other public position during his term of office; (8) every warrant for search or seizure shall be explicit and under oath; (9) no soldier shall be enlisted for a period of more than four years during time of peace; (10) no soldier shall be quartered in a private home during time of peace unless with the consent of the owner; (11) no mutiny bill shall continue in force longer than two years; (12) the freedom of the press shall be inviolably preserved; and (13) except in time of war, invasion or rebellion, the State Militia shall never be subject to martial law.[13]

Fifteen other reservations were rejected. These were intended to restrain the Federal Government from ordering the Militia beyond the border of a State except with the consent of the Governor or the Legislature; to prevent any change in the time, place or manner of holding elections for members of Congress unless a State should fail to make such regulations; to give the States full opportunity to collect any direct Federal taxes; to prohibit the President from commanding the Army in person except with the per-

---

[13] Jonathan Elliot, *The Debates in the Several State Conventions, on the Adoption of the Federal Constitution.* Vol. II, page 547.

mission of Congress; to prevent the maintenance of a standing Army during time of peace unless by a two-thirds vote of Congress; to make members of Congress ineligible to any other Federal office; to place all duties and imposts to the credit of the State in which collected; to prohibit a Federal poll tax; to prevent any treaty from repealing any provision of a State Constitution; and to guarantee full religious liberty.

The Majority members promised to support the first thirteen reservations, provided the Minority would not lay any others before the Convention; the Minority agreed if three additional reservations were added—*viz.*, regarding the control over the Militia, the elections for members of Congress, and the collection of direct Federal taxes. A vote was accordingly again taken on the three additional reservations. Trying his best to sweeten a bitter situation, Mr. Johnson voted to add these three to the original thirteen, but the scheme was rejected by a vote of 8 to 5.

High feeling now arose among the members of the committee. Some of the Federalists declared that they had voted through misconception and demanded that no report at all should be made to the Convention.

Meanwhile the members of the Convention were growing impatient. The official ratification of the Constitution was ordered sent to Congress. The Committee of Thirteen returned without being able to reach an agreement.

Mr. Paca read to the Convention the thirteen reservations which had originally been adopted and the three which had been rejected; but the stanch Federalists now affirmed that they would not give any further consideration to amendments. So, after passing a vote of thanks to President Plater, the Convention adjourned *sine die.*

The final motion to adjourn was adopted by a vote of 47 to 27, quite a few of the Federalists being willing to remain in session a few days longer to give further consideration to Mr. Paca's suggestions. Mr. Johnson was one of the Federal members who voted against adjournment— the only one of the four delegates from Frederick County to take this position. However, Johnson's course was thoroughly consistent throughout the Convention. While he had voted in favor of the three additional reservations, and against precipitate adjournment, at no time did he try to retard the ratification of the Constitution.

On April 28th Johnson subscribed his name to the Convention's certificate of ratification. This certificate was signed by the "virtuous sixty-three"—the men who had voted in favor of ratification—including Mr. Paca. It was a complete victory for the Federal cause. "The State," says one historian, "which was cradled in religious liberty gained the undisputed victory over the first velleity of the slave-holding States to form a separate Confederacy." [14]

Mr. Johnson refused, of course, to sign the Minority's Address to the people of Maryland. This report set forth Paca's amendments and maintained that the liberty and happiness of the people would be endangered unless the provisions of the proposed Constitution were greatly altered. As a lawyer of ability, Johnson was little worried by the objections and the mutterings of discontent that followed ratification. One Anti-Federal writer contended that the ratification by Maryland was not final since it altered the Constitution of the State and therefore needed the sanction of two successive General Assemblies. The same

[14] George Bancroft, *History of the Formation of the Constitution*, page 413.

writer made the complaint that had been advanced by the Anti-Federalists in Pennsylvania—that ratification had been procured by the aristocrats, while the "common class" knew practically nothing about the proposed Constitution. In some of the Counties of Maryland—in Frederick, for instance—the Opposition had not named any candidates at all to run against the Federalists; and out of a total of about 25,000 voters, declared the disgruntled writer, scarcely 6,000 men had voted in the elections in the State.[15]

However, the ratification by the Maryland Convention by a vote of nearly 6 to 1 was regarded by the friends of the Constitution as "a most conclusive proof" of the Federalism of Maryland. Everywhere in the State there was great rejoicing. "Maryland," said one of the happy Federalists, "has erected the seventh pillar upon which will be reared the glorious fabric of American greatness, in which fabric the rights of Mankind will be concentered as to their native home. O, may the happy moment soon arrive when the august Temple of Freedom shall be supported by thirteen pillars, with its gates unfolded to every part of Creation, may its duration be as permanent as Time and its period engulfed only in the bosom of Eternity!"[16]

Washington had always believed that the favorable action of Maryland would "most assuredly raise the edifice." So when the news reached Mount Vernon that the Convention had voted by a large majority in favor of the Union, he no longer doubted the triumph of the Constitution. He told Madison that the decisive majority for ratification at Annapolis was a thorn in the sides of the leaders of the Opposition in Virginia. "Should South Caro-

[15] *Maryland Journal,* May 16, 1788.
[16] *Maryland Journal.*

lina give as unequivocal approbation of the System,"
Washington asserted, "the opposition here must become
feeble for eight affirmatives without a negative carries
weight of argument if not eloquence with it that would
cause even the *unerring* Sister to hesitate.—Mr. Chase, it
is said, made a display of all his eloquence. Mr. Mercer
discharged his whole artillery of inflammable matter, and
Mr. Martin I know not what, perhaps vehemence; but no
converts were made—no, not one." At the same time the
Virginia chieftain also wrote to General Lincoln and
Gouverneur Morris, explaining that Maryland's acceptance
of the Constitution by a great majority would operate to
influence many of the wavering Virginians to vote in favor
of the Constitution and virtually assured the accession of
the Commonwealth.[17]

Washington's hopes were soon realized. "In his hours
of meditation," Bancroft observes, "he saw the movement
of the Divine Power which gives unity to the Universe, and
order and connection to events."[18] Down in South Carolina the influence of Maryland's action was shown by the
fact that a few days later one of the members of the Convention who had been opposed to the Federal plan arose
and declared that since the fiat of Maryland had been so
overwhelming in favor of ratification, he would cast his vote
for acceptance by South Carolina; and South Carolina by
a large majority became the eighth State to ratify the
new Constitution. On the 28th of May, Washington wrote
to his old Revolutionary friend, General Lafayette: "The
plot thickens fast. A few short weeks will determine the
political fate of America for the present generation, and

---

[17] *George Washington Letter Book,* Library of Congress, May 2, 1788.
[18] Bancroft, *History of the Formation of the Constitution,* page 414.

probably produce no small influence on the happiness of Society through a long succession of ages to come. Should everything proceed with harmony and consent, according to our actual wishes and expectations, it will be so much beyond anything we had a right to imagine or expect eighteen months ago, that it will, as visibly as any possible event in the course of human affairs, demonstrate the finger of Providence."

When the New Hampshire Convention reassembled in June, ratification was voted within a few days; and the Constitution was now ready to go into operation. The first nine States were followed shortly afterwards by Virginia.

And so, out of hopeless confusion, out of the jealousies of rival States, out of the chaos that threatened the life of the Nation, there arose a more perfect Union—the bulwark of individual rights, the guardian of the destinies of the Republic.

CHAPTER XXVIII

ALOOF FROM PUBLIC LIFE—PRESIDENT OF
THE POTOMAC COMPANY

"Consulting your domestic inclinations, and the state of your health, I yielded, on a recent occasion, to the opinions of some of your friends, who thought that you would not be prevailed on to leave your State to mingle in the administration of public affairs."
—*President Washington to Johnson, September 20, 1789.*

AFTER the adjournment of the Convention at Annapolis, Johnson returned to Richfield, his tranquil estate in Frederick County, hoping to spend the remainder of his days in private life. His home was to him a haven most dear, as Mount Vernon was to General Washington.

But neither Johnson nor Washington was allowed to remain long in their cherished tranquillity. Indeed, scarcely had the War Governor returned home before he was asked to fill a vacant seat in the Maryland Senate; but immediately he declined.[1]

During the Summer of 1788, the peaceful pleasures of Mount Vernon and Richfield were interrupted only when it was necessary to attend meetings of the Potomac Company. On the 2nd of June, Washington met Johnson and the other Directors of the Company—Lee and Gilpin—at Harper's Ferry, for the purpose of making an inspection of the canal on the Maryland side of the Potomac.[2] After

---

[1] *Votes and Proceedings of the Senate*, May 24, 1788; November 8, 1788.
[2] *The Diaries of George Washington*, edited by Fitzpatrick, Vol. III, page 361.

dinner they were ready to hear complaints that had been brought against Superintendent Richardson Stuart. Mr. Stuart failed to appear and it was impossible to consider the charges. However, being of the opinion that the Company was financially able to employ only one superintendent, the Directors decided to retain Superintendent Smith and to discharge Stuart; and Washington and the three Directors signed a letter to Stuart explaining that the action of the Board was not influenced in any manner by the alleged charges, but was done simply for the best interests of the Company.[3]

In August, at the annual meeting of the Company in Alexandria, Washington expressed in the report of the Board of Directors the hope that navigation—partial, even if not perfect—would be effected from the Great Falls to Fort Cumberland before Winter.

In the meantime, Johnson and other prominent statesmen were mentioning Washington for the position of President of the United States. Strange to say, a rumor had arisen that there had been an estrangement between Johnson and Washington: it had been averred that Johnson had been insulted by the letter received from Washington at the time of the opening of the Maryland Convention, and therefore had endeavored to give aid to the Anti-Federalists by placing obstructions in the way of ratification. Such a report, however, was entirely groundless. Johnson had been trying in the Convention simply to pour oil on the troubled waters: as Daniel Carroll, the young Maryland farmer who was one of the signers of the Constitution at Philadelphia, had explained to Madison, the whole truth was that "Mr. Johnson's accomodating dis-

---

[3] *Records of the Columbia Historical Society,* Vol. XV, page 173.

position, and a respect to his character lead the Majority into a Situation, out of which they found some difficulty to extricate themselves." [4]

Nor did Washington place any credence in the rumor that Johnson had been insulted by the appeal to expedite ratification. However, Washington directed to the former Governor the following letter of inquiry: [5]

GEORGE WASHINGTON TO THOMAS JOHNSON

Mount Vernon,
August 31st 1788.

Dear Sir,

I shall be obliged to you for informing me, what foundation there is for so much of the following extract of a letter from Doctr Brooks at Fredericksburg to Doctr Stuart of this County as relates to the officious light in which my conduct was viewed for having written the letter alluded to——

"Since then, I was informed by the Honourable James Mercer, that his Brother Colo John Mercer, who was at that time (July 10th) in this town, was furnished with documents to prove, that Genl Washington had wrote a letter upon the present Constitution, to Governor Johnson of Maryland, and that Governor Johnson was so much displeased with the officiousness of General Washington, as to induce him to take an active part in bringing about the amendments proposed by a Committee of the Convention of Maryland."

If the letter which I wrote to you at Annapolis, while the Convention of your State was in session, was so considered, I have only to regret that it ever escaped me. My motives were declared. Having such proofs as were satisfactory to me, that the intention of the leaders of opposition was to effect an adjournment of your Convention

[4] *Writings to Madison,* Library of Congress, Vol. XV, page 118, May 28, 1788.
[5] *George Washington Letter Book,* Library of Congress.

(if a direct attack should be found unlikely to succeed) I conceived that a hint of it, thereof could not be displeasing to the supporters of the proposed Constitution—in which light as well from a letter I had received from you, as from universal report and belief I had placed you—for I defy any Anti-Federalist to say, with truth, that I ever wrote to, or exchanged a word with him, on the subject of the New Constitution if the latter was not forced upon me in a manner not to be avoided. Nothing therefore could be more foreign from my desire than to attempt to make proselytes, or to obtrude my opinions with a view to influence the Judgment of any one. The first wish of my heart, from the beginning of this business, was that a dispassionate enquiry might . . . take place and an impartial Judgment formed of it.

I have no other object, Sir, for making this enquiry than merely to be satisfied whether the information (for information was all I had in view) was considered by you as an improper interference on my part—or that the *document* and *interpretation* of this matter by Col° Mercer is the effect of one of those mistakes which he is so *very* apt to fall into.

I am, Dear Sir,

Your most obedient Servant,

G° WASHINGTON.

In returning his assurance of sincere friendship, Johnson took the opportunity to say the Nation needed Washington for President. Said Johnson:[6]

THOMAS JOHNSON TO GEORGE WASHINGTON

Frederick 10 October 1788.

Dear Sir:

I lately received your Letter of the 31st of August, scarce any Thing could have surprised me more than the Occasion of it for instead of being displeased I thought myself much obliged by the

---

[6] *The Papers of George Washington, Library of Congress,* Manuscript Division.

Letter you wrote me in the Time of our Convention.—To strengthen the Friends of the new Constitution and expedite its Adoption I showed that, and other Letters, containing much the same Information and Sentim^ts, to some Gent. and mentioned them to others—a strange Conduct had I been under the Impressions suggested! Nor do I recollect any Conduct of mine which can be called active to bring about any Amendments—I was not well pleased at the manner of our breaking up, I thought it to our discredit and should be better pleased with the Constitution with some Alterations but I am very far from wishing all that were proposed to take place.

A conversation between us at Shennadoah relative to your Letter and my answering it was broke off, I believe, by some Body's coming up or a Call to Breakfast—when you first mentioned it I did not understand certainly what Letter you referred to but the one received when I was at the Convention I answered the same Evening that it came to my Hands—As my writing is pretty generally known and suspecting that curiosity might peep into it to see how Things were going on I got Mr. Mercer who was sitting by to direct and contrive it: I was the more solicitous that it should have reached you safely as the Declaration you made in yours, and which I am satisfied came from the Heart gave me Reflection enough to hint at the necessity we should be under for your farther Services—*We cannot Sir do without you and I and thousands more can explain to anybody but yourself why we cannot do without you.*

My acquaintance with Col^o Mercer is not of long standing or very close—he will never find me acting on a great public Question from such unworthy Motives nor I hope displeased with any Letter I may have the Honor to receive from you.

I am my dear Sir
With the sincerest Esteem & affection
Your most obed^t Servant
TH. JOHNSON.

One month after Johnson was urging Washington to sacrifice the pleasures of Mount Vernon for the Presidency, the people of Maryland were urging Johnson to return to

Annapolis to fill the office of Governor. Under the Maryland Constitution, Governor William Smallwood, the fourth Executive of the State, having served three consecutive terms, was ineligible for reëlection; and on November 10, 1788, Johnson was chosen by the Legislature to succeed him. In the hope of inducing the first Governor to return to the Executive chair, the House of Delegates suggested that the letter of notification be drafted by a special joint committee; but the Senate felt that the preparation of the communication should be left as usual in the hands of the President of the Senate and the Speaker of the House.[7]

But Mr. Johnson was becoming deeply engrossed again in private business. For illustration, the Land Records of Frederick County show that Johnson and three of his brothers bought from an ironmaster at this time four Negro slaves, as well as additional holdings of real estate.[8] His furnaces and farms, his legal affairs, and the work of the Potomac Company all required attention and justified him in declining the office of Governor. His letter of refusal was received by the Legislature on November 20th[9] and on the following day John Eager Howard was chosen as the fifth Executive of the State.

The Federal Constitution having been adopted as the organic law of the United States, the Maryland Legislature now made provision for the election in January, 1789, of Presidential Electors and members of the House of Representatives. Despite Johnson's known desire for retirement, his name was mentioned for both Elector and member of Congress. Indeed, even though he was not an aspirant for

[7] *Votes and Proceedings of the House of Delegates,* November Session, 1788, page 10; *Senate,* page 2.
[8] *Land Records of Frederick County,* Liber W. R., No. 8, folio 286.
[9] *Votes and Proceedings of the Senate,* page 4.

office, he received more than seven hundred votes for Elector in the State.[10]

All the while the tide of public sentiment was sweeping irresistibly in favor of George Washington for President. But the great Virginian realized that the organization of the new Republic was a stupendous undertaking, and he looked forward to his election with characteristic modesty and unfeigned reluctance. On account of his advancing years and the growing love of retirement, he declared that his wish was to live and die an honest man on his own farm. But Johnson and many other of his friends insisted that he was the only man upon whom the infant Nation could lean with confidence—and he heard the call of his distressed country again.

At the time of his inauguration in New York on April 30, 1789, President Washington considered Johnson for an important post in his Administration; but, after a conference with a number of their mutual friends, he felt it was useless to prevail upon the Marylander to leave home at a time when he was so anxious for retirement.

Several months later, however, the President sent a very urgent appeal to Johnson to serve as United States District Judge for Maryland. In his letter Washington said:[11]

PRESIDENT WASHINGTON TO THOMAS JOHNSON

New York,
Septr 28th 1789.

Dear Sir

In assenting to the opinion that the due administration of Justice is the strongest cement of good Government, you will also agree

[10] Scharf, *History of Maryland,* Vol. II, page 549.
[11] *George Washington Letter Book,* Library of Congress, Manuscript Division.

with me that the first organization of the Judicial department is essential to the happiness of our Country, and to the stability of our political system—hence the selection of the fittest characters to expound the Laws, and dispense Justice has been an invariable object of my anxious concern.

Consulting your domestic inclinations and the state of your health I yielded on a recent occasion, to the opinions of some of your friends, who thought that you would not be prevailed on to leave your State to mingle in the administration of public affairs. But I found it impossible, in selecting a character to preside in the District Court of Maryland, to refuse to, what I conceive to be, the public wish, and to the conviction of my mind, the necessity of nominating you to that office—and I cannot but flatter myself that the same reasons which have led you to former sacrafices in the public service, will now operate to induce your acceptance of an appointment so highly interesting to your Country.

As soon as the Acts, which are necessary accompaniments of these appointments can be got ready you will receive official notice of the latter. This letter is only to be considered as an early communication of my sentiments on this occasion and as a testimony of the sincere esteem and regard with which I am,

Dear Sir,

Your most Obed & Affect. Servt,

Go Washington.

At the same time President Washington was also urging Chief Judge Robert Hanson Harrison, of the General Court of Maryland, to serve as an Associate Justice of the United States Supreme Court. But both Mr. Johnson and Judge Harrison asked to be excused.

Judge Harrison was asked to reconsider his declination, which he did. But it was evident that any effort to draw Johnson from seclusion would be fruitless. Greatly did the President regret the positive declination, not only because he believed Johnson would make an able jurist, but also because of the apprehension that the return of commissions of high importance might have a tendency to bring the Government into disrepute. "Mr. Johnson's resignation came to hand too late," the President lamented,[12] "to admit of a new appointment, and information to be given of it before the time fixed by the Act for holding the first District Court in Maryland. However, if this had not been the case, I should hardly have hazarded a new appointment, for the reasons before mentioned, until I had good grounds to believe it would be accepted." Judge Alexander Contee Hanson also did not want to be District Judge, and the place was then offered to ex-Governor Paca, who served on the Federal District bench until the time of his death.

So it was that for a period of two years, following the ratification of the Federal Constitution, Mr. Johnson held aloof from public life; and the only office which he did agree to accept—and this was of a *quasi-public* nature— was that of President of the Potomac Company. Washington was unable to give adequate attention to the organization after his inauguration as President of the United States; and at the annual meeting of the stockholders in Georgetown in September, 1789, Johnson was elected as the second President of the Company.

Johnson accepted the duty at a time when insolvency was threatening the corporation. But navigation of the waterway—at least for the smaller boats—now seemed in sight; and the officers were directed to proceed by law to collect all amounts from delinquent subscribers due on their stock subscriptions. So the years went by and hundreds of thousands of dollars were spent in an effort to

---

[12] Scharf, *History of Maryland*, Vol. II, page 560. *Washington to Dr. McHenry*, November 30, 1789.

utilize the natural river bed of the Potomac as a channel of traffic. And while the project was eventually abandoned, it paved the way for the construction of the Chesapeake and Ohio Canal and the Baltimore and Ohio Railroad. Thus the Potomac Company not only led, as we have seen, to the adoption of the Federal Constitution, but also constituted an important step in the commercial development of the Nation.

CHAPTER **XXIX**

CHIEF JUDGE OF THE GENERAL COURT

R OBERT HANSON HARRISON, Chief Judge of the
General Court, died suddenly a short time afer he was
invited to become an Associate Justice of the United States
Supreme Court. And on April 20, 1790, Mr. Johnson was
chosen by Governor Howard to fill Judge Harrison's seat
on the General Court.

Under the Maryland Constitution of 1776, the Judicial Department of the State consisted of a General Court,
a Court of Chancery, a Court of Admiralty, and a Court
of Appeals. The General Court superseded the old
Provincial Court, and had original jurisdiction in both civil
and criminal causes arising on both the Western and
Eastern Shores.[1]

Strange to say, Johnson accepted the appointment to
the bench. Just why he accepted is difficult to explain, unless it was the natural desire of a lawyer in the latter part
of life to round out his life as a jurist.

Certain it is that in the closing years of the Eighteenth
Century, a seat on the General Court of Maryland was a
place of great responsibility. Before the tribunal there
came cases of great magnitude for decision. Roger Brooke
Taney once said that the members of the General Court

[1] *Maryland Constitution*, Article LVI.

were always selected from the eminent men of the Bar. "The extent of its jurisdiction, and the importance of the cases tried in it," declared the Chief Justice, "brought together, at its sessions, all that were eminent or distinguished at the Bar on either of the Shores for which it was sitting." [2]

The Associate Judges who served with Johnson were Robert Goldsborough and Jeremiah Townley Chase. Luther Martin was the Attorney-General of Maryland and the acknowledged head of the legal profession in the State. Among other lawyers of prominence who appeared before the Court were such brilliant lawyers as Chase, Cooke, Mercer, Pinkney, Key, and Kilty.

While Johnson remained on the bench of the General Court little more than a year, there came before him during this brief period several cases which called for interpretation of the Constitution of the United States.

The first case presenting a Constitutional question, *State of Maryland vs. Sluby*,[3] was a *scire facias* on a bond conditioned to pay duties on certain goods imported by Sluby into the State. The defendant, through Attorneys Key and Potts, interposed a demurrer, claiming that the Acts of the General Assembly allowing duties were repealed by Article I, Section 8, of the Federal Constitution, empowering Congress to lay and collect duties, imposts and excises and providing that all duties, imposts and excises should be uniform throughout the United States. In their reply, Attorney-General Martin and Mr. Chase, representing the State, contended that under Article I, Section 10, of the Federal Constitution, a State was entitled to lay imposts or duties when

<hr/>

[2] Samuel Tyler, *Memoir of Roger Brooke Taney*, page 58.
[3] *2 H. & McH. 322.*

necessary for executing its inspection laws. At the May Term of 1790, the General Court overruled the demurrer and directed issuance of the execution. Several years later the judgment was affirmed by the Court of Appeals. Some time later, the power of Congress to lay duties was construed as exclusive by the United States Supreme Court.[4]

Another case asking for construction of the Federal Constitution—*Donaldson vs. Harvey*—appeared at the October Term of 1790.[5] The action was a motion to set aside the return of the Sheriff of Washington County on a *fieri facias*. Under an Act of the Assembly of 1716, a Sheriff was required to seize personal property of a debtor and give it to the creditor. The plaintiff contended that the Act of 1716 impaired the nature of a contract by forcing a creditor to accept chattels in payment of debt; and therefore the Act was repealed by Article I, Section 10, of the Constitution, which prohibits any State from making anything but gold and silver coin a tender in payment of debts or from passing any law impairing the obligation of contracts. The defendant replied that the Constitution did not repeal the Act of 1716, so far as antecedent debts were concerned. The General Court took the view of the defendant and refused to set aside the Sheriff's return.

But the most important of all the cases that came before Johnson while he was Chief Judge of the General Court was the case of *Dulany vs. Wells*.[6] It was commonly known as the British Debt Case and its importance arose from the large amount of property that hinged on the decision of the Court. The case was an action of *debt* brought by Daniel Dulany, as administrator of Bladen, a British

---

[4] *Brown vs. Maryland, 12 Wheaton, 419.*
[5] *3 H. & McH., 8.*
[6] *3 H. & McH., 14.*

creditor, on a bond executed in 1775 by Wells, a Maryland debtor. Under an Act of 1780, citizens of the State who were indebted to British subjects were permitted to discharge their debts by making payment into the Treasury of the State. Mr. Wells's surety had availed himself of the provisions of this law and received a receipt in full from the Treasurer of the Western Shore. The lawyers for the British creditor's administrator maintained that, while the property of aliens was confiscated upon the declaration of war, the remedy of creditors was restored by the Treaty between Great Britain and the United States, which provided that creditors on either side should not meet with any lawful impediment to the recovery of *bona fide* debts theretofore contracted. Attorney-General Martin, representing Wells, contended in reply that Maryland citizens who had made payments to the State under authority of the law had discharged their debts; and the Treaty of Peace could not operate to destroy rights acquired under the existing laws of the State. The General Court at the October Term of 1790 held that the payments made into the Treasury were not valid, and Dulany was given judgment for the entire amount of the claim except interest during the period of the war.

Nearly five years later the decision of the General Court was reversed by the Court of Appeals; but the early British Debt case of *Dulany vs. Wells* is of interest in the study of the life of Johnson because of the fact that he was to be called upon within a few years to consider the same question as a member of the Supreme Court of the United States.

CHAPTER **XXX**

COMMISSIONER OF THE FEDERAL CITY

ON January 22, 1791, Johnson, then the Chief Judge of the General Court of Maryland, was appointed by President Washington as the head of the Board of Commissioners of the Federal City. Under the Residence Law—this Act of Congress, approved July 16, 1790, authorized the establishment of a permanent seat of Government along the Potomac—the Commissioners were empowered to purchase the necessary land and provide suitable buildings for the accommodation of Congress and the President. Named with Johnson on the Board were Daniel Carroll, of Maryland, and Dr. David Stuart, Washington's physician, who resided near Alexandria, Virginia. Johnson's executive ability and great energy had been shown in the work of the Potomac Company, and Washington also felt that an able Maryland lawyer "would be invaluable as legal adviser to the Commission and particularly in preparing the conveyances which would be required in carrying out his scheme for acquiring the site for the proposed city and in drafting such legislation as would be needed to facilitate the work of the Commission." [1]

Having been given the privilege of selecting the location of the Federal District, not exceeding ten miles square, at any place along the Potomac River between the Eastern Branch and the Conococheague, the President selected the

[1] Tindall, *History of the City of Washington,* page 49.

area including the thriving towns of Georgetown, Maryland, and Alexandria, Virginia. After Congress adjourned at Philadelphia in March, 1791, Washington arranged to meet the three Commissioners in Georgetown for a preliminary conference. They met on March 28th [2] and conferred with Major Andrew Ellicott, who had been engaged to make the first survey of the District, and Major Pierre Charles L'Enfant, the French engineer, who had served with credit in the American Revolution, and who now at the age of 37 was anxious to have the distinction of laying out the Federal City.

On the following morning—March 29, 1791—Washington and the three Commissioners set out on horseback with L'Enfant and Ellicott to inspect the proposed territory. That night they held a meeting to consider an amicable agreement between the Commissioners and the property holders; and on the 30th an agreement was signed by the nineteen men who owned practically all of the land within the District.

Washington looked to Johnson to expedite the consummation of the transactions. On the third of April, after his arrival at Mount Vernon, the President wrote as follows to the Commissioners: "If Mr. Johnson could conveniently undertake to prepare such a Deed as he thinks would answer all the purposes both of the public and the Grantees, I am sure it would be efficiently done. If this can not be, then it might be well to furnish the Attorney-General with a copy of the agreement, with the papers I left with you together with such other information as will enable him to do it." [3]

[2] *Washington's Diary.*
[3] *George Washington Letter Book,* Library of Congress, Manuscript Division, Vol. XI, page 128.

The second conference of the President and the Commissioners was held at Georgetown at the close of June,
1791. On the 30th of the month he set out shortly after
4 A.M., for Philadelphia, *via* York and Lancaster, and at
sundown arrived in Frederick, where he was entertained
at Mrs. Kimball's Hotel. Tradition says that one of
those who helped to entertain the President that night
was an attractive dark-haired girl of about twenty-four
named Hauer, who many years later was immortalized by
Whittier under her married name of Barbara Fritchie.
Washington spent the night with Judge and Mrs. Johnson
at Richfield; and on the following morning continued on
his journey to Philadelphia. He was accompanied by
Johnson and other Frederick countians as far as Terra
Rubra, the estate of Major John Ross Key, where the party
spent the night. Before leaving there on the next day,
Johnson announced to the crowds that had assembled outside the mansion that the President would say a few words
before departure. Washington then feelingly expressed his
thanks for the cordial reception given him in Maryland and
declared that in the darkest hours of the Revolution, the
succor and support he received from the people of Frederick
County always cheered him.[4]

Soon after his arrival in Philadelphia, the President received from Major L'Enfant a tentative plan of the Federal
City. The design showed the Congress House and the
President's House, connected by a broad avenue about a
mile in length, with broad avenues, intersecting streets, and
parks, somewhat like the plan of Versailles. Jefferson and
Madison also made an examination of L'Enfant's design.

The Commissioners met again in September, and it was

---

[4] Scharf, *History of Western Maryland*, Vol. I, page 553.

WARRANT,

Nº **311** _For One Thousand_ DOLLARS.

KNOW YE, That in conformity with the special trust repofed in us, and to further the views of Government respecting their permanent refidence, the underfigned commiffioners, by and with the approbation of the PRESIDENT OF THE UNITED STATES OF AMERICA, have fanctioned a loan to the city of WASHINGTON, to be applied to the sole improvement thereof in the fum of five hundred thoufand dollars.

The terms of the loan are, viz.

The evidence or titles fhall confift of 500 fhares, or certificates for 1000 dollars each, payable by inftalments at the bank of the United States of America, or at fuch other place or places as may be duly notified by the commiffion. The ftated periods for the inftalments on each fhare are as follows, viz.

On the 15th of June 1792, - - 100 dollars,		On the 15th of November following 200 dollars.
On the 15th of November following 100 do.		On the 15th of May 1794, - - 200 do.
On the 15th of May 1793, - - 200 do.		On the 15th of November following 200 do.

The intereft fhall be duly paid by the commiffioners, at the rate of fix per cent. per annum, half yearly, by a deduction from inftalments after the firft (while there are inftalments to be paid) and half yearly ever after till the principal fhall be redeemed; and the principal fhall be paid in fuch fums and times as the borrower fhall think proper, except that for the benefit of the lender, it is ftipulated that no part of the principal fhall be repaid before the year 1800, nor fhall there be repaid at any one time thereafter a fmaller portion than five per cent. on the capital.— And further for the benefit of the loaner, the PRESIDENT OF THE UNITED STATES OF AMERICA has executed a deed declaring that 3000 lots of public property in the faid city of WASHINGTON, north of a line drawn eaft and weft, through the fite of the Prefident's houfe, and 2000 lots fouth of the fame line, fhall be referved unfold, and fhall be held in truft as fecurity to infure the punctual payment of the principal as well as the intereft on the aforefaid loan, to the lender or loaners thereof.

BE IT KNOWN, _That Samuel Blodget, jun. of Boston, or his assigns,_ will be entitled to _____ SHARE Nº. _____ in the above loan: Provided always, that the inftalments fpecified fhall be punctually paid and regularly noted on this inftrument; and that every _affignment or transfer fhall be accompanied by a certificate from a Loan Officer of the United States of America, or from a duly qualified Notary Public residing at the place where fuch transfer or affignment may be made._

IN WITNESS _whereof, we have hereunto fet our hands and affixed our feals, this tenth_

Day of April 1792

figned May 18th 1792

S Blodget Jun

Th Johnfon

D. Stuart ⎱ Commiff.

Danl Carroll

CERTIFICATE OF LOAN TO THE CITY OF WASHINGTON

then that they agreed to give to the Federal City the name of *Washington*. Their desire to this effect was made known in the following communication to L'Enfant:

Georgetown, September 9, 1791.

Sir:

We have agreed that the Federal District shall be called "The Territory of Columbia," and the Federal City the "City of Washington." The title of the map will therefore be "A Map of the City of Washington in the Territory of Columbia."

We have also agreed that the streets be named alphabetically one way and numerically the other, the former to be divided into North and South, and the latter into East and West Numbers from the Capitol.

Major Ellicott, with proper assistance, will immediately take, and soon furnish you with the soundings of the Eastern Branch, to be inserted in the map. We expect he will also furnish you with the proposed post road, which we wish to be noticed in the map.

We are, respectfully yours,

Th. Johnson,
David Stuart,
Daniel Carroll.

CHAPTER **XXXI**

ASSOCIATE JUSTICE OF THE UNITED STATES SUPREME COURT

AT the time he was serving as Chief Judge of the General Court and as Commissioner of the Federal City, Johnson received still another call to public service. This was an invitation from President Washington to become an Associate Justice of the United States Supreme Court.

The President's invitation follows: [1]

PRESIDENT WASHINGTON TO JUDGE JOHNSON

Philadelphia,
14th July, 1791.

Dr Sir,

Without preface or apology for propounding the following question to you at this time, permit me to ask you with frankness, and in the fullness of friendship, whether you will accept an appointment on the Supreme Judiciary of the United States.

Mr. Rutledge's resignation has occasioned a vacancy therein, which I should be glad to see filled by you.

Your answer to this question by the Post (which is the most certain mode of conveying letters) as soon as you can make it convenient, will very much oblige, dear Sir,

Your most obed^t and affectionate h^{ble} Servt
G^o WASHINGTON.

[1] Scharf, *History of Western Maryland,* Vol. I, page 391.

At this time, the Justices, in addition to their work on the Supreme bench, were required to hold Circuit Courts in pairs, together with the Judge of the District in which the Court was held. Travel was slow, fatiguing, and dangerous; and Johnson, now approaching 59, wrote the President that he might consider serving on the Supreme bench were it not for the highly objectionable duty of circuit riding.

Washington replied as follows: [2]

PRESIDENT WASHINGTON TO JUDGE JOHNSON

Philadelphia, 7 August, 1791.

Dear Sir,

I have been duly favored with your letters of the 27th and 30th of July, the last of which came to hand while the Judges of the Supreme Court were with me on an invitation to dinner.

I took this opportunity of laying your letter before the Chief Justice (as you mentioned your having written to him and to Mr. Nelson on the subject) in order that it might be communicated to the other judges. After a few minutes' consultation together, the Chief Justice informed me that the arrangement had been, or would be, agreed upon, that you might be wholly exempted from performing this tour of duty at that time.

And I take the present occasion to observe that an opinion prevails pretty generally among the judges, as well as others, who have turned their minds to the subject, against the expediency of continuing the Circuits of the Associate Judges, and that it is expected some alterations in the Judicial System will be brought forward at the next session of Congress, among which this may be one.

Upon considering the arrangements of the Judges with respect to the ensuing Circuit, and the probability of future relief from these disagreeable tours, I thought it best to direct your Commission to be made out and transmitted to you, which has accordingly been done;

[2] Sparks, *The Writings of George Washington*, Vol. II, page 182.

and I have no doubt that the public will be benefited, and the wishes of your friends gratified, by your acceptance.

With sentiments of very great regard,
I am, Dear Sir,
Your most obed^t Servt,
G^o WASHINGTON.

The commission, dated August 5, 1791, was forwarded from Philadelphia by Jefferson; and Johnson, resigning as Chief Judge of the General Court, was succeeded by Samuel Chase, who was appointed October 7, 1791.

Johnson's appointment as Associate Justice of the Supreme Court was confirmed by the United States Senate on November 7th; and, although he had tried to escape the laborious duties in the Federal Circuit Court, he was called upon within a few weeks to sit on the Circuit Court bench at Richmond in the important British Debt case of *Ware, administrator of Jones, vs. Hylton et al.*[3] Soon after the establishment of the National Courts, a large number of suits were instituted by British creditors to recover debts contracted prior to the Revolution. One of these suits was brought in the Circuit Court at Richmond by William Jones, a British subject, against Dr. Thomas Walker, a citizen of Virginia. It was a test case, the decision of which involved immense sums of money. Justice Johnson was familiar with the questions involved: he had heard them argued in the General Court of Maryland.

The *cause célèbre* came on for argument on the 24th of November, 1791. With Johnson sat Associate Justice John Blair, a Virginian, and Judge Griffin, the Federal Judge of that District. The Court room was densely crowded, and

---

[3] 1 *Curtis*, 164.

the presiding jurists "relaxed the rigour of respect which they were in the habit of exacting, and permitted the vacant seats of the bench, and even the windows behind it, to be occupied by the impatient multitude." [4] The lawyers in the case were men of great ability. Representing the plaintiff—and incidentally other British creditors—were William Ronald, John Baker, John Wickham, and John Starke; while the defendant—and other debtors who were trying to uphold the law of Virginia—were represented by James Innis, Attorney-General of the Commonwealth, Patrick Henry, John Marshall, and Alexander Campbell.

Patrick Henry's great argument commenced on November 25th and continued for three days. He showed that confiscation had been practiced in England ever since the time of William I and he contended that the cruelty of George III justified the American people in confiscating debts. He also took the position that the debts had not been revived by the Treaty of Peace since this covenant had been violated by the British. According to one biographer, the case was "probably the most difficult and important in a legal aspect" of all the causes in which Mr. Henry ever took part as a lawyer in any period of his career.[5] Another biographer declares that Henry in this case made "his most distinguished display of professional talents." [6]

It was also this case in which John Marshall first won nation-wide reputation as an outstanding leader of the American Bar. Young Marshall's notable argument, says Beveridge, "carried his reputation beyond Virginia and won for him the admiration of the ablest men at the Bar,

---

[4] William Wirt, *Sketches of the Life and Character of Patrick Henry*, page 320.

[5] M. C. Tyler, *Patrick Henry*, page 359.

[6] Wirt, *Sketches of the Life and Character of Patrick Henry*, page 312.

regardless of their opinion of the merits of the controversy." [7]

Justice Johnson did not render a final opinion in the
case. Indeed, no decision was reached until 1794, and subsequently the Circuit Court was reversed by the Supreme
Court, which held that the debtors were liable for their
obligations on the ground that the Treaty annulled the laws
of the State.

Mr. Johnson, however, had the honor of writing the
first opinion in the Reports of the United States Supreme
Court. While he did not take his seat on the Supreme
Court bench until the August Term of 1792, there had been
as yet no written opinions of the tribunal. The February
and August Terms of 1790, which had been held in New
York, brought practically no work before the Supreme
Court. In 1791, when the jurists assembled in Philadelphia, there was still no important business to transact.

On account of indisposition—not to mention the unin-
viting roads and the severe Winter weather—Mr. Johnson
was prevented from going to Philadelphia to qualify as
Associate Justice of the Supreme Court at the February
Term of 1792. He sent his regrets to Chief Justice Jay,
who said in reply that he hoped Congress would soon free
the judicial system from the necessity of circuit riding. [8]

While there was little except routine business to be
transacted by the Supreme Court justices at the February
Term, and Johnson was actually not needed for any im-
portant judicial duties, his failure to make the journey to
Philadelphia at this time was a distinct disappointment to
President Washington. "That Mr. Johnson's health did

[7] Albert J. Beveridge, *The Life of John Marshall*, Vol. II, page 187.
[8] Johnson to Jay, February 3; Jay to Johnson, March 12. Original in
the Maryland Historical Society, Baltimore, Md.

not permit him to come to this City as he proposed and was expected," the President wrote Dr. Stuart, "is a matter of exceeding great regret, as many things relative to the Federal District—the City and the public buildings—might have been more satisfactorily arranged, and delays avoided; but as there is no contending against acts of Providence, we must submit as it becomes us so to do and endeavor to recover the time lost in the best manner we can." [9]

However, Johnson was just as keenly anxious as the President to expedite the erection of the Federal buildings. He had written a tentative draft of an advertisement asking for designs for a Congress House and forwarded it to the President for his criticism. With a few alterations the suggested advertisement was returned by Mr. Jefferson together with another advertisement for plans for a President's House. "Both of them," wrote Jefferson to the Commissioners under date of March 6th, "are subject to your pleasure, and when accommodated to that, if you will return them, they shall be advertised here and elsewhere." And so the Commissioners proceeded to announce a list of prizes for the best plans submitted for the Capitol and the President's House. It was about this time—early in March, 1792—that Johnson heard the news that President Washington had discharged Major L'Enfant on account of insubordination [10] and the President called upon the Commissioners for perseverance and vigorous exertions to combat the forces of jealousy and discontent. It appeared that many Pennsylvanians were scheming to retain the National Capital at Philadelphia, and Washington was

---

[9] *George Washington Letter Book*, Library of Congress, Manuscript Division.

[10] *Daniel Carroll to Johnson*, March 3, 1792. Original in Maryland Historical Society.

apprehensive that the enemies of the proposed Federal City would take advantage of the discharge of L'Enfant to trumpet the entire plan of the Commissioners as abortive in an attempt to retard the completion of the project. In April, the Commissioners received word from Jefferson that the financial situation was very unfavorable for securing a loan to the City of Washington, but Johnson and his associates were called upon to fix the enterprise in the public mind as stable and unalterable. "No doubt," says one writer, "the personnel of the Board had much to do with the enterprise escaping shipwreck on the rocks which were abundant enough in the course of an undertaking that was but meagerly supplied with funds and had hostile and jealous critics both at home and abroad." [11]

In August, Mr. Johnson felt sufficiently strong to make the journey to Philadelphia to qualify as Associate Justice of the Supreme Court. He took the oath of office before Chief Justice Jay on August 6, 1792. Shortly after this came Johnson's opportunity to write the first opinion. The case, in which the opinion is recorded, *State of Georgia, vs. Brailsford, et al.*,[12] was another proceeding involving the confiscation of British debts. In its bill filed in the Supreme Court, the State of Georgia set forth the fact that a law had been enacted by the Legislature to confiscate all British debts for the use of the State; that Brailsford, a British subject, whose bond had been sequestered by the State, brought suit notwithstanding against the debtor in the Federal Circuit Court; and that the Circuit Court had refused to allow the State of Georgia to become a part to the proceedings. The Supreme Court was asked for an

[11] W. B. Bryan, *A History of the National Capital*, Vol. I, page 122.
[12] 2 *Dallas*, 402.

injunction to stay further proceedings in the Circuit Court in order that the money would be retained for the State. The chief issue was whether there was need for the intervention of Equity, or whether there was adequate remedy at Law.

After the able arguments of Mr. Dallas, for the State of Georgia, and Mr. Randolph, then Attorney-General of the United States, for the defendants, the justices on August 11, 1792, delivered their opinions *seriatim*. Chief Justice Jay and Associate Justices Iredell, Blair and Wilson held that they had "no objection" to ordering the money held in the custody of the law until the Court could better satisfy themselves "both as to the remedy and the right." Justice Johnson and Justice Cushing dissented on the ground that the bill for injunction did not set up a sufficient foundation for the exercise of equitable jurisdiction.

Johnson's opinion is as follows:

"In order to support a motion for an injunction, the bill should set forth a case of probable right, and a probable danger that the right would be defeated, without this special interposition of the Court. It does not appear to me, that the present bill sufficiently claims such an interposition. If the State has a right to the debt in question, it may be enforced at Common Law, notwithstanding the judgment of the Circuit Court; and there is no suggestion in the bill, though it has been suggested at the bar, that the State is likely to lose her right by the insolvency either of Spalding, the original debtor, or of Brailsford, who will become her debtor for the amount, if he receives it, when in law he ought not to receive, or retain, it.

"Nor does the bill state any particular confederacy, or fraud. The refusal to admit the Attorney General as a party on the record, was the act of a competent Court; and it is not sufficient barely to allege, that the defendant has not chosen to sue out a writ of error.

"The case might, perhaps, be made better; but as I can only know, at present, the facts which the bill alleges, and which the affidavit supports, it is my opinion, that there is not a proper foundation for issuing an injunction."

At the February Term of 1793, in the absence of Justice Johnson, the injunction was continued and in August Justice Iredell concurred in the views expressed by Johnson. At the February Term of 1794, the suit was tried by a jury, to which Chief Justice Jay delivered a charge. Later the jury returned and asked the Court whether the Act of the Georgia Legislature vested debts in the State, and, if so, whether the Treaty of Peace revived the right of the defendants to the debt in controversy. The Chief Justice replied that it was the unanimous opinion of the Court that the Act did not vest the debts in the State, and that the return of peace revived the right of action to recover. There was thereupon a verdict against the State.

"It will thus be seen," says one writer, "that although in opposition to the views of Justice Johnson at the preliminary hearing a restraining order had been issued, the final decision of the Court, without dissent, was that the State of Georgia had no standing in Court." [13]

On account of failing health, Justice Johnson on January 16, 1793, sent to President Washington a letter of resignation.

Regretfully the President replied:

PRESIDENT WASHINGTON TO JUSTICE JOHNSON

Philadelphia, February 1, 1793.

Dear Sir—

Whilst I acknowledge the receipt of your letter of the 16th January, I cannot but express the regret with which I received the

[13] *Indexed Digest of the U. S. Supreme Court Reports,* Vol. I, xxxii.

resignation of your office, and sincerely lament the causes that produced it. It is unnecessary for me to say how much I should have been pleased had your health permitted you to continue in office; for besides the difficulty of providing a character to fill the distinguished and important station of Judge, in whom are combined the necessary professional, local, and other requisites, the resignation of persons holding that high office conveys to the public mind a want of stability in that Department, where perhaps it is more essential than in any other.

With sentiments of pure esteem and regard, and sincere wishes for your health and happiness,

I am Sir,

Your most obedient Servant,

Go Washington.

President Washington, in accepting Johnson's resignation, thereupon named William Paterson, of New Jersey, to fill the vacancy.

Chapter XXXII

AT THE CORNER STONE OF THE CAPITOL

RELIEVED of his judicial duties early in 1793, Johnson agreed to continue as a member of the Board of Commissioners of the Federal City. The work was not confining; indeed, Washington had arranged for the appointment of a superintendent to relieve the Commissioners from details and all sacrifices of time except the periodical meetings. The matter of compensation for the Commissioners was also adjusted.

The chief problem before the Commissioners in 1793 —the plan of Captain James Hoban for a President's House had already been approved—was the selection of a plan for the Capitol. The design of Stephen Hallet had been adjudged the best of all the plans submitted in the public contest and it would have been finally accepted had not Dr. William Thornton, a physician with drawing as a hobby, presented a design which was more pleasing to the President. Hallet had made alterations to meet the approbation of the President, who now suggested that Dr. Thornton's plan be accepted, but that as he was not a professional architect Hallet be engaged to perfect it. "We feel sensibly for poor Hallet," the Commissioners wrote to Jefferson under date of February 7, 1793, "and shall do everything in our power to soothe him. We hope he may be usefully employed notwithstanding."

In April the Commissioners notified Dr. Thornton that his plans had been given formal approval by the President, but in the months that followed Hallet made a number of alterations which were finally adopted.

Everything was finally in readiness for the laying of the corner stone of the Capitol on Wednesday, September 18, 1793. It was a beautiful Autumn day. And it was a most satisfactory day for Washington and Johnson, who had served together so long in helping to lay the foundation of the Nation. After President Washington had been escorted with pomp from his landing place on the North bank of the Potomac to the President's Square, the grand procession started on its way to the Capitol—with music playing, drums beating, colors flying, and spectators rejoicing—in the following order of march: Surveying Department of the City of Washington; Mayor and Corporation of Georgetown; Virginia Artillery; Commissioners of the City and their attendants; stone cutters and mechanics; two sword bearers; Masons of the fifth degree; Bibles on grand cushions; deacons with staffs of office; stewards with wands; Masons of the third degree; wardens with truncheons; secretaries with tools of office; paymasters with their regalia; treasurers with their jewels; band of music; Lodge No. 22, of Alexandria; corn, wine and oil; Grand Master *pro tem;* President Washington; and the grand sword bearer.

After the Grand Marshal ordered a halt at the Capitol, the marchers divided, forming two lines facing each other, through which the sword bearer marched followed by President Washington and all the others in the procession. As the artillery discharged their cannon, Washington stood in silence near the big corner stone. Johnson, Carroll and

Stuart, the three Commissioners of the Federal City, then received from Joseph Clark, grand master *pro tem*, a handsome silver plate to be laid upon the corner stone.

The plate bore the following inscription:

"This Southeast corner stone of the Capitol of the United States of America, in the City of Washington, was laid on the 18th day of September, 1793, in the eighteenth year of American Independence, in the first year of the second term of the Presidency of George Washington, whose virtues in the civil administration of his country have been as conspicuous and beneficial as his military valor and prudence have been useful in establishing her liberties, and in the year of Masonry 5793, by the President of the United States, in concert with the Grand Lodge of Maryland, several lodges under its jurisdiction, and Lodge No. 22, from Alexandria, Va.; Thomas Johnson, David Stuart, and Daniel Carroll, Commissioners; Joseph Clark, Right Worshipful Grand Master, *pro tempore;* James Hoban and Stephen Hallet, architects; Collin Williamson, master mason."

The Commissioners ordered the inscription to be read; the artillery discharged another volley; and the silver plate was then delivered to President Washington, who laid it upon the corner stone, after which it was covered with corn, wine and oil. The whole assemblage then joined in prayer, after which Grand Master Clark delivered the oration of the day. The occasion concluded with an ox barbecue.[1]

A few months later Johnson was definitely planning to resign as a member of the Board. He sent the following notice of his determination to the President:[2]

[1] *Columbian Sentinel,* Boston, Mass., October 5, 1793.
[2] *The Papers of George Washington,* Library of Congress, Manuscript Division.

JOHNSON TO PRESIDENT WASHINGTON

Washington, 23ᵈ Decemʳ 1793.

Sir

We are just about finishing the Business of this Meeting, it has been very important, much influenced by the Considerations hinted in our general Letter and I hope will meet your Approbation. Funds are now secured, I think, to carry on the public Buildings to a considerable Length under the most disagreeable Events and if our public affairs should brighten a powerful Influence is secured to do what is right and proper and which ought to have been done in the Outset.

Mr. Blodget has involved us in unpleasant circumstances. Doctʳ Stuart and I cannot quit our Post to our own Satisfaction till we see the present Lottery in a way of being settled and we had all determined that another should not be offered in the present Temper of the public or at all without a farther Security than mere Honor. I will deal frankly with you, Sir, tho' I dare say your own Observation renders mine unnecessary. Mr. Blodget will not be useful in the Affairs of the City he wants Judgment and Steadiness I cannot think of leaving him to a Successor we all wish to part from him and that quietly.

As soon as the Lottery Business is smoothed, and I hope it will be so by the first of March, I wish to be relieved: my affairs are pretty extensive and require much of my attention: I wish too to avail myself of the Moment which I saw and has almost past away to benefit myself by the rise of the City to which a long Friendship for Potomack and every Exertion in my power in it's favor fairly intitle me.

I am Sir,
With the most perfect Esteem and Respect
Your very affectionate Servant
TH JOHNSON.

The President urged Johnson to remain on the Board a little while longer. "With regret," said Washington, "I perceive your determination to withdraw from the Commission under which you have acted for executing the plan of the Federal City. My wish was, and still is, if it could be made to comport with your convenience and inclination, that it should be changed, or at least suspended; for I should be sorry to see others (coming in at the eleventh hour as it were) reap the fruits of your difficult labors." [3] Washington also asked Johnson to recommend a successor.

Johnson realized the difficulty that faced the President in trying to secure suitable men to serve as Commissioners and consented to remain on the Board a little while longer until a successor could be found. This delighted Washington. "For although I have no doubt," the President wrote on February 23, 1794, "with respect to the accomplishment of the law (establishing the permanent residence of Congress) nor of the execution of the plan of the City, yet a great and sudden change of the Commissioners appointed to conduct this business is not likely, in my opinion, to produce good, but on the contrary, evil consequences." [4]

Johnson then replied: [5]

JOHNSON TO PRESIDENT WASHINGTON

Frederick 6 February 1794.

Sir

Your Letter of the 23[d] of last Month came to Hand whilst I was attending on the Lottery Business at George Town: I forbore to answer it immediately hoping that a little Delay might enable me to do it more to your Satisfaction as well as my own for I could not think of any Gentleman of the neighborh[d] whom I could venture to

[3] *George Washington Letter Book,* Library of Congress, Manuscript Division.

[4] Original in New York Public Library, New York City.

[5] *The Papers of George Washington,* Library of Congress, Manuscript Division.

recommend to you and the Proprietors, amongst whom there is the most ability, have not lately gained in my Confidence. Reflection has not assisted me nor do I see a prospect of a favorable change unless from an Accession of Strangers several of whom it is said will be at the City in the Spring and amongst them I hope such as will be proper for your Choice. In the Mean Time, with your Approbation, I will continue to act for though I sh^d not suffer much in seeing the little credit I may have earned, transferred by common Opinion to a Successor I should be very sorry a change of Com^{rs} should injure the work I have very much at Heart.

I am Sir,
With the truest Respect,
Your affectionate Servant,
Th Johnson.

Mr. Johnson was hopeful that before he left the Board it would be possible for the President to have a final meeting with the Commissioners early in June. But on account of the delay of Congress Washington wrote from Philadelphia on June 27th that much to his regret he was unable to meet them at the Federal City on his way to Mount Vernon. The President also declared that he had not yet been able to secure Commissioners to fill the vacancies caused by the resignation of Johnson and Dr. Stuart; and, indeed, the President was still holding out a faint hope that Johnson might yet be induced to continue on the Board as a result of a report that Johnson was thinking of taking up his residence in the new City.[6]

But Johnson insisted that he must resign. Said he:[7]

[6] *George Washington Letter Book*, Library of Congress, Manuscript Division.

[7] *The Papers of George Washington*, Library of Congress, Manuscript Division.

JOHNSON TO PRESIDENT WASHINGTON

Washington 28 June 1794.

Sir

Disappointed by Mr. Greenleafs not coming and tired of stay-
ing here I had wrote to you Yesterday by Doct Stuart who will have
the pleasure of seeing you, and we were just separating this Morning
when I received your Letter of Yesterday. . . .

Your desire to retain me as principal gives me pleasure in this that
it evinces the satisfaction you have in my Endeavours to be useful:
but before I went so far as to mention with Doct^r Stuart 600 £ a
year as a moderate Compensation to each Commissioner who could
and would do his Duty my Resolution was finally taken, and I do
not know of any Event which would induce me to stand the Mark
of Calumny and gross Abuse as I have alone for near three years
past. Sincerely do I wish there was a greater quantity of Men for
choice who could and would do better; one of the Commissioners
ought to have legal knowledge deeper than the near Surface or else
be no Lawyer at all. I do not suppose that every Thing which has
past through my Hands will be free from Cavil but I have the
satisfaction that we have had fewer Disputes on them than might
have been expected under all circumstances. I begg you Sir that I
may be discharged by the first of August and I am the more earnest
in this Request because of my having openly said on several Occasions
that I should not act longer.

I always have pleasure in meeting you: circumstances would not
allow it on your way to Mount Vernon and I despair of seeing you
on your way to Philadelphia. Doct^r Stuart will inform you of the
Substance of a serious Convers^a we have had on levelling Streets and
allowing areas to be cut out of them.

I shall be glad to hear of your setting out for Philadelphia at
the Time you design, recovered perfectly from the Accident you met
with

And remain Sir,
With the truest Respect,
Your affectionate Servant,
TH JOHNSON.

It was not, however, until the middle of September, 1794, that President Washington was able to complete the personnel of the Board. He selected Gustavus Scott and Dr. William Thornton as the new Commissioners.

By this time the most difficult work in connection with the establishment of the Federal City on the Potomac had been completed. It had been a gigantic undertaking; but, through the farsightedness and resourcefulness of Washington and the indomitable energy and perseverance of Johnson and his associates, the plan of establishing the Capital City of the Nation had been launched successfully.

Chapter XXXIII

WASHINGTON'S LAST APPEAL

"No time more than the present ever required the aid of your abilities."
—*President Washington to Johnson, August 24, 1795.*

JOHNSON was not destined by Providence to enjoy long the tranquillity of Richfield. Scarcely had he laid down his work as Commissioner of the City of Washington and returned home, ere his faithful wife was stricken ill; and she passed away on the 22nd of November, 1794.

The War Governor was now given an invitation to live at Rose Hill with his daughter, Ann Jennings Grahame. Of his eight children, Mrs. Grahame was next to the eldest. His eldest child, Thomas Jennings, was twice married; the first wife was Charlotte Hesselius, of near Annapolis, who died at the birth of her daughter; the second was Elizabeth Russell, of Baltimore. The other six children were Rebecca, who died in infancy, Elizabeth, Rebecca, James, Joshua, and Dorcas. The Governor was particularly fond of his eldest daughter, Ann Jennings. At the time of her marriage in January, 1788, he gave her as a wedding present the tract of 225 acres of land known as Rose Hill,[1] and her husband, Major John C. Grahame, erected a beautiful mansion on the property for their home. Here,

---

[1] *Land Records of Frederick County,* Liber W. R., No. 7, Folio 665.

ROSE HILL MANSION

The home at Frederick, Maryland, where Johnson spent the last twenty-
five years of his life and where he died in 1819.

a mile North of Frederick, Johnson spent the last 25 years of his life.

Johnson had devoted practically his whole life to the public service, and he now felt it his duty to provide for himself and his children. He had purchased from James Greenleaf some lots of ground along Rock Creek in the City of Washington, hoping they would enhance in value; but the new Board of Commissioners took the position that they were "water lots" and therefore did not come within the selections to be made by Greenleaf and his associates. Johnson maintained that this restriction in the agreement between Greenleaf and himself did not apply to the section on Rock Creek but only to lots on the Potomac River. After Christmas, 1794, Johnson spent a number of weeks in the Capital City looking after his own property and also acting as an unofficial representative of the President. Under date of February 28, 1795, he wrote to the President from Georgetown that notwithstanding the quarrel with the Commissioners he was still interested in the Capital City. "The success of the City has now become important to your Reputation," wrote Johnson,[2] "it is a favorite Object with you and not less so with me though the Reward will be as unequal as our Powers and Merits for you will stand as the first Figure confessed to posterity the noblest Reward to inflame a generous Mind whilst I shall be Junk in the undistinguished Group in the back Ground. Need I tell you that I take the same Interest in your Success and Honor as in my own."

Washington, of course, regretted the dispute between Johnson and the Commissioners and hoped it could be amicably settled. "No opinion of mine, on the nature of

[2] Original in Historical Society of Pennsylvania, Philadelphia, Pa.

it, has yet been given," he replied to Johnson, "nor, if it respects property, or the construction of a contract, may there be propriety in my doing it." [3]

Johnson answered from Georgetown on March 21st that he never intended to give the President the trouble of investigating the dispute with the Commissioners. "And," wrote Johnson, "I am confident you will do me the Justice to believe, in general, that my Disposition did not lead me out of my way to look for an Occasion to quarrel with them: but things are brought to that state, without any fault I think in me, that they or I must retreat and it is not usual with me to give up the Ground I have once taken." After recommending several men to fill the place on the Board made vacant by the resignation of Daniel Carroll, Johnson soliloquized: "It is mortifying that an old man, having almost crossed the Stage, cannot quietly quit it without being kickt at behind by Envy personified in young Men, however some Times instead of the old Fellow falling on his Nose the Blade kicks so wanton and high that he falls on his Back and draws on himself the contemptuous Laughter of the Spectators." [4]

The Commissioners—Carroll, Scott and Thornton— held to their view that the lots situated on Rock Creek were to be considered as "water lots" under Greenleaf's contract and as such were of greater value than other lots. And so when Johnson filed a suit in Equity against the Commissioners, they retained William Pinkney and Luther Martin, two of the leading lawyers in the Nation, to represent them. But throughout the controversy President Washington took

[3] From original letter, Washington to Johnson, Philadelphia, March 6, 1795.
[4] From original letter, Johnson to Washington, Georgetown, March 21, 1795.

the view that the dispute was a legal question which he was unable to decide and so held aloof.

Nor did Washington think any less of Johnson for asserting his legal rights. Not long afterwards the President showed his unfailing regard for Johnson by inviting him to enter the Cabinet as Secretary of State.

Two years before—at the time Jefferson was retiring to private life—Johnson had been considered by the President for the portfolio. Mr. Jefferson asked the President if he had ever thought of Johnson as a suitable man to fill the office. "He said he had; that he was a man of great good sense, an honest man, and he believed, clear of speculations;"—thus Jefferson reports the conversation [5] —"but this, said he, is an instance of what I was observing; with all these qualifications, Governor Johnson, from a want of familiarity with foreign affairs, would be in them like a fish out of water; everything would be new to him, and he awkward in everything. I confessed to him that I had considered Johnson rather as fit for the Treasury Department. Yes, said he, for that he would be the fittest appointment that could be made; he is a man acquainted with figures, and having as good a knowledge of the resources of this country as any man. . . . I asked him whether he could not name Governor Johnson to my office, under an express arrangement that at the close of the session he should take that of the Treasury. He said that men never chose to descend; that being once in a higher Department, he would not like to go into a lower one."

Finally Edmund Randolph, of Virginia, was named as Secretary of State; but after serving two years was forced to resign on account of an alleged corrupt intrigue with the

[5] Jefferson's *Anas*, August 6, 1793.

French Minister. Washington turned to Johnson for help in the latest hour of trial. The following letter, a flattering testimonial of confidence and esteem, was the last of a long series of appeals that Johnson received from the Father of his Country: [6]

PRESIDENT WASHINGTON TO JOHNSON

Philad[a] 24 Aug. 1795.

My d[r] Sir,

The office of Secretary of State is vacant, occasioned by the resignation of Mr. Randolph. Will you accept it? You know my wishes of old, to bring you into the Administration; where then is the necessity of repeating them?

No time more than the present ever required the aid of your abilities, nor of the old and proved talents of the Country. To have yours would be pleasing to me, and I verily believe would be agreeable also to the community at large. It is with you to decide: if in the affirmative, return to me the enclosed letter, and I will communicate further with you on this subject the moment you inform me thereof. If it is in the negative, be so good as to forward the letter by the Post agreeably to its address; and at any rate write me the result of your determination as soon as you can after the receipt of this letter, as I only remain here to get this and some other matters arranged before I go to Virginia for my family.

With sincere esteem and regard,
I am, very dear Sir,
Your obedient and affectionate Serv[t]
G[o] WASHINGTON.

On account of growing physical infirmities, Johnson was constrained to decline this final appeal. He replied as follows: [7]

[6] *George Washington Letter Book,* Library of Congress, Manuscript Division.
[7] *Washington Papers,* Library of Congress, Manuscript Division.

JOHNSON TO PRESIDENT WASHINGTON

Frederick,
Saturday 29 Aug. 1795.

My dear Sir.

I have just received your Letters of the 24th and 26th and feel real Concern that my Circumstances will not permit me to fill the important Office you propose to me. I am far from being out of Humor with the World on my own Account; it has done me more than Justice in estimating my Abilities and more Justice than common in conjecturing my Motives. I feel nothing of fear either in hazarding again the little reputation I may have acquired for I am not conscious of having sought or despised applause. But, without Affectation, I do not think I could do credit to the Office of Secretary; I cannot persuade myself that I possess the necessary Qualifications for it and I am sure I am too old to expect Improvement. My Strength declines and so too probably will my mental powers soon. My views in this world have been some time bounded chiefly to my children, they yet for a little while may have me to lean on, being constantly with them adds to their Happiness and makes my chief comfort.

I send your Letter to Gen¹ Pinckney to the Post Office with this as you eventually desired.

Most sincerely wishing you less alloy in the Returns of this world and the fulness of Joy in the next

I remain with Truth
Your affectionate and most obed^t Servt
TH JOHNSON.

The offer of the portfolio was forwarded by Johnson to Charles C. Pinckney, of South Carolina; but, as he too declined, the vacancy was eventually filled by Timothy Pickering, of Pennsylvania.

Chapter XXXIV

A SOLEMN PANEGYRIC

WASHINGTON issued his immortal Farewell Address to the people of the United States in September, 1796, and upon being succeeded by John Adams in 1797 retired to spend the remainder of his days at Mount Vernon. But scarcely more than two years of rest were allowed him. Riding out one day on horseback he was overtaken by a storm which chilled him through, brought on a severe cold, and resulted in his death on the 14th of December, 1799. The news was a shock to America. Indeed, the whole world agreed with Lord Byron that the great American chieftain had been among patriots

"the first, the last, the best, The Cincinnatus of the West."

Congress, in addition to holding memorial services of its own, asked the American people to observe the 22nd day of February, 1800—the birthday of George Washington—as a day of mourning and prayer.

In accordance with the request of Congress, the people of Frederick made arrangements for a mock funeral. Johnson agreed to deliver the funeral oration.

It was one of the most impressive ceremonies on that day in the Nation. Once again there was an imposing procession—the last of the many in which Johnson participated during his lifetime. Accompanied by Governor Benjamin Ogle, ex-Governor Lee, and Congressman George Baer, he rode at the head of the procession in a carriage drawn by four white horses draped in black. Behind rode other prominent men, including Charles Carroll of Carrollton, General John Eager Howard, Colonel William Washington, and Sergeant Lawrence Everhart. Soldiers, a horse with an empty saddle draped in black, bands of music, the bier and pallbearers, and a number of delegations made up the line of march. Tradition says that 8,000 people witnessed the procession. If this be correct, there must have been many visitors in Frederick for the occasion; for the population of the town was only about 2,600 at that time. The procession moved down Market Street to the Square, and then up West Patrick Street, to the graveyard of the German Reformed Church. With great solemnity the bier was carried into the graveyard, after which three volleys were fired.

The memorial service was then held in the Church.[1] The building, which the Reformers (sometimes called *German Presbyterians*) had erected in 1764 for their house of worship—in its lofty steeple the town clock had lately been installed—was one of the most handsome edifices in Maryland.[2] The service was conducted by Rev. John William Runkel, the pastor of the Church. A native of the Palatinate, Rev. Runkel had been ordained at Carlisle, Pennsylvania, and had been called to Frederick in 1784.

The oration, delivered by Johnson on the Character and

---

[1] Scharf, *History of Western Maryland*, Vol. I, pages, 392, 510, and 553. Rev. E. R. Eschbach, D. D., *Historic Sketch of the Evangelical Reformed Church of Frederick, Maryland*, page 24. Williams, *History of Frederick County*, page 411.

[2] Now called Trinity Chapel. Rev. E. R. Eschbach, D.D., *Historical Sermon, The Town Steeple's Centenary Services*, page 10.

Public Services of George Washington, is unique in that it is the only one of Johnson's public speeches that History has preserved.

The panegyric follows:

FELLOW CITIZENS:

Long disused to speak in public, and never possessing talents equal to this solemn occasion, it would have accorded with my wishes that one more proper had been chosen for this task: a task arduous in itself, and rendered still more difficult from the fairest flowers having been already selected by the hand of genius: But, who can decline the place assigned him in the public demonstrations of respect, admiration and gratitude to the *beloved Washington?*

After the bursts of grief have subsided into calm and tender recollections of dear departed friends, it is soothing to hear their sayings repeated and their actions related, even in the homeliest language: untired with repetitions the theme is eloquence in itself; it sinks into the soul. So here, where I can add nothing to your information of the splendid qualities and finished patriotism of the great good man, my address can only be from the heart to the heart.

Scarce had Washington reached manhood, than the blossoms which have since ripened into the richest fruit drew on him the choice of his country to execute a delicate and important commission; he discharged it with the prudence of matured age. In his return, his caution secured him and his followers from preconcerted assassination in the woody way; his courage was fatal to the instrument sent forth for his destruction.

Braddock's defeat and the carnage of his troops, whose scattered bones still whiten the field of action and confusion, called forth the talents of the young warrior: he partly restored order and command, and drew off a remnant from the uplifted tomahawk of savage ferocity. But there could be no association between British pride and acknowledged merit: no talents could compensate the want of British birth: the army lost his services and he preserved his honor.

Most esteemed by those who best knew him, he often, perhaps constantly, filled with true dignity the most honorable post the people could then bestow; and when America trembled for her rights, we find him in the faithful band which composed the Congress of '74.

Britain would remit nothing of her unwarranted claim, and America was tenacious of her just rights: stifled rage filled the hearts of men, and like confined powder, struck by the spark from Lexington, burst into flame.

Half-armed, and disregarding even a thought on subsistence, a crowd collected and girt the British round about in Boston, Bunker's-Hill, where Warren fell, bore testimony to American valour.

In this state a real general, a man of war was wanted—Order, discipline, love, respect, and confidence were to be established—As if pointed out by Heaven, every heart and every voice called out— *Washington!*

Oft has his majestic figure, on his acceptance of the high commission, risen to my imagination: so strongly is the dear image imprinted on memory, methinks I can almost see him now: his manly form and graceful attitude, his piercing blue eyes softened by modesty, innate sweetness and harmony of soul; the fate of a nation attends him and hangs on his fortitude, his wisdom and his talents. Lisped and haled on his way, he is shouted at Boston, and enters on the arduous work of war. Order arises—discipline is improving—the temporary army becomes more and more confident and formidable— Dorchester Heights, as by enchantment, exhibit a threatening and unassailable aspect, and the British are suffered to evacuate under the condition of not destroying.

Shall we trace his steps, his plans for attack or defence, his toils, his successes and reverses, from Boston to York, with an army perpetually shifting, and at times so thin, that it is credibly said, even the sentinels at his door in Morris-Town left their arms and him. The compass of this address will not permit such particularity, and besides due justice in description or appreciation, requires more knowledge than we possess in the military art.

Deprived of the necessary means of defence, with a handful, he suddenly attacked the enemy at Trenton. The enraged Delaware detained half his force against the most painful efforts—broke his plan, and limited his success. Soon after, he surprised Princeton, where lamented Mercer fell, and cut his way to the favouring mountains.

Some of you, my hearers, saw him there in almost the destitute condition mentioned before, where the Maryland Militia made about half his force, opposed to three times his number, and those disciplined troops in different posts in his neighborhood.

Yet in those gloomy times his fortitude did not forsake him. Six long years did he maintain the dubious conflict with ill-paid or unpaid troops, at times destitute of almost every necessary, strengthened indeed now and then with short services of half-armed Militia, against a disciplined army generally much more numerous, and the best appointed and supplied, perhaps, that ever an army was; until, with the assistance of the French, Cornwallis with his army were captured at York.

Rapid as the flight of an eagle when nothing else could save: cautious, circumspect, and guarded, as the old Roman when his country's cause could be thus best saved: like him, too, his courage was proof against stinging imputations from rashness and folly. In the contending field he firmly meets the clash of arms and coolly points the battle, where to rage or follow: or, in retreat, securing points which safely cover his exhausted troops, he slowly retires.

Yes, *Washington!* thou art covered with true military glory: thou didst devote thyself to thy country: thy toils and thy victories were for her. Detaching Morgan with his corps, the strength and sinews of thine own army was the work of thy wisdom—retaining Greene in the service was thy doing: the convention of Saratoga and the battles of the Cowpens, Guilford and Eutaw, show thy just estimate of men and talents, and that thou knewest how to prepare the catastrophe which afterwards took place at York, ended thy military career, and sealed the liberty and independence of thy country.

Of all spectacles, merely human, that of General Washington's surrendering to Congress the power deposited in his hands, is, perhaps, the most interesting of any hitherto exhibited on the theatre of this world. Some of you, my hearers, may have been witnesses of this august ceremony. Devoid of pomp and splendid show, it worked in the heart, and plentifully effused the tears of joy, gratitude, and veneration: an instructive but disregarded lesson to mean pride and lawless ambition.

As, after a mighty collection of discordant matter is consumed or dispersed in a tremendous gust, the cheering sun and calm return: so the strife and rage of war have ceased; the roaring cannon, shrill fife, and rattling drum are heard no more; sweet peace advances in her downy step, with all her smiling blessings in her train.

From the iron field, Washington, the first in merit as in fame, seeks the rural scene—his constant wish: agriculture, and the improvement of inland rivers, there employ his useful thoughts. True sources of rational delight, and private and public wealth.

The pressure removed, he saw the old confederation, from the weakness of the cement, and the fragility of its materials, was crumbling and passing away: he presided in the general convention, and the letter of that body to Congress, accompanying the Federal Constitution, is strongly impressive of the sentiments which ought to be felt by every citizen.

Twice called by the unanimous voice of the nation to the Presidential Chair (painful pre-eminence!) he gave motion and harmony to a new government, of which himself was the great spring; his exercise of the constitutional check was appreciated by the public sentiment.—The much agitated question is now decided, and speculatists are taught that a representative government is not only practicable, but the best for virtuous citizens.

Of all the attributes of the Supreme, that of justice can be the nearest imitated by man: it is the obligation of Nations as well as individuals, stamped by the Great Creator on the human heart, and on none more legibly than that of Washington. As in his private, so in his public character, it was his invariable maxim, *To do justice to all*. Happy the nation that is governed by that rule!

Scarce was the new Government settled in action, than the devouring flames of war were lighted up in Europe. Unhappy Nation, O! how long, and to what extent, have they consumed: you had no Washington: The ways of Providence, hid from men, have not yet disclosed whether you are still to groan under the galling yoke of despotism, and leave your struggles as the remembrance of a passing dream.

Our relations with the warring powers rendered our situation delicate and embarrassing: neutrality was the right and interest of the nation: that ground was taken, approved by the legislature and

the people at large: it was sedulously endeavoured to be preserved
by the Executive. Those endeavours have so far prevailed hitherto,
that our country has not yet suffered the evils of a great and solemn
war, and notwithstanding the injuries we have received from both
sides, we feel ourselves happy on a comparison with others. The
pleasing hope is now reviving in an opening prospect that we may
settle differences and be restored to full peace—the wish of man.

After eight years devotement to the service of his country in the
Chief Magistracy, this great, good man retires again to his private
station and rural occupations; not without having given, however,
to the nation at large—in his excellent letter, generally called his
legacy—the clue of his political measures, and the matured wisdom
of many years experience. Can you find in it the marks of declined
mental faculties, or trace the imbecilities of old age? No, my
hearers: blessed by Heaven, every time he comes forth he shines in
still more brightness, and seems to transcend his former self.

Again he is called to the command of armies, and instantly obeys
the summons: true greatness of soul, his highest post of honour is,
where he can be most useful to his country.

But the scene is closing: approach his bed of death: no stings;
no painful recollections are attending. Perfectly sensible of his
extremity and near approaching dissolution, he calmly says "*I am not
afraid to die*"—and closing his mouth and eyes soon expired: his
mounting spirit, perhaps exclaiming—"*O death, where is thy sting?
O grave, where is thy victory?*"

He is gone! He is gone! Alas! to return no more: the man
"who take him for all in all, we ne'er shall see his like again."

Suffer me, fellow-citizens, to touch some of the less striking
though not less instructive traits of this great character. His modesty,
which was to a degree embarrassing, was perfectly natural; his long
and general acquaintance with the world and men, could not subdue it. His patience in enquiry to gain information and form a
right judgment was untired. His thoughts in the course of discussion,
were closed in his own breast without giving offence, thereby drawing out the reasons of others which he received and weighed with
candour. He compared things and took their difference with exact-

ness: he had, indeed, a most excellent judgment, which guided the decision to which he adhered.

Feeling in less degree the weaknesses of our nature, and undeviating from the line of rectitude himself, he was uncommonly indulgent to the mistakes, the failings, and the faults of others. With a gravity which did not distance confidence or decent freedom, he possessed a steady cheerfulness which did not invite to overfamiliarity: in this, perhaps, no temper was ever better balanced to gain and maintain respect.

His military exploits, his civil administration and his private virtues, are themes on which the world has delighted, and ingenuity has been exhausted: but the praises of a nation, and their echo from distant climes have not inflated him. We have seen him the same man throughout: his country's good was his fixed goal: he has won the prize of never-fading fame.

Let our hearts, my hearers, glow with gratitude to the Supreme, for the blessing bestowed on us in Washington: like this sound philosopher and practical Christian, let us refer the gift to the hand of Him whose governing Providence rules the fate of individuals and of nations: let us feel the weight of his advice, not disregard his exhortations to union.

Let us imitate the example we cannot but admire. We are citizens: we can all love our common country—if called on to defend it in arms, remember his patience, his deprivations, his fortitude, his courage in the field of battle and of death: his submission to civil authority—and, like him, to return the sword again to the country from whom you received it.—If called to the councils of the nation or the state, remember the sacredness of the deposit, equal his disinterested patriotism, and to the utmost of your power approach his calm, deliberate wisdom—increase in softness towards the faults of others—be not vain of real estimable qualities; remember the talent is lent, and its use must be accounted for.

We profess to be Christians; in a word, therefore, so live that we may be able to say with Washington, *"I am not afraid to die."*

CHAPTER **XXXV**

THE SUNSET AT ROSE HILL

"Statesman, yet friend to truth! of soul sincere,
In action faithful, and in honour clear;
Who broke no promise, served no private end;
Who gain'd no title, and who lost no friend;
Ennobled by himself, by all approved,
And praised, unenvied by the muse he loved."

THESE lines from Pope's *Epistle to Mr. Addison* express exactly Thomas Johnson's idea of a successful career. While he had never sought political power or fame, throughout his life he frankly admitted that one of his chief sources of happiness was the thought that he had served his country with honor and that his name would be revered by future generations. When, for example, at the age of 47, he was warmly praised by the Legislature of Maryland for the prudence, assiduity, firmness and integrity with which he had discharged the duties of Governor, he replied: "The favourable light in which you have been pleased to accept my endeavours for the public service, is the most noble and pleasing reward you could bestow; . . . it highly gratifies my ambition in handing me down as approved of by you and deserving well of posterity." The final years did not change this philosophy.

It is recorded that Johnson presided at a public meeting in the Frederick County Court House on April 28, 1798, when resolutions were adopted thanking President John

Adams for his endeavors to protect American commerce. But in the twenty years that followed—save only once when he delivered his eulogy of George Washington—he never emerged from seclusion. On March 3, 1801, he was appointed by President Adams as the first Chief Judge of the Circuit Court of the District of Columbia, and his nomination was promptly confirmed by the United States Senate, but as promptly he declined.[1] Even when he was "crouching under a load of more than eighty years," he was invited by a committee at Georgetown to attend a celebration commemorating American victories; but he replied that his physical strength was exhausted and his appearance would only "incite chilling reflections on the imbecility of an old man worn out." And in this reply he again proclaimed his philosophy: "I claim however the conscious merit of constantly wishing the liberty and prosperity of our Country, from a very early period in life to the present hour. May they again return and be perpetual! I have gained too the friendship and confidence of Washington, which I estimate beyond price; or would I part from the self-complacency I enjoy, for all the profit and power that can be acquired by fraud and deception; everything is quiet within. . . . I have no enemy that I know of, and I am sure I have nothing to ask or fear from the world." [2]

Again, when over eighty, he wrote to one of his grandchildren the same thought. "The notice taken of me lately in the newspapers adds nothing to my self-complacency; indeed, I wish, rather, that I had not been mentioned at all. . . . Though a very old man my mind is not so gone as to be flattered by praise. I love the good

---

[1] W. B. Bryan, *A History of the National Capital,* Vol. I, page 402.
[2] *Johnson to Messrs. R. Beverly and John Lee.*

opinion of the world when it *follows* my own, but I must be older before it *leads*. . . . I love and much appreciate family pride, to the extent as an additional guard against doing anything improper. I hope to leave to every descendant of mine the inheritance of not blushing for their blood having passed through my veins. . . . There needs no great cunning to go through the world with self-approbation and credit. Indeed, cunning will sometimes prevent a regard for truth and sincerity, which surpass in value all the cunning of the most dextrous politician and are open to the practice of every honest mind." [3]

While frail of body for many years before his death, Johnson's mind remained strong until the end. In his Church—he and his relatives were among the leading and most active members of All Saints Protestant Episcopal parish—as well as in the current events of the State and Nation he retained always a lively interest.

As late as the Spring of 1815 he granted the title of an island in the Potomac River to some of his descendants [4] but more than a year and a half later, when almost 84, he bought a small tract of land, paying for it more than a thousand dollars. [5] While his eyesight was dim, his mind was keen and his hearing "almost as perfect as ever and quicker now than most young people's." [6] He did not make his last will and testament until July 4, 1818. By this instrument he gave to his daughter, Rebecca, his undivided share in some Virginia land which he had held jointly with her deceased husband, Thomas James Johnson; to his son,

---

[3] Johnson to Mrs. Hugh W. Evans, of Baltimore (daughter of Thomas Jennings and Charlotte Hesselius Johnson), September 2, 1813.

[4] *Land Records of Frederick County,* Liber T. B., No. 1, Folio 480.

[5] Liber J. S., No. 3, Folio 718.

[6] *Johnson to Cousin James Johnson,* February 5, 1816. Original in the Historical Society of Pennsylvania, Philadelphia, Pa.

Joshua, half of all the residue of his real estate; and to his grandson, Thomas J. Grahame, the remaining half. His son and grandson were also named to serve as executors together with his son-in-law, Major Grahame. One of the witnesses to the will was Roger Brooke Taney, who was now a member of the Maryland Senate.[7]

The aged patriot finally slept away at Rose Hill mansion, in the 87th year of his age, on Tuesday morning, October 26, 1819.[8] In reporting his death, a Frederick newspaper paid him the following tribute: "His deeds are inscribed in the imperishable archives of his country; his wisdom, impartiality and integrity in the records of justice; his worth and virtues are preserved in the hearts of his countrymen; his kindness, affection and friendship in the memory of his family, relatives and friends; his trust for immortality rested in his Saviour and God. Washington was his friend. Eulogium can add no more." [9]

It was, indeed, an appropriate tribute—one that accorded so well with Johnson's philosophy. Washington's influence upon him had been profound. When near the end of life, he gave a relative two of the many letters he had received from Washington during their long and intimate friendship, he explained that he left them as "a rich legacy of Honour" to his descendants—not to swell them with pride but to stimulate them in the course of truth and virtue. "How I loved him, and how I love his memory! There were doubtless specs of our nature in him, but I am

---

[7] *Record of Wills,* Liber H. S., No. 2, Folio 312.

[8] He was buried in the family vault in the old Episcopal graveyard, on All Saints Street. After many years the grave became obscure and in 1894 a marble stone marking the spot was laid by the Daughters of the American Revolution. In 1913 the remains were removed to Mt. Olivet Cemetery, where a monument was erected.

[9] *Frederick-Town Herald,* October 30, 1819.

more and more fixed in the opinion that he nearer approached the order of Superior Beings than any man I ever personally knew. . . . That we are to pass into another state of being after death I hold for certain, and as certain, too, as that we shall be rewarded or punished according to our deeds in this life, the rewards liberal, the punishments mitigated by mercy. But in the manner of our future existence and the enlargement of capacity in the next superior class of beings we possibly cannot have adequate ideas in our present state. Some imagine that we shall have a remembrance of and something of the feelings of relationships and friendships in this life, with improved powers of communication. If this should prove to be the state of things, may I meet Washington beyond the grave!"

INDEX